D1286475

Rhetoric and Truth in France

DESCARTES TO DIDEROT

R. A. Houasse. *Eloquence*. (Musée de Brest)

Rhetoric and Truth in France

DESCARTES TO DIDEROT

PETER FRANCE

OXFORD
AT THE CLARENDON PRESS
1972

808.044
F81r

Oxford University Press, Ely House, London W. 1

GLASGOW NEW YORK TORONTO MELBOURNE WELLINGTON
CAPE TOWN IBADAN NAIROBI DAR ES SALAAM LUSAKA ADDIS ABABA
DELHI BOMBAY CALCUTTA MADRAS KARACHI LAHORE DACCA
KUALA LUMPUR SINGAPORE HONG KONG TOKYO

© OXFORD UNIVERSITY PRESS 1972

PRINTED IN GREAT BRITAIN
AT THE UNIVERSITY PRESS, OXFORD
BY VIVIAN RIDLER
PRINTER TO THE UNIVERSITY

PREFACE

No school subject is universally popular, but few can have excited as much distaste and derision as rhetoric. It is the art of seeming, the art which teaches you to put on a public mask of honesty and conviction, to weep when you are unmoved, to enter by deceit into the hearts of your unsuspecting audience. It teaches the art of flattery, how to adapt your matter and manner so as to ingratiate yourself with different hearers, how to speak to every man in the language he likes to hear. And it teaches the art of charming appearances, how to clothe your message in an attractive garb, how to dress yourself for polite society. It is, in short, a repellent art. But it is also indispensable; as soon as you talk to someone else, you are immediately involved with rhetoric. You cannot choose to do without it, for there is no such thing as non-rhetorical utterance. You can, however, become aware of your own position, choose among the many alternative rhetorical stances, and even, in a small way, create a new rhetoric. You can indeed come to value and love rhetoric, for if to some writers it was 'the mother of lies', to others it was 'my Lady Rhetoric', the beautiful young woman of the allegorical paintings.[1]

It is not my intention to prove the truth of one single thesis, nor to give anything like a complete account of the development of French rhetoric in the two centuries preceding the Revolution. The essays which make up this volume can be read separately as approaches to the persuasive stance and techniques of individual writers. It is my hope, none the less, that they will be read together and that taken as a whole they will suggest the value of using the concept and terminology of rhetoric when reading writers as different as Rousseau and Boileau. Of many of the writers discussed here it is more normal to ask such questions as: 'What does he mean?' 'Why does he say this?' 'What conditions influence the development of his ideas?'—or, more interestingly perhaps, 'What is the value of what he says?' 'Are his arguments sound?' 'Do his conclusions still hold true today?' These are the historical and

---

[1] The frontispiece to this book is a relatively late example of long and quite vigorous iconographical tradition.

UNIVERSITY LIBRARIES
CARNEGIE-MELLON UNIVERSITY
PITTSBURGH, PENNSYLVANIA 15213

(broadly speaking) the philosophical approaches, and the former at least is widely represented in present-day writing on such figures as Descartes or Diderot. I believe, however, that there is another set of questions which can be asked about anyone who writes or speaks in public, questions such as: 'Who does he think he is talking to?' 'What does it mean for him to write a book?' 'Why does he adopt this or that tone of voice?' It would be difficult to prove that either set of questions should take precedence over the other, just as it is difficult to say whether when talking to a man we should be more interested in what he means to say or in how he communicates with us. Obviously the two cannot be neatly separated; both come together in our attempt to understand and live with the man. But at least I would claim that a proper reading of Rousseau, for instance, demands not only that we clarify his terms and arguments and relate them to their intellectual and social context, but also that we become aware of the rhetorical dimension, and come to grips with Rousseau's problems and achievements as a man talking to other men.

In writing these essays, my purpose was nevertheless largely historical. I wanted to define and illustrate one aspect of the common mental equipment of one section of French society during a given period in time. Rhetoric (as it is described in Chapter 1) was an important element in that equipment; its influence could be traced equally in the actions and writings of men less well known than Racine or Montesquieu. Indeed it might be said that my historical purpose would have been better served by avoiding the outstanding writers, since in my view there is no necessary coincidence between the writers whom we most enjoy reading (or even the writers who have become standard classics) and those who can tell us most about their time. But of course my purpose was not *entirely* historical—nor can I attain the purity of literary history suggested by Valéry: 'une *Histoire de l'esprit en tant qu'il produit ou consomme de la "littérature"*, et cette histoire pourrait même se faire sans que le nom d'un écrivain y fût prononcé.' For me, it is more interesting and rewarding to concentrate on individuals and their specific responses to commonly experienced situations and problems. There is therefore an element of orthodox evaluation in my choice of subjects; the writers I discuss are all great masters of rhetoric, with the possible exception of d'Alembert, who owes his place partly to his representative status.

Some major figures are omitted, either because they would have
extended the book too far (Voltaire) or because they have already
been fully studied from a rhetorical point of view (Pascal, Montaigne). Other slightly less obvious figures would have been worth
further study (Malebranche, Condillac, Fontenelle, Maupertuis,
Buffon), but I could not discuss all of them and felt that the hints
contained in Chapter 3 would have to suffice. And, finally, if I am
asked why I did not extend the period covered to include the
nineteenth century, I can only say that that is another chapter (and
an interesting one) in the same story.

Neither the attempt to describe collective mentalities nor the
study of individual writers can lay claim to total objectivity. Any
historical analysis creates its own categories and speaks to and for
its own time. The problems which I discuss in these essays are ones
which, in a different form, have become acute in the literature of
our century (though less so, it seems, in our science, our history,
our social sciences, and even our philosophy—I do not know
about our preaching). It is likely that the imaginative writer of
today will feel quite as strongly as Descartes or Rousseau (though
for different reasons) the distaste for books, 'literary' style, and the
reading public which is expressed so memorably in Jean-Paul
Sartre's *Les Mots*. (This distaste or loss of faith may have been
stronger in French literature than in our own, since in England
the formalities of rhetoric have always been less obtrusive.) In a
way, as Rousseau knew, the proper outcome of the disgust with
rhetoric is silence, but few writers are sufficiently held by the myth
of Rimbaud to be able to put down their pens for good. More
usually, the discomforts of rhetoric may lead extremists to two
opposite positions, either the desperate quest for the mirage of
genuine, unmediated communication (which we shall see in Rousseau), or else the deliberate cultivation of self-proclaiming form,
the writing of literature which seeks to exorcize the demon of
rhetoric by openly designating itself as literature (we shall see this
in an attenuated form in Boileau). At all events, such ideas are an
inescapable part of our culture, and it is possible that they have
led me to overstate the strains and problems of rhetoric in an
earlier age. Once you have seen the power of rhetoric, it is hard
not to see it everywhere. I remain convinced, however, that these
problems were real ones for such men as Bossuet or d'Alembert—
as they themselves tell us.

The first part of this book is a descriptive account of rhetorical theory and teaching in pre-revolutionary France. This is intended to provide both a context and a starting-point for the consideration of individual cases; many of the points which it raises in a rapid or generalizing manner are extensively illustrated in the following chapters. These are arranged thematically rather than chronologically; the betrayals and triumphs of rhetoric are viewed from three different standpoints. Part II deals with the relations between rhetoric and philosophy, the problems of philosophical communication with a non-specialist audience. Part III is devoted to the social face of rhetoric, the tension between the language of magnificence or politeness and the claims of honesty and a world-denying religion. In the final part, I look at rhetoric in the way which is perhaps most familiar to us, as a routine curb on the self-expression of the original writer, who is driven to renew (but not to reject) the despised tool which tradition has put into his hands.

Rhetorical studies are not new today; I have indicated some of my debts in the bibliographical essay at the end of this volume. Similarly, in writing about the rhetoric of Descartes or Diderot, one is not in unexplored territory; rereading these essays, I have been conscious of the presence of Gouhier on Descartes, Truchet on Bossuet, Boudhors on Boileau, Dieckmann on Diderot, Starobinski and Ellrich on Rousseau, to name only a few. I also owe a great deal to discussion with colleagues, students, and friends in my own university and elsewhere; I should particularly like to thank Margaret McGowan, who read much of the manuscript and made many helpful suggestions. The rhetoric of preface-writing compels me to add that I bear the sole responsibility for any errors or absurdities contained in the following pages.

P.F.

University of Sussex, 1971

CONTENTS

I

THEORY

La loi de toute rhétorique, c'est qu'il faut mentir pour
être vrai.

(Jean-Paul Sartre : *Saint-Genêt*)

1. Rhetoric in the *ancien régime*

MOST people who know French know the fable of the wolf and the lamb. Before the Revolution, the educated minority learned to write such fables in Latin. If the *Novus Candidatus Rhetoricae* of the Jesuit Père Pomey is a reliable witness, they were first presented with the fable 'stylo simplici':

Siti Agnus aestuans, ad rivum venit; ad quem pariter accessit Lupus, ad bibendum. Cumque superior staret Lupus, et Agnus inferior; Ille tamen jurgii causam captans, Agnum accusat, quod turbet aquam pedibus. Hic modeste negat, fieri id posse, cum ab ipso Lupo rivi unda decurreret. At maledictis, inquit Lupus, me proscidisti ante sex menses. Neque id accidere potuisse, respondet Agnus, cum nondum natus esset id temporis. At tuus certe pater maledixit mihi, subdit ferox: atque ita correptum lacerat.

Sic adornare calumnias, et opprimere Innocentem non est difficile.

Then they were shown how this could be transformed 'stylo ornatiore'—the first three sentences alone give this:

Ad rivum Agnus venerat, sitis levandae causa. Lupus huc etiam accurrit, magis praedae, quam potus desiderio, ac potius stimulante fame, quam siti: Dum bibit Agnus, terribilem in aqua videt umbram Lupi, totisque contremiscens tenellis artubus, haeret perculsus ipso in vestigio, nec caudam caputve movere misellus audet. At Lupus fauce improba, rixas movens, illumque lacerandi occasionem aucupans: Heus, inquit, audacule, non cessabis mihi aquam turbulentam bibenti facere lutulentis pedibus tuis? Men' tu, o bone Lupe, audaculum appellas, qui prae timore tuique reverentia, vix pedibus consisto? Non absistes, inquam, reponit Latro, turbare aquam mihi? Cui Agnus, Qui possum, quaeso facere quod quereris, Lupe humanissime? Vix, heu primoribus labellis rivum attigi, vix extrema libavi undam lingula. Mentiris, impudens, turbasti latices; lutulentior ad me fluit aqua. Ah! quid ais, Lupe nobilissime? Non ego certe sum, nec esse possum. Nonne vides, a te decurrere liquorem ad meos haustus.[1]

This transposition is one of the first exercises in the rhetorical training to which not only La Fontaine but almost all the major

[1] F. Pomey, *Novus Candidatus Rhetoricae*, Paris, 1682 ed., pp. 15–16.

writers of pre-revolutionary France were subjected. Like many of
the less glamorous aids to writing, dictionaries, encyclopedias, and
the like, it was the object of much ingratitude, and was often
spurned by those who had most profited from it, but this did
not diminish its significance as a powerful force in the world of
writing and speaking, reading and listening. The purpose of this
introductory chapter is to give an idea of the nature of this discipline, its place in educational practice, and some of its constant
features.[2] The material discussed here may seem rather aridly
theoretical, but it should provide the necessary framework for the
subsequent chapters, which develop and illustrate by particular
cases the points which here remain mostly on the level of general
theory. General rhetorical theory is usually boring, when it is
not absurd, but the rhetorical behaviour of individuals is full of
interest.

Rhetoric was primarily a school subject, taught to boys who
were hardly even adolescents. It was one of the three elements of
the medieval *trivium*, the first cycle of Arts subjects which taught
the schoolboy to use Latin correctly and elegantly. After spending
some years on the grammar of the foreign but not yet dead language which was a gateway to advancement, the student learnt
in his rhetoric class some of the ways in which Latin can be used
to greatest effect; only then did he go on to study what was probably at this time the most important member of the trio, logic or
dialectic. There were attempts, at various times, to alter this order,
putting rhetoric after logic on the grounds that it was wrong to
learn the art of communication before you had anything solid to
communicate, but for the most part the medieval order persisted
up to the Revolution and beyond—the word 'rhétorique' was not
dropped from the school curriculum until 1902. After the rich
confusion of the early sixteenth century, it was the Jesuit colleges
above all which established a regular pattern of linguistic studies:
three years of Latin grammar, one year of 'humanities' or pre-
rhetorical literary studies, and a final year of rhetoric proper.
These linguistic studies were balanced by a philosophical and
scientific cycle, but many pupils did not go beyond rhetoric, which
appears therefore as the culmination of the basic cycle of studies.

---

[2] A bibliographical essay on rhetoric in France appears at the end of this book.
The spelling and punctuation of quotations and titles have been modernized throughout.

The Jesuit pattern was followed with variations in most of the other teaching establishments. Thus most boys who went to school had a thorough grounding in rhetoric by the time they were fifteen.

Of course the majority of French people at this time did not study rhetoric or anything else. Secondary schooling was confined to a small proportion of the population—on the eve of the Revolution more than half the population could not even sign their names. This does not mean necessarily that only the wealthy learnt rhetoric; the Jesuit colleges, for instance, gave free instruction to day-boys, and François de Dainville has shown that many children of shopkeepers, artisans, and peasants were able to take advantage of this.[3] It does mean, however, that rhetoric was a mark of social ascension, a key to relatively privileged sorts of employment and thus an integral part of the established order. It was also essentially a masculine subject, at any rate as far as school rhetoric was concerned, since such secondary education as was available to girls concentrated on what were regarded as more feminine accomplishments.

It should not be thought that rhetoric was a subject learnt at school and thereafter totally neglected. While such textbooks as Pomey's *Novus Candidatus Rhetoricae* are clearly manuals for classroom use only, there are others, from Erasmus's *De Duplici Copia* to Bernard Lamy's *De l'art de parler*, which appear to be directed at the cultivated adult reader as well as the schoolboy. This is most obviously the case with books written in French. At the time when rhetoric was an exclusively Latin subject in the schoolroom, there had been occasional attempts to make it accessible to those who could only read the vernacular. As early as the thirteenth century, Brunetto Latini's French encyclopedia, *Li Livres dou tresor*, included a large section devoted to Ciceronian rhetoric. At the same period Jean d'Antioche translated Cicero's *De Inventione* and the *Rhetorica ad Herennium* into French. In the sixteenth century there were one or two attempts to write French rhetorics, the best-known being Antoine Fouquelin's *La Rhétorique française*, an adaptation of Omer Talon's Ramist rhetoric. In the case of Fouquelin it is not quite clear what sort of audience he has in mind; his book does not appear to have been very successful and

---

[3] F. de Dainville, 'Collèges et fréquentation scolaire au XVIIe siècle', *Population*, 1957.

it has been suggested that rather than responding to consumer demand, Fouquelin was following the Pléiade programme of 'illustrating' the French language by using it for serious writing.[4]

It was only in the seventeenth century that there was a strong development of French rhetoric. The French Academy had as a part of its original programme the composition of a French rhetoric; working with its usual slowness, it was overtaken by events and never produced anything in this field. After 1650 a variety of individual writers rushed in to fill the gap. To quote only some of the more important, there were full-scale rhetorical treatises by La Mothe le Vayer (*La Rhétorique du Prince*, 1651), René Bary (*La Rhétorique française*, 1653), Le Gras (*La Rhétorique française*, 1671), Bernard Lamy (*De l'art de parler*, 1675), and the Abbé de Bretteville (*L'Éloquence de la chaire et du barreau*, 1689). The movement continues strongly in the eighteenth century with the treatises of Gibert, Rollin, and Crévier. In addition to actual treatises there was a host of less formal writings, reflexions on Aristotle, thoughts, poems, letters, and dialogues on various aspects of rhetoric.

These genuinely rhetorical writings shade off into what may be called a sub-rhetoric, the undergrowth of works on polite language, letter-writing, conversation, and the like. These manuals (which are by no means a prerogative of the seventeenth century) usually provide samples of correct and elegant usage; two typical specimens are La Serre's *Le Secrétaire à la mode, ou méthode facile d'écrire selon le temps diverses lettres de compliment, amoureuses ou morales*, etc. (1641), and a collection of model conversations by René Bary, 'rhéteur des Précieuses', entitled *L'Esprit de cour, ou les conversations galantes, divisées en cent dialogues* (1662). With such guides women who had had no formal education could pick up the appropriate rhetorics of polite society.

And eventually, of course, the Latin fortress of school rhetoric had to give way to this vernacular flood. From early in the seventeenth century it had been normal, even in the extremely Latin-centred Jesuit colleges, for illustrations from contemporary French literature to be used alongside examples from the Latin. Other

---

[4] See R. J. Leake, jun., 'The Relationship of Two Ramist Rhetorics: Omer Talon's *Rhetorica* and Antoine Fouquelin's *Rhétorique française*', *Bibliothèque d'Humanisme et Renaissance*, 1968; and W. J. Ong, 'Fouquelin's French Rhetoric and the Ramist Vernacular Tradition', *Studies in Philology*, 1954.

teaching establishments were more inclined than the Jesuits to favour the use of French, and gradually French rhetoric was established alongside Latin in all secondary schools. Rollin's *De la manière d'enseigner et d'étudier les belles-lettres*, first published in 1726 and purporting to record the practice of the University of Paris, includes a French rhetoric. The author explains that, although he could just as well have written it in Latin, he thinks it will be more useful in French. For the same reason he has illustrated it from French and Latin authors alike. Latin is still a central object of study, but it is losing ground as a medium of communication. Thus Rollin believes that the oral exercises, which had traditionally been in Latin, should really be in the vernacular: 'Le principal but qu'on se propose, c'est de les préparer aux emplois qu'ils doivent un jour exercer: instruire, plaider, faire le rapport d'une affaire, dire son avis dans une compagnie. Or, tout cela se fait en français et, à peu de chose près, de la manière dont on parle dans les exercices.'[5]

This movement reached its climax in the nineteenth century, when rhetoric, far from fading away as is sometimes supposed, retained a dominant place in the curriculum of the *lycées*—and it was now in large part French rhetoric. It is worth remembering that all the French writers of the nineteenth century who followed a full *lycée* course had devoted most of two years to the sort of study which the historian Ernest Lavisse describes with loving mockery:

La vraie fin des études d'alors, c'était la rhétorique, où les meilleurs élèves passaient deux ans. Dans la rhétorique, tout cédait au discours. Nous en composions deux par semaine, l'un en latin et l'autre en français . . . Je me souviens d'ailleurs d'une utilité maîtresse de cet exercice: il était le seul où nous apprissions à mettre et tenir nos idées en ordre et à les bien exprimer. M. Lemaire nous dictait des 'matières' qu'il fallait suivre rigoureusement, et qui se divisaient en trois, ou quatre, ou cinq paragraphes . . .[6]

The same picture could doubtless be drawn of many colleges before the Revolution.

[5] C. Rollin, *De la manière d'enseigner et d'étudier les belles-lettres*, Paris 1775 (1st ed., 1726), vol. IV, pp. 480–1. On the shifting balance between classical and French studies in the Jesuit colleges at the end of the seventeenth century see F. de Dainville, 'Le *Ratio Discendi et Docendi* de Jouvancy', *Archivum Historicum Societatis Jesu*, 1951. Dainville does well to remind us that the textbooks are one thing, the actual classroom practice another.

[6] Quoted in A. Prost, *L'Enseignement en France, 1800–1967*, Paris, 1968, pp. 62–3.

Lavisse's reminiscences give a faint idea of the nature of school-room rhetoric, but now we must try to fill out the picture. More than any other subject, rhetoric was a classical inheritance; what-ever modifications it might undergo, it built on the foundation of an ancient and rich tradition. Classical rhetoric, exemplified notably by Aristotle, Cicero, and Quintilian, had aimed to provide a comprehensive art of public speaking, to give the orator all the necessary materials for swaying an audience and speaking well on any subject. It would be wrong to imagine classical rhetoric as a unified body of precepts, all accepted by every rhetorician; never-theless, for our present purpose, it is possible to give an over-all picture of ancient rhetorical theory as it appeared to the peda-gogues of the seventeenth century. In doing so I shall draw largely on the *Institutio Oratoria* of Quintilian, a complete guide for the teacher of rhetoric written in the first century A.D., partly because it gives an exhaustive and orthodox account of the theory de-veloped over the preceding 500 years and partly because it was one of the most influential texts with post-Renaissance theorists. It is in fact a very interesting text; I must apologize if the need to summarize makes me present it in a schematic way. It is true that the mania for classification was the rhetorician's besetting sin, but the best treatises disguised the skeleton better than I can do here.

The first two books are mainly devoted to the training which precedes rhetoric proper.[7] This starts from the earliest lessons in speech and includes a variety of exercises based on models which the teacher has previously explained. This is followed by a lengthy discussion of the nature and definition of rhetoric: Quintilian prefers to call it 'ars bene dicendi', the art of speaking well, since the 'well' indicates for him that rhetoric is not morally neutral: 'no man can speak well who is not good himself' (II. xv. 34). After these or similar preambles, the traditional treatise divides rhetoric into five parts: *inventio*, the discovery of all the available means of persuasion; *dispositio*, the plan of the speech; *elocutio*, style; *memoria*, memory; and *pronunciatio*, delivery. At this point two other divisions are commonly made: (*a*) the three fields of oratory, the deliberative (where the aim is to determine future action), the judicial (where the aim is to prove something about the past), and the epideictic or demonstrative (where the aim is to distribute

---

[7] Translations of Quintilian are taken from the Loeb edition in four volumes by H. E. Butler, London, 1920.

praise or blame in the present); (*b*) the three duties of the orator, to instruct (*docere*), to move (*movere*), and to please (*delectare*).

Of the parts of rhetoric, *inventio* is often the most extensive. It teaches in the first place the importance of deciding what is at issue—Quintilian calls this the *status* of the case—for instance, whether the dispute concerns a matter of fact, of law, or of interpretation. Once this is done, the orator can think about the material at his disposal for persuading his listeners. His assets fall into three main groups: (*a*) the impression which he makes as a person; (*b*) the possibility of appealing to his audience's emotions; (*c*) last but not least, his proofs.

The first of these, generally expressed in French as *les mœurs*, is fairly simple; it depends a lot on style and delivery. It was considered normal for the orator to concentrate on establishing his own good character at the beginning of his speech. The *captatio benevolentiae*, as it was often called, involved a lot in the way of *précautions oratoires* and flattery. This enterprise, like the appeal to the emotions (or the passions, as they were usually called), called for some practical knowledge of human psychology. To this end rhetorical treatises—notably the *Rhetoric* of Aristotle—often contained a guide to the passions, showing how they can be stirred up, how they manifest themselves physically, and how they can be expected to vary according to the age and situation of the individual.

The section dealing with proofs was the most complex. The first point to be made here is that the proofs of rhetoric were not the same as those of logic; where logic aimed for certain deduction, rhetoric was content with probabilities. The syllogism of logic had its counterpart in the enthymeme of rhetoric. The enthymeme was originally a syllogistic argument based on merely probable premisses, although in the subsequent history of rhetoric it came to mean a syllogism of which either the major or the minor was not expressed. Of the other forms of rhetorical argument, the most important was undoubtedly the example, usually the argument from historical precedent.

A significant chapter of *inventio* was that devoted to the so-called *loci* or topics. These were a sort of check-list of the possible sources of material, the 'places' in which arguments were likely to be found. Thus, given a subject to treat, a war for instance, the orator should think of its causes, its effects, its similarity or dissimilarity with other matters, and so on, reminding himself of all the possible things to be said on his side. Similarly he might find assistance from the *loci communes, lieux communs* or commonplaces, those generally accepted pieces of wisdom such as the image of Fortune's wheel, which could do service in any number of causes.

Dispositio taught the order to be given to this material. The basic order, drawn in the first place from the pattern of judicial oratory, starts with the *exordium*, or general introduction, in which the speaker puts himself or his client forward in a favourable light and attempts to win the audience's goodwill. Then comes the statement of the case, often taking the form of a narration of events, followed by the arguments in favour of the speaker's position and a refutation of the points made by opponents. Finally, in the peroration, the speaker may briefly sum up what has been said, but above all he will try to sway the audience in his favour by appealing to their emotions. So much for the general order; within it, some rhetoricians were prepared to subdivide rigorously, but most favoured flexibility. In Quintilian's opinion the important thing is to follow 'the natural order, which demands that after dealing with this question [i.e. the principal question], he should then proceed to introduce the subsidiary questions, thereby making the structure of his speech as regular as that of the human body' (VII. x. 7).

Although reputable theorists normally warned against too great a preoccupation with *elocutio* for its own sake, it was generally agreed that it was in the field of style that study could make its greatest contribution. Apart from general recommendations about speaking clearly, correctly, and elegantly, rhetoric had a rich fund of advice on stylistic effectiveness. In the first place, a distinction was often made, notably by Cicero, between the three styles, the elevated, the temperate, and the humble. This division was universally accepted by French theorists, who were inclined to apply it more strictly than their classical predecessors, turning what had originally been a stylistic classification into a social hierarchy. Thus words were arranged on 'Virgil's wheel'; this device, based on the three works of Virgil, the *Aeneid*, the *Georgics*, and the *Eclogues*, placed words in one of the three classes—*equus*, elevated; *bos*, temperate; and *ovis*, humble.

The largest part of *elocutio*, however, was devoted to a classification of the figures of speech, the linguistic devices which enabled speakers to impress, please, or stir their audience. First came the tropes, defined by Quintilian as 'the artistic alteration of a word or phrase from its proper meaning to another' (VIII. vi. 1). The king of these is the metaphor, which Aristotle had described as the touchstone of a speaker's genius. Of metaphors the most striking are those which give life and action to an inanimate object. Their use is subject to many restrictions; in particular the speaker is warned off extended, over-frequent, low, or inappropriate metaphors. Next comes synecdoche, the substitution of the part for the whole, the whole for the part, the species for the genus, the genus for the species, and so on—thus *ferrum* for *gladium*. Closely connected is metonymy, where one word is replaced by another word standing in some close relation to it (other than that of resemblance, which is the distinguishing feature of metaphor). Indeed it might be possible to subsume synecdoche under metonymy and see metaphor and metonymy as the two basic tropes. In fact, however, the list given by most ancient rhetoricians is a long one, including, for instance, periphrasis or circumlocution and the epithet or superfluous adjective. What all the tropes have in common is that they contribute to embellishing the speaker's language, surprising and pleasing the audience by their distinguished elegance.

After the tropes come the figures, where instead of a change of meaning it is an artificial turn of phrase which attracts our attention. The figures too have a decorative function, but their role is above all to communicate emotion to the listener. A hazy border line divides figures into two sorts, the figures of thought, *figurae sententiae*, and the figures of speech, *figurae verborum*. The former are those which involve a departure from normal direct statement in such a manner as to express and provoke emotion. The most important of them are rhetorical questions, feigned hesitations, 'communication' or apparent appeal to one's audience, simulated exclamations, prosopopœia or impersonation (where the orator lends words to his adversary, the Gods, inanimate objects or the dead), apostrophe, irony, 'concession' (where the speaker begins by appearing to give something away to his adversary), and aposiopesis or interruption (where the orator interrupts the flow of his speech in order to give an impression of anger or passion). In all of these the emphasis is on dissimulation; it is assumed that the speaker deliberately chooses these figures to create a strong impression on his audience. Thus exclamation is only a figure when it is not a natural expression of emotion.

Of the *figurae verborum* the most important are those which depend on the arrangement of words. There are also, it is true, grammatical figures which are a deliberate departure from normal usage; in Quintilian's words, such figures 'relieve the tedium of everyday stereotyped speech' (IX. iii. 3). But more striking effects are achieved by the use of various patterns of language. These include repetition (which has many subdivisions), parallelism (where the same thought is repeated in different forms), asyndeton (the omission of conjunctions, as in 'veni, vidi, vici') and its opposite polysyndeton, enumeration and gradation (where the different elements of an enumeration are arranged so as to lead to a climax), various sorts of word play, and those figures which depend on symmetry of construction, notably antithesis.

An essential part of the *elocutio* section is that devoted to prose rhythm and the construction of the oratorical period. Quintilian uses a comparison with music to bring out the persuasive and emotive power of rhythm and harmony over men's minds. When there is a conflict between 'the natural order' and euphony, it is usually euphony which wins. At the same time, one of the most important conditions of a good prose style is that it should avoid the rhythms of verse. A second over-all recommendation insists on the adaptation of rhythm to subject; there is a distinction, for instance, between the formal rhythms of oratory and the more disjointed style which is appropriate to dialogues or letters. Inside a speech the periodic style is better suited to the peroration than to the exposition of facts. Above all, 'it is necessary to conceal the care expended upon it so that our rhythms may seem to possess a spontaneous flow, not to have been the result of elaborate search or compulsion' (IX. iv. 147).

The final two sections of rhetoric, memory and delivery, are usually more rapidly dealt with. Not that they are insignificant— Demosthenes is often quoted as saying that delivery is primordial —but they call for fewer precepts. There was, however, a fairly elaborate code of gestures and expressions which reinforced the purely verbal tropes and figures. In this, as in the techniques of oral delivery, the orator was often compared to the actor, the example always quoted being that of Cicero taking lessons from the actor Roscius. And so ends the standard textbook, though

Quintilian, for instance, devotes his final book to a discussion of the moral qualities and breadth of knowledge desirable in an orator, insisting that eloquence must be more than a mere knack and finally presenting oratory as 'the fairest gift of God to man, without which all things are stricken dumb and robbed alike of present glory and the immortal record of posterity' (XII. xi. 30).

Such was the traditional theory of rhetoric which was taught both in Latin and in the vernacular in the schools of France from the sixteenth to the nineteenth century. Aristotle, Cicero, and Quintilian were not always used directly, but they formed the basis of numerous manuals composed by teachers. The Jesuits, the dominant teaching order throughout this period, made extensive use of the useful compendium of the Spanish Father Soarez, *De Arte Rhetorica* (1562), and subsequently of the question-and-answer manuals of Père Pomey (*Novus Candidatus Rhetoricae*, 1659) and Père Jouvancy (*Candidatus Rhetoricae*, 1711). Obviously the study of the dry rules and classifications which I have outlined was not enough to make an orator. The formal treatises provided a framework for the course, but it was filled out with the close study of literary texts, including plays and poems as well as the inevitable orations of Cicero. This began well before the class officially known as rhetoric, in the 'humanities' or even earlier. The aim was to build up a 'copia verborum ac rerum', a rich stock of words, expressions, and erudition which would serve the orator well when he had to prepare a speech or speak impromptu. Characteristically the student reads 'la plume à la main', noting down anything which might come in useful; the result may be seen, for instance, in Racine's numerous annotations of classical literature, most of which date from his Port-Royal school-days. And naturally there were encyclopedic textbooks, such as Erasmus's *Adages* or Étienne Binet's *Essai des merveilles de nature et des plus nobles artifices* (1621), which did a lot of the student's compilation for him.

Sometimes this sort of study of classic texts enabled the master to initiate the pupil into literary criticism as it was then understood —and it was understood in a very rhetorical way. In his *Lettre sur les sourds et muets*, Diderot gives an example of this critical training at a Jesuit college in the early eighteenth century, by which time French texts were being studied alongside classical ones:

Mais si l'on nous faisait remarquer à Louis-le-Grand toutes les beautés de cet endroit de la tragédie de Racine, on ne manquait pas de nous

UNIVERSITY LIBRARIES
CARNEGIE-MELLON UNIVERSITY
PITTSBURGH, PENNSYLVANIA 15213

avertir en même temps qu'elles étaient déplacées dans la bouche de
Théramène, et que Thésée aurait eu raison de l'arrêter et de lui dire:
'Eh! laissez-là le char et les chevaux de mon fils, et parlez-moi de lui.'
Ce n'est pas ainsi, nous ajoutait le célèbre Porée, qu'Antiloche annonce
à Achille la mort de Patrocle. Antiloche s'approche du héros, les larmes
aux yeux, et lui apprend en deux mots la terrible nouvelle . . . 'Patrocle
n'est plus. On combat pour son cadavre. Hector a ses armes.' Il y a plus
de sublime dans ces deux vers d'Homère que dans toute la pompeuse
déclamation de Racine. 'Achille, vous n'avez plus d'ami et vos armes
sont perdues . . .' A ces mots, qui ne sent pas qu'Achille doit voler
au combat? Lorsqu'un morceau pèche contre le décent et le vrai, il
n'est beau ni dans la tragédie ni dans le poème épique. Les détails de
celui de Racine ne convenaient que dans la bouche d'un poète parlant
en son nom, et décrivant la mort d'un de ses héros.
   C'est ainsi que l'habile rhéteur nous instruisait.[8]

Fully as important as this close study of literary texts was the
practical training in writing and speaking. The schoolroom exercises were imitative in nature, their aim being to come as near as
possible to the beautiful latinity of the ancients. Translated into
Latin and adapted by various pedagogues, the *Progymnasmata*, or
elementary exercises of the Hellenistic rhetoricians, Hermogenes
and Aphthonius, did service for many generations; they taught
the schoolboy by example how to construct a fable, a narration,
and all the other constituents of a full-blown speech, how to vary
his style, how to transpose from verse to prose and back again,
how to turn a simple statement into a period of two, three, or four
members, and how to develop a *chria*. This last was an exercise in
which a brief sentence such as 'Lingua nihil peius' or (equally
probable) 'Lingua nihil melius' is expanded according to a strict
eight-part pattern:

1. Praise of the author of the sentence.
2. Paraphrase of the sentence.
3. Proof by cause.
4. Proof by contrast.
5. Comparison.
6. Illustration by example.
7. Quotation of authorities in favour of the sentence.
8. Concluding exhortation.

[8] *Lettre sur les sourds et muets*, ed. P. H. Meyer, *Diderot Studies*, VII (1965), pp. 79–80.

Having mastered these techniques in his humanities class, the young rhetorician was able to proceed to the composition of full-length speeches on the Ciceronian model. And to complete the practical training, there was a multitude of exercises, including the famous plays which the Jesuit fathers composed to give their pupils confidence and skill in oral performance.

So much may be said in general terms about rhetorical studies over two centuries or more. It would be a mistake, however, to imagine rhetoric as a fixed discipline. Although it was rooted in tradition, it changed with the times. In the heroic days of human-ism, the age of Erasmus, the dominant function of rhetoric was generally thought of as ornament. Erasmus's *De Duplici Copia*, composed at the beginning of the sixteenth century and reprinted some thirty times over the next fifty years, has the expressly declared aim of helping the young rhetorician to accumulate a rich stock of material for speaking or writing Latin. Erasmus gives the ritual warnings against decoration for decoration's sake, but his opening sentence makes it clear where he stands: 'Non est aliud vel admirabilius, vel magnificentius quam oratio, divite quadam sententiarum verborumque copia, aurei fluminis instar, exube-rans.'[9] What this means in practice is shown when Erasmus, after outlining some of the traditional means of making speech more impressive, lists no fewer than 158 variations on the simple phrase: 'Tuae litterae me magnopere delectarunt', starting from synonymic substitution, but gradually becoming more ornate as the various tropes and figures are brought into play, so that by the end the sentence has become, for instance: 'Quod apibus cytisum, quod salignae frondes capellis, quod urso mel, hoc mihi tuae sunt litterae.'[10] One is reminded of Ronsard's definition of 'élocution': 'Élocution n'est autre chose qu'une propriété et splendeur de paroles bien choisies et ornées de graves et courtes sentences, qui font reluire les vers comme les pierres précieuses bien enchas-sées les doigts de quelque grand seigneur.'[11] The programme of the Pléiade is in some respects a continuation of Erasmus's rhetoric.

This Renaissance stress on ornament was doubtless encouraged by Peter Ramus's redistribution of the subject-matter of rhetoric.

[9] Erasmus, *Opera Omnia*, Leiden, 1703, vol. I, p. 3.
[10] Ibid., pp. 23–5.
[11] Ronsard, *Œuvres*, ed. G. Cohen, Bibliothèque de la Pléiade, vol. II, p. 1000.

In his desire to map out the field of learning without overlap, Ramus found it necessary to transfer the first two parts of rhetoric, *inventio* and *dispositio*, to the province of logic. Under this dispensation the speaker as well as the philosopher went to logic for help in finding and distributing arguments; rhetoric was then concerned simply with *elocutio* and *pronunciatio*, style and delivery. It is true that Ramus's rhetoric was always taught alongside his logic, and in any case Ramus's classification was more influential in England than in France, where the Jesuits always taught a complete Aristotelian rhetoric, but nevertheless this amputation is symptomatic of the constant tendency in modern times to regard rhetoric merely as the theory of stylistic ornament. This tendency was strong at the beginning of the seventeenth century; one could speak of the dominance at this time of a baroque eloquence of display, a display which shows itself equally in a profusion of such figures as antithesis and hyperbole and in the extravagant use of classical erudition.

The next 150 years saw a gradual and at best spasmodic modification of rhetorical teaching so as to give less emphasis to such obvious forms of display. This does not mean that rhetoric did not continue to centre largely on questions of style and language, but rather that a new stress came to be placed on persuasion and the appeal to the emotions. I think it would be easy to exaggerate the significance of this movement; if one thing is constant, it is that rhetorical theory and practice are not the same thing. The most 'Asiatic' of writers, even at the beginning of the seventeenth century, will speak vigorously in favour of the 'Attic' style. If one can discern without difficulty a general shift in the stylistic norms of writing in French between, say, 1630 and 1730, it would be more difficult to plot this movement in rhetorical theory without a good deal of selection and distortion. Perhaps, rather than claim that the period saw a transformation of rhetoric, one should simply say that taste evolved away from exuberant display and Ciceronian magniloquence to a more subtle form of embellishment. Elegance and wit tended to replace pomp and splendour. Rhetoric did not so much create this movement as follow it, often with a considerable time-lag. There was of course a reciprocal influence between rhetorical teaching and fashionable taste, but rhetoric was always a conservative weight rather than a force for change. For our present purposes at least, the evolution of the stylistics of rhetoric is less significant than some of its constant, unchanging characteristics. Most of these have already been mentioned, but I should like to dwell a little on some of the more important of them.

In the first place, it is worth stressing that classical rhetoric, unlike most literary studies today, combined in one continuous process what one might call literary criticism and creative writing (or speaking). In the words of G. Genette, 'la rhétorique ancienne assurait à la fois une *fonction critique*, qui était d'étudier la littérature, et une *fonction poïétique* (pour parler comme Valéry), qui était de produire à son tour de la littérature en proposant des modèles.'[12] Thus the sort of textual criticism described by Diderot in the *Lettre sur les sourds et muets* was intended to lead not to the writing of critical dissertations (as it might today), but to the production of narrations based on imitation of the good and avoidance of the faulty. In this way, rhetoric launched writers directly into their career. Jean Bruneau, in his *Les Débuts littéraires de Gustave Flaubert*, shows how Flaubert's first writings, narrations such as 'L'Anneau du Chartreux', are in fact simply the exercises of *lycée* rhetoric. Similarly, in the *Progymnasmata* studied in the seventeenth century, the first exercise deals with the fable; the student is taught how to cover the skeleton of one of Aesop's fables, enlivening it with a variety of rhetorical devices—we saw above how this works for 'The Wolf and the Lamb'.

Sometimes the fair copy of the amplified version was taken from approved authors, rather than being simply the invention of the schoolmaster. Rollin, describing the practice of the University of Paris in the early eighteenth century, shows how selected passages from the classics may be reduced to their bare bones and given to the students to work on; then, 'après qu'ils auront fait quelque effort sur chaque partie, on leur lira l'endroit de l'auteur'—the method is not unknown to teachers of foreign languages today. In this manner the 'proposition simple':

Je souhaiterais pouvoir vous le représenter tel qu'il était, lorsqu'après les travaux du Palais, il allait passer les vacations à Basville. Vous le verriez tantôt s'appliquant à l'agriculture, tantôt méditant les discours qu'il devait prononcer à la rentrée du Palais, tantôt accommodant dans quelque allée de son jardin les différends des paysans

[12] G. Genette, 'Enseignement et rhétorique au xxᵉ siècle', *Annales E.S.C.*, 1966, p. 304.

corresponds to this passage from Fléchier's funeral oration for
Lamoignon (funeral orations were great favourites for these
exercises):

Que ne puis-je vous le représenter tel qu'il était, lorsqu'après un long
et pénible travail, loin du bruit de la ville et du tumulte des affaires, il
allait se décharger du poids de sa dignité et jouir d'un noble repos dans
la retraite de Basville! Vous le verriez, tantôt s'adonnant aux plaisirs
innocents de l'agriculture, élevant son esprit aux choses invisibles de
Dieu par les merveilles visibles de la nature; tantôt méditant ces éloquents et graves discours qui enseignaient et inspiraient tous les ans
la justice, et dans lesquels formant l'idée d'un homme de bien, il se
décrivait lui-même sans y penser; tantôt accommodant les différends
que la discorde, la jalousie ou le mauvais conseil font naître parmi les
habitants de la campagne; plus content en lui-même, et peut-être plus
grand aux yeux de Dieu, lorsque dans le fond d'une sombre allée, et sur
un tribunal de gazon, il avait assuré le repos d'une pauvre famille, que
lorsqu'il décidait des fortunes les plus éclatantes sur le premier trône
de la justice.[13]

In this way the writings of the classics are seen as amplifications
on a basic plan, usually, as here, in the proportion of three to one.
What the masters had done, the good student could hope to imitate.

A related and perhaps rather obvious point that should be made
here is that rhetoric, which strictly speaking was the theory of
spoken eloquence, had long since extended its field to cover written composition as well as speech, and verse as well as prose.
Written composition was considered an essential exercise in learning to speak well, but it was also clearly useful in its own right.
Rhetoric tended to blur the distinction between the written and
spoken word, which was in any case less apparent in the seventeenth century than it is today. Speech had much of the formality
which we usually associate with writing, but in return the work
of literature or even the private letter was more readily thought
of as a composition which needed to be read aloud in order to
make its full impact. If, as George Steiner says, a typical activity
of the modern European educated man is to sit by himself reading
a book in silence, the seventeenth century was still close to a time
when it was more normal for books to be read aloud, even by
solitary readers.[14] Although rhetoric might be associated with the

[13] Rollin, op. cit., vol. II, pp. 40–1.
[14] See G. Steiner, *Language and Silence*, London, 1967, p. 104, and W. J. Ong, *The*

pedantry of the schoolroom, it set against the dullness of the written word and the printed book the prestige of the living human voice.

It would be fascinating to follow in detail the changing relationship between poetics and rhetoric. The two had been clearly distinguished by Aristotle, but subsequent rhetoricians often confused them. They virtually merged in many medieval writings, with poetics becoming known as 'la deuxième rhétorique', adding to the precepts of prose rhetoric a collection of rules governing versification. In the period which concerns us, poetics consisted mainly in the establishment of norms for the various literary genres; in this it often echoed the terminology and the assumptions of rhetoric. One of the main interests of critics of poetry was always in questions of language, and in this field, criticism remained the tributary of grammar and rhetoric. As an art of writing, rhetoric contained many rules and techniques directly applicable to verse-writing; moreover, it taught the student to make the necessary distinction between the styles of poetry and oratory. Its examples were taken alike from prose-writers and poets, and its exercises included, though in a relatively minor way, the actual writing of verse. As Claude Fleury said, 'il ne faudrait pas beaucoup de préceptes de poétique à un homme qui saurait ceux de l'éloquence.'[15]

One of the constant characteristics of rhetorical theory is the insistence on things being said or written in the right order. This, of course, was peculiarly the concern of *dispositio*, the second part of rhetoric. To praise order is not necessarily to force all subjects, however different, into the same unchanging mould—although the unintelligent teacher may well give that impression. For example, the order of traditional civil rhetoric was not directly suited to pulpit eloquence, which was after all the most flourishing practical application of rhetoric in the age of Bossuet. In place of Quintilian's order, the preacher learnt to divide his subject, based on a Biblical text, into two or three symmetrical parts, set in the over-all frame of an exordium and a peroration. Not surprisingly, this division in its turn often became a pointless tyranny.

Nor were the theorists blind to the virtues of surprise and

Barbarian Within, New York, 1962, particularly chapters 5 and 12. Both these collections of essays are full of insights relevant to the present volume.
[15] C. Fleury, *Traité du choix et de la méthode des études*, Paris, 1686, p. 246.

shock; they knew that too mechanical an ordering of material is
tedious and therefore defeats the ends of the speaker. In his section
devoted to *dispositio*, Quintilian envisages all sorts of different
ways in which the material of a case can be presented. A distinction is commonly made, for instance, between the sort of dogmatic order which moves from general principles to detailed
examples—from the trunk to the branches to the twigs—and what
Bacon calls the 'method of probation',[16] whereby the listener or
reader is given the feeling of discovering something for himself,
starting with a given phenomenon and only gradually working
back to general principles. The same sort of distinction might be
made concerning artistic composition and the desirability of beginning sometimes from the beginning and sometimes *in media re.*

But however adaptable it might be, rhetoric always insisted that
the speaker should know where he was going. The audience also
should not be left too much in the dark; they might often be
surprised, but they should not be confused; thus for Bary, narrations should be clear, 'parce que la netteté contribue à l'intelligence des auditeurs, et qu'on écoute ordinairement sans ennui ce
qu'on entend sans embarras'.[17] This is perhaps the element of
rhetoric which lives on most strongly after the rhetoric class.
G. Genette has pointed out that modern literature teaching in
France, devoted to critical rather than creative writing, has tended
to concentrate on *dispositio*, on the virtues of the plan.[18] In this
way any subject can be divided into a number of clearly defined
parts and each part into a number of paragraphs, each containing
one distinct idea. Considered in this light, rhetoric has contributed
a great deal to the famous 'clarté française' and the supposedly
Cartesian spirit which was—and perhaps still is—the glory of the
French educational system.

If every paragraph must contain one important idea and only
one, then clearly that idea must be expanded to fill the space available. One of the key notions of rhetoric is that of *amplification*. In
Quintilian's rhetoric the word had been used to indicate the ways
in which a subject could be made to appear more impressive; this
might be done, for instance, by comparing it with something
smaller, or by enumerating its parts, preferably arranging them in

16 Francis Bacon, *Of the Advancement of Learning*, Book 2, XVII, 2–4.
17 René Bary, *La Rhétorique française*, 1673 ed., pp. 210–11.
18 Genette, art. cit.

ascending order of importance. In modern manuals, however, the meaning of the word is shifted and extended. In standard text-books such as Jouvancy's *Candidatus Rhetoricae*, it comes to mean not so much making an object appear bigger as making your speech longer. Where something could be said in a few words, it is amplified to fill several pages. We have seen how this operates in the building up of an eight-part *chria*; one can similarly see it at work in the use of the *loci*. The function of these 'places', it will be remembered, is to help the orator find something to say on any given point. The sixteen standard 'intrinsic' places are: definition, enumeration of parts, etymology, derivatives, genus, species, resemblance, dissimilarity, contraries, circumstances, antecedents, consequences, contradiction, causes, effects, and comparison. There is no need to explain all these in detail; an example will show better what they entail. Jouvancy demonstrates how the student, faced with a typical subject, will run through the check-list:

1. S'agit-il de faire l'éloge de l'éloquence? Tirez d'abord un argu-ment *de la Définition du Mot*. Dites que c'est l'art de persuader l'auditeur, ou bien de l'amener à changer de volonté. Qu'y a-t-il de plus noble, de plus utile au genre humain?

2. De *l'Énumération des Parties*. L'éloquence forme l'intelligence des enfants, dompte les passions de la jeunesse, règle les conseils de la vieillesse.

3. De *l'Étymologie du Nom*. Vous expliquerez le mot Éloquence

and so on, relentlessly, through all the *loci*.[19] Not that the rhetori-cian was expected to use material derived from *all* the places, but his immediate reaction when faced with a subject was supposedly to run through the list. It is noticeable that examples of the use of the places often come from the rather pointless subjects of epideictic oratory, the praise of eloquence, the condemnation of prodigality, and so forth. The connection between these and the set patterns of the epitaph, the panegyric, and the funeral oration is all too obvious.

The places were much criticized in the seventeenth century, perhaps most effectively in the *Logique* of Arnauld and Nicole and the *De l'art de parler* of Bernard Lamy. It was the places above all else which led to the disgrace of rhetoric, since the accumulation of

---

[19] J. Jouvancy, *L'Élève de rhétorique* (a trans. of his *Candidatus Rhetoricae* by H. Ferté), Paris, 1892, pp. 24–5.

commonplaces was clearly at odds with the demands of meaning-
ful communication. It was particularly repugnant to the philosophers whom I shall be discussing in the next two chapters,
whose concern was with things rather than words. Arnauld and
Nicole wrote: 'Rien n'étouffe plus les bonnes semences que
l'abondance des mauvaises herbes: rien ne rend un esprit plus
stérile en pensées justes et solides que cette mauvaise fertilité de
pensées communes. L'esprit s'accoutume à cette facilité, et ne fait
plus d'effort pour trouver les raisons propres, particulières et
naturelles, qui ne se découvrent que dans la considération attentive de son sujet.'[20] Nevertheless, in spite of all the attacks of the
Cartesians and the *philosophes*, the places held their own for a long
time. Writing as late as 1825, M. Andrieux gives an outline of
them in his *Préceptes d'éloquence*; he is distinctly apologetic about
them, but reminds his more mature readers that they are a very
useful aid to the inexperienced and the slow-witted.

When Pomey and Jouvancy speak of amplification, they are
usually thinking not so much of the *loci* as of various stylistic
means of magnifying a subject or spinning out a speech. They
both begin their sections on amplification with lists of words which
may prove useful, mainly nouns and adjectives which can be used
to praise, to blame, or simply to develop a subject at greater
length. Thus Pomey shows how someone who has to compose
a speech in praise of virginity could try out a series of words
beginning with 'a': *admirabilis, amabilis, argenteus, aureus, adamas,
agnus, ara, astrum, absconditus, abundans, adversarius, aeternus, arbor,
ars, arx, aula*, etc.[21] Some of these will prove more suitable than
others and can serve as a starting-point for interesting developments. Then he will try the figures, turning his subject in all directions and selecting whatever is most effective—to this end Pomey
gives thirty different figurative versions of the sentence: 'Pec-
catum fugiendum est, quia innumeras in hac vita poenas affert, et
aeternas in altera.'[22] Similarly he will learn how to develop a short
sentence into a period. Pomey calls this *dilatatio periodica*, and the
term seems entirely appropriate for the exercise which consists
of swelling 'Peccati gravitas maxima' into 'Tanta inest peccato
vel levissimo gravitas, tanta foeditas, tanta pestis, ut omnium

[20] A. Arnauld and P. Nicole, *La Logique ou l'art de penser*, ed. P. Clair and F. Girbal, Paris, 1965, p. 235.
[21] Pomey, op. cit., pp. 244–6. [22] Op. cit., pp. 254–64.

mortalium salus, et orbis universi conservatio unico sit, ut ita dicam, mendacio posthabendum'—and this is only a modest two-part period.[23]

It is hard for a modern reader to read the precepts of amplification with a straight face. They remind one of the *Exercices de style* of Raymond Queneau; they are all the funnier because they are meant seriously. But if one recalls that the aim was originally to give schoolboys a mastery of the resources of a foreign language, the method seems more appropriate. It is more dubious, perhaps, as a guide to writing and speaking one's native language and seems particularly ill-suited to the sort of communication which aims at practicality or meaningfulness, that of scientists, philosophers, or businessmen. The concept of amplification conflicts too with many widely held views about the nature of literary creation, and by itself it is clearly woefully inadequate to deal with a piece of writing such as *Bérénice*; yet it appears to be echoed in Racine's boast that 'toute l'invention consiste à faire quelque chose de rien'.[24] As in a *chria*, his subject is given him in a few words: 'Titus reginam Berenicen, cui etiam nuptias pollicitus ferebatur, statim ab Urbe dimisit invitus invitam.' His task as playwright is first to work this up into a complete plan and then to fill it out with the riches of *elocutio*.

It is particularly in the field of *elocutio* that one notices a further constant of ancient rhetoric, the notion, familiar to modern stylistics, of departure from a norm. I have already said a little about the Renaissance concept of rhetoric as ornament; even if the rhetoricians of subsequent centuries condemned the more ostentatious forms of ornamental language, they shared with the Humanists the belief that the aim of rhetoric is to teach people to speak in a peculiarly elevated or refined manner. There was of course a constant need to hold a balance between 'nature' and 'art'; all theorists were careful to protest that natural gifts are indispensable to the formation of an orator. At the same time, as theorists of

---

[23] Op. cit., pp. 159–60. The eccentric Nicolas de Hauteville, in the preface to his presentation of Raymond Lulle, *L'Art de bien discourir*, Paris, 1666, shows 'que sur la pointe d'une aiguille (qui est une matière fort déliée), on peut former des discours de six heures et même de dix jours entiers, et dilater les preuves du sujet proposé par une amplification si riche et si féconde, qu'on y pourra fournir plus de quatorze cents raisons'.

[24] Preface to *Bérénice*. See also Racine's 'canevas' for an unwritten play, *Iphigénie en Tauride*, in his *Œuvres*, ed. Picard, Bibliothèque de la Pléiade, vol. I, pp. 965–9.

a complicated art, they had obviously to claim that the eloquence which they taught did not come naturally. Quintilian says of *elocutio*: 'it is on this that teachers of rhetoric concentrate their attention, since it cannot possibly be acquired without the assistance of the rules of art' (VIII. Pr. 16).

There are certain difficulties in the way of this assertion. For one thing, the practice of eloquence preceded the theory of rhetoric, which therefore appears to be doing no more than codifying the natural laws of effective speech. Moreover, it is obvious to anyone who keeps his ears open that all the tropes and figures are in constant use in the street and the market-place. It is therefore unsatisfactory to define the figures of rhetoric by opposition to the normal way of talking. Yet to have any effect they must be perceived as in some way unusual or different. Different from what, then? Pierre Fontanier, whose work *Les Figures du discours* (1830) is the culmination of a long stylistic tradition, gives the following answer: 'Les figures du discours sont les traits, les formes ou les tours plus ou moins remarquables et d'un effet plus ou moins heureux, par lesquels le discours, dans l'expression des idées, des pensées ou des sentiments, s'éloigne plus ou moins de ce qui en eût été l'expression simple et commune.'[25] In other words there is an imagined or real *degré zéro* of simple expression on which figurative language is perceived as a variation. Fontanier goes on to exclude such grammatical figures as are imposed by the language, allowing the name of figure only to those turns of phrase which are the result of a free choice. This being so, the use of figures designates the speaker as someone who has chosen to speak in an unusual way. Rhetoric conceived in this way is essentially artificial, and rhetorical language proclaims its distance from an assumed norm.

This concept of rhetoric, which has recently been eloquently expounded by G. Genette in his collection of essays, *Figures*,[26] and in his introduction to Fontanier's *Les Figures du discours*, is by no means an exhaustive account. Indeed, taken by itself, it is a severe distortion of an art whose aim was originally and above all to persuade. Persuasion necessitated, so it was held, the appearance of sincerity. The orator, in order to be effective, must conceal as

[25] P. Fontanier, *Les Figures du discours*, ed. G. Genette, Paris, 1969, p. 64.
[26] G. Genette, *Figures*, Paris, 1966. See in particular the essay entitled 'Figures', pp. 205–11.

far as possible his artifices and use the figures in such a way as to make them seem the natural expression of his emotion rather than the weapons he has chosen or, worse still, the ornament he has bestowed on his ideas. To quote one example among many, Bernard Lamy declares: 'L'étude et l'art qui paraissent dans un discours peigné ne sont pas le caractère d'un esprit qui est vivement touché des choses dont il parle, mais plutôt d'un homme qui est dégagé de toutes affaires et qui se joue.'[27] The stress on emotion and the appearance of naturalness runs directly counter to Genette's notion of rhetoric as self-proclaiming artifice. Both have to be taken into account. Indeed one can attempt to reconcile them, saying, for instance, that it is only the abnormal, when not perceived as a deliberate trick, which can enable a speaker to work effectively on his audience. But this is still a long way from Genette's view of rhetoric as the art which taught how to signify that a piece of writing or speech was 'literature' and not simple communication.

This was indeed one of the great problems of rhetoric. It was attempting to play two different roles, which are not easily reconciled. The first was *l'art de persuader*, the art of effective communication, relying heavily on the appearance of sincere emotion on the part of the speaker. The second was *l'art de bien dire*, where the stress lay more on saying things as well as possible—and 'well' here tended to mean 'in a distinguished and elegant way'. As *l'art de bien dire* it favoured a deliberately literary use of language which set the speaker and the speech apart from and above the norms of simple communication. To see how this worked in practice one has only to look at the manuals of Pomey or Jouvancy. For theorists such as these the comparisons which come to mind to describe the figures of rhetoric are jewels and flowers. Less metaphorically, Jouvancy's catechism puts it this way:

C'est grâce aux figures qu'un discours a de la dignité, de la force et une certaine majesté qui distingue l'élocution oratoire.
— Qu'est-ce qu'une figure?
— C'est une forme de langage plus élégante que le langage ordinaire, auquel elle ne ressemble pas.[28]

[27] B. Lamy, *La Rhétorique ou l'art de parler*, 4th ed., Amsterdam, 1699; Sussex Reprints, 1969, p. 149. The original title was *De l'art de parler*.
[28] Jouvancy, op. cit., p. 54.

In many respects the notion of distinction coincides with that of amplification, notably in the widespread admiration for the elegant periphrasis. Thus Dumarsais, grammarian, *philosophe*, and author of the classic treatise *Des tropes*, quotes with approval these lines of the seventeenth-century poet Brébeuf, which refer to the Phœnician who was supposed to have invented writing:

> C'est de lui que nous vient cet art ingénieux
> De peindre la parole et de parler aux yeux,
> Et par les traits divers de figures tracées,
> Donner de la couleur et du corps aux pensées

—all this rather than say that he invented writing, 'ce qui serait une expression trop simple pour la poésie'.[29] Too simple for poetry and too simple for rhetoric, as we have seen in considering the *dilatatio periodica*. Not that distinction always involves circumlocution; so common is the use of embellishing figures that the simple statement acquires a particular force of its own. Thus it is that the 'Fiat lux' of Genesis and the 'Qu'il mourût' of Corneille's *Horace* are the invariably quoted examples of *le sublime*.

It would not be an exaggeration to see in this concern for distinction a sign of the social function of rhetoric. Learning to speak 'well' is like learning to dress and behave with the style which marks the well-bred man. We have seen how rhetoric shades off into an area of manuals on letter-writing, compliments, table-manners, and the like. Often rhetoricians compare the proper use of words to elegant clothing. Erasmus writes: 'Quod est vestis nostro corpori, id est sententiis, elocutio. Neque enim aliter quam forma dignitasque corporis, cultu habituque, itidem et sententia verbis vel commendatur, vel deturpatur.'[30] And more than three centuries later Andrieux reminds his reader that 'les bienséances oratoires ne sont autre chose que les bienséances sociales transportées dans le discours'.[31] For the *notable* of the nineteenth century, a training in rhetoric, like a knowledge of Greek and Latin, set him apart from his less fortunate fellow citizens. In the same

---

[29] C. C. Dumarsais, *Des tropes*, 3rd ed., Paris, 1775, p. 35.
[30] Erasmus, op. cit., p. 8.
[31] M. Andrieux, *Préceptes d'éloquence*, 2nd ed., Paris, 1838, preface, p. v. Roland Barthes remarks that 'dans la société bourgeoise, l'art de parler selon certaines règles est à la fois un signe de pouvoir social et un instrument de ce pouvoir' ('L'analyse rhétorique' in *Littérature et société*, Éditions de l'Institut de sociologie de l'Université libre de Bruxelles, 1967).

way, as Georges Snyders has pointed out in his study of the
pedagogy of the *ancien régime*, the study of rhetoric took its place
alongside the study of the ancient world and the closed boarding
system to separate the life of the Jesuit college from the world
outside.[32] In this case, however, it must be said that in intention
(if not in effect) this separation was dictated by moral and religious
rather than social aims.

At all events, both the reliance on amplification and the notion
of departure from a norm of simplicity caused many writers to
criticize rhetoric as trivial or artificial, less concerned with truthful
communication than with sterile word-games. This was very much
Descartes's idea of the art, and Descartes's ideas were echoed over
the next two hundred years by generations of philosophers and
scientists. Their objections are easy to imagine; they mocked at
the precocious ability of children to juggle with words before they
had any ideas to express and they exposed the distortion of simple
truth in the name of fluency and elegance. It is enough to quote
one of the most vehement opponents of school rhetoric, the
Encyclopedist d'Alembert, whose views on the subject are discussed at greater length in Chapter 3:

On donne à ces discours le nom d'*amplifications*; nom très convenable
en effet, puisqu'ils consistent pour l'ordinaire à noyer dans deux
feuilles de verbiage ce qu'on pourrait et ce qu'on devrait dire en deux
lignes. Je ne parle point de ces figures de rhétorique si chères à quelques pédants modernes, et dont le nom même est devenu si ridicule,
que les professeurs les plus sensés les ont entièrement bannies de leurs
leçons.[33]

To this the defenders of rhetoric would have replied, like
Diderot's Maréchale: 'Voilà bien les abus; mais ce n'est pas la
chose.' Indeed almost all theorists warned their readers against
what was commonly called 'la fausse rhétorique'. By this they
meant the futile art of decorative word-spinning which did not
contribute to the true end of rhetoric, persuasion. In this connection it is interesting to examine the controversy which blew up
towards the end of the seventeenth century about the place of
rhetoric in preaching.[34] This had always been a tricky problem.

[32] G. Snyders, *La Pédagogie en France aux xviie et xviiie siècles*, Paris, 1965. See in
particular part 1, chapter 5.   [33] *Encyclopédie*, article 'Collège'.
[34] See B. Munteano, *Constantes dialectiques en littérature et en histoire*, Paris, 1967,
pp. 354–60.

The theoretical solution seemed to have been given once and for all by Saint Augustine in his *De Doctrina Christiana*; his teaching allows rhetoric a place, but insists that it should be of the functional sort, the servant rather than the mistress of subject-matter. In 1694 some of Augustine's sermons were translated by Goibaud Dubois, who used his preface as an occasion to attack 'la fausse rhétorique', as he calls it. His attack was renewed by the Benedictine François Lamy in the fifth book of his *De la connaissance de soi-même* (1700). What Dubois and Lamy call false rhetoric is 'l'art d'aller à l'esprit par le cœur et d'aller au cœur par l'imagination'. They think that the preacher should stick to the straightforward exposition of the truth—according to them, this, and this alone, is true rhetoric. This attack provoked a number of replies,[35] all of which insist that if the term 'false rhetoric' is used, it should be applied only to decorative and ineffectual rhetoric. The sort of emotive and imaginative persuasion which had been criticized by Lamy and Dubois was, according to Antoine Arnauld, absolutely essential to rhetoric. In an ideal world, simply to tell the truth might be enough; in a fallen world persuasion inevitably involved the use of irrational means.

The emphasis on irrational persuasion is one of the most important constants of rhetorical theory. As we have seen, it often conflicts with the notion of rhetoric as the sign of the artificial. It is hard to weigh up the relative importance of these two elements. On the one hand, it seems likely that the sort of school exercise which I have discussed was calculated to instil into the schoolboy an image of rhetoric as something quite distinct from ordinary persuasive communication. Learning to build up a *chria* or to make stylistic variations on a piece of general wisdom seems a far cry from getting your neighbour to do what you want. But later in life, seeing the persuasive effect of a sermon or a barrister's harangue, a man might come to accept something of the exaggerated claims for the power of formal eloquence which theorists were naturally keen to put forward.

Some striking things were said about oratory. A sixteenth-century Jesuit father speaks in these terms of the ideal orator:

C'est une chose humainement divine et divinement humaine de savoir dignement manier d'esprit et de langue un sujet, le concevoir en l'âme

---

[35] See in particular A. Arnauld and others, *Réflexions sur l'éloquence*, Paris, 1700.

avec de belles et judicieuses pensées, ranger ses pensées d'une sage
ordonnance, les revêtir d'un riche langage, et les porter à l'oreille de
l'auditeur avec une mémoire ferme, une voix vivement éclatante et
doucement pénétrante, et d'une pareille séance de tout le corps, se
faire efficacement entendre, planter de nouvelles opinions et nouveaux
désirs ès cœurs et en arracher les vieux, fléchir et plier les volontés
raidies, s'adresser et raidir les tortues et lâches et victorieusement
persuader et dissuader ce qu'on veut.[36]

This clearly echoes the enthusiasm of Cicero and Quintilian. It
reminds one too of Du Bellay's very rhetorical notion of the ideal
poet, 'qui me fera indigner, apaiser, éjouir, douloir, aimer, haïr,
admirer, étonner, bref, qui tiendra la bride de mes affections,
me tournant çà et là à son plaisir'.[37] Du Bellay ends his *Défense
et illustration* with the image of the 'Hercule gaulois', dragging
men along by chains attached to his tongue, a symbol of
eloquence which was often used in sixteenth-century France.
It was used in the following century too, for instance by
the Abbé d'Aubignac in his *Discours académique sur l'éloquence*.
The Abbé describes how the orator 'remplit si adroitement
l'imagination de ses auditeurs de tout ce qui peut charmer,
que le jugement ne se peut appliquer sur les autres objets
extérieurs'.[38]

Here the emphasis is on imagination, 'cette partie dominante
de l'âme, cette maîtresse d'erreur et de fausseté'.[39] Bacon too had
stressed the central role of the imagination in persuasion: 'the
duty and office of rhetoric is to apply reason to imagination for
the better moving of the will.'[40] Where pure logic would present
the facts of the case in a disembodied way, rhetoric aims to conjure
up images before the mind's eye, painting vivid pictures of happiness or misery. The process is described in hostile terms by a
philosopher who had no love for rhetoric, Malebranche. In a section of *De la recherche de la vérité* entitled 'De la communication
contagieuse des imaginations fortes', he shows how in society the
man with a vivid imagination is better able to persuade others:

[36] Quoted by F. de Dainville, 'L'évolution de l'enseignement de la rhétorique au
xvii⁰ siècle', *Dix-septième Siècle*, nos. 80–1, 1968, p. 20.
[37] J. du Bellay, *La Défense et illustration de la langue française*, ed. H. Chamard, Paris,
1948, p. 179.
[38] F. H. d'Aubignac, *Discours académique sur l'éloquence*, Paris, 1668, p. 15.
[39] B. Pascal, *Pensées*, ed. L. Lafuma, Paris, 1951, para. 81.
[40] Bacon, op. cit., Book 2, xviii, 2.

'Quoique sa rhétorique soit souvent irrégulière, elle ne laisse pas d'être très persuasive.'[41]

A few pages earlier we read: 'Les personnes passionnées nous passionnent.'[42] Clearly there is no sharp distinction between what philosophers then called the appeal to the imagination and the appeal to the passions. In presenting an absent scene to our imagination, the orator is in fact aiming to stir up desire, love, fear, hate, indignation, or some other emotion in his audience. And the rhetoricians knew, as La Rochefoucauld knew, that 'les passions sont les seuls orateurs qui persuadent toujours'.[43] A speaker may speak with the tongue of angels, he will achieve nothing if he does not command our emotions. For this reason rhetoric had always given a good deal of attention to a study of the passions. Aristotle in particular had devoted most of his second book to this subject; his remarks were regularly repeated in modern treatises. Balthasar Gibert, who wrote a critical history of rhetoric at the beginning of the eighteenth century, noted that Soarez's manual was good on all aspects of rhetoric except the passions,[44] but this deficiency was remedied in the practice of the Jesuit colleges of the seventeenth century. François de Dainville, who has studied the manuscript notes of the rhetoric courses which were actually taught at this period, concludes that 'la conviction qu'ils ont que la rhétorique est moins un art de prouver qu'un art de persuader, les conduit à apprendre à leurs élèves à faire moins appel aux arguments de raison qu'aux émotions qui entraînent le cœur'.[45] The same tendency is found in French rhetorics, notably in Bernard Lamy's *De l'art de parler*, which compares the orator to a soldier using the figures of rhetoric as weapons to compel the submission of his enemy.[46] Thus the perfect orator must be able to predict and play on the likely emotional reactions of his audience. But above all he must be able to simulate passion himself, since, as Bernard Lamy says, echoing Horace's 'Si vis me flere' for the thousandth time, 'on ne peut pas toucher les autres, si on ne paraît touché'.[47] So rhetoric teaches the speaker to show emotion even if he does not feel it, and indicates some of the

[41] N. Malebranche, *Œuvres complètes*, sous la direction d'André Robinet; vols. I, II, III, *De la recherche de la vérité*, ed. G. Rodis-Lewis, Paris, 1962-4, vol. I, p. 329.

[42] Ibid., p. 324.   [43] La Rochefoucauld, *Maximes*, no. 8.

[44] B. Gibert, *Les Jugements des savants sur les auteurs qui ont traité de la rhétorique*, Paris, 1713-19, vol. III, pp. 43-4.   [45] Dainville, op. cit., p. 30.

[46] Lamy, op. cit., pp. 137-41.   [47] Op. cit., p. 111.

figures—such as hesitation or exclamation—which make this easier. At this point the orator is close to the actor, whose task is to move the theatre audience with his own simulated emotion, and to the playwright, who gives him the words which make this simulation possible.

Together with the appeal to the passions and the imagination Malebranche mentions the appeal to the senses. This can mean various things. It can indicate the power of harmony over men's minds, springing, for instance, from the 'plaisir sensible . . . de la mesure des périodes',[48] which brings the orator close to an Orphic enchanter. Or else it may refer to the use of tropes such as the metaphor, which often evoke an attractive physical object in the place of the more abstract real subject of discourse, since, as Lamy says:

Les hommes pour l'ordinaire ne sont capables de comprendre que les choses qui entrent dans l'esprit par les sens. Pour leur faire concevoir ce qui est spirituel, il se faut servir de comparaisons sensibles, qui sont agréables, parce qu'elles soulagent l'esprit et l'exemptent de l'application qu'il faut avoir pour découvrir ce qui ne tombe pas sous les sens.[49]

In both cases there is a connection here between the two potential enemies, the eloquence of display and the appeal to the emotions. What might seem trivial may turn out to be effectively persuasive.

The appeal to the passions, the appeal to the imagination, and the appeal to the senses, all these made rhetoric suspect to philosophers, whose model of communication was rather the pure rationality of mathematical symbols. Rhetoric, with its reliance on the probable as opposed to the certain, could easily be seen simply as a knack, which was morally neutral and could as well be used in the cause of evil as in the cause of good. As such it had been attacked by Plato, most vehemently in his *Gorgias*, where he equates rhetoric with beauty-culture and cookery, both of them arts which pander harmfully to men's depraved tastes, rather than sticking to what is true or real. As beauty-culture is to athletics, so is rhetoric to proper debate. A similar attack is launched many years later in the *Phaedrus*; here, it is true, Plato is willing to envisage the possibility of a reformed rhetoric, but this turns out to be so close to simple truth-telling as hardly to be a rhetoric at all. And of course from his absolute standpoint Plato was right.

[48] Malebranche, op. cit., vol. 1, p. 178. [49] Lamy, op. cit., p. 106.

Rhetoric does indeed advise a regrettable departure from the ideal of plain speaking. All the theorists of the subject, from Aristotle on, repeat piously that rhetoric's true place is as the servant of truth, and that the good orator must necessarily be a good man. But this is no more than wishful thinking and professional self-defence. In the end rhetoric remains characteristically intent above all else on swaying a public. It is less concerned with the discovery of the truth than with the means of successfully communicating any belief, whether true or false.

The final constant of rhetoric, which I shall discuss very briefly, is the notion of adaptation to an audience. This is implicit in a good deal of what I have already said, concerning both stylistic 'bienséances' and the appeal to the emotions. Whereas the logician is concerned with the techniques of discovering new truths, the rhetorician is interested in the transmission of any message. His image of speech or writing is that of a communicator constantly aware of his audience's reactions and expectations, and ready to adjust to changing circumstances. A primordial condition of per-suasion is that the persuader should know his audience and know what sort of concessions he needs to make to their tastes, habits, and prejudices. He may wish to change their minds on a specific issue, but he will normally be able to do this only if he respects their opinions on other issues. His language must always be fundamentally the language which is expected of him in a given situation; he may shock his audience for certain strong effects, but only in the context of an over-all linguistic conformity. To put it crudely, the disciple of rhetoric had to be a flatterer.

Nothing could be further from the spirit of rhetoric than the romantic notion of writing or speaking as self-expression. If rhetoric seems to be sincere, this is a calculated sincerity, designed to impress an audience. Again, nothing could be less like the image of the orator than the unvarying man of integrity. The orator may be an honest man, but he will know how to clothe his honesty in the appropriate costume, how to wear a mask if need be. From the beginning of his speech, his first task is to capture the goodwill of his hearers, and this means speaking their lan-guage, accepting their criteria, and himself appearing to be the sort of man whom his audience like and trust. Even if he wants to tell the truth, he has to know that, as Sartre puts it, 'la loi de toute rhétorique, c'est qu'il faut mentir pour être vrai'.

Here, I think, we have the common feature of the various aspects of rhetoric which I have touched on. They all involve some sort of lie, some departure from a vision of straight, honest speaking. Of course, such a vision is utopian. All systems of verbal communication appear to contain an element of distortion. But rhetoric, as I have described it, carries this distortion further than most systems. It does this partly in the name of pleasure, the pleasure which comes from mastering words and playing with them or from enjoying this mastery in others. But primarily the distortion is designed to make persuasion more effective. Without it, according to the rhetorician, truth will go unheard in the wicked world where people are swayed by the senses, the imagination, and the passions rather than by pure reason. With it, the speaker will be able to compete equally, to make himself heard, and to carry the day.

For the serious writer or speaker, however, the cost of this persuasion and this pleasure is high. The message of truth becomes dissolved in a worldly ritual of elegant words or grandiose amplification; the sincere belief is compromised by the reliance on irrational means of persuasion. To accept any rhetoric wholeheartedly is felt to be a betrayal of the truth, but to reject all rhetoric seems impossible this side of silence. What the speaker or writer must do is to be conscious of the rhetoric he is using, ridding it as far as he can of those elements which are an embarrassment to him, creating where possible his own rhetoric, or at any rate modifying the traditional rhetoric. Often indeed the most effective communication rests on an apparent denial of rhetoric, but it must not be imagined that this *degré zéro* is not a rhetoric too, and one which can become as tarnished as the old one—'unaccustomed as I am to public speaking . . .'

Most writers of seventeenth- and eighteenth-century France stopped a long way short of any *degré zéro*, but all were more or less conscious of the sort of problems which I have been outlining. For some the dilemmas of rhetoric presented themselves in dramatic terms, for others they were rather the object of amused interest. The aim of the following chapters is to examine the reactions of a number of important writers and speakers to their rhetorical situation and the ways in which they attempted to resolve the contradictions of rhetoric and truth.

II

PHILOSOPHY AND
PERSUASION

SOCRATES: What I call oratory is a branch of something
which certainly isn't a fine or honourable pursuit.

GORGIAS: What do you mean, Socrates? Speak out and
don't be afraid of hurting my feelings.

SOCRATES: Well, Gorgias, the whole of which oratory is
a branch seems to me to be a pursuit which has nothing
to do with art, but which requires in its practitioners a
shrewd and bold spirit together with a natural aptitude
for dealing with men. The generic name which I should
give it is pandering; it has many subdivisions, one of
which is cookery, an occupation which masquerades
as an art but in my opinion is no more than a knack
acquired by routine. I should classify oratory and
beauty-culture and popular lecturing as species of the
same genus.

(Plato: *Gorgias*)

PHILOSOPHY and rhetoric had long been enemies.[1] Plato had stated in all their force the philosopher's objections to rhetoric as the adulteration of truth in the name of pleasure and persuasion. It is not surprising that the philosophers of the seventeenth and eighteenth centuries took a similar line. Their concern, as they often repeated, was the search for truth, and by this they often meant scientific certainty—it is as well to remember at the outset that at this time there was no sharp distinction between what we should now call science and philosophy. From the time of Francis Bacon on, the search for truth, whether about the mind of man or the universe around him, was increasingly seen as proceeding by observation and experiment rather than by debate and exegesis. Thinkers attempted to give to their theories the irrefutability of mathematics. The dialectic of the preceding centuries was condemned as useless for the discovery of new truths; at best it was no more than an instrument for communicating or debating what was already known. Nevertheless, although the emphasis was on the new methods of discovery, communication remained a necessity. Some sort of rhetoric was unavoidable. But could the rhetoric of scientific and philosophical communication be the same as the traditional rhetoric of the law courts, the pulpit, and the public assembly, an art which was primarily oral and which aimed to win the assent of a large, unspecialized audience by any available means? Or was it possible to evolve a new technique which appealed not so much to the imagination, the senses, and the passions as to the rational side of man's nature?

We have seen that even in the field of preaching, an oral activity where the old lessons of rhetoric were notably appropriate, certain extremists advocated a non-emotive form of communication.[2] If the preacher could in theory get along without appealing to the

---

[1] A valuable introduction to this question as it affected Renaissance England is provided by W. S. Howell, *Logic and Rhetoric in England, 1500–1700*, New York, 1956. See also W. J. Ong, *Ramus, Method and the Decay of Dialogue*, Cambridge, Mass., 1958, and B. Munteano, *Constantes dialectiques en littérature et en histoire*, Paris, 1967.

[2] See above, pp. 27–8.

irrational, one might expect that the philosopher-scientist, whose concern was not to win men's souls but to convey, usually in writing, his quasi-mathematical certainties, would use a plain method of exposition. And in fact we do find something like this, particularly in the English scientific movement of the seventeenth century. Members of the Royal Society were expected to keep to 'a close, naked, natural way of speaking; positive expressions; clear senses; a native easiness: bringing all things as near the mathematical plainness as they can; and preferring the language of Artisans, Countrymen and Merchants before that of wits and scholars'.[3] But many difficulties remained. Not all philosophy is capable of such plain exposition; if in the field of natural philosophy (i.e. natural science) it is often possible to communicate without touching the emotions of the audience, the same is less likely to be true of moral or metaphysical philosophy. Moreover, not all philosophical communication is conducted between members of the Royal Society. Different audiences, more or less learned, demand different techniques of communication or persuasion—and even the most learned men are not disembodied minds.

Francis Bacon, one of the originators of the new scientific philosophy, has some interesting things to say about the problems of communication.[4] While he rejects much of traditional rhetoric— and particularly the Renaissance conception of rhetoric as ornament—he is very much aware of the obstacles (or 'Idols') which stand in the way of acceptance of the truth. He therefore sees the need of an art which will help to break down these obstacles; this art is rhetoric, which teaches us to enlist the imagination on the side of reason in its battle against the passions of men. This involves various practical recommendations, one of the most important being the suggestion of different orders of exposition for different subjects and audiences.

Some valuable work has been done on English contributions to the theory of learned communication.[5] My aim in this section is to explore how things were ordered in France. Clearly, I cannot

---

[3] Thomas Sprat's *History of the Royal Society* (1667), quoted in Howell, op. cit., p. 390.

[4] Bacon, *Advancement of Learning*, Book 2, XVII–XVIII. See K. R. Wallace *Francis Bacon on Communication and Rhetoric*, Chapel Hill, N.C., 1943.

[5] See W. S. Howell, op. cit. and 'John Locke and the New Rhetoric', *Quarterly Journal of Speech*, 1967, and R. F. Jones and others, *The Seventeenth Century*, Stanford, Cal., 1951.

hope to cover the field exhaustively; this would involve an extensive treatment of the theory and practice of the Port-Royalists,
Malebranche, Fontenelle, and Condillac,[6] to mention only the
most important. I have chosen rather to concentrate in the first
place on Descartes as the philosopher who commands our immediate attention. I shall try, with all the hesitations of one who is
not a professional philosopher, to show what were his solutions,
both theoretical and practical, to the problems of philosophical
communication. Then, in the first part of Chapter 3, I shall deal
more rapidly with the ensuing alliances and dissensions of rhetoric
and philosophy—since in most cases a fuller consideration would
mean repeating what had already been said in relation to Descartes—and finally, in the second and third parts of the same
chapter, I shall examine the writings of two prominent enlighteners, Montesquieu and d'Alembert, who had to face the
rhetorical problems of an age when philosophy was becoming
triumphantly popular.

[6] Malebranche, Fontenelle, and Condillac are briefly discussed in Chapter 3; they
would repay more detailed study.

2. Descartes: *la recherche de la vérité*

> Ceux qui ont le raisonnement le plus fort, et qui digèrent
> le mieux leurs pensées, afin de les rendre claires et intel-
> ligibles, peuvent toujours le mieux persuader ce qu'ils
> proposent, encore qu'ils ne parlassent que bas breton, et
> qu'ils n'eussent jamais appris de rhétorique.
>
> (Descartes: *Discours de la méthode*)

PERHAPS we can start from Descartes's notions concerning poetry, remembering that poetics and rhetoric were almost twin sisters in his day.[1] From time to time Descartes speaks highly of the poetic faculty. In his account of Descartes's dream, Baillet records the philosopher's belief in the poet's ability both to find the truth and to imprint it on men's minds; this power stems from 'la divinité de l'inspiration' and 'la force de l'imagination', which can reveal truth more easily than 'la Raison dans les Philosophes' (*Alq.* 1. 56–7).[2] And much later, in 1649, Descartes speaks again, though perhaps mainly in order to flatter Princess Elizabeth, of the 'emportement' of the poet, which he takes as 'une marque d'un esprit plus fort et plus relevé que le commun' (*Corr.* VIII. 142). It will be noticed that the later passage no longer attributes to the poet the vision of the truth, and in general this Ronsardian idea of the poet as seer is absent from Descartes's writings and far removed from his way of thinking, his constant concern being to develop a method for the advancement of knowledge which would have the rational certainty of mathematics.

Not that the philosopher did not enjoy poetry. In the *Discours*

---

[1] Among the vast number of books devoted to René Descartes and his philosophy, the most relevant to the subject of this essay is the excellent work of H. Gouhier, *La Pensée métaphysique de Descartes*, Paris, 1962, particularly chapters 3 and 4, to which I am indebted on various points.

[2] Descartes's works are referred to wherever possible in the recent edition of F. Alquié, *Œuvres philosophiques*, Paris, 1963–7 (cited as *Alq.*). Works not contained in the two volumes of this edition which have so far appeared are referred to in the following editions: *Œuvres*, ed. C. Adam and P. Tannery, Paris, 1897–1913 (cited as *A.T.*), and *Correspondance*, ed. C. Adam and G. Milhaud, Paris, 1936–63 (cited as *Corr.*). The French translations of Descartes's Latin writings are in all cases those given in these editions.

de la méthode he describes himself as having been 'amoureux de la poésie' and well aware that it possesses 'des délicatesses et des douceurs très ravissantes', but poetry is seen here as a giver of delight, something the young man will grow out of together with the pleasures of bookish humanism: 'je croyais avoir déjà donné assez de temps aux langues, et même aussi à la lecture des livres anciens, et à leurs histoires, et à leurs fables' (*Alq.* I. 572–4). Later on, he and Huyghens seem to share a sort of amused contempt for poetry as a juvenile occupation—though Huyghens dabbles in it far more than Descartes (*Corr.* VI. 133). Similarly, having been drawn into discussing a love-song at some length and with apparent seriousness, Descartes stops short and laughs at his subject: 'Mais qu'ils meurent donc, ces diseurs de riens, si cela leur plaît; nous cependant ne faisons qu'en rire.' (*Alq.* II. 297.) Aesthetic matters cannot be examined scientifically,[3] and as for the song itself, the philosopher may be amused by it, but he will not let it get in the way of the real business, the search for truth.

In poetry then, Descartes was chiefly conscious of what is decorative and beguiling. It is the same with rhetoric. I have spoken of the emphasis placed on *elocutio* or style in the rhetorical theory of this period; in the early seventeenth century it was customary to regard rhetoric as an ornamental art, whose main function was to clothe the naked body of speech in various pleasing frills so as to make it acceptable to polite society. Descartes had no time for this sort of thing—or so he affirmed. Several times he proclaims his disdain for the fine colours of eloquence; thus to Chanut, about his philosophical writings in general: 'Je les ai fait sortir en public sans être parés, ni avoir aucun des ornements qui peuvent attirer les yeux du peuple, afin que ceux qui ne s'arrêtent qu'à l'extérieur ne les vissent pas, et qu'ils fussent seulement regardés par quelques personnes de bon esprit.' (*Corr.* VII. 199.) This could be seen, of course, as no more than a well-known rhetorical move; similarly, when attacking other writers, Descartes is quick to point to their use 'des feintes et des déguisements de la rhétorique'. He scoffs at the theatrical nature of Père Bourdin's objections to the *Méditations* and refuses to treat Gassendi's *Cinquièmes Objections* seriously, pointing out several of the devices used by his opponent, parodying him and affirming that 'il ne se veut pas lui-même servir de cette candeur

[3] See on this subject a letter of 1630 to Mersenne (*Alq.* I. 251).

philosophique, ni mettre en usage les raisons, mais seulement donner aux choses le fard et les couleurs de la rhétorique' (*Alq.* II. 790).

Rhetoric on this view is essentially deceptive or at best frivolous, and the serious writer naturally wishes to dissociate himself from it. But in Descartes's case the attack on rhetoric appears to be more than the orator's conventional preamble. It corresponds rather to a distaste for the whole world of books. Descartes did not wish to be taken for a 'faiseur de livres'; again and again he denies that he is an author, 'ce qui n'est ni mon humeur ni ma profession' (*Alq.* I. 533). He disdains the concern for stylistic detail which marks the professional writer, and we may reasonably suspect him of mock modesty when he apologizes for 'la rudesse de mon style et . . . la simplicité de mes pensées' (*Alq.* I. 776) to Guez de Balzac, who was generally acknowledged to be an outstanding example of the fine writer.[4]

Again, the disdain for the pedantic or affected writer was one of the clichés of the French aristocratic tradition and is often to be met with on the printed page (the example of Montaigne springs to mind). With Descartes, however, it is primarily intellectual in origin. For one thing, he knew that he would not find the truth by reading books; Baillet, in his life of the master, tells how, when asked to show his library, he pointed to the animal he was dissecting.[5] Neither did he wish to waste his time writing books for others to read. His letters and contemporary remarks about him give us a picture of a studious man, avoiding pointless human contact in his Dutch solitude and devoting himself to his scientific and philosophical investigations.[6] He often talks of his laziness and his love of the quiet life. But above all, particularly in the period of extensive scientific research preceding the *Discours de la méthode*, he was unwilling to take time off from his pursuit of knowledge to communicate his findings to the public. In 1630 he writes to Mersenne of his reluctance to continue his treatise on physics, which we now know as *Le Monde*: 'Je prends beaucoup plus de plaisir à m'instruire moi-même, que non pas à mettre par écrit le peu que je sais.' (*Alq.* I. 255.) Similar remarks occur in many letters. Later he became more concerned to communicate

---

4 See also a Latin epistle to Balzac (*A.T.* I. 7–12).
5 A. Baillet, *La Vie de Monsieur Descartes*, ed. La Table Ronde, p. 227. On Descartes's distaste for reading see a letter to Huyghens (*Alq.* II. 112).
6 See, for instance, the evocative letter of 1631 to Guez de Balzac (*Alq.* I. 291–3).

his ideas, as we shall see, but until the end of his life we hear the same refrain from time to time, particularly in moments of discouragement.

But more frequently, as Descartes grows older, we hear a different note. Now he says that he would willingly write, but that it is not worth it if the public is going to be indifferent or hostile. In 1646 he confesses to Chanut: 'Je serais maintenant d'humeur à écrire quelque autre chose, si le dégoût que j'ai de voir combien il y a peu de personnes au monde qui daignent lire mes écrits ne me faisait pas être négligent.' (*Corr.* VII. 83.) A similar doubt had worried him even before he started to publish his philosophy; it springs directly from his perception of the eternal differences of philosophers and the uncertainty of their opinions. It was this area of uncertainty and disagreement which he aimed to eliminate or reduce in his scientific and philosophical work, hoping to establish truths which would be clear and indubitable. But for all his confidence in his own rightness, a confidence which never deserted him, Descartes could not fail to be aware that his own ideas would not automatically meet with immediate acceptance. And for him it was all or nothing, at least in the letter he wrote to Mersenne in 1633: 'Il y a déjà tant d'opinions en Philosophie qui ont de l'apparence, et qui peuvent être soutenues en dispute, que si les miennes n'ont rien de plus certain et ne peuvent être approuvées sans controverse, je ne les veux jamais publier.' (*Alq.* I. 488.) It was probably this feeling as well as fear resulting from the condemnation of Galileo which led him to delay publication of *Le Monde*—the two reasons being linked in that the official rejection of the Copernican world-system brought home to him with particular force the possibility of total disagreement between men of good faith.

In the letter just quoted, the words 'sans controverse' are essential. If Descartes was reluctant to write, he was even more reluctant to enter into debate. This was mainly because his notion of debate was largely formed on the model of the scholastic disputation, an exercise which seemed to him useless for the advancement of learning, because each contestant is concerned above all to win. Again and again Descartes uses military metaphors to describe intellectual argument. It is not surprising then if in 'la chaleur de la dispute', 'l'on n'a pas assez de temps pour peser les raisons de part et d'autre' and 'la honte de paraître vaincus, si les nôtres étaient les plus faibles, nous en ôte souvent la volonté' (*Alq.* ii. 919). Perhaps he was unaware of it, but he might almost be describing his own polemical activity, where he often shows himself brutal and unscrupulous, not only in his legal action against Voëtius, but equally in his philosophical disputes with such contemporaries as Gassendi, Roberval, Bourdin, or Hobbes. Descartes may have been blind to this failing in himself, but he was all too conscious of it in others. In this perspective, the pursuit of truth seemed an impossible task; each new debate, rather than contributing to scientific progress, only served to obscure things still further. Descartes frequently claimed that the objections of his contradictors had taught him nothing. His reply was to withdraw from sterile debate and say nothing to an audience who instead of accepting his clear and evident truths would seek to undermine them out of spite or vanity. He condemns the whole race of disputatious pedants and with them their prime instrument, the dialectic of the Schools: 'Je pris garde que, pour la logique, ses syllogismes et la plupart de ses autres instructions servent plutôt à expliquer à autrui les choses qu'on sait ou même, comme l'art de Lulle, à parler, sans jugement, de celles qu'on ignore, qu'à les apprendre.' (*Alq.* i. 585.)[7]

Such were the reasons which made Descartes prefer solitary research to writing and debate. But this is only part of the picture. He may have been unwilling to expose himself to time-wasting discussion, but he was not blind to the advantages of some sorts of communication. For all his dislike of the disputation, he often refers to the value of discussion. He regularly invites objections to his philosophy, saying, for instance, apropos of the *Septièmes Objections*: 'je ne souhaite rien tant que d'éprouver la certitude de mes opinions, et de me confirmer dans leur vérité, si, après avoir été examinées par tous les savants, elles se trouvent à l'épreuve de leurs atteintes, ou d'être averti de mes erreurs, afin de m'en corriger.' (*Alq.* ii. 1074–5.) As this suggests, Descartes's attitude to objections is not always as open as it might be; he often uses

---

[7] See also a passage in the *Regulae* (*Alq.* i. 130); in this work Descartes attacks dialectics rather than logic; later, commenting on the passage quoted above from the *Discours*, he distinguishes between the two: 'Ceci est plutôt la dialectique, puisqu'elle nous enseigne à discourir de toutes choses, tandis que la logique donne de toutes choses des démonstrations' (*Entretien avec Burman*, trans. and ed. C. Adam, Paris, 1937, p. 117). On the relation between logic and dialectics see Ong, *Ramus*, chapter 4 and *passim*.

them merely as a way of making his own philosophy look more secure, without really meeting the points raised. At the end of his replies to Gassendi's objections he proclaims with satisfaction: 'J'ai été ravi qu'un homme de son mérite, dans un discours si long et si soigneusement recherché, n'ait apporté aucune raison qui détruisît et renversât les miennes, et n'ait aussi rien opposé contre mes conclusions à quoi il ne m'ait été très facile de répondre.' (*Alq.* II. 838.) Still, there is another sort of discussion in which the objections are taken seriously and provoke a clarification or a correction of the original thought; we shall see that in the *Principes*, Descartes takes advantage of previous objections to make his exposition more convincing. And when the objector is courteous and fairly docile, when Descartes is convinced that his interlocutor is not a scholastic pedant who is arguing for argument's sake, then he warms to the discussion and comes out from behind his defences of reserve and aggressive polemic. This is the case in his written exchanges with Princess Elizabeth, Henry More, Père Mesland, Père Mersenne, Antoine Arnauld, and many other correspondents. It is interesting, moreover, to find him, in a letter to Arnauld, speaking in favour of the real discussion which is possible between two people in the same room: 'Je crois qu'on peut agir plus sûrement par lettres avec ceux qui aiment la dispute; mais pour ceux qui aiment la vérité, l'entrevue et la vive voix sont bien commodes' (*Corr.* VIII. 45–6)—once again the same distinction between dispute and discussion. A letter to Chanut goes further than this and tells us that conversation with decent men of learning is 'le plus grand bien de la vie' (*Corr.* VII. 29). And in the record of Descartes's conversation with Burman and the fictitious dialogue of *La Recherche de la vérité* we see philosophy once again in the form of a Socratic discussion rather than a heroic, solitary exploit.

So Descartes's philosophy was not for his own use only; in certain conditions he was willing and glad to impart it to others. But conversation is one thing and publication another. As far as publication is concerned, there is an interesting development of Descartes's attitude between about 1630 and 1645. In 1630 he had already thought of publishing his *Dioptrique* to test public opinion: 'J'éprouverai en la *Dioptrique* si je suis capable d'expliquer mes conceptions, et de persuader aux autres une vérité, après que je me la suis persuadée; ce que je ne pense nullement.' (*Alq.* I. 287.)

But the *Dioptrique* was not published and neither was the full-scale treatise *Le Monde*—for reasons which we have already seen. Only in 1636 did Descartes decide to publish some samples of his philosophy, together with a preface, the *Discours de la méthode*. In the sixth book of the *Discours* (*Alq.* 1. 632–47) he describes his changing attitude towards publication, his reasons for keeping *Le Monde* to himself and only giving fragments to the public. He first declares his constant distaste for 'le métier de faire des livres'; however, he continues, he had become aware some years ago that his discoveries and above all his principles were so different from what had been believed and potentially so valuable to mankind that it would be a crime to keep them hidden.[8] If they were published, they might lead through collective research to much greater progress than he could hope to achieve by working alone. But then various reasons had led him to change his mind, in particular the thought of time-wasting controversy. Objections, he says, have hardly ever been any use to him, being mainly either malicious or obvious. Moreover, he does not really think that anyone could develop his principles as successfully as he himself—haughtily, he compares disciples to the ivy growing on a great tree. All these reasons had contributed to prevent him from publishing *Le Monde*. Nevertheless, he says, he has broken his resolution never to publish, partly in order to defend his reputation and partly because he feels obliged to tell the public in what ways they can help him. This has led him to 'choisir quelques matières qui, sans être sujettes à beaucoup de controverses, ni m'obliger à déclarer davantage de mes principes que je ne désire, ne laisseraient pas de faire voir assez clairement ce que je puis, ou ne puis pas, dans les sciences'. In this hesitant way, committing himself as little as possible and waiting to see how the public will react, Descartes enters the arena. But once in, there is no turning back. As he makes disciples and sees the possibility of establishing his philosophy as the alternative or even the successor to the reigning Scholasticism, he is inevitably led further and further into controversy, and the need to persuade becomes more and more urgent.

---

[8] Baillet tells us that the Cardinal de Bérulle made it a matter of conscience with Descartes to persevere and adds: 'Les instances que ses amis renouvelèrent pour le presser de communiquer ses lumières au public, ne lui permirent pas de reculer plus loin.' (*Vie*, pp. 73–4.)

Whereas the *Discours* and the accompanying essays had been somewhat tentative offerings, the *Méditations* are already a full-scale exercise in persuasion and aim to establish a firm metaphysical base for Descartes's science. Descartes had deliberately avoided describing the earlier work as a 'Traité de la méthode' so as to indicate 'que je n'ai pas dessein de l'enseigner, mais seulement d'en parler' (*Alq.* I. 521-2); it was intentionally incomplete. But of the *Méditations* he writes to the Sorbonne: 'j'ai travaillé de tout mon possible pour comprendre dans ce traité tout ce qui s'en peut dire' and 'j'ai traité les premières et principales [raisons] d'une telle manière que j'ose bien les proposer pour de très évidentes et de très certaines démonstrations.' (*Alq.* II. 386.) Even so, the title of the *Méditations* and its form avoid the more rigid forms of didactic writing, which Descartes was to come to at last in his *Principes*. In this last work we see at its clearest the desire to imprint his philosophy victoriously on the minds of men. Already the essay *Des météores*, which accompanied the *Discours*, had been laid out in such a way as to invite comparison with the standard educational treatises on the subject; remarking on the success of his book, Descartes writes to his former philosophy teacher at the Jesuit college of La Flèche: 'je vois déjà que tant de personnes se portent à croire ce qu'il contient, que (particulièrement pour les *Météores*) je ne sais pas de quelle façon ils pourront dorénavant les enseigner, comme ils font tous les ans en la plupart de vos collèges, s'ils ne réfutent ce que j'en ai écrit, ou s'ils ne le suivent.' (*Alq.* I. 798.) The idea of introducing his philosophy into the Jesuit colleges, one of the bastions of Scholasticism, attracts him; the letters written during the controversies following the *Méditations* show him evolving the plan of a work which will finally silence his adversaries and end all controversy; in particular, in the important letter to Père Dinet, he announces: 'j'ai résolu de donner au public tout le peu que j'ai médité sur la philosophie, et de travailler de tout mon possible pour faire que mes opinions soient reçues de tout le monde, si elles se trouvent conformes à la vérité.' (*Alq.* II. 1084.) The isolated philosopher of 1630 is by now a committed persuader.

Descartes's first and constant notion of persuasion is one in which he will state the truth firmly and clearly and everyone will agree. Although he makes suitable protestations of modesty ('si elles se trouvent conformes à la vérité'), his confidence that he is right is virtually unshakeable. Where Gassendi ends his *Cinquièmes Objections* on a note of relativity and uncertainty (a somewhat aggressive uncertainty, be it said), Descartes ends his replies with the affirmation of his rightness. Nor is he in the least worried when Regius points out to him that any madman can claim that his ideas are perfectly clear; he simply returns the accusations to Regius (*Corr.* VI. 270–2). Frequently he refuses to believe that anyone can in good faith refuse to see and accept the truth of his ideas. In particular his aim is to give to his proofs the certainty of mathematics. I do not wish to discuss his success in doing this, but merely to observe that he himself was convinced that he had done it. In the final section of the *Principes*, after admitting that some unverifiable hypotheses have been used, he goes on to say that his ideas have as much moral certainty as the affirmation that Rome is in Italy by someone who has not been there; in fact the certainty is more than moral, since God will not have deceived him and he has used his reason rightly, deducing everything 'par les principes de la mathématique ou par d'autres aussi évidents et certains' (*A.T.* IX, *Princ.* 322–4). Where the reasoning is sound and the truths mathematically deduced, there should be no possibility of doubt or controversy and no need of persuasive rhetoric. Eloquence and sound reasoning are more or less equated in the *Discours de la méthode*: 'ceux qui ont le raisonnement le plus fort, et qui digèrent le mieux leurs pensées, afin de les rendre claires et intelligibles, peuvent toujours le mieux persuader ce qu'ils proposent.' (*Alq.* I. 574.) There is no need for any particular preparation of the audience or any appeal to the imagination, the passions, or the senses (as traditional rhetoric put it); the method is rhetoric enough.

And yet experience showed Descartes that people did not always accept the truth, that not all readers were as docile as he might expect. The man who has sailed round the world may know quite well what he has done, but will he be able to convince others? (*Alq.* II. 845.) Descartes admits to Père Mesland, one of his most receptive readers: 'Je sais qu'il est très malaisé d'entrer dans les pensées d'autrui, et l'expérience m'a fait connaître combien les miennes semblent difficiles à plusieurs.' (*Corr.* VI. 140.) The philosopher who is content simply to state his arguments clearly and logically, relying on his audience to see the light, may well be neglected, misunderstood, or ignored. It might be possible to do without rhetoric if there were a universal language, based on philosophical analysis and thus aiding human judgement, 'lui représentant si distinctement toutes choses, qu'il lui serait presque impossible de se tromper' (*Alq.* 1. 231). This was a common dream in the seventeenth century. But Descartes, while claiming that this language could be devised, did not believe that it would ever actually come into being, since its creation would presuppose the existence of an earthly paradise. Meanwhile the difficulties of communication remained, and Descartes was led to reflect on the obstacles in the way of the reception of the truth and the techniques of philosophical persuasion.

In general, the obstacles to persuasion are similar to the causes of error, which Descartes treats very thoroughly. The main cause of error is the gap between the understanding ('entendement') and the will ('volonté');[9] if we make mistakes it is because we seek to affirm more than is clear to us. It is also possible for the human will, in its freedom, to refuse the evidence of the understanding, or at any rate to direct the attention of the mind elsewhere. The persuader then must seek both to enlighten the understanding and to curb the tendency of the will to assert itself in hasty judgement. In more practical terms there are a certain number of precise obstacles—akin to the 'Idols' of Francis Bacon. Awareness of these will enable the persuader to point them out to his audience— which is the beginning of the cure—and to develop techniques of counter-attack.

One of the main obstacles is the strength of our childhood prejudices—which are, in Descartes's terminology, judgements in which the will has outstripped the understanding. These deep-rooted opinions may make it difficult for the adult to accept such propositions as the movement of the Earth, the soullessness of animals, or the immateriality of the mind. Descartes never tires of attacking this obstacle, one of his most important weapons being to show his own progress from childhood prejudice to true philosophy.[10] Assent to new ideas is also hampered by our deference to authority. Descartes, with the example of Galileo before him, is keenly aware of this difficulty and seeks to counter it by winning

---

[9] On this subject see the interesting pages of G. Rodis-Lewis, *Descartes et le rationalisme*, Paris, 1966, pp. 41–50.

[10] See Gouhier, *Pensée métaphysique*, chapter 2.

over authority to his side. This may be an unphilosophical thing
to do, but experience shows it to be necessary. It is for this reason
that Descartes prefaces the *Méditations* with a letter to the Sorbonne and works hard to bring his various Jesuit acquaintances
to declare their support for his ideas. As well as matching authority against authority, Descartes attempts to convince those who
are shocked by the apparent newness of his ideas that it is in fact
scholastic philosophy which is the innovator, whereas he is con-
tinuing an ancient line. He is very concerned that his opinions
should not seem to be wilful paradoxes. Conversely, another
difficulty he encounters is that although his ideas may shock at first,
when they are assimilated they seem so plain and straightforward
that they no longer hold the reader's interest, 'à cause que le
naturel des hommes est tel qu'ils n'estiment que les choses qui leur
laissent de l'admiration et qu'ils ne possèdent pas tout à fait'
(*Corr.* VIII. 194). The remedy may lie in various rhetorical devices
which are designed to hold the attention, though this is a compromise which Descartes is not always willing to accept. Finally,
though this does not exhaust the list of obstacles, there is the
perverse human will; the persuader has to contend with the vanity,
the obstinacy, the spite, and the vested interests of professional
philosophers. Descartes never ceases to denounce the pedants,
covering them with mockery and appealing over their heads to
the common sense of the general public.

Such, in brief, are the obstacles in the way of effective communication. Later in this chapter I shall examine in more detail
some of the corresponding techniques of persuasion as we see
them in Descartes's writing. But before doing this I should like
to look at the more positive side of Descartes's theory of persuasion. The first thing to be noticed is his consciousness of the
different needs of different audiences—this being one of the
fundamental aspects of traditional rhetoric. At its simplest, this
expresses itself in the choice of French or Latin as a means of
communication; the choice is made with a particular audience in
mind. Quite apart from the choice of language, the same problem
constantly confronts the philosopher; as Descartes puts it in a
letter to Desargues, 'vous pouvez avoir deux desseins, qui sont
fort bons et fort louables, mais qui ne requièrent pas tous deux
même façon de procéder. L'un est d'écrire pour les doctes . . .
l'autre est d'écrire pour les curieux qui ne sont pas doctes.' (*Alq.*

II. 133.) In fact most of his works are destined for a mixed audience and not just for professionals. Although the *Méditations* were originally addressed to those who knew Latin—this allowed the author more freedom than he had had in his *Discours*—he welcomed the translation of both the *Méditations* and the *Principes*. In practice we shall see his feeling for his audience, his constant concern to control their reactions.

Descartes's most complete theoretical treatment of the question of adapting one's method and style to the audience is to be found at the end of his replies to the second series of objections to his *Méditations* (*Alq.* II. 581–3). It concerns the manner of exposition. While there may be only one way of finding the truth, the Method, there are two opposed ways of communicating it; the choice between these will depend on the audience. The first of these he calls analysis, and it is akin to what Ramus called the 'prudential' or 'crafty' method (he rather distrusted it) and what Bacon called the 'probative' method. It consists in following 'la vraie voie par laquelle la chose a été méthodiquement inventée', allowing the reader to retrace the steps of discovery. This method, however, may not convince 'les lecteurs opiniâtres ou peu attentifs', who will fail to follow it in all its detail. For them the author will need to use synthesis (similar to Ramus's 'natural' method and Bacon's 'magisterial'), which entails 'une longue suite de définitions, de demandes, d'axiomes, de théorèmes et de problèmes'. This method 'arrache le consentement du lecteur, tant obstiné et opiniâtre qu'il puisse être', but on the other hand 'elle ne donne pas . . . une entière satisfaction aux esprits qui désirent d'apprendre, parce qu'elle n'enseigne pas la méthode par laquelle la chose a été inventée'. In general Descartes seems to favour analysis, since, as he often says, philosophy is not a form of knowledge which can simply be handed over; each man must do it for himself.

This is Descartes's most important theoretical statement on the methods of communication. Reading his letters and his philosophical writings, one finds a great many less important remarks, all of them stemming from the awareness of audience demands and audience response. Some of the most interesting ones are those where the philosopher, for all his rejection of 'le fard et les couleurs de la rhétorique', accepts the need to please. In particular Descartes often comes back to the need for brevity and incompleteness—and attacks the long-windedness of his opponents.

Sometimes this incompleteness is malicious; the *Géométrie*, he says, has been left deliberately incomplete so as to sort out the sheep from the goats (*Corr.* VIII. 26–7). But more often the aim is to avoid tedium, to give the audience the pleasure which comes from collaboration; he says in *Le Monde*, addressing himself with typical directness to his reader: 'Ce sera assez que je vous ouvre le chemin, par lequel vous les pourrez trouver de vous-même, quand vous prendrez la peine de les chercher. La plupart des esprits se dégoûtent, lorsqu'on leur rend les choses trop faciles. Et pour faire ici un tableau qui vous agrée, il est besoin que j'y emploie de l'ombre aussi bien que des couleurs claires.' (*Alq.* I. 364.)

If here he points to the need to make the exposition piquant, in other places he advises against shocking the listener or reader. Again and again he returns to the need for adequate preparation of the audience. Writing to Regius, he distinguishes between the thesis, which shocks by being as paradoxical as possible, and his own method: 'quant à moi, je pense que je ne dois rien éviter davantage que de laisser paraître paradoxales mes opinions.' (*Corr.* VI. 262.) To avoid shocking the audience one must even descend to the niceties of style; Descartes comments on a book by Regius: 'le style n'est pas assez châtié en bien des endroits'—though he does say that this is 'peu de chose' (*Alq.* II. 932). He is even worried lest the title of the French translation of his *Principia* should seem too pedantic and put off the general reader (*A.T.* IX, *Princ.* I).

Having attempted to sum up Descartes's feelings and ideas about persuasion, I should like now to turn to his practice as a persuader. In what ways does he woo his audience to his way of thinking? Clearly this is a vast subject, and I can do no more than point to some of the dominant features of it here. In particular I shall confine myself to what may be called the rhetorical side of Descartes's writing. Thus I shall take it for granted that much of his persuasive power comes simply from the fact that many of his premisses or intuitions seem to us to be true, that many of his demonstrations are conducted with a logic to which we can assent, and that many of his conclusions are supported by empirical observations which we can share (also, of course, that many of these premisses, demonstrations, and observations do not in fact command our assent). However, it is also true that just as Descartes's theory of communication goes beyond sound reasoning to include a great deal of what one must call rhetoric, so in practice Descartes does more than simply demonstrate. To imprint his demonstration on the minds of his audience, he uses a variety of techniques which are rhetorical rather than logical.

We can begin by observing Descartes at his most rhetorical, as a polemicist. We have seen that he frequently talks about his philosophical disputes as battles or duels; this being so, it is not surprising if his posture is often aggressive. In this sort of debate it is quite legitimate to object when the other man misunderstands or distorts your ideas. Many of Descartes's replies to Hobbes, Gassendi, or Bourdin are taken up with just this sort of objection. But there are different ways of doing this, and Descartes's way is not always sweetly reasonable. To take one example, in the *Septièmes Objections*, Bourdin argues that Descartes's hyperbolic doubt leads him to assert not only that commonly held beliefs (e.g. $2+3 = 5$) are uncertain, but even that they are false and that their opposite is true. Now it is true that in doing so Bourdin exaggerates, but his argument is soundly based on certain passages in the First Meditation. Descartes, however, nettled by the objection, rounds on his opponent:

Lorsque j'ai dit qu'il fallait pour quelque temps tenir les choses douteuses pour fausses, ou bien les rejeter comme telles, j'ai donné si clairement à connaître que j'entendais seulement que, pour faire une exacte recherche des vérités tout à fait certaines, il ne fallait faire non plus de compte des choses douteuses que de celles qui étaient absolument fausses, qu'il me semble que tout homme de bon sens ne pouvait autrement interpréter mes paroles, et qu'il ne pouvait s'en rencontrer aucun qui pût feindre que j'ai voulu croire l'opposé de ce qui est douteux . . . à moins qu'il n'eût point honte de passer pour un cavillateur ou pour une personne qui dit les choses autrement qu'elles ne sont; et, bien que notre auteur n'assure pas ce dernier, mais qu'il le propose seulement comme douteux, je m'étonne toutefois qu'une personne comme lui ait semblé imiter en cela ces infâmes détracteurs, qui se comportent souvent de la même manière qu'il a fait . . .

(*Alq.* II. 959–60)

Like Bourdin, Descartes is exaggerating here; his way of stating his case is obviously highly rhetorical. One notices in particular the hyperboles: 'j'ai donné si clairement à connaître', 'tout homme de bon sens', and the insults: 'cavillateur', 'infâmes détracteurs'. Insult is a constant feature of Descartes's polemic. One of its more effective forms is the insolent refusal to take objections seriously, implying that the objector is either a fool or a knave. This method is often used against Hobbes; thus, when Hobbes questions the ontological proof and Descartes's views on essence and existence, Descartes simply cuts him short: 'La distinction qui est entre l'essence et l'existence est connue de tout le monde' (*Alq*. II. 628), hardly a philosophical answer.

Gassendi too comes in for his share of abuse; in particular he is accused of repeating himself, a fair accusation, but Descartes uses it to dodge questions: 'Je ne m'arrête pas ici sur des choses que vous avez tant de fois rebattues, et que vous répétez encore en cet endroit si vainement; par exemple, qu'il y a beaucoup de choses que j'ai avancées sans preuve, lesquelles je maintiens néanmoins avoir très évidemment démontrées.' (*Alq*. II. 833–4.) Against Gassendi and Bourdin, Descartes reinforces argument with irony and mockery—or sometimes substitutes mockery for argument. He obviously enjoys making his opponents look foolish.[11] Where they attempt to entertain the audience, Descartes tries to turn the laugh on them. Bourdin had enlivened his objections with imagined dialogue and Descartes goes one further, seeing Bourdin as a comic actor fighting a battle against a shadow (*Alq*. II. 1017). Gassendi had mocked Descartes by addressing him as 'soul', so Descartes addresses Gassendi as 'flesh', laughing at him rather than answering him: 'Tout ce que vous alléguez ici, ô très bonne chair, ne me semble pas tant des objections que quelques murmures qui n'ont pas besoin de repartie.' (*Alq*. II. 799.)

These are all the customary weapons of polemic. They do not exactly tally with the image of the modest philosopher, inviting objections to help him in his search for truth, but it would be unreasonable to expect pure reason from a philosopher at all times. It is more rewarding, however, to read Descartes when he is being not so much aggressive as earnestly persuasive—he is far more impressive in his *Méditations*, for instance, than in his ensuing polemic with Gassendi. In the first place, we have seen that the fundamental principle of rhetoric is awareness of the audience. In all Descartes's writings we can detect the desire to keep in touch with his audience, helping them, guiding them, reassuring them, flattering them.

---

[11] See, for example, his glee at the discomfiture of his arch-enemy Voëtius (*Alq*. II. 932).

Like the traditional orator, Descartes cannot do without his *précautions oratoires*. Although modesty is not his dominant characteristic, he begins the *Discours de la méthode* with suitable protestations: 'Toutefois il se peut faire que je me trompe, et ce n'est peut-être qu'un peu de cuivre et de verre que je prends pour de l'or et des diamants.' (*Alq.* I. 570.) And when he comes to the *Cogito*, Descartes seems to hesitate before expounding his 'premières méditations', 'car elles sont si métaphysiques et si peu communes, qu'elles ne seront peut-être pas au goût de tout le monde' (*Alq.* I. 601–2). The dogmatic *Principes* finishes on a similar note. Throughout Descartes's work there is a juxtaposition of confident assertion and protestation that the author is not so arrogant as to think that he alone knows the truth. In some of his writings he insists on the speculative nature of his theories, presenting them more than once as a 'fable', notably in *Le Monde*, where he describes a hypothetical world which resembles the actual world. In this case, as in the third book of the *Principes*, the reason for the precaution is clear: Descartes does not want to enter into open dispute with the Church's official views on cosmology—'je m'avance masqué'. Such self-deprecating devices are necessary above all when Descartes is addressing a particular audience on whom he depends. The letter to the Sorbonne which precedes the *Méditations* combines flattery of the theologians with a certain philosophical modesty. It is true that the dominant note of this letter is the familiar one of self-confidence, but Descartes has the tact to add that, 'ayant connaissance non seulement de mon infirmité, mais aussi de mon ignorance' (*Alq.* II. 388), he would be grateful if the Sorbonne could correct his mistakes.

If it is desirable for the persuader to placate his audience by modesty, he must also predispose them in his favour by giving them a good opinion of his competence. One of the most important aids to this is reputation, as Descartes was well aware. In his many polemics he was always anxious not only to be right, but to be seen to be right, and one can see how this serves him to advertise his wares in the preface to the *Traité des passions*. This preface is in the form of an exchange of letters between Descartes and an admirer (probably Picot), the longest letter being one from the admirer asking Descartes to publish his treatise. This letter is presumably not Descartes's own work and one cannot be sure that he wanted it published—he himself says not in one of his letters.

But it appears as if the opposite were true; for the letter repeats things that Descartes often says elsewhere, talking of his tendency to keep his philosophy to himself and his reluctance to persuade. What concerns us here, however, is that the letter uses Descartes's reputation to prepare the ground for a favourable reception of his new treatise; in particular it points out, as Descartes himself often does, that the failure of the Jesuits to refute his ideas tells in their favour. The whole preface reminds one of what Descartes says about Galileo's dialogues: 'sa façon d'écrire par dialogues, où il introduit trois personnes qui ne font autre chose que louer et exalter ses inventions chacun à son tour, aide fort à faire valoir sa marchandise.' (*Alq.* II. 92.)

A third element in the preparation of the audience is flattery. In his dedication of the *Principes* to Elizabeth of Bohemia (*A.T.* IX, *Princ.* 21–3), Descartes announces that the philosopher cannot flatter, but this is only the traditional prelude which makes what follows all the sweeter, for the body of the dedication is, as the genre demands, a full-scale eulogy of the princess (a eulogy which is probably quite sincere). In his private letters Descartes often says that he cannot bring himself to write the normal compliments, yet in fact he showers praise on the geometer Fermat—of whom he had a fairly low opinion—and produces sweetly fulsome little letters for Elizabeth's young sister Sophia. It is instructive to compare the two letters he wrote to Chanut, the French ambassador in Sweden, in reply to Christina of Sweden's invitation to visit her (*Corr.* VIII. 191–5). One letter is to be shown to the Queen; the other, for Chanut only, says what Descartes really thinks. In all this Descartes is doing no more than all letter-writers normally do.

What is more important, in his philosophical writings Descartes flatters the general public, the mixed audience of professional teachers, amateur philosophers, and interested men of the world to whom he addressed most of his works. The notion of flattery does not here imply insincerity, but simply the desire to make the public feel well disposed to the author's ideas by insisting on the fact that, as Descartes saw it, there was no need of great learning to understand them. 'Le bon sens est la chose du monde la mieux partagée' (*Alq.* I. 568), and the philosopher has no qualities of mind which he does not share with everyone else. He has simply had, as he says, 'beaucoup d'heur' (*Alq.* I. 570), which has enabled him to find the correct way of using his mind. And so he is able to reassure diffident readers of the French version of the *Principes*: 'Je voudrais assurer ceux qui se défient trop de leurs forces, qu'il n'y a aucune chose en mes écrits qu'ils ne puissent entièrement entendre, s'ils prennent la peine de les examiner' (*A.T.* IX, *Princ.* 13)—although in fact, as we have seen, Descartes often complained that very few readers really did understand his works.

In works addressed to a large public, Descartes appeals to the widespread dislike of the pedant, the professional scholar, the 'faiseur de livres'. He often compares the sound sense of the *honnête homme* with the twisted mind of the university teacher, appealing to the common sense of the former against the pedantic quibbles of the latter. A particularly good example of this procedure is the unfinished dialogue *La Recherche de la vérité par la lumière naturelle*, which is specifically designed to show the ease with which an *honnête homme* can learn to philosophize. Descartes paints a glowing picture of Poliandre, the man of the world, who with only a little prompting progresses rapidly along the road which Descartes himself follows in his *Méditations*. Meanwhile Epistémon, the scholar, raises petty objections, which Eudoxe, who seems to represent the author, disposes of as follows:

Je conviens avec vous, Epistémon, qu'il faut savoir ce que c'est que le doute, la pensée, l'existence, avant d'être entièrement convaincu de la vérité de ce raisonnement: *je doute, donc j'existe*; ou, ce qui est la même chose: *je pense, donc j'existe*. Mais n'allez pas vous imaginer que pour acquérir ces notions préalables il faille violenter et torturer notre esprit pour trouver le genre le plus proche et la différence essentielle, et de ces éléments composer une véritable définition. Laissons cette tâche à celui qui veut faire le professeur ou disputer dans les écoles. Mais quiconque désire examiner les choses par lui-même et en juger selon qu'il les conçoit, ne peut être d'un esprit si borné qu'il n'ait pas assez de lumière pour voir suffisamment, toutes les fois qu'il y fera attention, ce que c'est que le doute, la pensée, l'existence, et pour qu'il lui soit nécessaire d'en apprendre les distinctions. (*Alq.* II. 1135–6)

Now all this is what Descartes in fact thought, but it is presented in such a way as to please the ordinary reader and encourage him to give his assent.

This sort of 'flattery' of the public is reinforced by the personal contact which Descartes establishes between himself and his audience. As we read the *Méditations*, the *Discours*, or even the *Regulae* or the *Principes*, we find ourselves listening to a man like ourselves, someone who, instead of laying out his ideas in an impersonal way, is all the time saying: 'je', 'vous', or 'nous'. In conversation the 'moi' may sometimes be 'haïssable', but this is by no means true of persuasion. The 'I' of the *Discours* and the *Méditations* seems to appeal for our sympathy, inviting us to put ourselves in his place, showing us that he too has been the way he invites us to go. The *Principes* uses the first person singular much less; this is a didactic work, but the tone is that of the teacher sharing in the investigation with his pupils; now it is the 'nous' which establishes a human link between writer and reader and appeals to our common experience. Similarly the 'vous' which we find in much of Descartes's scientific popularization sets up a conversational tone and helps to overcome the reader's resistance. When in addition Descartes asks questions, it is very much the orator that we hear: 'Pensez-vous, lors même que nous ne prenons pas garde à la signification des paroles, et que nous oyons seulement leur son, que l'idée de ce son, qui se forme en notre pensée, soit quelque chose de semblable à l'objet qui en est la cause?' (*Alq.* I. 317.)

In these various ways Descartes attempts to set up a current of sympathy between himself and his reader, just like the orator in his exordium. He also does a great deal to make things easy for the reader. To start with, he indicates in some cases how the book should be read. The *Principes* should be read first of all like a novel, straight through, then a second time, paying attention to detail, and finally a third time, to clear up any remaining difficulties! (*A.T.* IX, *Princ.* 11–12.) The *Méditations* on the other hand, as its name might suggest, calls for a different technique, in particular the First Meditation: 'je voudrais que les lecteurs n'employassent pas seulement le peu de temps qu'il faut pour la lire, mais quelques mois, ou du moins quelques semaines, à considérer les choses dont elle traite, auparavant que de passer outre; car ainsi je ne doute point qu'ils ne fissent bien mieux leur profit de la lecture du reste.' (*Alq.* II. 552.)

Once the reader has embarked on the book in hand, Descartes, again like an orator, attempts to make it easy for him to follow and give his assent. One notices the way in which he forestalls objections, particularly in such works as the *Principes* and *La Recherche de la vérité*, where he has learnt from the polemic which followed the *Méditations*. However much Descartes may claim to disdain most objections, we find that he uses them to set up a sort of didactic dialogue and to build into the *Principes* chapters such as 'D'où vient que tout le monde ne la connaisse pas de cette façon' (*A.T.* IX, *Princ.* 30). I spoke earlier of some of the obstacles and prejudices which Descartes saw as preventing the acceptance of his ideas; an important persuasive weapon is to point out to the audience its own prejudices. Thus in Book I of the *Principes* there are two chapters entitled 'Que la première et principale cause de nos erreurs sont les préjugés de notre enfance', and 'Que la seconde est que nous ne pouvons oublier ces préjugés'. These are amply illustrated in the subsequent books—a chapter on the vacuum begins characteristically: 'Nous avons presque tous été préoccupés de cette erreur dès le commencement de notre vie.' (*A.T.* IX, *Princ.* 72.)

Everything is done to make the reader feel that he is in safe hands. The author announces that what we are about to read is the unembroidered truth; thus the *Traité des passions* is prefaced by the remark that its style is 'si simple et si bref, qu'il fera connaître que mon dessein n'a pas été d'expliquer les passions en orateur, ni même en philosophe moral, mais seulement en physicien' (*A.T.* XI. 326). There was nothing new in this sort of claim and we shall see later to what extent it is true of Descartes's writing as a whole, but it can be said now that in that part of his work (and it is a very important part) which we might call science for the general reader, in *Le Monde*, the *Traité des passions*, and much of the *Principes*, he does in fact employ the sort of plain style which the English Royal Society might have approved. Later, the elimination of the first person came to be regarded as an essential feature of the scientific style, a sign of objectivity. Descartes does not go as far as this— indeed we have seen that he puts the first person to good use—but he inculcates confidence with the logical unemotive language which is seen at its best in the *Traité des passions*. We may take one example among hundreds:

Après avoir ainsi considéré toutes les fonctions qui appartiennent au corps seul, il est aisé de connaître qu'il ne reste rien en nous que nous devions attribuer à notre âme, sinon nos pensées, lesquelles sont principalement de deux genres: à savoir, les unes sont les actions de l'âme, les autres sont ses passions.   (*A.T.* XI. 342)

On the face of it, there is nothing here to shock or puzzle the reader. The tone is calm, the ideas clearly expressed, the logical links well to the fore, and the confident 'il est aisé de connaître'— a typical Descartes expression—serves to confirm the appearance of obvious rightness. The combination of straightforwardness and affirmation encourages us to place our faith in the author—and this, of course, was to be one of the dominant features of scientific writing in subsequent centuries.

But it is above all in Descartes's choice of a form of exposition that we see his concern to control his audience. I have outlined the basic distinction in Descartes's theory between the analytic and synthetic modes of communication. In his philosophy he rarely gives us anything like the full-blown synthetic method; his reduction of the *Méditations* to an apparently geometric scheme of 'définitions', 'demandes', 'axiomes', 'propositions', and 'démonstrations' is not at all convincing (*Alq.* II. 586–98). In general he seems to prefer the analytic method, which allows the reader to follow the same path as the author, thus really making the conclusions his own. But this method is not always possible or appropriate, and Descartes adjusts his method to the occasion and the audience.

The analytic method is seen, for instance, in the section on the rainbow in *Des météores* (*Alq.* I. 749–61), but best of all in the *Méditations*. Here, as Descartes frequently points out to his correspondents, his aim is not to set out his philosophy as succinctly as possible, but to involve the reader in a process of meditation and discovery which will affect him fundamentally. Thus when Hobbes objects that the notion of universal doubt is an old one, Descartes can reply: 'je m'en suis servi, non pour les débiter comme nouvelles, mais en partie pour *préparer les esprits des lecteurs* [my italics] à considérer les choses intellectuelles et les distinguer des corporelles.' (*Alq.* II. 600.) He is asking his reader to 'méditer avec moi sérieusement' (*Alq.* II. 393), and so he introduces his subject very slowly, repeating himself where necessary to bring his ideas home more lastingly to the reader, since 'il ne suffit pas d'avoir fait ces remarques; il faut encore que je prenne soin de m'en souvenir' (*Alq.* II. 411). It is possible, for instance, to understand in this way the introduction of the 'mauvais génie' after the 'Dieu trompeur'; Gouhier suggests that Descartes's aim here is not so much to move to a different plane of meditation as to make sure that the reader has really come to doubt the existence of the physical world and the truths of mathematics.[12] Similarly the second proof of God's existence in the Third Meditation is not really called for by the rigour of the argument, but is a concession to the audience. And of course the dominant feature of the *Méditations* is the autobiographical method (which Descartes had already used, in a rather different way, in the *Discours de la méthode*). Descartes shows himself in the process of inventing his metaphysics; the reader follows him along the road he traces for us day by day, shares with him the attempt to fight off the prejudices of childhood, the discouragement of universal doubt, and the triumphant rebuilding of certainty, 'en sorte que, si le lecteur la veut suivre, et jeter les yeux soigneusement sur tout ce qu'elle contient, il n'entendra pas moins la chose ainsi démontrée et ne la rendra pas moins sienne, que si lui-même l'avait inventée' (*Alq.* II. 582).

Descartes could doubtless have said the same thing about the dialogue *La Recherche de la vérité*, if he had finished it. In this work he had in mind a less specialized audience than in the *Méditations*; this led him to compose it originally in French rather than Latin and to choose a form which would appeal to a large public: 'Aussi me suis-je efforcé de les rendre également utiles à tous les hommes; et pour cet effet, je n'ai point trouvé de style plus commode, que celui de ces conversations honnêtes, où chacun découvre familièrement à ses amis ce qu'il a de meilleur en sa pensée.' (*Alq.* II. 1108.) The dialogue form brings in a certain additional liveliness (though Descartes's dialogue is not particularly convincing as a rendering of conversation), but essentially it follows the same initiatory order as the *Méditations*. Just as in the *Méditations* we see Descartes building his philosophy from the foundations up, so here we see the *honnête homme* Poliandre going through the same stages. The only difference is that he and his mentor Eudoxe have to answer the objections of Epistémon—the dialogue was probably composed round about the time of the polemic following the *Méditations*. The dialogue form is particularly apt for dealing with objections, and in this respect Descartes uses it in very much the same way as Berkeley or Malebranche, or Plato in his more didactic dialogues.

The first book of the *Principes* again covers the same ground as the *Méditations* and *La Recherche de la vérité*, dealing with the

---

[12] Gouhier, *Pensée métaphysique*, chapter 5.

material in much the same order, but the manner of exposition is quite different. Descartes writes to Mersenne in 1640 that he has decided to 'écrire ma Philosophie en tel ordre qu'elle puisse aisément être enseignée. Et la première partie, que je fais maintenant, contient quasi les mêmes choses que les *Méditations* que vous avez, sinon qu'elle est entièrement d'autre style, et que ce qui est mis en l'un tout au long est plus abrégé en l'autre, et vice versa.' (*Alq.* II. 307.) Descartes is now writing a school manual, which calls for less preparation of the audience (one notices that the 'mauvais génie' does not appear in the *Principes*) and more attention to definitions and objections. (In fact, here, as in the *Traité des passions* and *Le Monde*, he is using something like what he calls the synthetic method—as he explains to Burman in their conversation of 1648.[13]) For instance, where each Meditation had been designed to be read at one go, absorbing the reader and changing his way of thinking, the same material is chopped up in the *Principes* into short sections, each with a helpful title. As often as not the title is presented, rather in the manner of some children's encyclopedias, as the answer to a question, for example: 'D'où vient qu'il y a des montagnes dont il sort quelquefois de grandes flammes' (*A.T.* IX, *Princ.* 242). Everything is ordered by the desire to give a clear and concise formulation of his thought.

Up till now I have mainly shown Descartes making things easier for his audience, encouraging them to follow him, but not really compromising himself with the 'worst' side of traditional rhetoric. We have seen that the reason why so many philosophers and theologians disliked and distrusted rhetoric was that it appealed not to men's reason, but to their senses, their imagination, and their passions. To what extent does Descartes, in his philosophical writing, call in these dubious allies in his assault on men's minds?

Part of the answer to this question has been touched on already. We have seen that a great deal of Descartes's force comes from his strong personal presence in his writing. We hear the unmistakable individual voice of a man speaking to us, telling us his whole intellectual history (in the *Discours*) and the story of his metaphysical discoveries (in the *Méditations*). In these two works in particular the 'je' is not just an impersonal philosopher figure; he is presented to us in the *Méditations* 'assis auprès du feu, vêtu d'une robe de chambre, ayant ce papier entre les mains' (*Alq.* II. 405).

[13] *Entretien avec Burman*, p. 27.

In particular the use of past, present, and future tenses in these works emphasizes the reality of Descartes's situation; thus the beginning of the Second Meditation: 'La Méditation que je fis hier m'a rempli l'esprit de tant de doutes, qu'il n'est plus désormais en ma puissance de les oublier. Et cependant je ne vois pas de quelle façon je les pourrai résoudre.' (*Alq.* II. 414.)

Above all, as we see in this passage, Descartes acts on the reader's emotions. Like the traditional rhetorician who moves his audience by a display of his own passions, Descartes involves his readers in the discouragement and expectant pursuit of his Second Meditation:

Et comme si tout à coup j'étais tombé dans une eau très profonde, je suis tellement surpris, que je ne puis ni assurer mes pieds dans le fond, ni nager pour me soutenir au-dessus. Je m'efforcerai néanmoins, et suivrai derechef la même voie où j'étais entré hier, en m'éloignant de tout ce en quoi je pourrai imaginer le moindre doute, tout de même que si je connaissais que cela fût absolument faux; et je continuerai toujours dans ce chemin, jusqu'à ce que j'aie rencontré quelque chose de certain, ou du moins, si je ne puis autre chose, jusqu'à ce que j'aie appris certainement, qu'il n'y a rien au monde de certain. (*Alq.* II. 414)

and in the triumph as he reaches the end of the Third Meditation:

Il me semble très à propos de m'arrêter quelque temps à la considération de ce Dieu tout parfait, de peser tout à loisir ses merveilleux attributs, de considérer, d'admirer et d'adorer l'incomparable beauté de cette immense lumière, au moins autant que la force de mon esprit, qui demeure en quelque sorte ébloui, me le pourra permettre.

Car, comme la foi nous apprend que la souveraine félicité de l'autre vie ne consiste que dans cette contemplation de la Majesté divine, ainsi expérimentons-nous dès maintenant qu'une semblable méditation, quoique incomparablement moins parfaite, nous fait jouir du plus grand contentement que nous soyons capables de ressentir en cette vie. (*Alq.* II. 454)

These are not entirely typical passages. This sort of emotional force is rare in most of Descartes's scientific work, where he is more concerned to inspire confidence in his plain honesty. It is to be found rather in the metaphysical and moral writings and in those prefaces and discourses (e.g. the preface to the *Principes*) where Descartes is concerned to win over the reader to his conception of philosophy. And although it would clearly be absurd to confine our attention to such passages (making a sort of poetic anthology of Descartes), I think it is fair to say that these powerful and memorable passages are the nails which attach the average reader's attention to Descartes's philosophical enterprise—and this is rhetoric at its best.

If we attempt now to examine in a little more detail the reasons for Descartes's power as a writer, I think we must concentrate on two elements, both of which are illustrated in the foregoing passages: the use of metaphor or comparison (which contemporary theory would have described in terms of the appeal to the imagination), and the effect of the rhythms of prose (the appeal to the senses). Since both of these are best studied in the original languages used by Descartes, I shall confine myself in the following remarks to those works which were originally composed in French, in particular the *Discours de la méthode*.

In Descartes's time, metaphor and comparison were normally considered as flowers of rhetoric, with which the author or orator might decorate his material. This conception will hardly do now; any discussion of Descartes's imagery[14] must take account of at least two functions, the illustrative and the emotive. Descartes himself speaks only of the former; he was aware of the value of images in making abstract or difficult ideas more comprehensible. On the other hand, there are fields of thought where he rejects the help of the imagination—in theory at least. In 1639 he writes to Mersenne: 'Car la partie de l'esprit qui aide le plus aux mathématiques, à savoir, l'imagination, nuit plus qu'elle ne sert pour les spéculations métaphysiques.' (*Alq.* II. 151.) More than once Descartes comes back to this distinction. But if images are a hindrance for those regions of philosophy where, according to Descartes, the mind must fight free of the material world, they are invaluable as aids to exposition in many other matters. Thus there are many illustrative figures in the mathematical *Regulae*, though in this case Descartes regards such illustrations as concessions to human weakness. The true doctrine is completely intellectual, but 'j'entends l'habiller et la parer, de manière à la pouvoir mieux accommoder à l'esprit humain' (*Alq.* I. 94). Similarly in the treatise on universal physics, *Le Monde*, there is a constant appeal to the

---

[14] On Descartes's imagery see the contribution of T. Spoerri to the Royaumont colloquium ('La puissance métaphorique de Descartes') and the following discussion in *Descartes* (Cahiers de Royaumont, II), Paris, 1957.

reader's homely experience: 'si vous daignez regarder ces petits corps qu'on nomme communément des atomes . . .' (*Alq.* I. 328), 'si vous mettez, par exemple, de la poudre en quelque vase . . .' (*Alq.* I. 331), etc. And he makes still further concessions when he goes beyond illustration by example to illustration by analogy; thus in the sequel to *Le Monde, L'Homme*, he begins a paragraph in the same way, appealing to the reader's experience: 'Si vous avez jamais eu la curiosité de voir de près les orgues de nos églises . . .' (*Alq.* I. 436), and goes on to a detailed comparison between the operation of a church organ and the operation of the human body.

The *Discours de la méthode* is rich in illustrative comparisons of this sort. For the most part, as has often been observed, Descartes uses simile rather than metaphor; or perhaps it would be truer to say that the most obvious and longest comparisons (e.g. that of the philosopher with the architect or town-planner) are presented as illustrations, with linking expressions such as 'à l'exemple de quoi', 'comme', or 'en même façon que'. There are, however, many metaphors in Descartes's writing. Some of these are fossilized metaphors, metaphors which have so passed into the language as to have lost their original metaphorical force; almost all abstract words (for example, the word 'abstract') have a forgotten physical origin. But in Descartes's writing, as in Racine's tragedies, there are many of these metaphors which are not really dead, but are waiting to be re-animated by contact with their surroundings. Thus when Descartes writes: 'je pense avoir eu beaucoup d'heur, de m'être rencontré dès ma jeunesse en certains chemins' (*Alq.* I. 570), these paths have a definite physical reference, because the road is so important a theme in Descartes's writing. In any case, it would be over-simple to suppose that there is always a great difference in effect between a metaphor and a simile, as if the mere introduction of a 'comme' introduced an intellectual element which reduced the comparison to a purely illustrative function. Almost all Descartes's comparisons are illustrative, but their importance often lies equally in their emotional effect on the reader. Thus whether he uses a simile: 'Mais, comme un homme qui marche seul et dans les ténèbres, je me résolus d'aller si lentement, et d'user de tant de circonspection en toutes choses, que, si je n'avançais que fort peu, je me garderais bien, au moins, de tomber' (*Alq.* I. 584), or a metaphor: 'tout mon dessein ne tendait qu'à m'assurer, et à rejeter la terre mouvante et le sable, pour trouver le roc ou l'argile' (*Alq.* i. 599), the image in either case has an equal emotive force.[15] This force is due in the first place—if the reader has read a certain amount of Descartes—to the links we establish between these images and others which recur throughout his works and which seem to correspond to some of his fundamental feelings—the desire for security and solidity, the perception of life and philosophy as a forward march. And in the second place— and this is doubtless a condition of the first—these images wake resonances in us, since Descartes's feeling for movement and construction corresponds to some of our own deepest impulses.

The use of images is the most obvious way in which the philosopher calls in the imagination and the emotions to help his reasoning. It is impossible to estimate these things at all objectively, but it seems to me that an even more important persuasive element—though less immediately obvious—is the rhythm of Descartes's sentences. It is true that the firm logical structure of his sentences and his paragraphs seems to appeal above all to our reason, but this is not all. As opposed to the relatively short, down-to-earth sentences of the *Traité des passions*, which seek to win our confidence with their plain honesty,[16] the *Discours de la méthode* has many long sentences which in their rhythms mime the marching confidence of Descartes's thought. Let us take one example:

Ces longues chaînes de raisons, toutes simples et faciles, dont les géomètres ont coutume de se servir, pour parvenir à leurs plus difficiles démonstrations, m'avaient donné occasion de m'imaginer que toutes les choses, qui peuvent tomber sous la connaissance des hommes, s'entresuivent en même façon et que, pourvu seulement qu'on s'abstienne d'en recevoir aucune pour vraie qui ne le soit, et qu'on garde toujours l'ordre qu'il faut pour les déduire les unes des autres, il n'y en peut avoir de si éloignées auxquelles enfin on ne parvienne, ni de si cachées qu'on ne découvre. (*Alq.* i. 587)

Not only does the sentence resemble in its shape one of the 'chaînes de raisons' which Descartes describes, it also rouses in the reader the emotion of buoyant confidence which is so typical of

---

15 The image of the tree in the preface to the *Principes* has a similar impact, I think.
16 There are, of course, exceptions to this generalization, notably the emotive and eloquent conclusion to Book II of the *Traité*, 'Que l'exercice de la vertu est un souverain remède contre les passions' (*A.T.* xi. 441-2).

its author. At first the rhythm is steady, reflective, and balanced—
the reader is kept in suspense—but then in the second half it rises
steadily in the accumulation of clauses to the triumphant symmetrical conclusion. The reader's attention does not flag; he is
carried on and up. The same could be said of larger units in Descartes's writing. The paragraph which introduces the *Cogito* in
the *Discours* is a particularly striking example of the exhilarating
march, taking in on the way all sorts of loops and parentheses, but
gradually gaining impetus until it reaches its final goal. And in
larger terms still, we can perceive the same rhythm in the construction of the first three meditations if we read them together
as a single unit. I think there can be no doubt that this distinctive
and contagious confidence contributes a great deal to Descartes's
power as a persuader.

None of this is what Descartes called 'le fard et les couleurs de
la rhétorique'. He is not the frivolous decorative rhetorician,
adorning his thoughts so as to win praise as a man of letters.[17]
Neither is he the court-room orator, hastily intent on swaying his
audience by any means, fair or foul. His writing is rhetorical in a
far more effective way. His is the persuasion of the philosopher
who knows when to put forward his ideas plainly and unemotion-
ally and when to appeal to the irrational sides of human nature.
Nor is this appeal ever carried to excess; it is kept in its place and
made to appear natural. Indeed, much of Descartes's eloquence
(his mastery of prose rhythm, for instance) was presumably
natural, but this natural gift was put to advantage by a writer who
had thought a good deal about the problems of communication
and persuasion. He may have been reluctant to admit the need for
persuasive tactics, but there is no question that if he still commands
the attention and even the assent of many readers (including those
non-specialist readers of whom he had so high an opinion), it is
not only because of the soundness of his intuitions and deduc-
tions, but also because he is able to communicate them with all the
skill of the traditional orator.

[17] It is interesting to note a contemporary comparison of the Latin styles of Gassendi and Descartes: 'Je me plais davantage au style doux et riant de Gassendi tout
impregné de belle littérature . . . Descartes manque trop de cette littérature polie, qui
n'a jamais été une entrave à un homme bien né et instruit quand il écrit, et sa façon de
philosopher me semble se ressentir quelque peu de l'humeur mélancolique.' (*Corr.*
v. 317, note.)

3. The Rhetoric of Enlightenment

En Angleterre, on se contentait que Newton fût le plus
grand géomètre de son siècle; en France, on aurait aussi
voulu qu'il fût aimable.

(D'Alembert: *Essai sur la société des gens de lettres
avec les grands*)

A. SCIENCE AND SOCIETY

IN Descartes's writings we can distinguish two important notions
of philosophical communication. The first is the impulse to bring
philosophy as close to mathematics as possible, attempting to rid
philosophical language of the impurities of common speech. The
second is the belief that philosophy is not the exclusive province
of the professional, but should be accessible to all men of common
sense—Descartes's only dialogue is entitled *La Recherche de la
vérité par la lumière naturelle qui toute pure, et sans emprunter le secours
de la religion ni de la philosophie, détermine les opinions que doit avoir un
honnête homme, touchant toutes les choses qui peuvent occuper sa pensée,
et pénètre jusque dans les secrets des plus curieuses sciences.*

These two positions are not necessarily contradictory. Indeed,
they come together in hostility to a common enemy, the unnecessary verbiage—as it seemed to Descartes—of scholastic philosophy. Both stress the need for simplicity, clarity, and certainty.
But there quickly comes a point where the two aims diverge. The
ordinary man of common sense may welcome clarity in the treatment of philosophical questions, but he is likely to be less willing
to follow the philosopher in his creation of a pure quasi-mathematical form of discourse, uncomfortably remote from the ordinary language of communication. He may, moreover, expect of the
philosopher certain concessions to his taste for elegance, harmony,
and urbanity, which the austere philosopher may be unwilling to
make. The present chapter looks in a general way at the theoretical
treatment of this question in the century following Descartes's
death and examines how Montesquieu and d'Alembert set about
reconciling professional rigour and the appeal to a broad public.

Many philosophers of the seventeenth and eighteenth centuries
spoke of the need for a reform of the language of philosophy; the
more extreme would have liked to extend this reform to all sorts
of language. In France, as in England, the misuse of language was
seen as one of the greatest obstacles to philosophical progress.
Condillac, a tireless enemy of verbal confusion and misplaced
imagination, repeatedly exposed the perils of imprecise speech.
In a very Cartesian passage of his *Essai sur l'origine des connaissances
humaines* he explains the inadequacy of normal speech:

Ce qui accoutume notre esprit à cette inexactitude, c'est la manière
dont nous nous formons au langage. Nous n'atteignons l'âge de raison
que longtemps après avoir contracté l'usage de la parole. Si l'on excepte
les mots destinés à faire connaître nos besoins, c'est ordinairement le
hasard qui nous a donné occasion d'entendre certains sons plutôt que
d'autres, et qui a décidé des idées que nous leur avons attachées. Pour
peu qu'en réfléchissant sur les enfants que nous voyons nous nous
rappelions l'état par où nous avons passé, nous reconnaîtrons qu'il n'y
a rien de moins exact que l'emploi que nous faisons ordinairement des
mots.[1]

This was what the philosopher had to contend with; the language
of children must be replaced by the language of thinking men.
For Condillac, as for most philosophers and scientists of the time,
the most valuable form of thought was analysis, the breaking
down of compound ideas into simple ideas, the simplest ideas
being generated by sensations and corresponding to real things
in the world of nature. The ideal philosophical language would
therefore consist of signs, each of which corresponded to one
simple idea. These signs would then be arranged in what was
considered by many as the 'natural' order of subject, verb, and
predicate; even those such as Condillac, who did not believe that
this was the actual way we think, still regarded this order as the
most suitable for the philosophical deployment of thought in
time.[2]

[1] Condillac, *Œuvres philosophiques*, ed. G. Le Roy, Paris, 1947–51, vol. I, p. 105.
For a general view of eighteenth-century theories of language see F. Brunot, *Histoire
de la langue française*, vol. VI, part 2: 'La langue post-classique' by A. François (Paris,
1932), pp. 863–925; M. Foucault, *Les Mots et les Choses*, Paris, 1966, chapter 4;
E. Cassirer, *The Philosophy of Symbolic Forms*, vol. I: 'Language', tr. R. Manheim,
New Haven, Conn., 1953, pp. 117–47.
[2] On Condillac and the 'ordre naturel' see U. Ricken, 'La *liaison des idées* selon
Condillac et la *clarté* du français', *Dix-huitième Siècle*, no. I, 1969, pp. 179–93. For
a more general treatment see N. Chomsky, *Cartesian Linguistics*, New York, 1966.

Such a language would greatly facilitate the task of the philosopher. Indeed, Condillac goes so far as to say that a science is no more than a well-made language.[3] Conversely, one sees that the lack of precise terminology was a great obstacle to the progress of the analytical natural sciences. It is considerations such as these which lay behind the recurrent efforts of philosophers of this period to create artificial languages as tools for philosophy, languages such as the one described in the *Encyclopédie* article 'Langue nouvelle'. But the creation of new languages remained a fringe enthusiasm, although an interesting and significant one. Most philosophers concluded, as Descartes had done in his letter to Mersenne, that such an innovation 'n'est bon à proposer que dans le pays des romans';[4] one had simply to make the best of existing languages.

Latin seemed to many to be the obvious choice. Here was a language which for all its shortcomings (such as its 'unnatural' word-order) was at least dead and so capable of lending itself for use as a non-emotive international language of learning. To a certain extent, it still had this function in the middle of the eighteenth century, and such prominent enlighteners as Diderot, d'Alembert, and Maupertuis argued that its position should be strengthened. But once again, this was largely wishful thinking; in the Preliminary Discourse of the *Encyclopédie*, d'Alembert has to accept that 'les philosophes, comme les autres écrivains, veulent être lus, et surtout de leur nation', even though they ought really to use 'une langue universelle et de convention' such as modern Latin.[5] D'Alembert, Maupertuis, and Diderot all used the vernacular, and this not only when they were writing for a large lay public, but also in such relatively specialized pieces as d'Alembert's *Traité de dynamique*. Maupertuis's *Système de la nature* was published first in Latin (in 1751), then in Latin and French at the same time, and finally in French alone (in 1754). The realistic philosopher had little choice; to have any effect, he had to use the vernacular.

Unfortunately, the existing modern languages were very far from the imagined ideal languages. Measured against the yardstick of general grammar and analytic philosophy, they were

3 Condillac, *Œuvres philosophiques*, vol. ii, p. 420.
4 *Œuvres philosophiques*, ed. F. Alquié, vol. i (1963), p. 232.
5 J. d'Alembert, *Œuvres*, ed. Bossange and Belin, Paris, 1821-2, vol. i, p. 76.

primitive instruments in which any one sign might convey a variety of different ideas and in which the word-order was far from conforming to the approved pattern. The basic trouble, from the philosophical point of view, appeared to be that languages retained too many traces of their original character. Condillac, like many others, believed that human language was originally poetic language, better suited to express emotion in a synthetic way than to analyse concepts. Gradually, however, prose diverged from poetry, which after the invention of writing had become increasingly cut off from its original philosophical function and confined to the 'choses de pur agrément'[6] (this is a typically eighteenth-century distinction between serious rational discourse and pleasant, but essentially frivolous, poetry). Thereafter human history showed a progressive refinement of language as an instrument of analytic thought—the French naturally considered that this process had gone furthest in France, though the English thought differently.

Most French philosophers who thought about language in the eighteenth century agreed about the state of their own tongue. With greater or lesser sincerity they expressed regrets at its decline as a poetic language, but held that in return it had developed in such a way as to make it more suitable than any other for conveying philosophical thought. To quote just one such opinion, Condillac states that 'la nôtre [langue], par la simplicité et par la netteté de ses constructions, donne de bonne heure à l'esprit une exactitude dont il se fait insensiblement une habitude, et qui prépare beaucoup les progrès de l'analyse; mais elle est peu favorable à l'imagination'.[7] Its main quality, whether inherent or acquired, was probably its famous 'natural' word-order—even Diderot suggests that Cicero must have thought in the French order before expressing himself in the Latin.[8] In addition it possessed certain less clearly defined qualities, 'la netteté, la clarté, la précision'. The polite form of the language was observed to show a marked resistance to fanciful metaphors and other figures which impeded clear communication. All this was good, but in spite of its clear philosophical potential, the language as

---

[6] Condillac, Œuvres philosophiques, vol. I, p. 81. See also Fontenelle, De l'origine des fables, and J.-J. Rousseau, Essai sur l'origine des langues.

[7] Condillac, Œuvres philosophiques, vol. I, p. 102.

[8] Diderot, Lettre sur les sourds et muets, ed. P. H. Meyer, Diderot Studies, VII (1965), pp. 57–60.

it was commonly used in polite society still had many grave defects.

One of the most significant of these was its intolerance of technical terms. If words are to correspond to ideas and ideas to things, then the exploration of the physical world will call for the creation of a vast number of appropriate terms. The norms of polite French, on the other hand, were laid down by the amateurish *honnête homme*—or rather, according to many witnesses, by his female counterpart. Montesquieu notes in his *Pensées*: '*Savants. On voudrait que, dans les livres, ils eussent appris le jargon des femmes*',[9] and what Montesquieu says concisely is spun out into an eloquent diatribe by many of his contemporaries. This fashionable world was hostile to precise technical terms, which smack of anti-social pedantry. The Physiocrats, for instance, met the same sort of mockery as tended to greet the sociologist in the England of the mid-twentieth century.[10] Philosophers and scientists were naturally sensitive to this kind of attitude, and many of them did their best to conform to the literary expectations of the general public. Buffon advocated the noble or general term in preference to the particular,[11] and d'Alembert, in his *Encyclopédie* article 'Éléments des sciences', spoke against the neologism: 'Les mots nouveaux, inutiles, bizarres ou tirés de trop loin, sont presque aussi ridicules en matière de science qu'en matière de goût.' This cautious approach led to the resistance of the Académie des Sciences to Lavoisier's attempt to remodel the language of chemistry; they felt that the last word should lie not with the professionals but with the general public.[12] Not surprisingly, many intellectuals disagreed with this position. One might quote the *Logique* of Port-Royal, Voltaire, the *Journal des Savants*, or, to give just one example, the *Encyclopédie* article 'Langue française', in which the author (de Jaucourt) protests that 'il est honteux qu'on n'ose aujourd'hui confondre le français proprement dit avec les termes des arts et des sciences, et qu'un homme de la cour se défende de connaître ce qui lui serait utile et honorable'. He

---

[9] Montesquieu, *Œuvres complètes*, ed. A. Masson, Paris, 1950–5, vol. II, p. 264.

[10] See F. Brunot, *Histoire de la langue française*, vol. VI, part 1, pp. 49–99 and *passim*.

[11] See D. Mornet, *Les Sciences de la nature au XVIIIe siècle*, Paris, 1911, pp. 198–200.

[12] See F. Brunot, *Histoire de la langue française*, vol. VI, part 1, section 1: 'La langue des sciences' by M. Fuchs (Paris, 1930), pp. 658–75. Fuchs's contribution to the *Histoire* is very important for the subject of this chapter.

concludes that 'la langue des Français polis n'est qu'un ramage faible et gentil'.

The question of the technical term is clearly only one aspect of a bigger problem, the relation between the world of learning and the world of fashion. It would have been simple if philosophers could have developed their own specialized vocabulary when talking to colleagues and followed 'le bon usage' of polite society when off duty. To a certain extent they did vary their style according to the occasion and the audience, but this sort of separation does not seem to have been so easy in the eighteenth century as it is today. For one thing, there was not yet anything like the modern university community in which scholars can operate together without having to face laymen, and where reputations do not necessarily depend on the normal skills of social communication. Eighteenth-century France had universities, of course, but these were not centres of intellectual life. There were, too, centres of learning such as the Benedictine monasteries or the medical school of Montpellier; here and in their private letters and personal contacts, scholars could in theory be as technical and abstruse as they pleased. But the main institutions of the new learning appear to have been the various academies, both Parisian and provincial. It was here in the first place that new ideas were tried out on a public; inevitably, therefore, these institutions did a lot to influence the way in which ideas were presented in book form to a wider public. It would be unwise to generalize too much about the academies, whose activity is in many cases only just beginning to be seriously explored,[13] but one can at least say that they were a sort of meeting-place between the man of learning and the world. They did a lot of serious work, but at the same time they had a certain number of non-playing members, mainly from the upper reaches of society, who added dignity to the proceedings. They held open sessions for the pleasure and instruction of a wider public, they conducted their business orally and fairly stylishly, and generally they encouraged the insertion of philosophy into polite society.

Academies are only one instance of the constant intermingling of scholars and laymen. One might also cite the presence of men of

[13] On the activity of provincial academies see D. Roche, 'Milieux académiques provinciaux et société des lumières', in *Livre et société dans la France du xviiie siècle*, ed. F. Furet, Paris, 1965.

letters in various *salons* and worldly gatherings (where new works might well be read aloud), the lack of any specialized periodical press until about the middle of the eighteenth century (the *Journal des Savants* was a popularizer and conscious of being so), the absence of a specialized book-buying public (nothing like the present-day captive audience of university libraries and university students), and the relation of patronage which still prevailed in the eighteenth century, even if in the modified form which we see in Diderot's connection with Catherine of Russia. Scientists needed public support, both moral and financial, and, as Fontenelle says, they were prepared to make concessions.[14] In this way many different factors encouraged the man of learning to combine what Hume calls 'the two greatest and purest pleasures of human life, study and society',[15] making his work as agreeable and accessible as possible to the uninitiated. He had the more reason to do this as increasingly he felt that his role was to enlighten his fellow men, to spread the new word of truth—and here we come back to Descartes's insistence on the possibility of making the new science available to any ordinary educated man.

It would be wrong to suggest that all scientists and philosophers were eaten up with the desire to enlighten. Many were content, like the Benedictine scholars, to work by themselves, devoting their lives to scholarly research which had no immediate impact on the public consciousness. Nor was the urge to spread the word comparable to the crusades for popular education of the nineteenth century. Popularization stopped a long way short of the peasant, who might be inclined to abandon the soil, once he had eaten the forbidden fruit. For all this, the eighteenth century was undoubtedly a great age of popularization; one need only think of such classics as the *Entretiens sur la pluralité des mondes* of Fontenelle, the *Éléments de la philosophie de Newton* of Voltaire, the *Spectacle de la nature* of the Abbé Pluche, the *Histoire naturelle* of Buffon, and of course the great *Encyclopédie*, the most famous of thousands of dictionaries, digests, compilations, and manuals. Grimm notes ironically in his *Correspondance littéraire* that 'la fureur

[14] See L. M. Marsak, *Bernard de Fontenelle; the Idea of Science in the French Enlightenment*, Philadelphia, 1959.
[15] Hume, *Dialogues concerning Natural Religion*, ed. N. Kemp-Smith, Oxford, 1935, p. 158.

des dictionnaires est devenue si grande parmi nous qu'on vient d'imprimer un *Dictionnaire des dictionnaires*'.[16]

Although Grimm, the professional reviewer, was naturally ferocious in his treatment of the many tedious compilations and digests which came his way, this does not mean that he scorned popularization as such. Not surprisingly, he did everything he could to push his friend Diderot's *Encyclopédie*. And the *Encyclopédie* in its turn sang the praises of the great enlighteners. Typically, the Preliminary Discourse of d'Alembert celebrates the example of Fontenelle:

Supérieur dans l'art de mettre en leur jour les idées les plus abstraites, il a su, par beaucoup de méthode, de précision et de clarté, les abaisser à la portée des esprits qu'on aurait cru les moins faits pour les saisir. Il a même osé prêter à la Philosophie les ornements qui semblaient lui être les plus étrangers, et qu'elle paraissait devoir s'interdire le plus sévèrement; et cette hardiesse a été justifiée par le succès le plus général et le plus flatteur.[17]

It is by following this example that d'Alembert's co-editor hopes that 'en multipliant le nombre des vrais savants, des artistes distingués et des amateurs éclairés, il répandra dans la société de nombreux avantages'.[18]

But the name of Fontenelle immediately suggests the difficulties of popularization. Against the praise of d'Alembert must be set the reservations expressed in his *Éloge de Fontenelle* and echoed by journalists and writers of all parties. Fontenelle worried them, and particularly his elegant *Entretiens sur la pluralité des mondes*. If they admitted the value of his personal achievement, they made up for this by condemning him as a model for others. In Grimm's words, 'son style, son coloris et sa manière d'écrire offrent une vaste carrière au faux bel esprit'.[19]

It was a tricky problem. On the one hand, the world being what it was, every rhetorician knew that it was necessary to deck philosophy out in a few ornaments to get it admitted to society. Thus the *Mémoires de Trévoux* for 1751 (to quote one among many) contains this rather charming description of the rhetoric of philosophy:

---

[16] M. Grimm and others, *Correspondance littéraire*, ed. M. Tourneux, Paris, 1877–82, vol. IV, p. 29.   [17] D'Alembert, *Œuvres*, vol. I, pp. 76–7.
[18] *Encyclopédie*, article 'Encyclopédie'.
[19] *Correspondance littéraire*, vol. III, p. 338.

Quand on observe, dans un laboratoire de physique, quand on démon-
tre dans le secret d'un cabinet, tout est dans la simplicité de la nature
et de la raison; mais quand on vient à communiquer au public le succès
des tentatives et l'avantage des nouvelles découvertes, c'est le moment
de parler aussi un peu à l'imagination, d'emprunter des couleurs, de
répandre des nuances, de peindre en un mot avec grâce. Les sciences
sont amies des belles-lettres.[20]

And Grimm, for all his severity to the school of Fontenelle, raps
Condillac over the knuckles for his tedious style: 'N'en déplaise
à M. l'abbé de Condillac, quand on veut être lu, il faut savoir
écrire.'[21]

'Savoir écrire'—what sort of meaning can be attached to these
words in a philosophical context? As we have seen, it might
mean the light-weight wit of a Fontenelle. One of the most
celebrated moments of his *Entretiens* is the passage where the
narrator is attempting to impress on the 'marquise' (and Fontenelle on his reader) the relativity of our notion of time:

Les anciens étaient plaisants de s'imaginer que les corps célestes étaient
de nature à ne changer jamais, parce qu'ils ne les avaient pas encore vu
changer. Avaient-ils eu le loisir de s'en assurer par l'expérience? Les
anciens étaient jeunes auprès de nous. Si les roses qui ne durent qu'un
jour faisaient des histoires, et se laissaient des mémoires les unes des
autres, les premières auraient fait le portrait de leur jardinier d'une
certaine façon, et de plus de quinze mille âges de roses, les autres qui
l'auraient encore laissé à celles qui les devaient suivre, n'y auraient rien
changé. Sur cela elles diraient, 'Nous avons toujours vu le même
jardinier, de mémoire de rose on n'a vu que lui, il a toujours été fait
comme il est, assurément il ne meurt point comme nous, il ne change
seulement pas.' Le raisonnement des roses serait-il bon?[22]

This passage is referred to in one of the dialogues of Fontenelle's
greater successor, Diderot. In the *Rêve de d'Alembert* the lay-
woman, Mademoiselle de Lespinasse, wonders why philosophers
do not always write as charmingly as this, but her interlocutor, the
doctor Bordeu, explains that 'franchement, je ne sais si ce ton
frivole convient aux sujets graves'.[23] This is perhaps an indication

[20] *Mémoires de Trévoux*, Apr. 1751, pp. 796-7.
[21] *Correspondance littéraire*, vol. III, p. 113.
[22] Fontenelle, *Entretien sur la pluralité des mondes*, ed. R. Shackleton, Oxford, 1955,
p. 141.
[23] Diderot, *Œuvres complètes*, ed. J. Assézat and M. Tourneux, Paris, 1875-7, vol. II,
p. 134.

that the times have changed—in 1769 it is no longer necessary to sugar the pill as thickly as in 1686. Nevertheless, Fontenelle's style shows several of the qualities which recur in philosophical popularization of the eighteenth century: the tendency to replace the treatise by dialogue, the spoken tone with variety of sentence length and urbane banter such as 'les anciens étaient plaisants', the use of questions (exclamations sometimes have a similar effect), the avoidance of technical terms, the use of elegant comparison, extended here to allegorical anecdote. One might add to this list, from other sources, the use of the pronouns 'je' and 'vous' to give a personal sound to the writing, or the affectation of a sweet disorder which shows the writer to be more than a mere pedant. Always the effort is to capture the natural tone, the tone of conversation; such classics as Montaigne, the Pascal of the *Provinciales*, and Madame de Sévigné provided models.

Most important of all is the stress on euphony and symmetry, the insistence which is so characteristic of this age of academies and salons that everything should *sound* right. Diderot noted regretfully that sense often gave way to sound: 'une des choses qui nuisent le plus dans notre langue et dans les langues anciennes à l'ordre naturel des idées, c'est cette harmonie du style à laquelle nous sommes devenus si sensibles, que nous lui sacrifions souvent tout le reste.'[24] At its extreme this leads to the rich sonorities of poetic prose, the ternary constructions, symmetries, enumerations, and generally ecclesiastical tone of this passage from Buffon's *Histoire naturelle*:

La Nature, indépendamment de ses hautes puissances auxquelles nous ne pouvons atteindre, et qui se déploient par des effets universels, a de plus les facultés de nos Arts, qu'elle manifeste par des effets particuliers; comme nous, elle sait fondre et sublimer les métaux, cristalliser les sels, tirer le vitriol et le soufre des pyrites, etc. Son mouvement plus que perpétuel, aidé de l'éternité des temps, produit, entraîne, amène toutes les révolutions, toutes les combinaisons possibles; pour obéir aux lois établies par le souverain Être, elle n'a besoin ni d'instruments, ni d'adminicules, ni d'une main dirigée par l'intelligence humaine: tout s'opère, parce qu'à force de temps tout se rencontre, et que, dans la libre étendue des espaces et dans la succession continue du mouvement, toute matière est remuée, toute forme donnée, toute figure imprimée; ainsi tout se rapproche ou s'éloigne, tout s'unit ou se fuit, tout se

---

[4] *Lettre sur les sourds et muets*, ed. P. H. Meyer, *Diderot Studies*, VII, p. 68.

combine ou s'oppose, tout se produit ou se détruit par des forces
relatives ou contraires, qui seules sont constantes, et, se balançant sans
se nuire, animent l'Univers et en font un théâtre de scènes toujours
nouvelles, d'objets sans cesse renaissants.[25]

Even as an introduction, this may seem somewhat out of place
in a treatise on sulphur.

Both to the flower chains of Fontenelle and to the organ music
of Buffon there were strong reactions. Many writers inclined to an
out-and-out rejection of rhetoric, not just the old and disreputable
rhetoric of the class-room, but the far more acceptable compromises with the demands of polite taste. The fear that these
might turn philosophy into a frivolous social game spurred them
to reassert its integrity and independence in linguistic terms.
Grimm, for instance, is constantly warning against the dangers
of paying too much attention to the demands of the public, even
though his position as purveyor of literary news to the crowned
heads of Europe was not without its ambiguities. In the *Correspondance littéraire*, and particularly in the recurrent doubts about
the wisdom of founding new academies, there is a vision of the
devaluing of science by excessive exposure to the lay public.
Science had become so fashionable that public interest was likely
to waste the philosopher's time and lower his standards.

The desire to avoid the dangers of popularization sometimes
led to the adoption of an austere tone, characterized by a wealth
of technical terms (as opposed to noble, general terms) and by the
absence of certain figures, metaphor and simile above all, but also
the various pattern figures, antithesis, symmetry and gradation,
and the care for harmonious sentence construction. Once again the
rhetoric of fine writing is despised and feared. One is reminded
of the pope who committed solecisms on religious principle,
or the deliberate 'bad writing' (by the standards of a certain
social group) which is often adopted in political texts. Somewhat
self-consciously, many eighteenth-century writers proclaimed
their disregard for the footling expectations of a certain sort of
reader.

Bougainville, giving the account of his voyage round the world,
makes it clear in his preliminary discourse that 'on ne doit pas
en regarder la relation comme un ouvrage d'amusement'. With

---

[25] Buffon, *Histoire naturelle des minéraux*, vol. II (Paris, 1783), p. 107. This sort of
eloquence is not the norm in the *Histoire naturelle*, but is deployed at strategic points.

apparently false modesty he points out that 'ce n'est ni dans les forêts du Canada ni sur le sein des mers, que l'on se forme à l'art d'écrire'.[26] There is some exaggeration in this posture of almost primitive innocence, but the result is indeed a fairly straightforward account, bristling with nautical terminology. It is, as Diderot put it, 'sans apprêt; le ton de la chose, de la simplicité et de la clarté, surtout quand on possède la langue des marins'.[27] It is interesting, however, that when he comes to the most attractive part of his travels, Tahiti ('la nouvelle Cythère'), Bougainville allows himself the luxury of a more elegant, even lush, style.

Bougainville's attitude could be paralleled in the prefaces of many more or less technical works, where the author feels himself obliged to assert from the outset his stylistic independence. As Diderot says in his article 'Encyclopédie', it is right that a serious work should be written in a serious style, 'et qu'il en reçût quelque austérité, même dans les endroits où les couleurs les plus brillantes et les plus gaies n'auraient pas été déplacées'. But here again the difficulty of sustaining a coherent position is suggested by the subsequent remark that an encyclopedia should be well written, since 'plus une route doit être longue, plus il serait à souhaiter qu'elle fût agréable'.

Obviously, it is easy to sound intransigent about your style and equally easy to fall into the traps of rhetoric. The rejection of ornament, and in particular the refusal to appeal to the senses and the imagination, had been seen most clearly perhaps in Malebranche's *La Recherche de la vérité*, which I mentioned briefly in an earlier chapter.[28] Malebranche's reputation in the eighteenth century is an interesting example of the gap between theory and practice. Although it may be incorrect in some respects to call him a Cartesian, he certainly followed Descartes in his ideas on communication—for example, he feared the power of the imagination to corrupt the understanding. The chapter entitled 'De la communication contagieuse des imaginations fortes' in the *Recherche* shows how eloquence seduces us and leads us away from the truth. An examination of the appeal of three arch-rhetoricians, Tertullian, Seneca, and Montaigne, reveals that

---

[26] Bougainville, *Voyage autour du monde*, ed. M. Hérubel, Paris, 1966, p. 51.
[27] Diderot, *Œuvres complètes*, vol. II, p. 208.
[28] See above, pp. 29-31.

'tous les divers styles ne nous plaisent ordinairement qu'à cause de
la corruption secrète de notre cœur'.[29] He notes too the way in
which 'le plaisir sensible de la mesure des périodes' influences our
judgement. This being so, the communicator can take up various
positions. Arnauld and Nicole, in the *Logique* of Port-Royal, while
deploring the fact that people let worldly taste affect the workings
of reason, nevertheless concede that we owe it to readers not to
shock them unnecessarily.[30] Malebranche, however, preserves a
theoretical purity, declaring himself interested not in expression,
but in truth.[31] This is a ridiculously vulnerable position. Journalists
and critics of the eighteenth century had no difficulty in showing
the difference between Malebranche's theory and his practice.
The Abbé Dubos remarks, to his own obvious satisfaction, that
'c'est à notre imagination qu'il parle contre l'abus de l'imagination'.[32] And indeed it is easy to show his affection for imagery,
his apparent care for the cadences of prose, his tendency to a
rather *précieux* wit, and in several of his works the concern for
attractive presentation which leads him to prefer the dialogue to
the treatise. As the *Mémoires de Trévoux* puts it, comparing him to
Rousseau, 'on a dit du Père Malebranche que *l'imagination servait
un ingrat*'.[33]

It is unrewarding to mock at the gap between rhetorical theory
and practice. Clearly the serious writer of the eighteenth century
had problems. How far could he satisfy the linguistic expectations
of an audience of amateurs? Did he owe it to his subject to express
himself as splendidly or as elegantly as was compatible with the
demands of truth? Or was it not his job to take up a moral stand
against the corruption of polite taste, choosing rather to shock
or disappoint his audience than to flatter it? Was it possible to
create a hierarchy of forms and styles for different subjects and
situations? These are questions one could ask of almost any
philosopher or scientist of the time. I should like now to look at
the writings of two *philosophes* whose writings were widely read
and admired, to show how they themselves saw their rhetorical

---

[29] N. Malebranche, *Œuvres*, vol. I, p. 360.

[30] A. Arnauld and P. Nicole, *La Logique*, ed. P. Clair and F. Girbal, Paris, 1965,
pp. 287–9.   [31] Op. cit., vol. I, p. 22.

[32] Abbé J.-B. Dubos, *Réflexions critiques sur la poésie et la peinture*, 7th ed., Paris,
1770, vol. I, p. 298.

[33] *Mémoires de Trévoux*, Feb. 1751, p. 505. Voltaire repeats this 'idée reçue' in his
1755 letter to Rousseau (*Correspondance*, ed. Bestermann, vol. XXVII, p. 232).

situation and to analyse the ways of writing and speaking which
they in fact adopted.

'De l'esprit sur les lois', said Madame du Deffand.[34] La Harpe put
her fairly firmly in her place, remarking that she was not even
capable of reading *De l'esprit des lois* and understanding it. Nevertheless, the smear was not quite washed away. For posterity, and
not just for Brunetière, Montesquieu has remained an ambiguous
figure, the legislator and the sage, but also the wit. We may make
allowances for Voltaire's critical (not to say malicious) turn of
mind, when he writes:

J'ai trouvé l'esprit de l'auteur, qui en a beaucoup, et rarement l'esprit
des lois; il sautille plus qu'il ne marche; il brille plus qu'il n'éclaire;
il satirise quelquefois plus qu'il ne juge; et il faut souhaiter qu'un si
beau génie eût toujours plus cherché à instruire qu'à surprendre[35]

but Voltaire was not alone. Many contemporary readers saw in
Montesquieu's masterpiece a turning-point in the study of human
society and a lesson to kings and princes—they were particularly
inclined to see it in this way when they were writing to congratulate the author on his achievement. Others, however, were more
sensitive to the formal qualities of the work, noting its 'grâces'
and its 'élégance, finesse, justesse et noblesse'. Significantly, the
Lois was defended by Fontenelle, who is reported to have
remarked 'que cet auteur répand tant d'agrément sur tout ce
qu'il écrit qu'il en mettrait même dans un livre de géométrie, s'il
s'avisait d'en faire un' (III. 1177).[36] Or again, 'c'est le seul livre
de ce genre qu'on puisse lire avec autant de plaisir que de fruit'
(III. 1233). Some time afterwards, Montesquieu wrote to d'Alembert: 'Dites ... à Madame du Deffand que si je continue à écrire
sur la philosophie, elle sera ma marquise' (III. 1479)—and so

34 This remark, and Montesquieu's changing reputation, are discussed in the
article of D. C. Cabeen, 'The "Esprit" of the *Esprit des Lois*', *P.M.L.A.*, 1939. On
the whole not much attention has been paid to Montesquieu's style, particularly when
considered from a rhetorical point of view. See, however, A. Chérel, *De Télémaque à
Candide*, Paris, 1958, pp. 286–95.
35 In *L'A. B. C.*, *Œuvres complètes*, ed. Moland, vol. XXVII, p. 321.
36 References are to the *Œuvres complètes*, ed. A. Masson, 3 vols., Paris, 1950–5. Note
that vol. I of this edition is divided into three books with separate pagination (the
original 3 volumes of the 1758 edition).

places himself, at least in joke, in the tradition of Fontenelle's
Entretiens sur la pluralité des mondes.

It will be remembered that many of the *philosophes* were divided
in their assessment of Fontenelle, and regretted that he had
sacrificed so much to 'bel esprit'. Similarly, Helvétius, who was
a friend of Montesquieu, but far from a disciple, says in a letter
to Saurin that 'sa manière est éblouissante' but cannot ultimately
conceal the errors of his philosophy. In the end, he says, 'notre
ami Montesquieu, dépouillé de son titre de sage et de législateur,
ne sera plus qu'homme de robe, gentilhomme et bel-esprit' (III.
1540). This is the Montesquieu whom his correspondents addressed
as 'mon cher Uzbek' or 'mon petit Romain', the academician of
Bordeaux, man of the *salons* and author of the *Lettres persanes*—
not to speak of the *Temple de Gnide.*

For other readers, who had perhaps less of an axe to grind than
Helvétius, Montesquieu was a model of sensible writing, an
example of 'le ton de la chose' to be set against the extravagances
of fine writers such as Buffon. The *Correspondance littéraire* notes
ironically: ' "Le style du président de Montesquieu!" disait il y a
quelque temps avec dédain M. de Buffon; "mais Montesquieu
a-t-il un style?" N'aurait-il pas mérité qu'on eût osé lui répondre:
"Il est vrai, Montesquieu n'a que le style du génie, et vous, monsieur, vous avez le génie du style"?'[37] Yet Buffon had himself
advocated 'le ton de la chose' in his Academic Discourse, which
contains a transparent critical allusion to *De l'esprit des lois.* It is no
good looking for any sort of consensus in this most personal of
questions, the appreciation of style.

Montesquieu was thus perceived by his contemporaries both as
serious philosopher and as wit. Posterity has not always agreed
which of these is the dominant element. I shall not attempt to adjudi-
cate between the two parties, or to decide whether Montesquieu's
attempts to charm his reader are acceptable in a serious thinker,
since their acceptability obviously depends on a number of subjective
factors in any given reader. My intention is rather to describe how
he himself saw his rhetorical position and to examine, particularly
in the *Lois,* the ways in which he adjusted his message to his public.

It is by no means easy to pick out a coherent rhetoric from
Montesquieu's scattered statements on the subject. A good

[37] *Correspondance littéraire,* vol. xv, p. 220.

example of his approach can be seen in the *Essai sur le goût*, written at the end of his life as a contribution to the *Encyclopédie*. Successive chapters begin respectively: 'Mais s'il faut de l'ordre dans les choses, il faut aussi de la variété' (I. iii. 619) and 'J'ai dit que l'âme aime la variété; cependant, dans la plupart des choses, elle aime à voir une espèce de symétrie' (I. iii. 621). Montesquieu's mind is well balanced almost to excess; his attitude to rhetoric shows very clearly his tendency to see both sides of a question.

In the first place, he frequently expresses a dislike for ostentatious wit. Rica of the *Lettres persanes* notes, without great originality, that 'la fureur de la plupart des Français, c'est d'avoir de l'esprit' (I. iii. 132), and the Montesquieu of *Mes pensées* goes one stage further: 'Quand on court après l'esprit, on attrape la sottise' (II. 406). At one level, it looks as if this attitude stems from personal feeling; Montesquieu simply does not like showy talk and writing. But it is clearly more than the perception of a failing in others; he sees it too as a danger for himself: 'Je suis (je crois) presque le seul homme qui ait fait des livres, ayant sans cesse peur de la réputation de bel-esprit.' (II. 87.) This is why he attempts to head off criticism in the preface to the *Lois* with the disclaimer: 'On ne trouvera point ici ces traits saillants, qui semblent caractériser les ouvrages d'aujourd'hui.' (I. i. lx.) This attempt to dissociate himself from 'le bel esprit' was not always successful with his contemporaries, but it shows at least that he wanted to avoid being considered a flashy writer. Rather he wanted to be the *honnête homme*, good company because he does not try to dazzle: 'Ceux qui m'ont connu savent que, dans mes conversations, je ne cherchais pas trop à le paraître [bel-esprit], et que j'avais assez le talent de prendre la langue de ceux avec qui je vivais.' (II. 87.) This judgement is confirmed fulsomely in the *Éloge* written by Montesquieu's son: M. de Secondat notes that 'la facilité de plaire lui en inspirait le désir' and that 'on ne sortait point d'avec lui sans être plus content de soi-même et sans reconnaître en même temps sa supériorité'.[38] And such indeed is the image of Montesquieu which emerges consistently from his letters and the descriptions of his talk.

The correspondence, for instance, is unremarkable compared with that of Diderot or Voltaire. We do not hear an insistent

---

[38] *Éloge historique de Monsieur de Montesquieu par Monsieur de Secondat, son fils*, in Montesquieu, *Œuvres complètes*, ed. D. Oster, Paris, 1964, p. 18.

single voice; the writer remains elusive, adapting his letters to
their recipients, saying the right thing in the right place, doing
what he can to amuse his correspondents and to avoid boring
them. In a very early letter he strikes a characteristic note: 'J'ai
pris la liberté de varier mon style pour vous ôter la fatigue d'une
longue prose.' (II. 731.) Style is here, as so often in the eighteenth
century, an instrument which is picked up, changed, and dis-
carded in accordance with quite deliberate rhetorical intentions.
Montesquieu is a good performer. He knows the value of the
society game to him and he enjoys playing it. He is good at the
academic game too and adept at turning neat compliments when
it is his turn to distribute the prizes. All these contexts—the letter,
the academic gathering, and the fashionable drawing-room—
called for wit, not perhaps the ostentatious display which Montesquieu repudiated, but at least the perception of nuances of
language and the ability to manipulate words so as to please
people who were not professional writers.

Perhaps the dominant note here is the avoidance of tedium.
This mattered a lot to Montesquieu personally, quite apart from
the need to please listeners and readers. While he was capable of
long and concentrated effort in one area—as *De l'esprit des lois*
demonstrates—he also appears as someone constantly searching
out new things, the indefatigable traveller, never stopping long
in any one place, but hurrying on to see all that can be seen. His
travel diaries and his letters bear witness to this formidable
curiosity; he writes from Italy of 'cette satisfaction que l'on a
lorsqu'on voit de belles choses qui sont nouvelles' (III. 934).
We understand how Madame de Lambert could write to him:
'ce qui vous plaît ne vous plaît pas longtemps' (III. 925). With personal knowledge of the lure of variety and the horror of monotony,
he was anxious not to be considered a 'conteur ennuyeux', like the
poor man in the *Histoire véritable* who loved telling long stories but
could never find anyone to listen to them. This character eventually learns to speak concisely, but still complains comically: 'je ne
comprenais pas que ce style raccourci, ni ces récits secs et décharnés
pussent plaire' (III. 346). Here Montesquieu might be describing
his own way of writing as it struck many contemporaries, the
laconic force which he contrasts more than once with the amplifications of rhetoric.

Avoiding tedium did not always involve using the 'style coupé' (which is often associated with Montesquieu's name); above all, it meant rejecting the predictable drone of pedantic school rhetoric and preferring, in accordance with a more evolved rhetoric, a style which is original, lively, and often goes against the rules of fine writing. A passage from his *Pensées* puts this with some force:

Quand on me demande si une diction est bonne, je n'y puis répondre, à moins qu'elle ne choque la grammaire. Je ne puis savoir le cas où elle sera bonne, ni l'usage qu'un homme d'esprit en pourra faire: car un homme d'esprit est, dans ses ouvrages, créateur de dictions, de tours, et de conceptions; il habille sa pensée à sa mode, la forme, la crée par des façons de parler éloignées du vulgaire, mais qui ne paraissent pas être mises pour s'en éloigner. Un homme qui écrit bien n'écrit pas comme on a écrit, mais comme il écrit, et c'est souvent en parlant mal qu'il parle bien.   (ii. 219)

Speech and writing alike call for the sparkle of individual character, careless of rules, but still keen to please. In writing, this often meant giving the feeling of familiar conversation—the quality which Montesquieu's son, and other less partial critics, praised in the *Défense de l'Esprit des lois*, 'ouvrage peut-être plus admirable que *L'Esprit des lois*, parce que, sans y penser, Monsieur de Montesquieu s'y est peint au naturel et qu'il était supérieur à ses ouvrages mêmes. C'est le ton de la conversation, c'est lui-même.'[39] Notice that the social man is characteristically preferred to the writer.

This 'society' style flourishes in the *Lettres persanes*, which made Montesquieu's reputation as a wit. For his friends in the 1720s he was a clever writer and an ornament to society, whether in the Academy of Bordeaux or the *salons* of Paris. This is the Montesquieu of the *Temple de Gnide*. But the young wit was conscious of carrying within himself a more serious purpose. In 1725 he wrote to a correspondent: 'je sens que si je suis fou quelquefois et même les trois quarts du temps, il y a néanmoins chez moi un fonds de sagesse en réserve que je pourrai faire valoir quelque jour.' (iii. 779.) The image we are given is the traditional one (as in Rabelais's prologue) of a flippant surface and a solid kernel. The two coexist, but separately, at different levels. Montesquieu is not the man to deny the flippant side. In his *Essai sur les causes qui peuvent affecter les esprits et les caractères* he talks of the twofold

---

[39] *Éloge historique*, op. cit., p. 17.

education necessary to form the 'homme d'esprit'. Formal education gives a respect for truth and the habit of making distinctions,
the education of polite society teaches us to adapt to our surroundings, and 'ces deux éducations nous font connaître, au
juste, ces deux valeurs, et l'esprit nous fait mettre l'une ou l'autre
en usage selon le temps, selon les personnes, selon le lieu'
(III. 418).

So far, so good; the academician will be able to relax gracefully. But what happens in his serious writings? Do they too need
to put on a smiling face? For Montesquieu the problem did not
present itself as dramatically as I may have suggested in the first
part of this chapter. While condemning the sort of clever writing
which is in any case incompatible with the stance of *honnête homme*,
Montesquieu quite naturally assumes that the thorns of philosophy should be hung with flowers. His own way of writing is
unlike that of Fontenelle, but his notion of the rhetoric of
enlightenment is close to that of the master. A short discourse
on the motives which should lead us to scientific study concludes
with some fairly traditional ideas on the relation between science
and letters. 'Belles-lettres', says Montesquieu, apart from the
pleasure they give, inculcate the habit of presenting our ideas
more effectively: 'les sciences gagnent beaucoup à être traitées
d'une manière ingénieuse et délicate; c'est par là qu'on en ôte
la sécheresse, qu'on prévient la lassitude, et qu'on les met à la
portée de tous les esprits.' (III. 226.) And out come the expected
examples, Malebranche and Fontenelle. Here, at least, there is no
suggestion that this sort of presentation might debase the sciences
and betray the cause of truth.

During his two years of European travel, Montesquieu kept a
diary, most of which has survived. In this he noted, as straight-
forwardly as possible, all the things of interest which he saw or
heard. Thus, in Venice, one example among a thousand:

J'allai, le 20 août, voir les manufactures de verre et de glaces.
    Il n'y a que deux fourneaux pour les glaces. Ils en font de deux
longueurs de bras et demie de hauteur, et d'une longueur et demie de
largeur, uniquement de soufflées, à ce qu'ils disent; mais je n'en ai
point vu là. Ils ont, d'ailleurs, environ 18 fourneaux où se fabriquent
verres et verroteries pour les Nègres. Tout cela peut faire une trentaine
de fourneaux. (II. 986)

Here Montesquieu is operating at the *degré zéro* of style, apparently with no concern for effect, and this for the most part is the language of the travel diaries. Nevertheless, a diary is rarely written without thought of an eventual or imaginary reader. Montesquieu clearly had thoughts of using his notes as the basis of a published book, and the diary shows this in places. From time to time a 'vous' figure is addressed, and occasionally a passage appears to be designed to amuse or impress, thus: 'A Rome, il n'y a rien de si commode que les églises pour prier Dieu et pour assassiner les gens.' (II. 1109.) Without necessarily being conscious of a reader at this point, the diarist is sliding naturally into the rhetorical habits to which he has been bred.

A further degree of elaboration appears in the *Lettre sur Gênes*, which is the subsequent working-up of earlier notes on Genoa, again probably with an eye to publication. It has been conjectured that Montesquieu intended to give this epistolary form to all his travels.[40] The most obvious difference between the notes and the letter is that the original untidy jottings have been ordered more or less logically and the paragraphs made longer. Apart from this, there is a certain amount of modest embellishment. Some passages from the notes go straight into the letter without alteration; these include an already evocative section on the unsociable character of the Genoese:

Vous ne sauriez croire à quel point va la parcimonie de ces princes-là. Il n'y a rien dans le monde de si menteur que leurs palais. Vous voyez une maison superbe, et, dedans, une vieille servante, qui file. Dans les grandes maisons, si vous voyez un page, c'est qu'il n'y a point de laquais. (II. 1060, 1308)

Other passages, originally more scrappy, are altered and improved. Thus the following notes:

Cependant, on a augmenté le Vieux-Môle, du côté du levant, de 80 pans (un pan est moins d'un pied), et on a remarqué que cela faisait beaucoup de bien; ce qui fait que l'on a résolu de travailler à diminuer encore cette ouverture; ce qui ne se peut faire qu'avec des frais et des peines immenses, parce que la mer y est très profonde, et qu'il y faut jeter un nombre innombrable de pierres.

La mer est plus profonde au Môle-Neuf qu'au Vieux.

On fait, avec du ciment, une espèce de maçonnerie dans un bateau. On envoie des plongeurs pour raccommoder le lieu qui doit servir de

lit pour cette maçonnerie, et ensuite on la laisse tomber dans l'eau.
Il y a tel de ces bateaux qui coûte 1000 francs.   (II. 1052)

give this:

Comme la mer est moins profonde au Môle-Vieux qu'au Neuf, les
Génois viennent de faire une prolongation au Môle-Vieux de 80 pans,
et l'on remarque que cela fait un très bon effet, et que les vaisseaux sont
un peu plus sûrs; ce qui fait qu'on a dessein de continuer. Mais cela
coûte beaucoup: car il faut faire, avec du ciment, une espèce de
maçonnerie dans des bateaux faits exprès. On envoie des plongeurs
voir et accommoder le lit où doit être assise cette maçonnerie. Ensuite,
on la laisse tomber, avec le bateau, dans le lieu convenable, où elle
s'enfonce de son propre poids.   (II. 1304)

The differences are not startling. The order is clearly improved.
Certain details have been left out—the definition of a 'pan' has
been relegated to a footnote. The sentences, and particularly the
first sentence of the second version, have been rearticulated in the
cause of oratorical harmony. In small ways the language has
become more elegant—'l'on' for 'on' after 'et', 'un très bon effet'
for 'beaucoup de bien', elimination of the repeated 'ce qui' and
of 'nombre innombrable'. The paragraph has been given a more
satisfying conclusion than the original notation of price. But all
in all, it is a modest 'toilette stylistique'; Montesquieu has brushed
his clothes, but not put on any new ornaments. There is no
question of any display of wit or eloquence.

Similarly, it seemed to some contemporaries that the *Considérations sur les causes de la grandeur des Romains et de leur décadence* did
not make enough advances to the reader and that it failed to live
up to the *Lettres persanes*. Voltaire wrote to Thériot that it was
'less a book than an ingenious *table des matières* writ in an odd
style'.[41] By this 'odd style' I think we must understand a laconic
manner, omitting the smooth transitions and flourishes of modern
rhetoric. The first paragraph of the work is notably undemon-
strative:

Il ne faut pas prendre, de la ville de Rome, dans ses commencements,
l'idée que nous donnent les villes que nous voyons aujourd'hui; à
moins que ce ne soient celles de la Crimée, faites pour renfermer le
butin, les bestiaux et les fruits de la campagne. Les noms anciens des
principaux lieux de Rome ont tous du rapport à cet usage.   (I. iii. 351)

---

41 Voltaire, *Correspondance*, ed. Bestermann, vol. III, p. 326.

No exordium here, but apparently the first of a series of historical notes. In a way it is a deceptive beginning, for Montesquieu subsequently brings to his subject more of the expected beauties of language. As his narration carries him to the great climaxes of Roman history, his eloquence swells occasionally to rival that of a Bossuet (whose *Discours sur l'histoire universelle* was inevitably in his mind as he wrote). Listen to the accumulations of clauses, the antitheses, the exclamations, and the rhetorical questions of the following passage, one of the high points:

C'est ici qu'il faut se donner le spectacle des choses humaines. Qu'on voie, dans l'histoire de Rome, tant de guerres entreprises, tant de sang répandu, tant de peuples détruits, tant de grandes actions, tant de triomphes, tant de politique, de sagesse, de prudence, de constance, de courage; ce projet d'envahir tout, si bien formé, si bien soutenu, si bien fini; à quoi aboutit-il, qu'à assouvir le bonheur de cinq ou six monstres? Quoi! ce sénat n'avait fait évanouir tant de rois, que pour tomber lui-même dans le plus bas esclavage de quelques-uns de ses plus indignes citoyens, et s'exterminer par ses propres arrêts? On n'élève donc sa puissance, que pour la voir mieux renversée? Les hommes ne travaillent à augmenter leur pouvoir, que pour le voir tomber contre eux-mêmes dans de plus heureuses mains?   (i. iii. 453)

This is all very splendid and traditional; the first sentence suggests that it is in fact a deliberate moment of self-indulgence. After the 'spectacle' it is striking how Montesquieu brings his readers back to a much drier, unemotional tone, how symmetry and harmony give way to the forceful brevity of the 'style coupé'. The next paragraph reads:

Caligula ayant été tué, le sénat s'assembla pour établir une forme de gouvernement. Dans le temps qu'il délibérait, quelques soldats entrèrent dans le palais, pour piller: ils trouvèrent, dans un lieu obscur, un homme tremblant de peur; c'était Claude: ils le saluèrent empereur.

This is the sort of prose we associate with the name of Montesquieu. Here it gains its full effect from being placed after a passage of rolling eloquence. The *style coupé* is perhaps not what one normally calls a stylistic affectation—though this is how it appeared to many contemporaries—but it undoubtedly contributes strongly to the impact of the passage. It should not therefore be confused with the plain style which we noted in the travel journals. In writing laconically Montesquieu is not eschewing rhetoric but using it to good effect.

The *Considérations* was a sort of preview of *De l'esprit des lois*; it is in this master-work above all that we can study the ways in which Montesquieu wooed, or declined to woo, his public. He was well aware of the rhetorical problems inherent in so long a book. The *Invocation aux Muses*, that curious piece which Jacob Vernet dissuaded him from including in the final printed version, restates in lyrical prose some of the ideas of his *Pensées*. He prays to the Muses:

> Mais si vous ne voulez pas adoucir la rigueur de mes travaux, cachez le travail même. Faites que je réfléchisse et que je paraisse sentir. Faites que l'on soit instruit et que je n'enseigne pas, et que, quand j'annoncerai des choses utiles, on croie que je ne savais rien et que vous m'avez tout dit . . .
>
> Muses charmantes, si vous jetez sur moi un seul de vos regards, tout le monde lira mes ouvrages, et ce qui ne devait être un amusement sera un plaisir.[42]

There is nothing new here for the student of rhetoric. It is in a way surprising that Montesquieu, the hard-working scholar, is so anxious to avoid the stance of pedant, so classically concerned to couple 'plaire' with 'instruire', but he was after all a man of the academies and the *salons*. His great book, moreover, was not simply a report on work done, it was designed to persuade. His readers saw in the author a legislator and counsellor of kings, and indeed the *Lois* is permeated by the desire to win over the reader to belief and even to action. Thus, although Montesquieu may decline to amuse his readers with 'saillies', he must attract them, keep their attention, and charm them into agreement. In order to do this more effectively, he was always remarkably docile and ready to follow the advice of readers of all kinds; his relation with his audience was of prime importance to him.

One of the first things one notices about the *Lois* is its disjointedness. Ever since it appeared, readers have been arguing about its order or lack of order. This is not an argument that I

---

[42] For Vernet's opinion of this 'pièce bizarre' see his letter to Montesquieu (III. 1098). Montesquieu defended it, noting that 'il n'y a point d'ouvrage où il faille plus songer à délasser le lecteur que dans celui-ci, à cause de la longueur et de la pesanteur des matières.' (III. 1097–8.) I quote the *Invocation* in the version printed at the head of vol. I of the Masson edition.

want to pursue, since my interest is not so much in the theoretical coherence of the book as in the way it may be expected to work on a reader. And seen in this light, the disorder of the *Lois* should perhaps rather be called variety.

Montesquieu's chapters are mostly short, often very short, so much so that Voltaire, for instance, saw in this a frivolous affectation unbecoming a serious subject. Chapter 13 of Book V reads:

Idée du despotisme

Quand les sauvages de la Louisiane veulent avoir du fruit, ils coupent l'arbre au pied, et cueillent le fruit. Voilà le gouvernement despotique.

(I. i. 78)

Voltaire thought this was a fraud.[43] The notion contained in the metaphor seemed to him dubious, one of Montesquieu's typical unverified travellers' tales, but he recognized that such short chapters were effective. It is certainly true that this presentation has a considerable visual impact, forcing the attention and giving a constant impression of new ideas and new departures. Inside the longer chapters, the material is divided into very short paragraphs; like the short chapters, these encourage the reader of what is, after all, a very long book to feel that he is being spared the tedium of amplification. This pregnant brevity, whether real or illusory, is flattering in that it appears to leave a good deal to the imagination.

In fact, for all its undoubted achievements as a systematic study, the *Lois* often resembles a series of travel notes. Variety, discontinuity, and brevity make it read like Montesquieu's diaries, never staying very long in any one place, but galloping on in search of new sights and new ideas. This, as we have seen, corresponds to Montesquieu's own temperament; it reflects too the taste of many of his contemporaries. In his *Éloge*, Montesquieu's son remarks: 'Si ce désordre apparent n'est pas un effet de l'art, c'est une ressemblance fort heureuse de l'ouvrage avec son auteur. . . . L'attention du lecteur, qui succomberait sous tant de méditations, est ranimée par les idées riantes qui sont semées à chaque pas.'[44]

'Les idées riantes'—it is not enough for the long work to be broken up into short and varied chapters. Inside the chapters also

[43] *Commentaire sur l'Esprit des lois*, in Voltaire, *Œuvres*, ed. Moland, vol. xxx, p. 423.
[44] *Éloge historique*, op. cit., p. 18.

the reader must be charmed. What is meant by these 'idées riantes'? While it might be possible to approach such a question by way of a statistical survey of the whole book, I think it can be more economically and effectively tackled by examining a single chapter. The problem is to choose a reasonably typical one. Too short a chapter will not provide enough information, whereas a long and important one such as that devoted to the English Constitution is hardly typical. But by taking an example somewhere between the extremes of short and long, dry and eloquent, and checking our findings against the rest of the work, we can perhaps see more clearly how Montesquieu set about making his material agreeable to his readers. Let us take then the fifth chapter of Book III, entitled 'Que la vertu n'est point le principe du gouvernement monarchique':

Dans les monarchies, la politique fait faire les grandes choses avec le moins de vertu qu'elle peut; comme, dans les plus belles machines, l'art emploie aussi peu de mouvements, de forces et de roues qu'il est possible.

L'État subsiste, indépendamment de l'amour pour la patrie, du désir de la vraie gloire, du renoncement à soi-même, du sacrifice de ses plus chers intérêts, et de toutes ces vertus héroïques que nous trouvons dans les anciens, et dont nous avons seulement entendu parler.

Les lois y tiennent la place de toutes ces vertus, dont on n'a aucun besoin; l'état vous en dispense: une action qui se fait sans bruit, y est en quelque façon sans conséquence.

Quoique tous les crimes soient publics par leur nature, on distingue pourtant les crimes véritablement publics d'avec les crimes privés, ainsi appelés parce qu'ils offensent plus un particulier, que la société entière.

Or, dans les républiques, les crimes privés sont plus publics; c'est-à-dire, choquent plus la constitution de l'État, que les particuliers; et, dans les monarchies, les crimes publics sont plus privés; c'est-à-dire, choquent plus les fortunes particulières, que la constitution de l'État même.

Je supplie qu'on ne s'offense pas de ce que j'ai dit; je parle après toutes les histoires. Je sais très bien qu'il n'est pas rare qu'il y ait des princes vertueux; mais je dis que, dans une monarchie, il est très difficile que le peuple le soit.

Qu'on lise ce que les historiens de tous les temps ont dit sur la cour des monarques; qu'on se rappelle les conversations des hommes de tous les pays sur le misérable caractère des courtisans: ce ne sont point des choses de spéculation, mais d'une triste expérience.

L'ambition dans l'oisiveté, la bassesse dans l'orgueil, le désir de s'enrichir sans travail, l'aversion pour la vérité, la flatterie, la trahison, la perfidie, l'abandon de tous ses engagements, le mépris des devoirs du citoyen, la crainte de la vertu du prince, l'espérance de ses faiblesses, et, plus que tout cela, le ridicule perpétuel jeté sur la vertu, forment, je crois, le caractère du plus grand nombre des courtisans, marqué dans tous les lieux et dans tous les temps. Or il est très malaisé que la plupart des principaux d'un État soient malhonnêtes gens, et que les inférieurs soient gens de bien; que ceux-là soient trompeurs, et que ceux-ci consentent à n'être que dupes.

Que si, dans le peuple, il se trouve quelque malheureux honnête homme, le cardinal de Richelieu, dans son testament politique, insinue qu'un monarque doit se garder de s'en servir. Tant il est vrai que la vertu n'est pas le ressort de ce gouvernement! Certainement elle n'en est point exclue; mais elle n'en est pas le ressort. (I. i. 31–2)

Montesquieu's aim in this chapter was twofold. He was adding another brick to his theoretical construction; he was also taking an opportunity of discreetly criticizing the French monarchy as he knew it. The chapter is both expository and emotive. The expository side is evident in the comparison of the first paragraph. This is the normal didactic simile; it makes no emotional impact, but aims simply to make clearer the idea preceding it. Whether it in fact does this is dubious, but at least it shows the reader that the author is on his side and willing to help him. It is, however, the only comparison or metaphor which one notices in this passage. As in any piece of prose, there are a number of fossilized metaphors, but nothing is done to bring these back to life. In general, tropes are not frequent in the *Lois*. From time to time, but by no means in every chapter, Montesquieu makes a formal comparison which acts as a brief resting-place along the way, but the basic texture of his language remains quite literal. This is the style of the philosopher; 'comparaison n'est pas raison'[45] and similes or metaphors can only be admitted at infrequent intervals. Yet the language is not too insistently philosophical. Technical terms are kept to a minimum, and there is certainly nothing abstruse about the vocabulary of this chapter. Like many of his contemporaries, Montesquieu wanted to do

---

[45] Montesquieu notes that 'les comparaisons ne sont bonnes que dans l'art oratoire et dans la poésie et ne servent qu'à dire la même chose, et plus mal' (II. 322). Voltaire might have been taking up this point when he criticizes one of Montesquieu's similes—'ce n'est pas là le style d'un législateur' (*Œuvres*, ed. Moland, vol. xxx, p. 413).

his technical work with the unpretentious clarity of the *honnête homme*.

More important than any trope as a way of pleasing the reader is the author's personal presence in what he writes. The 'moi' is a great weapon of persuasion; it is the sign of the human being, conscious of his own failings and not attempting to disguise his presence in the pompous impersonality of the philosopher. Here the 'je' is brought forward to plead with the public: 'Je supplie qu'on ne s'offense pas de ce que j'ai dit.' He is not dogmatic, but reasonable and modest. Again, in the middle of the eloquent development of the eighth paragraph, a discreet 'je crois' tempers the rhetorical insistence; the author is not talking grandly into the distance, but speaking directly to the reader. Several times the exposition is enlivened by a touch of irony or a hint of personal emotion. Montesquieu the man of feeling is heard in such wry phrases as 'quelque malheureux honnête homme', 'ce ne sont point des choses de spéculation, mais d'une triste expérience', and 'toutes ces vertus héroïques que nous trouvons dans les anciens, et dont nous avons seulement entendu parler'. Emotion is rendered more directly in the long enumeration of the eighth paragraph, which for all its modest 'je crois' carries a heavy charge of scorn and hate.

This oratorical period, emotional as it is, shows also one of the dominant elements in Montesquieu's rhetorical appeal, that of harmony and symmetry. At the same time as the reader perceives, and perhaps shares, the emotions of the author, he will also take pleasure in the way the words are arranged, the neat balance of the first two phrases, prolonged but slightly attenuated in the next two phrases, varied by the three plain abstract nouns which stand without conjunctions in the middle of the sentence ('la flatterie, la trahison, la perfidie'), and then taken up again in the four final parts of the enumeration, culminating in the crucial word 'vertu'. These are the old musical pleasures of prose and belong to an age when writing was not yet very far removed from speech. We know that Montesquieu thought highly of such qualities; he remarks in his *Pensées*: 'Bien des gens en France, surtout Monsieur de la Motte, soutiennent qu'il n'y a pas d'harmonie. Je prouve qu'il y en a, comme Diogène prouvait à Zénon qu'il y avait du mouvement en faisant un tour de chambre.' (II. 158.) As well as sonorous enumeration, we notice the swaying symmetry of sentences such as this one: 'Qu'on lise ce que les historiens de tous les temps ont dit sur la cour des monarques; qu'on se rappelle les conversations des hommes de tous les pays sur le misérable caractère des courtisans: ce ne sont point des choses de spéculation, mais d'une triste expérience.' These are not ostentatious mirror reflections which might be branded as mere 'bel esprit', but there is satisfaction, both aural and visual, in the way the longer symmetrical clauses are followed by the clinching antithesis.

In all this Montesquieu is by no means original. His individual voice is heard more clearly in the laconic style which counterbalances the eloquence of the periodic style. As I have said, it is his habit to divide his already short chapters into very short paragraphs, often no more than a single sentence. He is the man of good company, not tediously insisting on saying everything, but relying on his intelligent reader to fill out such rapid indications as those of the third paragraph. In this paragraph too the *style coupé* contrasts agreeably with the build-up of the preceding paragraph. This broken style is the small-scale equivalent of the division into short chapters; it conveys an impression of lively agility and perhaps too the feeling of honesty, as if the author was reluctant to inflate his ideas in accordance with the old methods of rhetoric. It is clearly a rhetorical weapon and tends towards the 'saillie' or epigram.

In his preface Montesquieu claims that his work contains no 'saillies'. In his *Pensées* he notes that 'On est trop frappé de ce genre de beauté qui fait qu'on désire que tout finisse en épigramme. Tout ne doit pas finir en épigramme.' (II. 501.) Yet Voltaire and other readers made a great deal of the epigrammatic brilliance of the *Lois*. There are obviously problems of definition here, but however we define such terms, there can be little doubt that Montesquieu has an affection for the epigrammatic conclusion which surprises a reader into attention, thought, and perhaps even agreement. Thus a paragraph describing the numbing effect of a cold climate on our ability to feel pain ends: 'Il faut écorcher un Moscovite, pour lui donner du sentiment' (I. i. 308). That may fairly be called a 'saillie', I think; in the chapter which we are considering there are no shock effects of this sort, but the last paragraph designates itself as a conclusion, with its brief exclamation ('Tant il est vrai que . . .') and its final antithesis, not unduly clever, it is true, but sufficiently clipped to impress and please the reader who is amenable to rhetoric—and what reader is not?

This fairly persuasive chapter from *De l'esprit des lois* is more obviously dressed up for effect than some of the more factual chapters which are so numerous later in the work. I do not think it gives an impression of forced elegance; like the rest of the book it shows the author adapting his manner and tone to his subject, writing 'eloquently' where his theme requires it (as here) and more drily where this sort of eloquence would seem out of place (as in Book XXII, which deals with financial matters). But everywhere the academician naturally writes to please, finding what appears to be a happy compromise between the language of the study and the tastes of his public. And this in turn corresponds to his characteristically eighteenth-century attitude to books. For him personally the writing of the *Lois* was an enterprise of the first importance; to it he was willing to sacrifice many years of life, his health, and his eyesight. Yet for the others, his readers, it was of course only a book, a lesson to princes perhaps, but also one of the many *divertissements* offering themselves to the cultivated man of leisure. It is true that 'Il ne faut donc pas regarder, dans une grande nation, les sciences comme une occupation vaine; c'est un objet sérieux.' (II. 279.) But did not Montesquieu also write, with splendid ease: 'L'étude a été pour moi le souverain remède contre les dégoûts de la vie, n'ayant jamais eu de chagrin qu'une heure de lecture ne m'ait ôté' (II. 85)?[46]

C. D'ALEMBERT

Like Montesquieu, d'Alembert was an academician.[47] He was indeed a member of several academies. He was only twenty-one when he made his first communication to the Académie des Sciences, where his mathematical and scientific work soon won him a place as *adjoint* and then *associé*. In the 1740s he produced a series of works on dynamics and related subjects which gave him a European reputation; before long he was a member of the

---

[46] A. Dupront quotes this remark in his interesting conclusion to *Livre et société dans la France du XVIIIᵉ siècle* and comments: 'La lecture de Montesquieu est une lecture de cabinet, et surtout une lecture d'homme de loisir. Lecture aristocratique s'il en fut et peut-être par cela cathartique.'

[47] For an account of d'Alembert's career and an introduction to his writings see R. Grimsley, *Jean d'Alembert*, Oxford, 1963.

Royal Society of London and the Royal Academy of Prussia. But after beginning his career strictly as a scientist, he became joint editor of the *Encyclopédie* and a frequenter of the *salons*.[48] The author of the Preliminary Discourse of the *Encyclopédie* became identified with the *philosophe* movement, and it was as a *philosophe* that in 1753 he allowed his name to be put forward, strongly backed by Madame du Deffand, for a seat in the Académie française. He was elected in 1754 and quickly made his mark as a conscientious member, ready to perform all sorts of relatively trivial duties of a mainly literary kind, such as speeches of adjudication and prize-giving for competitions of poetry or prose eloquence.

D'Alembert's two French academies pursued quite different ends: the encouragement of good writing and speech, and the advancement of scientific learning. They had, it is true, a good deal in common. The Académie des Sciences, in particular, seems to have felt itself obliged in public session to comply with some of the standards of eloquence upheld by its sister academy.[49] This was not a two-way process, however. Before d'Alembert's time, the Académie française took little interest in philosophy or science; he himself worked hard to give some philosophical body to its dignified proceedings. Thus, although we should not talk in sensational terms of a great gap between two cultures in eighteenth-century France, it may be said that d'Alembert moved in two different worlds. His successor as secretary of the Académie française, Marmontel, himself only a *littérateur*, gives us a glimpse of this double life as it appeared round about 1750: 'J'étais content, j'étais heureux, lorsque dans la petite chambre de d'Alembert, chez sa bonne vitrière, faisant avec lui tête à tête un dîner frugal, je l'entendais, après avoir chiffré tout le matin de sa haute géométrie, me parler en homme de lettres, plein de goût, d'esprit et de lumières.'[50]

[48] The literary d'Alembert can best be seen in his letters to Madame du Deffand and, to a certain extent, in those to Voltaire and Frederick of Prussia; see *Œuvres complètes*, ed. Bossange and Belin, 1821–2, vol. v. In this section references are to this edition; it does not include the scientific writings. For the *Traité de dynamique*, I refer to M. Solovine's edition, 2 vols., Paris, 1921 (cited as *T.D.*).

[49] See, for instance, the description of the Academy's resistance (on grounds of good taste) to Lavoisier's new chemical nomenclature given by M. Fuchs, 'La langue des sciences', in F. Brunot, *Histoire de la langue française*, vol. II, part 2, sect. 2, pp. 658–74.

[50] Marmontel, *Mémoires*, ed. M. Tourneux, Paris, 1891, vol. I, p. 280.

'Sa haute géométrie'—this was what had made d'Alembert's name, and it appears that, for all his literary activities, this continued to be the work he valued most. Indeed, if we are to believe Condorcet's *Éloge*, it was the only work he valued, the rest being hardly more than a frivolous pastime:

Ses ouvrages mathématiques étaient les seuls auxquels il attachât une importance sérieuse; il disait, il répétait souvent qu'il n'y avait de réel que ces vérités; et tandis que les savants lui reprochaient son goût pour la littérature, et le prix qu'il mettait à l'art d'écrire, souvent il offensait les littérateurs, en laissant échapper son opinion secrète sur le mérite ou l'utilité de leurs travaux.   (I. xxiii)

If, then, we are to study the rhetoric of d'Alembert's writings, we should look first of all at his most serious work, the *Traité de dynamique* (1743), which sets out the principle for which his name is still known to scientists.

The *Traité* opens with a preliminary discourse which is quite separate from the body of the work and which d'Alembert later incorporated with some alterations in his *Éléments de philosophie*. I shall discuss this work later, so for the moment I shall confine my attention to the treatise itself—but it should be remembered that it did in fact appear in public with an introduction which is much more accessible to the average reader than what follows it. The *Traité* proper is written to be read by experts; it makes few concessions to the demands of literary taste. It is, however, written in French rather than Latin, which is already something of a concession. D'Alembert states the case for scientific Latin in his essay *Sur la latinité des modernes*:

Mais autant il serait à souhaiter qu'on n'écrivît jamais des ouvrages *de goût* que dans sa propre langue, autant il serait utile que les ouvrages *de science*, comme de géométrie, de physique, de médecine, d'érudition même, ne fussent écrits qu'en langue latine, c'est-à-dire dans une langue qu'il n'est pas nécessaire en ces cas-là de parler élégamment, mais qui est familière à presque tous ceux qui s'appliquent à ces sciences, en quelque pays qu'ils soient placés.   (IV. 25)

But as he admitted, most scientists did in fact use their own vernacular by 1750, and he himself invariably does so. By so doing he was consenting to be governed by the norms of correct and even elegant French usage; he declares in his *Réflexions sur l'élocution oratoire* that although the style of the orator, the historian, and the philosopher may differ, 'l'élocution n'a pour tous qu'une même règle; c'est d'être claire, précise, harmonieuse, et surtout facile et naturelle' (IV. 290).

Clarity and precision, rather than harmony and ease, are the dominant qualities of the *Traité*. It begins impeccably with a set of basic definitions, of impenetrability, body, place, rest, and so on. The 'définitions et notions préliminaires' are given in a language accessible to any educated man. The French is correct, unpretentious, and as clear as the subject allows. Gradually the reader is led to more complex notions; at the same time the language departs from that written or spoken by those who are not mathematicians or scientists. This is evident in the growing frequency of mathemetical symbols, which are at first placed mainly in the notes, but quite soon make up an integral and unavoidable part of the argument. It is in this above all that d'Alembert reveals that he is writing for colleagues and not for the general public. Nevertheless, these colleagues were academicians and they too appreciated good writing—and indeed good speaking, for it is interesting to note that a good deal of the *Traité* was in fact read out in front of the Académie des Sciences (*T.D.* I. 81). The academicians could hardly object to equations, but they naturally expected a speaker's prose to be correct, and as clear and easy on the ear as possible. And this is more or less what they got; to take an example free from mathematical symbols, we read:

Du mouvement en lignes courbes et des forces centrales

33. Comme un corps tend de lui-même à se mouvoir en ligne droite, il ne peut décrire une ligne courbe qu'en vertu de l'action d'une puissance qui le détourne continuellement de sa direction naturelle. On peut déduire de l'article précédent les principes du mouvement d'un corps sur une courbe.

Il est démontré qu'un arc infiniment petit d'une courbe quelconque peut être pris pour un arc de cercle, dont le rayon serait égal au rayon de la développée de cet arc de la courbe. On réduit par ce moyen le mouvement d'un corps sur une courbe quelconque au mouvement de ce même corps sur un cercle dont le rayon change à chaque instant. (*T.D.* I. 43)

The exposition proceeds steadily and logically; the sentences are well formed and grammatically irreproachable. This is the admirable basic scientific style of the eighteenth century. It can best be characterized in negative terms—the language of ordinary speech, but pruned of a number of undesirable elements.[51]

The first of these undesirable elements is the trope. The didactic or illustrative simile and the ennobling metaphor and metonymy are all virtually excluded from the *Traité*. Neither is there any place for the elegant periphrasis or euphemism. D'Alembert believes in avoiding technical terms where this can be done without detriment to the scientific value of his work: 'on ne doit pas surtout exprimer d'une manière savante ce qu'on dira aussi bien par un terme que tout le monde peut entendre. On ne saurait rendre la langue de la raison trop simple et trop populaire.' (1. 134.) In this treatise, however, there can be no question of avoiding the technical. I have already noted the heavy reliance on the symbols of algebra. Similarly, d'Alembert attaches the appropriate formal labels to the different sections of his demonstration—'loi', 'corollaire', 'remarque', 'théorème', 'scolie', 'lemme'—and numbers his paragraphs. The reader must also have some acquaintance with mathematical terminology; in the passage just quoted we have 'développée', 'arc', and 'rayon'. Obviously no elegant circumlocution could replace these.

As undesirable as the tropes are those figures of speech which organize language so as to affect the ear, the pattern figures. This does not mean that the speaker must try to sound unpleasant, but that he must avoid any turns of phrase which might appear to be stylistic frills. The prose of the *Traité* is totally bare of the symmetrical harmonies which we noted in a chapter from Montesquieu's *Lois*. In the passage quoted above the sentences march forward, without any of the figures which make language dance by setting up a balance between one clause and another. Consider, for instance, the first sentence with its series of three clauses which merely follow one another, without there being any attempt to build them up to a climax. The sentences in these two paragraphs are all reasonably short and thus avoid any disagreeable awkwardness, but in other places d'Alembert is led by his argument into long and even graceless sentences which run counter to the norms of classical rhetoric. But if symmetrical patterns are avoided, so too are the deliberately irregular constructions which were often used for oratorical effect—anacoluthon, asyndeton, inversion, and

---

[51] Compare Bossuet's description of the relation between logic and rhetoric, quoted below p. 129 n. 16.

others. It will be remembered that for the *philosophes* one of
the virtues of French was precisely the 'natural' word-order
(subject–verb–predicate), which distinguished it from the ancient
languages. It is not surprising, therefore, if d'Alembert constructs
almost all his sentences on the approved model.

Inversion and similar turns of phrase were to be avoided because
they were unnatural, but also because they were associated with
the emotive style of poetry and oratory. Similarly, we shall not
expect to find in a book like the *Traité* any of the exclamations,
apostrophes, and other figures which were the normal vehicle
for the *chaleur* which d'Alembert distrusted. It is worth noting,
however, that the didactic question appears from time to time;
the author takes into account the facts of communication and
attempts to forestall the response of the reader:

On pourrait faire ici une difficulté qu'il est bon de prévenir . . . Comment
accorder ces deux propositions? La réponse est très simple. (*T.D.*
I. 33)

Here the tone becomes slightly less impersonal for a moment; the
same is true of the passages where the normal 'on' or 'nous' gives
way to 'je'. 'Je' is in fact quite frequent in this work (more so than
it would be in an equivalent work written today), but it is still
a fairly impersonal pronoun. 'Je' is the author of the treatise, who
explains why he has set out his material in this or that way ('Je
ne m'étendrai pas davantage sur les lois de l'équilibre dans cette
première partie' (I. 78)). It is a hand holding a pen, never a man
with an existence outside the field of mathematics. That sort of
'je' could only confuse things.

In a word, then, the *Traité de dynamique* does without rhetoric,
if by rhetoric we understand the system of departures from an
imagined norm which was taught in the schools of eighteenth-
century France. D'Alembert more than once dismisses school-
room rhetoric, most forcefully in his *Encyclopédie* article 'Collège'.[52]
It was easy enough to ridicule the subject. It was more difficult,
however, not to conform in some respects to its teaching, particularly when you were writing for a wider public than that which
could understand the *Traité de dynamique*.

D'Alembert was an academician, an encyclopedist, and an
enlightener. For all his love of higher mathematics, he was more

---

[52] The relevant passage from this article is quoted in Chapter 1 above, p. 27.

committed than most of his contemporaries to spreading the new philosophy among amateurs.[53] It was for them that he wrote many of his most famous works, notably the *Éléments de philosophie*, the Preliminary Discourse of the *Encyclopédie*, and the *Éloges* of dead academicians. He was as aware as anyone of the dangers of popularization which I discussed in the first part of this chapter. Above all, he feared the influence of the great and warned eloquently against it in his *Essai sur la société des gens de lettres avec les grands* (1753), which reflects its author's experience as a favourite of the Paris *salons*. According to d'Alembert, great men were still inclined, even in this age of philosophy, to treat men of letters as entertainers. They were, moreover, poor judges of literary productions and, worse still, had a bad influence on French style, encouraging frivolity, servility, and affectation. Little wonder that in the *Encyclopédie* article, 'Figure de la terre', d'Alembert excludes from his readership 'cette partie du public indifférente et creuse, qui, plus avide du nouveau que du vrai, use tout en se contentant de tout effleurer'.

It is the same with the *Éléments de philosophie* (1759). His readers are, he supposes, 'des personnes à qui d'autres occupations ne permettent pas de s'appliquer à ces sciences et d'en faire leur objet' (1. 288). His duty, therefore, as he says in the 'Avertissement', is to write in a language both intelligible and acceptable to the non-specialist. This does not, however, open the door to the dilettante: 'On croit devoir avertir ceux qui ne cherchent qu'à s'amuser dans leurs lectures, qu'ils peuvent se dispenser d'entreprendre celle de ce volume.' (1. 116.) So while d'Alembert is willing elsewhere to admit that it is necessary for the Académie française to preserve purity of language and good taste, and even (albeit ironically) that the courtier members of the Academy have their value in maintaining taste by talking elegant nothings, his insistence in his own philosophical popularization is always on the austere truth. He distinguishes again and again between the 'ouvrage de goût' and the 'ouvrage philosophique', between the orator and the philosopher—thus on the crucial question of harmony:

L'arrangement harmonique des mots ne peut quelquefois se concilier avec leur arrangement logique; quel parti faut-il prendre alors? un

[53] For a description of d'Alembert's activity as a public figure see Grimsley, *Jean d'Alembert*, ch. 4.

philosophe rigide ne balancerait pas; la raison est son maître, je dirais presque son tyran. L'orateur soumis à l'oreille autant que le philosophe l'est à la raison, sacrifie suivant le cas, tantôt l'harmonie, tantôt la justesse. (IV. 286–7)

Whatever the orator or poet may be allowed to do, the philosopher is the servant of truth. If he is eloquent, d'Alembert insists that his eloquence will come from his subject alone, not from any added graces. Neither will he allow himself that personal warmth which gives a spurious persuasive force to arguments. Thinking perhaps of Jean-Jacques, whom he sometimes cites as an example of fraudulent enthusiasm, he distances himself from such tricks in the 'Avertissement' to the *Éléments de philosophie*:

On ne parle aujourd'hui que de *chaleur*; on en veut jusque dans les écrits qui ne sont destinés qu'à instruire . . . Pour moi . . . je n'ai jamais eu pour point de vue dans mes écrits que ces deux mots, *clarté* et *vérité*; et je me tiendrais fort heureux d'avoir rempli cette devise, persuadé que la vérité seule donne le sceau de la durée aux ouvrages philosophiques; qu'un écrivain qui s'annonce pour parler à des hommes ne doit pas se borner à étourdir ou amuser des enfants; et que l'éloquence est bientôt oubliée quand elle n'est employée qu'à orner des chimères.
(I. 116–17)

Note the characteristic comparison of the child and the adult; d'Alembert knows all too well which is the world for him.

There is, inevitably, a certain variety in the rhetoric of the *Éléments*. Predictably, the opening pages contain more clearly than the body of the work the sort of writing that a non-specialist audience may have expected from d'Alembert. Similarly, he writes in a 'nobler', more animated way when dealing with general philosophical questions than when he is on his home ground of mathematics. If we look at the chapter entitled 'Mécanique', which is a slightly modified version of his original Preliminary Discourse to the *Traité de dynamique*, we find that although there are no mathematical symbols and not many technical terms, there is also very little of the rhetorical embellishment whose absence we noted in the *Traité* itself. It is the honest, clear style of the philosopher. At most, one might point to a certain care for the sound of the sentences; there are no elaborate verbal patterns, but there is often a sober harmony which is not so easily to be found in the *Traité*. Take the following paragraph:

Comme le rapport des parties du temps nous est inconnu en lui-même,
l'unique moyen que nous puissions employer pour découvrir ce
rapport, c'est d'en chercher quelque autre plus sensible et mieux
connu, auquel nous puissions le comparer. On aura donc trouvé la
mesure du temps la plus simple, si on vient à bout de comparer, de la
manière la plus simple qu'il soit possible, le rapport des parties du
temps avec celui de tous les rapports qu'on connaît le mieux. De là
il résulte que le mouvement uniforme est la mesure du temps la plus
simple. Car, d'un côté, le rapport des parties d'une ligne droite est celui
que nous saisissons le plus facilement: et de l'autre il n'est point de
rapports plus aisés à comparer entre eux, que des rapports égaux. Or,
dans le mouvement uniforme, le rapport des parties du temps est égal
à celui des parties correspondantes de la ligne parcourue. Le mouvement uniforme nous donne donc tout à la fois le moyen, et de comparer
le rapport des parties du temps au rapport qui nous est le plus sensible,
et de faire cette comparaison de la manière la plus simple; nous trouvons
donc dans le mouvement uniforme la mesure la plus simple du temps.
(I. 302–3)

There is certainly no suspect 'chaleur' here, but there is a dignified
and reassuring balance of clauses and at the same time the variety
(short sentences and long sentences) which rhetoric always
recommended. The first two sentences, solid and steady, lead up
to an emphatic short sentence which contains the central assertion
of the paragraph. This is then expanded and explained in a series
of symmetrical sentences, which lead again to the satisfying
reappearance of the main theme: 'nous trouvons donc dans le
mouvement uniforme la mesure la plus simple du temps.' The
whole paragraph is built of two blocks, the one seeming to echo
the other; within this division other discreet but agreeable symmetries find their place. It can be read aloud with satisfaction.
And all this is done without any sacrifice of truth; there can
be no question of 'fausses fenêtres pour la symétrie', but the
patterning may be felt as a bonus by the stylistically conscious
reader.

   In other places d'Alembert goes a little further—and particularly at the beginning of the work, where his aim is to capture
the interest of the reader. In the 'Avertissement', as we have seen,
he issues stern warnings to the frivolous, but even so the first
few chapters do make certain concessions, if not to frivolity, then
at least to fine writing. There is still nothing that could really be
called 'chaleur', no attempt on the author's part to rouse our

emotions by showing his own involvement with the subject. The tone remains agreeably cool, with a slight tendency, much less pronounced than in Montesquieu, to the witty turn of phrase— thus on metaphysics, in the tradition of Voltaire but with less sparkle: 'On peut dire en un sens de la métaphysique que tout le monde la sait ou personne, ou pour parler plus exactement, que tout le monde ignore celle que tout le monde ne peut savoir.' (I. 180.) But it is the metaphor and the simile which are the chief mark of fine writing here. D'Alembert uses these figures in a completely unoriginal way; the same old comparisons occur, used in the same old ways, their function being not to illuminate the argument, but to give dignity to the proceedings. Thus history, which he feels obliged to say something about, even though it is far from the centre of his interests, calls forth images of this sort: 'Les hommes placés sur la scène du monde sont appréciés par le sage comme témoins, ou jugés comme acteurs.' (I. 127.) It is at such points in the *Éléments* that the voice of the honest philoso- pher gives way to the more pompous voice of the public speaker, that d'Alembert becomes, in the words of an enemy, 'un joli pédant, géomètre orateur'.[54]

What we see then in the *Traité* and the *Éléments* is a limited hierarchy of styles, ranging from the rebarbatively technical to the grandly general. We can extend this range by considering works which are less narrowly philosophical, the Preliminary Discourse of the *Encyclopédie* and the *Éloges* of former academi- cians. These were all part of d'Alembert's campaign for the new philosophy. The *Discours préliminaire* is intended not only to explain the plan of the *Encyclopédie*, but equally to provide an imposing entrance gate and to fire readers for the greatness of the cause. Thus d'Alembert is led to depart yet further from the plain writing which is his staple. Noting the different ways in which Buffon and Fontenelle had made philosophy attractive, he himself writes up for the occasion. Not unduly so, of course; the *Discours* displays primarily the good sense of a philosopher talking to *honnêtes gens*, explaining elegantly, but not too wittily, the founda- tions of the encyclopedic enterprise. There are moments, however, when the subject calls forth in d'Alembert something not far removed from the suspect 'chaleur'. Significantly, this is less apparent in the methodological section of the *Discours* (which

<hr/>

[54] Quoted by Grimsley, op. cit., p. 102.

resembles the *Éléments*) than in the historical sketch of the progress
of philosophy. Here d'Alembert is drawn towards the oratorical
style of the traditional historian. Francis Bacon, the hero of the
encyclopedists, is introduced in these terms:

A la tête de ces illustres personnages doit être placé l'immortel chan-
celier d'Angleterre, François Bacon, dont les ouvrages si justement
estimés, et plus estimés pourtant qu'ils ne sont connus, méritent
encore plus notre lecture que nos éloges. A considérer les vues saines
et étendues de ce grand homme, la multitude d'objets sur lesquels son
esprit s'est porté, la hardiesse de son style qui réunit partout les plus
sublimes images avec la précision la plus rigoureuse, on serait tenté
de le regarder comme le plus grand, le plus universel, et le plus éloquent
des philosophes. Bacon, né dans le sein de la nuit la plus profonde,
sentit que la philosophie n'était pas encore, quoique bien des gens sans
doute se flattassent d'y exceller; car plus un siècle est grossier, plus il
se croit instruit de tout ce qu'il peut savoir.   (i. 63)

The language is a long way from the modest honesty which
d'Alembert tends to recommend. We notice the nobly abstract
vocabulary, the banal epithets of greatness ('immortel', 'illustre',
'sublime'), and the conventional images, particularly that of 'la
nuit la plus profonde', which helps to emphasize the struggle of
light and darkness that is the dominant metaphorical theme of the
Discours. But it is the oratorical patterning which above all gives
this passage its grandiose tone. Like any public speaker, d'Alembert arranges his sentences according to the traditional symmetry,
which centres round the alternation of antithetical constructions
and threefold enumerations. Most typically, two ternary constructions balance one another; the enumeration of 'les vues saines
. . . la multitude d'objets . . . la hardiesse de son style' is set against
the threefold glorification of Bacon, 'le plus grand, le plus universel, et le plus éloquent des philosophes'.

In an essay on style, d'Alembert speaks scornfully of 'ce langage
figuré, poétique, chargé de métaphores et d'antithèses, qu'on
appelle, je ne sais par quelle raison, *style académique*, quoique les
plus illustres membres de l'Académie Française l'aient évité
avec soin et proscrit hautement dans leurs ouvrages', and goes on
to assert, in his partisan way, that 'on l'appellerait avec bien plus
de raison *style de la chaire*' (iv. 289). Nevertheless, we can identify
the praise of Bacon as a mild example of this style, whether we call
it academic or not. That it has something to do with academies,

and with the Académie française in particular, is suggested by a reading of d'Alembert's *Éloges*.

The majority of these were designed to be included in a history of the Academy which d'Alembert undertook as its secretary, and were read out by their author at fashionable open sessions. Condorcet notes that these pieces are less uniformly noble in tone than earlier 'éloges', such as that of Montesquieu, which were composed shortly after the death of their subject, and that they include anecdotes and 'traits plaisants' which certain readers considered misplaced (I. xxiv). Since the subjects had been dead for many years, the author was less tied to the solemnity of the funeral oration and did what he could to enliven a potentially monotonous series of panegyrics. He tells us in his *Réflexions sur les éloges* that he has deliberately varied his style and, more generally, 'je n'ai rien négligé pour soutenir et intéresser l'attention des gens de lettres' (II. 153). The *Éloges* are usually built on a foundation of dignified but straightforward narration, the standard style of historical writing. This is constantly enlivened, however, by anecdotes, jokes, and a familiar tone, or embellished by the noble ornaments and even the would-be 'chaleur' of what d'Alembert would have had to call the 'style de la chaire'. In the *Réflexions* he himself says that in some of his panegyrics he had adopted the style of his subject; in this way, after several rather chatty portraits of minor seventeenth-century academicians, he lets himself go in a flood of traditional rhetoric to honour the great orator Bossuet.

The *Éloge de Bossuet* is a good example of the way in which eloquence comes in to fill gaps, even for d'Alembert.[55] We have reason to suppose that Bossuet was not an object of true admiration for him, but the job had to be done and the panegyrist goes dutifully through the motions of the sublime—seasoned, however, with a few anecdotes. Bossuet's religious controversies, which seemed puerile to d'Alembert the philosopher, gave d'Alembert the academic secretary an opportunity to show that he too could speak like an angel:

[55] In the *Encyclopédie* article 'Élocution', after stating that all true eloquence is natural, d'Alembert admits that rhetoric may have a minor role to fulfil: 'les règles de l'élocution n'ont lieu, à proprement parler, et ne sont vraiment nécessaires que pour les morceaux qui ne sont pas proprement éloquents, que l'orateur compose plus à froid, et où la nature a besoin de l'art.' (IV. 521.) In the same way, rhetoric helps the philosopher to talk about subjects which are really beneath his interest.

Là, on le voit sans cesse aux prises, soit avec l'incrédulité, soit avec l'hérésie, bravant et repoussant l'une et l'autre, et couvrant l'Église de son égide contre ce double ennemi qui cherche à l'anéantir. Son goût pour la guerre semble le poursuivre jusque dans les pièces qu'il a consacrées à l'éloquence; il oublie quelquefois qu'il est orateur, pour se livrer à cette controverse qu'il chérit tant; et du trône où il tonne, daignant descendre dans l'arène, il quitte, si on peut parler ainsi, la foudre pour le ceste: mais il reprend bientôt cette foudre, et le dieu fait oublier l'athlète. (II. 255)

Here it appears that the academic rhetoric of symmetry and metaphor is the product of d'Alembert's lack of interest, or even embarrassment; it serves at the same time to conceal his true feelings from those who do not want to take the hint and to convey an ironic judgement to those who are willing to accept it.

The *Éloges* display their author's stylistic versatility. They are almost his furthest venture away from the plain style of the honest philosopher. The furthest ventures of all are probably the two short pieces in memory of Julie de Lespinasse, *Aux mânes de Mademoiselle de Lespinasse* and *Sur la tombe de Mademoiselle de Lespinasse*, both written in 1776. There is nothing philosophical about these pieces; they are highly personal, full of the 'je' who had to be excluded from philosophy, and aiming to express what we must presume to be genuine emotions of love, regret, and jealousy with all the 'chaleur' that their author felt. But if the subject is personal, the style is literary; d'Alembert not only quotes freely from the modern classics (Racine in particular), but he adopts all the ways of classical tragic rhetoric, apostrophe, exclamation, repetition, and indeed all the elements whose absence we noted in the *Traité de dynamique*: 'Adieu, adieu, pour jamais! hélas, pour jamais! ma chère et infortunée Julie!' (III. 731.) Only the alexandrines are missing.

D'Alembert was not a versifier. Grimm said of him that he had no style.[56] He himself characterized his style as 'serré, clair et précis, ordinairement facile, sans prétention quoique châtié, quelquefois un peu sec, mais jamais de mauvais goût . . . plus d'énergie que de chaleur, plus de justesse que d'imagination, plus de noblesse que de grâce' (I. 10)—and it is remarkable how close this is to the definition of the ideal style of philosophical com-

---

56 'Son style n'a point de caractère' (*Correspondance littéraire*, vol. IV, p. 158). Grimm puts him on the same level as Maupertuis.

munication which he gives when talking about Malebranche in the preface to his *Éloges*, 'méthodique sans sécheresse, développé sans verbiage, intéressant et sensible sans fausse chaleur, grand sans effort, et noble sans enflure' (II. 158). It is impossible to pick out any of his different styles as his 'true' style—in speech he appears to have been far more of an individualist, far more witty and disconcerting than he ever is on paper.[57] Where he is writing on his own subjects, as in most of the *Éléments*, his style is much as he describes it; at most one might question the word 'énergie'. Like a true academician, however, he was prepared to dress up for the occasion, as we have seen in the *Discours préliminaire* and the *Éloges*. But he stops short of verse, which was for him the final step in rhetorical embellishment. Yet if he did not actually write verse, he was led by his academic life to think and write *about* it, and what he says on the subject is both curious and characteristic of the man and his times.

Reading d'Alembert on philosophy and poetry is rather like reading a modern exposition of the 'two cultures' question. He was first and foremost a scientist, anxious to defend the value of science and the 'esprit philosophique'. One of his aims was to conquer the Academy for the new philosophy, but he knew that poetry and oratory occupied a place of eminence; moreover, as a member of the Académie française, he became interested in gaining a reputation as a man of taste and eloquence. He therefore set out to reconcile the two enemies. (A title of one of his typical academic performances is: *Dialogue entre la poésie et la philosophie, pour servir de préliminaire et de base à un traité de paix et d'amitié perpétuelle entre l'une et l'autre.*) In order to do this, he must show that philosophers can appreciate poetry, that the vogue of scientific philosophy is not detrimental to literature (though he does in fact admit this charge in his *Discours préliminaire*),[58] and that

---

[57] An exception to this generalization is provided by his letters, for instance, those addressed to Voltaire, where he is seen as the lively, clever cynic, speaking with a voice quite different from any we hear in his published writings. Clearly, for d'Alembert, publication implied a seriousness which is strange in one whose professed faith (to Voltaire) was that the world is only fit for laughing at. D'Alembert was good at wearing different hats.

[58] 'Cet esprit philosophique, si à la mode aujourd'hui, qui veut tout voir et ne rien supposer, s'est répandu jusque dans les belles lettres; on prétend même qu'il est nuisible à leurs progrès, et il est difficile de se le dissimuler. Notre siècle, porté à la combinaison et à l'analyse, semble vouloir introduire les discussions froides et didactiques dans les choses de sentiment.' (I. 78.)

the philosopher has qualities which the man of letters should respect.

Basically, for him, the appeal of poetry lay in difficulty conquered. He believed that it was the ability to dance gracefully in chains which distinguished the good poet: 'moins nous adoucirons la rigueur de nos lois poétiques, plus il y aura de gloire à les surmonter' (IV. 296). Pleasing the reader of taste is like running an obstacle-race: 'On impose au poète les lois les plus sévères; et pour comble de rigueur, on lui défend de laisser voir ce qu'il lui en a coûté pour s'y soumettre' (IV. 300). But this pleasure in the harmony of a virtuoso performance is not enough to satisfy the adult reader. D'Alembert notes repeatedly—though perhaps not correctly—that poetry has fallen out of favour in his century; this is because philosophy has taught men that a poem must be judged not only by its own standards of beauty, but by the standards of sense which apply equally to prose writing. So, as well as being pretty, poetry must be worth reading for its ideas, taking 'ideas' in its broadest sense; the most valuable poet (and Virgil and Homer do badly on this test) is the one who best survives translation:

Les vers qu'on retient avec facilité, qu'on se rappelle avec plaisir, sont ceux dont le mérite ne se borne pas à l'arrangement harmonieux des paroles. Un sentiment confus semble nous dire, qu'il ne faut pas mettre à exprimer les choses plus de peine et de soin qu'elles ne valent; et que ce qui paraîtrait commun en prose, ne mérite pas l'appareil de la versification. Toute poésie, on en convient, perd à être traduite; mais la plus belle peut-être est celle qui y perd le moins. (IV. 301)

The way to reconcile poetry and philosophy is therefore to make poetry philosophical. Although d'Alembert is anxious not to put his case too crudely or to condemn pleasant novelties, his real preference is for instructive verse; here is the doctrine expressed in its classic form:

C'est avec cette sévérité que le philosophe examine et juge les ouvrages de poésie. Pour lui le premier mérite et le plus indispensable dans tout écrivain, est celui des pensées: la poésie ajoute à ce mérite celui de la difficulté vaincue dans l'expression; mais ce second mérite, très estimable quand il se joint au premier, n'est plus qu'un effort puéril dès qu'il est prodigué en pure perte et sur des objets futiles. (IV. 292)

There is a note of contempt here and elsewhere which makes one suspect that the praise which d'Alembert of the Académie

française gives to poetry is often but patronizing lip-service. Just
as he is willing to go through the motions of eloquence in his
own popularization, so he is willing to allow publicly the value
of an activity which he really rather despises. His attitude is not
unlike that of the adult Descartes—but Descartes had the good
fortune not to be an academician. And it is perhaps the same with
the theatre. Although he went along with Voltaire in calling for
a theatre in Geneva, d'Alembert seems to have had a low opinion
of dramatic art; his defence of it is to describe it as a toy for sick
children.[59] The child needs toys, plays and poems; the adult
philosopher will not mind humouring the child. One understands
why Diderot exclaimed in exasperation, after hearing about one
of his colleague's ventures into literary theory: 'Qu'il s'en tienne
aux équations. C'est son lot.'[60]

Perhaps examples are never really typical; Montesquieu and
d'Alembert are certainly not typical *philosophes*. They were public
figures, noted academicians, and we should expect them to be
readier than some of their contemporaries to adopt the dignified
or charming rhetoric of public speaking. It would be possible
to select other, less prestigious, *philosophes*, the authors of the in-
numerable works on botany, political economy, or metallurgy, the
obscure but useful writers who are so often disdained in Grimm's
Correspondance littéraire. However, a cursory reading in this area suggests that even the obscure felt the double pull of philosophical
honesty and social graces. In this age of academies and oral performance, when the book was largely destined for the consumption
of a class with plenty of spare time and a literary education, fine
writing extended its influence in all directions. In this, if not in their
eminence, Montesquieu and d'Alembert are characteristic figures.

It would be interesting to study the rhetoric of other enlighteners. There is Buffon, one of the scientific best-sellers of the century,
whose reputation as a stylist was already arousing doubts among
the Encyclopedists; they called him 'le grand phrasier', and he
has remained, perhaps unwarrantably,[61] an example of vulnerable

[59] See Grimsley, op. cit., p. 137.
[60] Diderot, *Correspondance*, ed. G. Roth, vol. III, p. 46.
[61] J. Roger, in the introduction to his edition of Buffon's *Époques de la nature* (Paris,
1962), makes a strong case for revising some of the accepted notions of Buffon's
style, which are reflected, for instance, in 'La Puce' of Paul Reboux and Charles
Muller (*A la manière de . . .*).

grandiloquence, a natural victim for the parodist. There is Helvétius, essentially a boring writer, but conscious of the need to embellish his works in the approved manner. There is Maupertuis, a good example (as d'Alembert says in his *Discours préliminaire*) of the happy marriage of science and readability.[62] And above all, there is Voltaire, too vast a subject for my present undertaking; his constant rhetorical awareness is reflected in a stylistic versatility which deserves detailed investigation. In the writings of all these *philosophes* and many others, one can see the influence of the demands of the audience which I outlined in the first part of this chapter.

In some ways, seen from the universities of the twentieth century, the philosophical writing of the eighteenth century seems admirable. It would be good if scholars today still brought truth and beauty together with the apparent ease of the great enlighteners. We have lost something of the innocence of the academicians, we are more ready than they were to suspect that what is made attractive is thereby debased. We know that good writing is the writing appreciated by a dominant class, and many feel the need to reject a rhetoric which places the writer at the service of established society. We have seen so much debased rhetoric that for us the writer's duty is as much to shock and flout as to conform to the stylistic expectations of polite, educated readers. It is more natural today than it was in eighteenth-century France to distrust the writer who, like Montesquieu or d'Alembert, changes his style according to the occasion. Whether in the name of individualism, or in reaction to the oppressions of society, we are perhaps more inclined to value the abrasive than the smooth. Not that such feelings were absent in eighteenth-century France; we have seen that the adjustments of rhetoric were often scorned by the scholar as they were by the preacher. For the *philosophes*, as for Descartes, truth was supposedly enough. But in the end, the dominant role of rhetoric in the education of French writers of the *ancien régime* and the position of the scientist in the society of *honnêtes gens* seem to have made it easier for them to move from one register to another without strain, instructing as they pleased · and combining, as Hume says with enviable blandness, 'the two greatest and purest pleasures of human life, study and society'.

III

THE RHETORIC OF
GRANDEUR

⟡

KENT: Sir, 'tis my occupation to be plain:
  I have seen better faces in my time
  Than stands on any shoulder that I see
  Before me at this instant.
CORNWALL: This is some fellow,
  Who, having been prais'd for bluntness, doth affect
  A saucy roughness, and constrains the garb
  Quite from his nature: he cannot flatter, he,
  An honest mind and plain, he must speak truth:
  An they will take it, so; if not, he's plain.
  These kind of knaves I know, which in this plainness
  Harbour more craft and more corrupter ends
  Than twenty silly-ducking observants,
  That stretch their duties nicely.
KENT: Sir, in good sooth, in sincere verity,
  Under the allowance of your grand aspect,
  Whose influence, like the wreath of radiant fire
  On flickering Phoebus' front,—
CORNWALL: What mean'st by this?
KENT: To go out of my dialect, which you discommend
  so much.

                    (Shakespeare: *King Lear*)

UNIVERSITY LIBRARIES
CARNEGIE-MELLON UNIVERSITY
PITTSBURGH, PENNSYLVANIA 15213

T H E fine words of the orator were often likened to the fine clothes of the courtier. Rhetoric, as we saw in Chapter 1, had a social function, fitting the speaker and the writer to take their place in polite society. If rhetoric is often described in terms of a departure from a norm, then in this context the norm is the plain speaking of the honest man, and the rhetorical departure the amplification or embellishment which suited splendid audiences, kings, courts, and fashionable society. We have already seen something of this in the attempts of philosophers to dress up their philosophy for consumption by the lay public. For other writers, the problem was more acute. The preacher delivering a funeral oration on the high and mighty, the court poet dedicating his works to a noble patron, the historiographer writing the history of the reigning monarch, all had to satisfy a much more specific and much more worldly audience than the philosopher, who could at least claim to be writing primarily for his colleagues.

The reign of Louis XIV, when royal power extended to the regimentation and payment of flocks of eulogizing writers, provides a classic example of the tensions between flattery and truth. The truth might be the truth of religion, or it might be the simpler truth of the honest man, but in either case it was difficult for it to survive unscathed. The preacher or the poet was not only compelled to tell lies and disguise the truth, he had also to use a language which he knew to be inflated and insincere.

Jan Kott, writing in *Shakespeare our Contemporary* of the Fool in *King Lear*, declares that 'the profession of a jester, like that of an intellectual, consists in proving entertainment. His philosophy demands of him that he tell the truth and abolish myths.' Many of those who wrote and spoke to the high society of seventeenth-century Paris shared the discomfort of Jan Kott's jesting intellectual.

4. Bossuet: the Word and the World

Le magnifique témoignage de notre néant
(Bossuet: *Oraison funèbre du Prince de Condé*)

THE philosopher had to reconcile the search for truth and the language of persuasion. The preacher's task was perhaps even more delicate; he had to marry the word of God to the words of men. For some Christians in seventeenth-century France silence was better than speech. The dangers of the word were recognized above all by the monastic orders, for whom a lesser or greater degree of silence was an essential part of Christian discipline. Rancé's reformed Trappist monk has become for subsequent generations an archetype of the total silence which indicates a total rejection of the pleasures and temptations of a reprobate world. Here, questions of rhetoric are a part of wider questions concerning the relation of Christian faith and worldly pursuits.[1]

Although rejection of the world was an important part of the Christian tradition, the founder of Christianity was an incarnate God, the Word who had become flesh and dwelt among us. Christians were not to be of the world, but they had to live in the world. The two cities of Augustine, the city of men and the city of God, were inextricably entangled as long as life on earth lasted. One of the dominant problems for serious Christians in seventeenth-century France was exactly this: how should I live in the world? How should the Christian regard political power, money, human virtue, natural beauty, civilized politeness? To questions such as these there was a great range of answers, from the extreme denial of Rancé or Barcos to the caricatural laxity of Pascal's Jesuit. In the middle, seeking to adapt the religion of poverty and persecution to a situation in which it was allied to wealth and

---

[1] The bibliography of this vast subject is proportionately large: H. Brémond, *Histoire littéraire du sentiment religieux en France*, 11 vols., Paris, 1916–33, is, for all its bias, a storehouse of information and ideas. The first volume, devoted to 'l'humanisme dévot', is a good introduction to the subject, but the subsequent volumes are also relevant. See also, among many others, L. Cognet, *La Spiritualité française au* XVIIe *siècle*, Paris, 1949; L. Goldmann, *Le Dieu caché*, Paris, 1955; J. Orcibal, *La Spiritualité de Saint-Cyran*, Paris, 1962.

power, were the many theorists who in some way reconciled faith
and worldliness, asserting the possibility of salvation even for
the powerful and the rich. St. François de Sales is the great
example.[2] Without any really scandalous concessions, he shows
that a man may live devoutly in the world and that worldly life
has certain claims on the Christian. Although he knows all about
the insidious corrupting power of worldly satisfactions, he still
manages, in a way which strikes an outsider as entertaining, to
allow his *dévot* a fair share of money: 'Être riche en effet et pauvre
d'affection, c'est le grand bonheur du chrétien; car il a par ce
moyen les commodités des richesses pour ce monde et le mérite
de la pauvreté pour l'autre.'[3] And as he speaks about the Last
Judgement or Original Sin, he indulges in the pleasure of an old-
fashioned, flowery style, which often jars oddly with the subject
of his writing.

These compromises of St. François de Sales are a good starting-
point for thinking about the attitude of Christian theorists to the
arts of the word. The respect for silence did not keep them from
using the word and thinking about it. Rancé, the outstanding
example of retreat to the desert for the age of Louis XIV, while
he imposed silence on his monks, was far from silent himself; his
extremist rejection of the world only provided him with a greater
audience for his writings. And like Rancé, almost all intellectual
Christians felt themselves to be charged with the task of persuasion
or conversion. Even Barcos, for whom silent contemplation was
the highest good, admitted that the Church would cease to exist
if priests did not allow themselves to be forced out of their retreat
by their pastoral work.[4] And how could this work be carried on
without recourse to the arts of the word, whether in writing or
in speech, in the composition of treatises or letters of spiritual
direction, in the delivery of homilies or funeral orations?

For the more extreme, this recourse to the word was a necessary evil which should not be aggravated by any of the care for
correctness or beauty of diction demanded by the traditional art
of persuasion, profane rhetoric. Others were less intransigent.
The seventeenth century saw a long, inconclusive battle over the

---

[2] For an introduction to this aspect of St. François de Sales see R. Bady, 'François de Sales, maître d'honnêteté', *Dix-septième Siècle*, 1968.
[3] St. François de Sales, *Introduction à la vie dévote*, ed. C. Florisoone, 2 vols.,
Paris, 1961, vol. II, p. 30.
[4] Martin de Barcos, *Correspondance*, ed. L. Goldmann, Paris, 1956, pp. 109–10.

place of profane rhetoric in religious persuasion. This naturally centred on preaching, but it also touched on all the forms of oral and written communication. Thus Barcos, whom we can take as a representative of the extremist position, scolds La Mère Angélique of Port-Royal for worrying about the way she expresses herself in a letter to him—and one notices that he practises what he preaches:

Comme il y a une sagesse qui est folie devant Dieu, il y a aussi un ordre qui est désordre; et par conséquent il y a une folie qui est sagesse, et un désordre qui est un règlement véritable, lequel les personnes qui veulent suivre l'Évangile doivent aimer, et j'ai peine de voir qu'elles s'en éloignent et qu'elles le fuient, s'attachant à des ajustements et à des agréments qui ne sont pas dignes d'elles, et qui troublent la symétrie de l'esprit de Dieu, et causent une disproportion et une difformité visible dans la suite de leurs actions et de leur vie, n'y ayant nulle apparence de suivre d'un côté la simplicité et la naïveté de l'Évangile et d'un autre la curiosité et les soins de l'esprit du monde.[5]

One might quote parallel passages from many Christian intellectuals of the time, in particular the Jansenists. But, to take the Jansenists as our example, it would be a mistake to see them lined up solidly against rhetoric.[6] Although Arnauld and Nicole in the *Logique* follow Descartes in the rejection of the mere probabilities of rhetoric, neither Arnauld nor Nicole is inclined to forget the importance of language in persuasion. When, near the end of the century, the old quarrel about pulpit rhetoric flared up again between Dubois and François Lamy on the one hand and Sillery and Gibert on the other, Arnauld intervened with a defence of rhetoric in which he recognized the need for an appeal to the imagination and not merely the reason if persuasion was to be effective.

Thus, although for many Jansenists there was something slightly shameful about an interest in language, they were in practice ready to compromise. Barcos may have confined himself mainly to letters (already a compromise?), but the Messieurs de Port-Royal produced volume after volume of polemic, treatises,

[5] Op. cit., p. 140.
[6] H. M. Davidson, *Audience, Words and Art*, Ohio, 1965, by concentrating on the *Logique* of Port-Royal, seems to me to underplay the importance of orthodox rhetoric at Port-Royal, though of course the *Logique* was a very influential work. Pascal is a special case; his approach to persuasion is described in a balanced way by P. Topliss, *The Rhetoric of Pascal*, Leicester, 1966.

textbooks, translations, and even poems. In all these writings they accepted and put into practice the middle-of-the-road view of rhetoric, which teaches that the persuader will do well to conform to certain of his audience's expectations in order to sway them more effectively. In the field of translation, for instance, where one might have expected them to come down on the side of faithfulness, they were more inclined to follow the example of Perrot d'Ablancourt's 'belles infidèles', even when the text to be translated was the Bible, the word of God.[7] Bossuet warned the Maréchal de Bellefonds that their version of the New Testament 'affecte trop de politesse'.[8] Their model of style—and they were mocked for it—was the worldly and ornate Guez de Balzac, whom we shall also find, even more unexpectedly, recommended by Bossuet as a source of fine expressions. Generally speaking, the Jansenists' stylistic theories were considerably more austere than their practice. In this they were entirely typical of their time. It is easy to speak out against the tricks and frills of rhetoric, far more difficult to do without rhetoric, or even to devise a rhetoric more innocent than the one you have just condemned.

In matters of language, as in other things, the Jansenists were far from forming a compact block. There was a wide range of opinion. But with very few exceptions, they were willing—sometimes all too willing—to couch their austere message in a form acceptable to a society which put a high value on such qualities as correctness and elegance of expression. It was the same with the Church as a whole. By the seventeenth century Augustine's two cities were inextricably involved with each other. The Church, however much it might see itself as the enemy of the world, was bound up with it at all points, socially, politically, morally, stylistically. At the extreme, this involvement could scandalize—as when La Bruyère points to the false position of the fashionable convent: 'Il s'est trouvé des filles qui avaient de la vertu, de la santé, de la ferveur, et une bonne vocation, mais qui n'étaient

[7] See B. Munteano, *Constantes dialectiques en littérature et en histoire*, Paris, 1967, pp. 251-72.
[8] *Corr.* 1. 334. Bossuet's works are cited in the following forms: *Corr.*, *Correspondance*, ed. C. Urbain and E. Levesque, 15 vols., Paris, 1909-25; *O.F.*, *Oraisons funèbres*, ed. J. Truchet, Classiques Garnier, Paris, 1961; *O.O.*, *Œuvres oratoires*, ed. J. Lebarq, 7 vols., Lille, 1890-7. The revised edition of Lebarq (ed. C. Urbain and E. Levesque, 7 vols., Paris, 1914-26) contains other material besides sermons; I refer to it where necessary as *O.O. revised*.

pas assez riches pour faire dans une riche abbaye vœu de pauvreté.'[9]

In speech and writing there were points of extreme stress at
which the Church's concessions to worldliness might be expected
to shock the austere. The funeral oration was one of these. But
even where the issues were not so dramatically tense as this, the
problems of the word constantly presented themselves to the
religious persuader. How could he make his persuasion most
effective? What sort of concessions was he justified in making to
an audience whose demands were often highly profane? At what
point did he cease to be a persuader and become simply another
entertainer? And however hard he hit, was it not possible for his
audience to neutralize his blows, allowing the fulminating preacher
his preordained place in the rituals of society and appreciating
the zeal with which he played his part—but not believing a word
of it? What I want to do now is to explore these problems as they
are reflected in the writings of Bossuet. In doing so, I shall be
interested not so much in the details of his debt to rhetoric or his
rhetorical skill (I think these may be largely taken for granted)
as in his attitude to more general questions involving the rhetoric
of religious communication.[10]

Of course, it is impossible really to know Bossuet as he was.
He was not an expansive man. One may gather enough hints from
his letters, his sermons, and his many other writings to be able to
see some of the things which worried him, pleased him, or dis-
pleased him. But that is a long way from knowing just how far
he let problems concern him, how weak or strong he felt in front
of his many tasks, how attractive or distasteful the world appeared
to him. There are great variations in Bossuet's attitude to such
things as literary culture, philosophical speculation, or even the
theatre; it would be quite wrong to fix him permanently as the
author of the puritanical letter to Caffaro—or equally as the academician whose 'agréable épanouissement de cœur et de visage'
(*O.O. revised*, VI. 12) was observed by his new colleague Char-

9 La Bruyère, *Les Caractères*, ed. R. Garapon, Classiques Garnier, Paris, 1962,
p. 423.
10 Like Descartes, Bossuet has a large bibliography. Two theses illuminate the
subject of this chapter from different directions: J. Truchet, *La Prédication de Bossuet*,
2 vols., Paris, 1960, and T. Goyet, *L'Humanisme de Bossuet*, 2 vols., Paris, 1965. See
also, on a more limited subject, J. Truchet, *Bossuet panégyriste*, Paris, 1962.

pentier. Again, it would be a mistake to insist too strongly on the
pull between God and the world in Bossuet's thought; there is
a temptation to over-dramatize the issue (as Bossuet himself does
in sermon after sermon), whereas in actual practice he may have
been capable of a fairly happy reconciliation of our two apparent
opposites. Still, the preaching of the word to the world did raise
problems, both theoretical and personal. My aim is simply to
point to some of these.

I do not wish to study Bossuet comparatively. Much has been
done by recent historians to correct the over-simple view which
attributed to Bossuet alone attitudes and achievements which he
shared with many of his contemporaries. We know, for instance,
that he was not the only one to use the funeral oration for edifying
purposes or to tell home truths to the King. If we want to see
what distinguishes Bossuet from Bourdaloue, Fléchier, Massillon,
Senault, and the hundreds of less memorable figures who fill the
pages of the histories of preaching, it goes without saying that
we should compare his sermons carefully with theirs. But this is
not the aim of the present study. Here I want to look at an aspect
of Bossuet's writing and speech which could be paralleled more
or less effectively in the writings of many contemporary preachers
or religious writers. I have chosen to write about Bossuet partly
because his writings and sermons are readily accessible and still
have many readers (willing and unwilling), partly because his
voluminous works give us a very clear picture of the problems of
religious communication in his day.

Finally, I should make it clear that I shall be looking mainly
at Bossuet the preacher. All kinds of writing and speaking, even
highly personal works such as the *Méditations sur l'Évangile*, called
for concessions to this world, but the pulpit was the real battle-
ground. Particularly in Paris and at court, face to face with an
audience of great worldliness and himself a participant in a ceremony which for most of those present was only nominally religious, the preacher was in an exposed position that might well
demand considerable heart-searching and sacrifice of integrity.
This was especially true of those who delivered the funeral orations of the high and the mighty—and if Bossuet became an
undoubted classic in the French schools, it was primarily because
of his performances on such occasions. Of all his orations, perhaps the best-known is that for 'Très haut et très puissant Prince

Louis de Bourbon, prince de Condé, premier prince du sang' (O.F. 369).

Condé, one of the military heroes of his century, had died in December 1686; three months later, on the King's orders, Notre-Dame was prepared for a grand memorial ceremony. The previous twenty years had seen some striking examples of the new Italian style of funeral architecture, introduced by the Jesuit Ménestrier and perfected by the court decorator Bérain. The show for Condé was, according to the art historian Tessier, 'la plus colossale de ces décorations qui ait jamais été faite'.[11] Bossuet himself gives a brief impression of it in his oration: 'des titres, des inscriptions, vaines marques de ce qui n'est plus; des figures qui semblent pleurer autour d'un tombeau, et des fragiles images d'une douleur que le temps emporte avec tout le reste; des colonnes qui semblent vouloir porter jusqu'au ciel le magnifique témoignage de notre néant' (O.F. 407–8). It was all much admired by the people of Paris, who, according to the custom, paid to come and look at the church when the décor was being assembled. The final result seemed to Madame de Sévigné well worth the 100,000 francs which it had cost Condé's son.[12]

At the centre of this theatrical setting, face to face with a noble audience in which Louis had assembled 'ce que son royaume a de plus auguste' (O.F. 370), Bossuet preached his famous funeral oration. As orator it was his task—as it was the decorator's—to orchestrate the grief of the congregation, recalling the greatness of the dead man and lamenting his loss. But as a Christian preacher he had another obligation—to turn this magnificent tragic spectacle to the edification of his audience. To do this was not difficult; it was enough to insist on the human greatness of Condé in the first part of the oration, only to show in the second part the vanity of such greatness compared with solid Christian piety and a 'good death'. Such in fact was the basic pattern of many funeral orations of the time.

11 A. Tessier, 'Le genre décoratif funèbre, esquisse d'une histoire de ses débuts en France', Revue de l'art ancien et moderne, 1924–5. A description of the decoration was published in 1687 under the title Honneurs funèbres rendus à la mémoire de Monseigneur Louis de Bourbon, prince de Condé, dans l'église métropolitaine de Notre-Dame de Paris.

12 Madame de Sévigné, Lettres, ed. Gérard-Gailly, Bibliothèque de la Pléiade, 3 vols., Paris, 1953–63, vol. III, pp. 149–50. The whole of the first paragraph of this letter is worth reading as an indication of a contemporary reaction to 'la plus belle . . . la plus magnifique et . . . la plus triomphante pompe funèbre qui ait jamais été faite depuis qu'il y a des mortels'.

Speaking of Condé Bossuet does in the end subordinate everything else to the instruction of his audience. Even so, the speech
creates an impression of tension, for praise and lamentation of
the merely human pull strongly against the moral lesson. Bossuet,
carried away perhaps by his close memories of the dead man,
evokes at great length his military and personal qualities. With
all the resources of historical rhetoric he celebrates the deeds of
'cet autre Alexandre'. The *récit* of the battle of Rocroi is very like
the magnifying description of Rodrigue's victories in *Le Cid*,
though elsewhere, like Boileau and other contemporaries, Bossuet
expresses a lower opinion of 'les César et les Alexandre, et tous
ces autres ravageurs de provinces que nous appelons conquérants'
(*O.O.* 1. 264) and mocks those who compose panegyrics for them.
The universality of the prince's gifts is evoked in extravagant
terms:

Quel astre brille davantage dans le firmament que le prince de Condé
n'a fait dans l'Europe? Ce n'était pas seulement la guerre qui lui
donnait de l'éclat; son grand génie embrassait tout, l'antique comme
le moderne, l'histoire, la philosophie, la théologie la plus sublime, et les
arts avec les sciences. Il n'y avait livre qu'il ne lût; il n'y avait homme
excellent, ou dans quelque spéculation, ou dans quelque ouvrage,
qu'il n'entretînt; tous sortaient plus éclairés d'avec lui, et rectifiaient
leurs pensées, ou par ses pénétrantes questions, ou par ses réflexions
judicieuses. (*O.F.* 393)

He even paints Condé walking with his friends 'dans ces superbes
allées au bruit de tant de jets d'eau qui ne se taisaient ni jour ni
nuit' (*O.F.* 386). Then, of course, with the great traditional turning movement, Bossuet overturns this grandeur and celebrates
Condé's piety. Even here, however, the dominant note is one of
panegyric, panegyric not only of the dying Condé, but also of his
King, whose courage in undergoing a painful operation receives
unexpected but enthusiastic praise in the middle of the evocation
of Condé's last days. Louis, like Condé and like the hero of a
novel, is fleetingly glimpsed moving through his 'jardins enchan-
tés' (*O.F.* 398).

But what strikes one most is the verbal splendour. Whether
Bossuet is singing the greatness of his hero, lamenting his loss,
or spelling out the moral, his words match the pomp of the decorations of Bérain. It is here above all that the old clichés about
Bossuet's magnificent music ring true—as Bossuet summons the

peoples and princes of the earth to contemplate their nothingness:

Venez, peuples, venez maintenant; mais venez plutôt, princes et sei-
gneurs, et vous qui jugez la terre, et vous qui ouvrez aux hommes les
portes du ciel, et vous plus que tous les autres, princes et princesses,
nobles rejetons de tant de rois, lumières de la France, mais aujourd'hui
obscurcies et couvertes de votre douleur comme d'un nuage: venez
voir le peu qui nous reste d'une si auguste naissance, de tant de grandeur, de tant de gloire. (O.F. 407)

It is fine, too fine. However correct the sentiments, their orchestra-
tion turns the speech into something which an audience can take
pleasure in, as it can take pleasure in the setting. Preachers of the
time tell us how fashionable audiences came flocking to the
ceremonies of death and renunciation, ceremonies which were
meant as a condemnation of the world, yet were assimilated by the
world and made a part of its pompous rituals. Bossuet repudiated
the tragic theatre, and yet the part he played on occasions such
as this was not unlike that played by the tragic actor—not for
nothing did contemporaries comment on the similarity of the
professions of actor and preacher.[13] We cannot know what went
on in the minds of the various members of his audience, but in
another funeral oration of Condé, part of a much less magnificent service, the Abbé du Jarry pointed out the dangers of such
ceremonies:

Au lieu de considérer cette pompe funèbre par ce qu'elle a de triste,
nous ne la regardons que par ce qu'elle a d'éclatant: la vanité des
grandeurs humaines se cache même sous un spectacle qui devrait nous
la découvrir . . ., et ces restes déplorables d'un prince dont la grandeur
va disparaître pour jamais avec ce dernier éclat, nous éblouissent encore
au lieu de nous instruire.[14]

Surely Bossuet could have said the same. Indeed, the end of his
peroration announces his intention of retiring from this worldly
sort of oratory and devoting his failing voice to his pastoral duties
at Meaux. As if to confirm this, the Condé funeral oration is nearly
the last complete sermon of Bossuet's which has been preserved
as a work of literature. It presents us dramatically with a tension

---

[13] See Spanheim's remarks on Racine, quoted below, p. 174.
[14] Quoted by Truchet in his edition of the *Oraisons funèbres*, p. 366.

between the World and the Word of God which we can now
explore in Bossuet's earlier speech and writing.

Bossuet was successful in the world. Socially he rose in the
same sort of way as Boileau or Racine, starting from the solid
Dijon bourgeoisie and reaching the highest circles as court
preacher, member of the Academy, bishop, and tutor to the Dauphin. His position as tutor brought him into constant contact
with the royal family; he was the King's director for a brief period
round 1675. In the 1670s he lived at court, and even when he had
taken up his pastoral duties at Meaux, he spent a good deal of
time in Paris and Versailles. This success seems to have been to
his taste. It would be excessive to paint him as the provincial
dazzled by the splendours of Versailles, but his relations with such
great figures as Condé were naturally flattering to him. He enjoyed
being a member of the Académie Française and gave himself
willingly to a fairly active intellectual and literary life. And he
liked living well, eating and drinking with relish. When he
became Bishop of Meaux, he devoted quite a lot of time to
embellishing his country residence at Germigny, borrowing an
expert from Condé to install fountains on the model of Chantilly.
'Le monde', in its two senses of human activity and high society,
had a lot to recommend itself to him.

It is of course possible and normal to reconcile Christian faith
with a fair degree of worldliness. As we have seen, it was the
endeavour of François de Sales and many others to implant
Christianity in the world and not just in the cloister. But frequently in the seventeenth century one encounters a much more
radical attitude, involving a total rejection of a corrupt world, an
attitude which is best expressed in the notion of the retreat to the
desert. Bossuet was not immune from this. Indeed, as one reads
not only his sermons but also his correspondence and such
relatively private works as the *Traité de la concupiscence*, one comes
to feel that he was haunted by the mirage of detachment. Naturally
the ideas he expresses vary considerably. In sermons the occasion
and the audience determine in part the degree of his intransigence.
In his *vêtures* (sermons for the taking of the veil) he has no call to
make concessions to the world. But equally in his sermons to the
court, his typical posture is one of total repudiation of worldliness.
Often he seems to realize that his demands appear excessive to the

ordinary man; in imaginary dialogues he makes his recalcitrant listener protest: 'Quels exemples nous proposez-vous! Voulez-vous déserter le monde?' (*O.O.* v. 412.) 'N'y a-t-il donc que des excès dans l'Évangile?' (*O.O.* v. 639.) And generally the reply is that this sort of excess is what Christianity is about.

Such an absolute position was perhaps what was expected of the preacher in his official capacity, but it goes deeper in Bossuet. Without dwelling on the *Traité de la concupiscence,* which represents the extreme point of Bossuet's anti-worldliness, we may consider the fascinating letters which he wrote between 1672 and 1676 to the exiled Maréchal de Bellefonds. Bossuet seeks in these letters to use Bellefonds's disgrace to lead him to salvation; this brings him to talk of the dangers of court life, and as he does so, his direction of conscience resembles a confession of the difficulties of living in the world. In theory, as we know, it is possible for the saint to live pure in an impure world—Bossuet had shown how this was possible in such discourses as his panegyric of St. François de Paule. But he himself is not a saint. Although he attempts to justify his acceptance of a fat benefice ('je perdrais plus de la moitié de mon esprit, si j'étais à l'étroit dans mon domestique' (*Corr.* I. 255)), he is aware of the subtle infiltration of 'l'air du monde' (one of the commonplaces of seventeenth-century preaching) and longs to be clear of it all. Accepting to live at court, he feels himself emptied of substance, separated from reality, an actor and a hypocrite: 'Oh! quand sera-ce que je songerai à être en effet, sans me mettre en peine de paraître ni à moi ni aux autres?' (*Corr.* I. 314.) And as Louise de la Vallière, under his guidance, prepares to make her spectacular retreat, he envies her: 'J'ai les discours, elle a les œuvres.' (*Corr.* I. 315.) It is with lyrical fervour that he envisages his escape into solitude and silence—a state he was never to reach except by snatches. So we see that for all his cheerful concessions to the world, he maintained intact— whether in good or bad faith we cannot tell—the call of total retreat.

This brief sketch of Bossuet's relation to the world of men and the court of Louis XIV will serve to introduce a consideration of his theory and practice as a persuader. Indeed, these are insepar-able from it; his attitude to speech and writing is only a part of his attitude to life in society.

Deep down in Bossuet, side by side with his rejection of the

world of men, is a distrust of words. It is not simply that, as he said
to the Academy, 'telle est tout ensemble la grandeur et la faiblesse
de l'esprit humain, que nous ne pouvons égaler nos propres
idées' (*O.O. revised*, VI. 10). More than this, the tongue is an instrument of pride, leading men away from their true centre, which is
God, inclining man to love the creature (and in particular himself)
rather than the creator. The ideal state, he often suggests, is one
of non-verbal communication with God, 'car appartient-il à la
langue, qui n'aime pas elle-même, de parler d'amour?' (*Corr.* I.
56.) He recommends silence equally to the Maréchal de Bellefonds and the Ursulines of Meaux.

But for someone living in the world this is not enough. Man
has been given the use of speech so that he can communicate the
truth to others: 'La vérité est un bien commun; quiconque la
possède, la doit à ses frères.' (*O.O.* IV. 36.) It is the preacher's
duty to imitate the Incarnation; just as Christ manifested himself
to men, so he, however imperfectly, must manifest Christ to
other people:

O sainte vérité! . . . Je vous dois le témoignage de ma parole. O vérité,
vous étiez cachée dans le sein du Père éternel, et vous avez daigné, par
miséricorde, vous manifester à nos yeux. Pour honorer cette charitable
manifestation, je vous dois manifester au dehors par le témoignage de
ma parole. (*Panégyrique de sainte Catherine, O.O.* IV. 42)

And this duty corresponds to another side of Bossuet's nature.
For all his aspiration to silence, he clearly loved using words, as
he self-mockingly admitted to Bellefonds in a letter of 1672:

Je ne parle point ici; il faut donc bien que j'écrive, et que j'écrive,
et que j'écrive. Hé! ne voilà-t-il pas un beau style pour un si grand
prédicateur? Riez de ma simplicité et de mon enfance, qui cherche
encore des jeux. (*Corr.* I. 258)

Speech is justified, then, but its dangers remain, the great danger
being that it may cease to be an instrument and become an end in
itself, a source of pleasure and vanity, a way of winning praise and
favour. The ideal of evangelical speech is one of self-effacement;
Bossuet uses the images of the canal and the mirror:

Tout appareil lui est bon, pourvu qu'il soit un miroir où Jesus-Christ
paraisse en sa vérité, un canal d'où sortent en leur pureté les eaux
vives de son Évangile, ou, s'il faut quelque chose de plus animé, un

interprète fidèle qui n'altère, ni ne détourne, ni ne mêle, ni ne diminue, sa sainte parole. (*Sur la parole de Dieu, O.O.* III. 577)

This was the ideal. What did it mean in practice? Bossuet, like all contemporary preachers, had to grapple with the problem of sacred and profane rhetoric. What place could be given to the arts of the word in the propagation of the word of God?

The first part of the answer was easy. It did not call for any originality to say that the preacher must not use the sort of eloquence which aims to entertain rather than to convince. If preaching is to be a pure canal, it must obviously avoid being a display of skill: 'Laissons, laissons, s'il vous plaît, aux orateurs du monde la pompe et la majesté du style panégyrique; ils ne se mettent point en peine que l'on les entende, pourvu qu'ils reconnaissent que l'on les admire.' (*O.O.* I. 200.) In particular the preacher must shun the verbal ingenuity which Bossuet describes variously as 'les afféteries de la rhétorique' (*O.O.* I. 167), or 'éloquence affectée' (*O.O.* I. 416), and which includes 'cadences harmonieuses', 'vaines curiosités', and 'vains ornements' (*O.O.* II. 302). Naturally, as Bossuet repeats several times, you must not flatter your audience; neither should you indulge in the subtle form of flattery that consists in satisfying the stylistic expectations of a worldly audience—you must reject 'cette douceur agréable, avec cette égalité tempérée que nous admirons dans les orateurs' (*O.O.* II. 302).

Nevertheless, Bossuet does not expect all preachers to follow this line unswervingly—nor could he bring himself to condemn splendid church music entirely, though it seemed very suspect to him.[15] Although it was wrong to make the audience's pleasure your chief aim, certain concessions could be made to the linguistic demands of a polite audience. When asked about pulpit style by the young Cardinal de Bouillon, Bossuet wrote a few pages of advice (*O.O. revised*, VII. 13–20) which suggest that the preacher should take some care over his language. In terms which recall the somewhat *précieux* position of such rhetoricians as René Bary, he states that in public speaking one must not merely express oneself correctly ('ce qui ne manque presque jamais à ceux qui sont nés et qui ont été nourris dans le grand monde'), but also that 'il faut trouver le style figuré, le style relevé, le style orné, la variété,

[15] *Maximes et réflexions sur la comédie*, in *L'Église et le Théâtre*, ed. C. Urbain and E. Levesque, Paris, 1930, p. 225.

qui est tout le secret pour plaire, les tours touchants et insinuants'.[16] He even goes so far as to recommend—with considerable reservations—the reading of Guez de Balzac. But this is the furthest that Bossuet goes in his concessions to polite style, and it would be wrong to take this little piece as an indication of his constant position.[17] In general he is far less inclined than many theorists (Fénelon, for instance) to compromise with politeness. Instead, he sets against flowery modern rhetoric the rude simplicity of the New Testament—above all in the *Panégyrique de saint Paul* and the two sermons, *Sur la parole de Dieu* and *Sur la prédication évangélique*.

In these sermons, following the teaching of Monsieur Vincent and many other theorists who had attempted to introduce something like evangelical simplicity into seventeenth-century preaching, Bossuet shows how God disdained the normal channels of persuasion. Thus St. Paul had none of the normal advantages of personal impressiveness, attractive subject-matter, or ingenious presentation, yet he and the uncouth apostles by their preaching changed the face of the world. The reason for this was above all the force of the truth in what they said. In a way, then, the praise of St. Paul is equivalent to the condemnation of rhetoric as it is normally understood; just as the folly of the Cross defeated the philosophy of the Greeks, so Paul's plain and uncultivated speech triumphed over the eloquence of the world. And yet, 'la véritable éloquence se moque de l'éloquence'; however damaging the example of Paul may be to a worldly notion of rhetoric, he was in

---

[16] It is interesting to observe that when Bossuet comes to explain the way he taught rhetoric to the Dauphin, he uses the traditional metaphor of bones and flesh: 'Nous avions coutume, en lisant les discours qui nous émouvaient le plus, d'en ôter les figures et les autres ornements de paroles, qui en sont comme la chair et la peau, de sorte que, n'y laissant que cet assemblage d'os et de nerfs dont nous venons de parler, c'est-à-dire les seuls arguments, il était aisé de voir ce que la logique faisait dans les ouvrages et ce que la rhétorique y ajoutait.' (*Corr.* II. 155.) This reminds one immediately of Ramus, but also, more generally, of the whole tradition of school-room amplification.

[17] T. Goyet makes rather too much of it in her *Humanisme de Bossuet*, vol. I, pp. 46-57. Some, but not all, of the apparent vacillations in Bossuet's rhetorical theory can be explained in terms of a chronological development, moving from an early taste for a rather ostentatious form of eloquence, through the period in which the puritan influence of St. Vincent de Paul was strong, to a more tolerant attitude in the 1670s. But it would be wrong to over-simplify this development. In the same way, it is as well to be wary of any over-simple schemes of the evolution of Bossuet's pulpit style. The variety of his style is primarily to be understood in terms of his different subjects and different audiences.

fact highly eloquent, as Fénelon pointed out to good effect in his
Dialogues sur l'éloquence.[18] Bossuet does not reject all forms of
eloquence; he repudiates the footling rhetoric which many contemporaries called 'la fausse rhétorique', but he clings to the
eloquence whose aim is to move rather than to dazzle. In this
he is in the central Augustinian tradition and stops short of the
rationalist rejection of emotive rhetoric which we find in Dubois
and François Lamy.

The preacher, then, must set out to move his audience. In order
to create emotion, and thus conviction, he will find all he needs
in the Bible. The sermon *Sur la parole de Dieu* gives us an eloquent
picture of what should happen:

Ils doivent rechercher, mes sœurs, non des brillants qui égayent, ni
une harmonie qui délecte, ni des mouvements qui chatouillent, mais des
éclairs qui percent, un tonnerre qui émeuve, un foudre qui brise les
cœurs. Et où trouveront-ils toutes ces grandes choses, s'ils ne font
luire la vérité, et parler Jésus-Christ lui-même? (*O.O.* III. 575)

If the preacher concentrates on the truth as it is found in the
Bible—preferably using the actual expressions of the Bible—
eloquence will come naturally to him. Bossuet quotes Augustine:
'la sagesse marche devant comme la maîtresse; l'éloquence s'avance
après comme la suivante.' (*O.O.* III. 576.)

This grounding of sacred eloquence on the word of God seems
to provide strong enough guarantees against the human tendency
to put personal vanity above the service of God. But the emphasis
on emotion conceals further dangers. Of course it is better to
move your audience than merely to appeal to their taste for pretty
language. It is only through emotion that most men can be
changed and persuaded. But emotion does not automatically lead
to conversion. If the preacher is not careful, it can become an end
in itself, with the orator complacently revelling in the tears of the
multitude. This, incidentally, is the sort of image presented by
Monsieur Vincent, who spoke to his disciples of the pleasure of
swaying an audience: 'N'est-il pas vrai que souvent vous voyez
votre auditoire en larmes?'—he went on, however, to stress the
need for something more solid than this.[19]

We know that Bossuet was a man of strong emotions. He knew
the way in which emotion spreads; in his quarrel with Caffaro

18 Fénelon, *Dialogues sur l'éloquence*, third dialogue.
19 St. Vincent de Paul, *Correspondance*, ed. P. Coste, vol. XI, p. 283.

about the virtues and vices of the theatre, he showed himself far more aware than his opponent of the contagious power of passion, even when it is only simulated by an actor.[20] Emotion was a powerful force and a dangerous one; when it was misdirected, as Bossuet thought it was in the theatre, the result could be disastrous. On the other hand, Bossuet was also aware that the emotions we feel in the theatre are apt to disappear when we leave the theatre; powerful and agreeable for a time, the emotional effect of tragedy is often short-lived. So it was not enough for the preacher simply to move his audience to tears; the playwright and the actor could do that. If preachers and actors were often compared, Bossuet, who placed the pulpit alongside the altar as the twin poles of Christian worship, was bound to react vigorously against the idea that the sermon was like a theatrical performance. His position is clearly stated in the sermon *Sur la parole de Dieu*. Having spoken, as we have seen, of the preacher's duty to move and the audience's duty to be moved, in his third point he reflects on the ambiguity of some audience reactions. After a striking analysis of the sort of emotion aroused by contemporary tragedy, he continues:

Quand le docte saint Chrysostome craignait que ses auditeurs n'assistassent à ses sermons de même qu'à la comédie, c'est que souvent ils semblaient émus; il s'élevait dans son auditoire des cris et des voix confuses qui marquaient que ses paroles excitaient les cœurs. Un homme un peu moins expérimenté aurait cru que ses auditeurs étaient convertis; mais il appréhendait, chrétiens, que ce ne fussent des affections de théâtre, excitées par ressorts et par artifices; il attendait à se réjouir quand il verrait les mœurs corrigées, et c'était en effet la marque assurée que Jésus-Christ était écouté.   (*O.O.* III. 587)

This is the crux of the matter. The preacher must aim neither to satisfy his congregation's taste for wit and elegance, nor to engender the sort of strong emotions which are the great attraction of *Bérénice* or *Le Cid*, but to convert. He must not flatter the old man, he must create a new man.

So much for the theory; it is clear enough and fairly uncompromising. But if one thing is constant in rhetoric, it is the gap between theory and practice. Everyone agrees that certain forms of eloquence are out of place in certain contexts, and just as

[20] Bossuet, *Lettre à Caffaro*, in *L'Église et le Théâtre*, pp. 123–34.

invariably everyone uses these forms. Perhaps the natural childish-
ness of word artists is to blame, perhaps their conformism or
sociability, perhaps also their vanity, their desire for applause
even at the cost of compromise. Whatever the other causes, it is
clear that audiences play a large part in determining the final
result. Writers and speakers would not compromise with their
principles if they did not feel compelled to do so by their probable
audiences. They may be wrong about their audiences; what
matters is that their notion of audience demands influences the
form—and thus the nature—of the message they wish to communicate. Some are more ready than others to do whatever is
necessary to please; others, more conscious of their own individual
value or the value of their subject-matter, are unwilling to go so
far; but all, if they put pen to paper or open their mouths to speak,
are conditioned by their idea of what the public expects of them.
As Bossuet puts it, 'ce sont les auditeurs qui font les prédicateurs' (*O.O.* vi. 26.)

The power of the audience over the writer was stronger in
seventeenth-century France than it is today, since the social relations between the two sides were much closer. Writers actually
knew quite an important section of their public; they read their
poems face to face with the men of birth and wealth who protected
them and pensioned them. Today the relation has changed; the
writer is further from his public and less subordinate to it. But
the public speaker is as dependent as ever. His audience is there
in front of him, reacting to all he says, showing its approval and
disapproval, interest and boredom. This is how it was for Bossuet. More than this, he had time to get to know certain audiences
quite well when he preached before them several times in quick
succession (as in the *Carêmes* and the *Avents*), or when he saw them
year after year (as at Metz and, to a certain extent, at the court of
Louis XIV).

Of course, Bossuet's audiences varied greatly.[21] The ones which
are of most interest for the present chapter are those which gave
an exemplary form to the demands of worldliness, those in whom
the two meanings of *le monde* met, the fashionable Paris congrega-
tions. Bossuet seems first to have confronted such an audience
when he preached the *Carême des Minimes*; he was to become used
to it in all the sermons he preached before the court. It goes

[21] On Bossuet and his audiences see Truchet, *Prédication de Bossuet*, vol. ii.

without saying that people came to these sermons for many reasons; it does not mean that everyone was motivated by 'unworthy' reasons if one says, as one must, that to go to a sermon at court, or even to follow the *Carême des Minimes*, was more likely to be a ceremonial duty for members of an officially Christian society than a committed act of individual piety. La Bruyère probably gives a stylized and biased form to the reality of church-going when he describes his courtiers in the Versailles chapel ranged in a circle of adoration before the King, who in his turn adores God, or when he paints 'un beau salut':

La décoration souvent profane, les places retenues et payées, des livres distribués comme au théâtre, les entrevues et les rendez-vous fréquents, le murmure et les causeries étourdissantes, quelqu'un monté sur une tribune qui y parle familièrement, sèchement, et sans autre zèle que de rassembler le peuple, l'amuser, jusqu'à ce qu'un orchestre, le dirai-je? et des voix qui concertent depuis longtemps se fassent entendre.[22]

Still, many testimonies, often from the preachers themselves, bear out a version of his critical view. It was a difficult sort of audience to set about converting.

Bossuet was very conscious of the pressure such a congregation put on the preacher to become a performer, and he fought back hard. Like many preachers then and now, he scolded his audiences for their unserious attitude to church services in general and sermons in particular. Thus to his average listener at the Minimes he exclaims: 'Nous ne sommes point dans les bals, dans les assemblées, dans les divertissements, dans les jeux du monde; c'est la prédication que tu entends.' (*O.O.* III. 324.) He is shocked —or appears shocked—at the frivolity of audiences whose only reaction to his attempt to convert them is this sort of stylistic fault-finding: 'Quoi, cette période n'a pas ses mesures, ce raisonnement n'est pas dans son jour, cette comparaison n'est pas bien tournée.' (*O.O.* III. 330.) Small wonder that his preaching has little

---

[22] *Caractères*, p. 419. Compare the description of fashionable sermons given by Rapin, talking of a slightly earlier period: 'Ne voit-on pas tous les jours de jeunes prédicateurs sans vertu et sans science monter en chaire, comme monte un comédien sur le théâtre, pour y jouer son personnage. On y invite les amis par billets, on fait un grand cercle de la parenté et une grande assemblée d'honnêtes gens pour parer l'auditoire et pour encourager le jeune déclamateur.' (*Réflexions sur l'usage de l'éloquence*, Paris, 1672, p. 67.) A great deal of evidence confirms this impression; see A. Hurel, *Les Orateurs sacrés à la cour de Louis XIV*, 2 vols., Paris, 1872, vol. I, introduction.

effect, 'que nous recevons assez de compliments, et que nous ne voyons point de pénitence' (O.O. III. 331). The same complaints occur again and again; Bossuet condemns or mocks his audience's taste for fashionable portraits, clever psychological analysis, ingenious wit, or caressing harmonies. And in his Easter sermon of 1681, when he was no longer a regular court preacher, he greeted his audience with the old refrain:

Reprendre la parole après tant d'années d'un perpétuel silence, et avoir à contenter la délicatesse d'un auditoire qui ne souffre rien que d'exquis; mais qui, permettez-moi de le dire, sans songer autant qu'il faudrait à se convertir, souvent ne veut être ému qu'autant qu'il le faut pour éviter la langueur d'un discours sans force, et, plus soigneux de son plaisir que de son salut, lorsqu'il s'agit de sa guérison, veut qu'on cherche de nouveaux moyens de flatter son goût raffiné; ce serait une chose à craindre . . . (O.O. VI. 49)

Here we see the second temptation of rhetoric; the audience wants not just elegant language, but an agreeable stirring of the emotions —as in the theatre.

I think it is fair to hear in these protests the exasperation of someone who knows that he is being pushed away from the evangelical simplicity he hankers after. He criticizes his audience partly because he is annoyed with himself. For in practice, objectively viewed, Bossuet's sermons certainly do give away a good deal to the taste of his hearers. Kick as he might against the situation, he was in fact an entertainer.

Already for many of his contemporaries his eloquence was something to be admired and savoured. In their remarks we find a hint of the way in which future generations would look at Bossuet, paying less attention to his aim (conversion) than to the means employed. The words which were spoken for immediate effect are transmuted into the literature which will be enjoyed and analysed by posterity. This was how Madame de Sévigné read his funeral orations:

Nous relisons aussi, à travers nos grandes lectures, des rogatons que nous trouvons sous notre main, par exemple toutes les belles oraisons funèbres de Monsieur de Meaux, de M. l'abbé Fléchier, de M. Mascaron, du Bourdaloue; nous repleurons M. de Turenne, Mme de Montausier, Monsieur le Prince, feu Madame, la reine d'Angleterre; nous admirons ce portrait de Cromwell: ce sont des chefs-d'œuvre d'éloquence qui charment l'esprit.[23]

[23] *Lettres*, vol. III, pp. 647–8.

She does not single out Bossuet from his contemporaries; all equally give her pleasure. Later Bossuet was to be exalted above the rest, and again for literary reasons. Voltaire consecrated this eminence in a well-known paragraph of his *Siècle de Louis XIV*, where it is clear that Bossuet has now entered the ranks of the classics of literature; he is mentioned in the chapter entitled 'Des beaux-arts', and his greatest genre, the funeral oration, is compared to the tragic theatre:

Les sujets de ces pièces d'éloquence sont heureux à proportion des malheurs que les morts ont éprouvés. C'est en quelque façon comme dans les tragédies, où les grandes infortunes des principaux personnages sont ce qui intéresse davantage.[24]

This is the ever-recurring comparison which Bossuet tried to avoid.

If we look now at some of the qualities in Bossuet's eloquence[25] which might conceivably interfere with his edifying purpose, I think the first to be considered is a certain grandiloquence, what Voltaire describes as 'une grandeur majestueuse qui tient un peu de la poésie'. Bossuet shared this quality with many of his contemporaries, though he was more inclined to what was called the *sublime* than Bourdaloue, for instance. An anonymous contemporary hints that his style in the funeral oration for Henriette d'Angleterre was considered 'trop poétique'.[26] And for the average twentieth-century reader Bossuet is probably first and foremost the author of resounding passages such as this:

Viendra, viendra le temps, Monseigneur, que non seulement les histoires, et les marbres, et les trophées, mais encore les villes, et les forteresses, et les peuples et les nations seront consumés par le même feu; et alors toute la gloire des hommes s'évanouira en fumée, si elle n'est défendue de l'embrasement général par l'humilité chrétienne.

(*Premier Panégyrique de saint François de Paule*, O.O. II. 17–18)

Humility, but nobly expressed. It is unnecessary to analyse the rhetoric of a passage such as this to see that it uses all the resources

---

[24] Voltaire, *Œuvres complètes*, ed. Moland, vol. XIV, p. 543.

[25] It is important to remember, when discussing the style of Bossuet's sermons, that the words we read, although written by Bossuet, may not in fact have been spoken by him, since like any seasoned orator he did not keep slavishly to a prepared text. It does appear, however, to judge from the notes taken by those who heard him, that the gap between the manuscript and the spoken words was not great. See J. Lebarq, *Histoire critique de la prédication de Bossuet*, 2nd ed., Paris, 1891, pp. 43–4.

[26] Quoted by Goyet, *Humanisme de Bossuet*, vol. I, p. 65.

of the grand style. But to what effect? Is it really more persuasive to speak like this than to say more simply that human honours cannot last? Or is the style not rather dictated by a notion of necessary grandeur? And if so, whose grandeur? One could say that the subject treated calls for a certain magnificence; Bossuet often talks of the challenge to human rhetoric offered by the sublime matters he has to deal with. Similarly, he says that churches should be decorated with proper splendour: 'la magnificence sied bien dans les temples.' (*O.O.* III. 299.) But this magnificence should belong to God rather than to men—let the church be fine and the clothes of the congregation plain. Following the analogy through, there is at least a suspicion that this grandiloquence is designed to magnify man as much as God; it appears first in a compliment addressed to the Maréchal de Schonberg and later in a direct address to Louis XIV. God may not be a respecter of persons, but Bossuet undoubtedly was. We may notice in passing the efficiency with which he always pays the standard compliments to any outstanding members of his audience, praising above all their piety, but contriving also to mention their wordly honours. He knew the dangers of this procedure, and describes them in his *Vêture de Mademoiselle de Bouillon*:

Je n'ignore pas néanmoins que j'en pourrais parler plus librement à une personne qui les quitte et les foule aux pieds, et qu'on peut en discourir de la sorte pour en inspirer le mépris. Mais cette manière détournée d'en parler en les rabaissant ne me semble pas encore assez pure pour la prise d'habit d'une Carmélite. (*O.O.* III. 516)

Silence is better. Nevertheless, although Bossuet knew 'combien les prédicateurs doivent être réservés sur les louanges' (*O.O.* III. 234), he normally made his compliments both acceptable and splendid.[27]

The splendour of Bossuet's style may then be seen in part as a concession to his audiences. Certainly it makes it more difficult to accept at their face value Bossuet's presumably sincere protestations of modesty. Take, for instance, the opening paragraph of the *Panégyrique de saint Paul*, where Bossuet proclaims the inadequacy of his own eloquence (this by way of prelude to a consideration of Paul's practice as a preacher). In the second sentence

---

[27] See, for instance, *O.O.* I. 164; III. 359; V. 271.

the self-confident symmetry of the style pulls oddly against the
ostensible message:

Quand je rappelle à mon souvenir tant de peuples que Paul a conquis,
tant de travaux qu'il a surmontés, tant de mystères qu'il a découverts,
tant d'exemples qu'il nous a laissés d'une charité consommée, ce sujet
me paraît si vaste, si relevé, si majestueux, que mon esprit, se trouvant
surpris, ne sait ni où s'arrêter dans cette étendue, ni que tenter dans
cette hauteur, ni que choisir dans cette abondance; et j'ose bien me
persuader qu'un ange même ne suffirait pas pour louer cet homme du
troisième ciel. (*O.O.* II. 294)

It is the same when Bossuet announces that he will do without
the figures of rhetoric and talk straight; in the following example
from his sermon for All Saints' Day 1669 we see him simply
abandoning one metaphor for another:

Si le fondement est solide, un coup de foudre viendra d'en haut qui
renversera tout de fond en comble. Je veux dire simplement et sans
figure, que les malheurs nous assaillent et nous pénètrent par trop
d'endroits, pour pouvoir être prévus et arrêtés de toutes parts.

(*O.O.* V. 511)

In fact, for all his protestations, his sermons afford many of the
traditional pleasures of literature.

After the grandiloquence one may notice the ingenuity which
Bossuet so frequently displays in the disposition of his subject into
three parts—this is a quality (or a failing) which he shared with
most of his contemporaries. Let us look at the way he introduces
his Good Friday sermon in 1662. Taking as his text 'Hoc est
sanguis meus Novi Testamenti', he dwells on the word 'testament':

Il y a dans un testament trois choses considérables: on regarde en
premier lieu si le testament est bon et valide; on regarde en second
lieu de quoi dispose le testateur en faveur de ses héritiers; et on regarde
en troisième lieu ce qu'il leur ordonne. Appliquons ceci, chrétiens, à
la dernière volonté de Jésus mourant: voyons la validité de ce testament mystique, par le sang et par la mort du testateur; voyons la
munificence de ce testament, par les biens que Jésus-Christ nous y
laisse; voyons l'équité de ce testament. par les choses qu'il nous y
ordonne. (*O.O.* IV. 278)

One could take much more complex examples from some of the
earlier sermons, but even this quite modest one shows clearly

how a device which is intended to make the sermon easier to
assimilate can become a sort of show-piece. One can imagine that
on hearing this for the first time the audience would wait eagerly
to see how the speaker would complete his division with the
ingenuity and symmetry to which they were accustomed (in the
more blasé, eagerness may have been replaced by boredom).

Cleverness of this sort is more usual at the beginning of sermons
and is generally followed by a more forceful attack. Even so, the
ingenuity which we have seen in the division is also evident in
the body of Bossuet's sermons, notably in the elegant and antithetical paradoxes which often sum up the Christian lesson. These
are the old reversals of the mighty and the humble, the first and
the last, wisdom and folly, riches and poverty, sight and blind-
ness, freedom and slavery. Here, for instance, is the play on
captivity which recurs practically every time Bossuet preaches
a *vêture*:

Au milieu de tant de captivités, les hommes du siècle s'estiment libres,
parmi toutes ces lois et toutes ces contraintes du monde . . . Que si le
monde a ses contraintes, je vous estime heureuse, ma sœur, qui estimant
trop votre liberté pour la soumettre aux lois de la terre, professez
hautement que vous ne vous voulez captiver que pour l'amour de
celui qui étant le maître de toutes choses, s'est rendu esclave pour nous,
afin de nous tirer de la servitude.   (O.O. II. 192)

This is, of course, not a paradox of Bossuet's invention, but a
perfectly orthodox position with strong Biblical backing. Nevertheless, one is reminded of those master–slave paradoxes which
flower so freely in the tragedy of the time. Seventeenth-century
audiences loved antithesis.

A more important feature of Bossuet's language is his constant
use of metaphor and comparison. His images are no more original
than those used by most writers or speakers of his day, but he
stands out from his contemporaries in the metaphorical richness
of his sermons. So natural was this way of speaking to him that,
as we saw in an example just quoted, even when he says he is
abandoning figurative language, he merely moves from a rather
obvious metaphor to a relatively effaced one. Often his images
are prolonged into great allegories which weave in and out
through the whole of a sermon—we saw that his Good Friday
sermon of 1662 is founded on the Biblical metaphor of the last
will and testament. These prolonged metaphors may be quite

conventionally developed, so that they contribute little to the sermon except a certain feeling of dignity (the sort of dignity we associate with the 'ship of state', the 'helmsman', and the 'stormy seas'). At other times they make the sermon memorable. Thus the Panegyric of St. Andrew begins with the word-play of the New Testament: 'Venite post me, et faciam vos fieri piscatores hominum.' (It may be noted in passing that many of the attractive qualities of Bossuet's speech, his metaphors, his paradoxes, his pattern rhetoric, owe a great deal to the Bible, which lends a kind of respectability to what might otherwise look like an all-too-worldly pleasure in the clash and roll of fine words.) Bossuet makes of this metaphor the dominant motif of his sermon, developing it with the ingenuity we have noted, and holding his audience (or so one supposes) with vivid passages such as this:

> Laissons-nous prendre; et tant de fois pris par les vanités, laissons-nous prendre une fois à ces pêcheurs d'hommes et aux filets de l'Évangile, 'qui ne tuent point ce qu'ils prennent, mais qui le conservent; qui font passer à la lumière ceux qu'ils tirent du fond de l'abîme, et transportent de la terre au ciel ceux qui s'agitent dans cette fange' . . .
> Laissons-nous tirer de cette mer, dont la face est toujours changeante, qui cède à tout vent, et qui est toujours agitée de quelque tempête. Écoute ce grand bruit du monde, ce tumulte, ce trouble éternel; voyez ce mouvement, cette agitation, ces flots vainement émus qui crèvent tout à coup, et ne laissent que de l'écume.   (O.O. v. 349)

In passages such as this, we not only see the vivid beauty of some of Bossuet's conventional imagery, but we can hear, as we heard in the evocation of destruction which I quoted earlier in the chapter, the swelling cadences which are so typical of Bossuet's grand style. The repetitions, the enumeration, the gradation, the beautiful effects of balance, the sonorous harmony, these are the qualities which in a debased form have made formal eloquence so ridiculous and even repulsive in our day. Yet this sort of eloquence can work, and it does work in Bossuet in that it often compels our attention and makes his sermons satisfying and memorable experiences, however little we may be in sympathy with his message. Yet although they may affect us, it may be doubted whether they are likely to convert. Even if we hear in them not only the eloquence of the speaker, but the compelling expression of something we recognize as a reality, there is at least a danger that the former may neutralize rather than intensify the latter. It is all too easy to react as many of Bossuet's audiences reacted—with congratulations rather than action.

But what chiefly distinguishes Bossuet from many of his contemporaries is his unremitting and vehement assault on what theorists used to call the passions, hope, fear, pity, admiration, indignation, love, and so on. As we have seen, this appeal to the emotions was more acceptable to contemporary theory than the qualities of splendour or ingenuity. Bossuet, although he had reservations about the value of certain emotional reactions, always combined doctrinal teaching with a direct personal appeal. As he himself frequently complained, it was not easy to get much response from his hard-boiled upper-class audiences—he cries to his congregation at the Minimes on Good Friday 1660:

Quoi! je vois encore vos yeux secs? Quoi! je n'entends point encore de sanglots! Attendez-vous que je représente en particulier toutes les diverses circonstances de cette sanglante tragédie? Faut-il que j'en fasse paraître successivement tous les différents personnages?

(O.O. III. 375)

This suggests that a measure of theatricality may be needed to get through to certain listeners. Great sentences or striking imagery may help, but the audience is most likely to be moved by the appearance of emotion in the preacher. And so Bossuet constantly brings himself into it, using the first person, exclaiming, questioning, engaging in imaginary dialogue with his listeners, crying out passionately for an emotion to match his. Thus his Good Friday sermon continues with an evocation of Christ on the Cross:

Contemplez cette face, autrefois les délices, maintenant l'horreur des yeux; regardez cet homme que Pilate vous présente. Le voilà, le voilà, cet homme; le voilà, cet homme de douleurs: *Ecce homo, ecce homo*: 'Voilà, l'homme!' Eh! qui est-ce? un homme ou un ver de terre? est-ce un homme vivant ou bien une victime écorchée? On vous le dit, c'est un homme: *Ecce homo*: 'Voilà l'homme!' Le voilà, l'homme de douleurs . . .

Ô plaies, que je vous adore! flétrissures sacrées, que je vous baise! ô sang qui découlez soit de la tête percée, soit des yeux meurtris, soit de tout le corps déchiré, ô sang précieux, que je vous recueille! Terre, terre, ne bois pas ce sang! (O.O. III. 376–7)

To present-day ears this is perhaps too violent to be effective. It is hard to say how it affected its first hearers. They were used to

vehemence in the pulpit, just as they were used to high rhetoric
on the stage. So they probably did not feel that there was anything
excessive about Bossuet's eloquence here. Nevertheless, there is
clearly something theatrical about this passage with its repetitions,
its exclamations, and its apostrophes—one could find parallels
in contemporary tragedy without difficulty. Bossuet was undoubtedly sincere, but in order to communicate with his audience,
he found it necessary to project his emotion into a dramatic form,
playing a part he believed in so as to make a more powerful impact
on his hearers. Perhaps those who officiate in religious ceremonies must always do something of the sort, as must politicians
and other public men. It is a commonplace to say that if the theatre
imitates society, society also imitates the theatre—or at least that
many of the public manifestations of social life bear a disquieting
resemblance to theatrical performances. Those who take part
may not like to regard themselves as performers, but to those
who watch (in this case Bossuet's congregation) the performance
is something to be enjoyed—and judged—in its own right.
This was the public of whom Bossuet said that it 'ne veut être
ému qu'autant qu'il le faut pour éviter la langueur d'un discours
sans force'. In spite of himself, in his most vehement appeals to
the passions, Bossuet was providing this sort of pleasure.

Let us now return to the funeral oration.[28] It is apparent that
this merely presents in an extreme form the problems posed by
preaching of all kinds. The difficulties inherent in the form were
recognized by those who wrote about it in the seventeenth century. In the first place they knew that the ceremony which should
denounce worldly vanity can be made to serve worldly vanity.
It was well known that funeral orations lied like epitaphs—
'menteur comme une oraison funèbre', quotes Furetière in his
dictionary. Many of the great departed had lived lives which
called for satire, not eulogy, or which at best were striking rather
than edifying. Bossuet voices a commonly held opinion in his
funeral oration for Père Bourgoing:

Je voux avoue, Chrétiens, que j'ai coutume de plaindre les prédicateurs
lorsqu'ils font les panégyriques funèbres des princes et des grands du
monde . . . il arrive ordinairement que Dieu a si peu de part dans de

[28] A good brief treatment of this subject will be found in J. Truchet's introduction
to his edition of Bossuet's *Oraisons funèbres*.

telles vies qu'on a peine à y trouver quelques actions qui méritent d'être louées par ses ministres. (O.F. 43)

The unfortunate preacher had to step carefully in his attempt to please the family of the dead man, the audience, and God.

But the most universal problems of the genre were presented not so much by the claims of truth and flattery as by the choice of style and tone for the speech. The *Dissertation sur les oraisons funèbres* by the Abbé du Jarry is interesting on this point.[29] Given the bad reputation of the funeral oration at the time, this work is largely defensive in tone; it attempts to justify the use in Christian funeral services of the grandiloquence which was traditionally associated with the *genre démonstratif* or epideictic oratory. He shows the orator negotiating between two camps, aiming to 'satisfaire les oreilles savantes et chrétiennes sans blesser les polies et les délicates', adopting a style combining 'de la politesse, de la religion, de la majesté, de la tristesse, ou plutôt un certain mélange de tout cela'. And although he gives due prominence to the edifying nature of the occasion, it is the magnificence which comes out on top:

La singularité de l'action, la sainteté du lieu, la préparation des esprits, la grandeur du sujet, le choix de l'auditoire, tout cela demande du grand et du sublime. On écoute avec indignation un homme qui au milieu des sacrés mystères interrompus, en présence de ce que le siècle a de plus grand, et de ce que la religion a de plus auguste; parmi cet éclatant et triste assemblage d'inscriptions, de chiffres, de mausolées, de sceptres, de couronnes, de flambeaux, de deuil et de larmes, glace les esprits par des morales froides et les fatigue avec des citations importunes.[30]

It will be seen that what is wanted is not simply splendid language, but a high tragic eloquence, since the orator is the 'organe de la douleur publique', who provokes the tears of the august assembly with his noble grief. It is like a parody of Racine's 'tristesse majestueuse qui fait tout le plaisir de la tragédie'. More conscious of the absurdity of such ceremonies, the Abbé Boileau gives us the other side of the coin:

L'éloge des grands est prononcé par certains orateurs qui songent quelquefois plus à leur propre réputation qu'à celle du héros qu'ils ont à louer. Ces discours si châtiés n'affligent le cœur que pour réjouir

[29] Abbé du Jarry, *Dissertation sur les oraisons fenèbres*, included in P. d'Ortigue de Vaumorière, *Harangues sur toutes sortes de sujets*, 3rd ed., Paris, 1713.
[30] Op. cit., p. 376.

l'imagination; et leurs pensées leur sont plus chères que les actions du mort.[31]

The funeral orator was open to all the temptations of literary vanity, the more so since many funeral orations were designed for posterity and published almost as soon as they were spoken. As du Jarry said, they were 'faites autant pour être lues que pour être entendues'.[32]

Such were the problems of the genre in which Bossuet had his greatest success as an orator. As Jacques Truchet points out in the introduction to his edition of the *Oraisons funèbres*, Bossuet was lucky in his subjects; he did not have to praise anyone who was totally unworthy of it. He did, however, have to deal tactfully with certain aspects of his heroes' careers—the irreligion and rebellion of Condé, the rumours surrounding Henriette d'Angleterre and Louis XIV, the neglect of Marie-Thérèse, the unedifying early life of the Princesse Palatine. This he did on the whole with dignified restraint, avoiding the twin perils of misplaced criticism and insincere flattery. In the case of the Princesse Palatine, he actually dwells on her misspent youth, the better to insist on her exemplary conversion. But if Bossuet avoids the more obvious pitfalls, it must be said that in some cases he seems to give excessive weight to various human qualities which in Christian terms are of doubtful value. The Condé oration has given us examples of this. Of course, in the end death and piety triumph, but I am not sure that the evocation of Condé's military skill is really affected by this. The same is true of the praise of Louis XIV which is so prominent in the oration for Queen Marie-Thérèse (it also finds a place in many other orations). Here again the greatness is set against the nothingness of human life—'l'inévitable néant des grandeurs humaines'—but this does not prevent Bossuet from praising Louis's military achievements in the same sort of way as the poets recruited by Chapelain:

Jamais on n'a fait la guerre avec une force plus inévitable, puisqu'en méprisant les saisons, il a ôté jusqu'à la défense à ses ennemis. Les soldats, ménagés et exposés quand il faut, marchent avec confiance sous ses étendards; nul fleuve ne les arrête, nulle forteresse ne les effraye. On sait que Louis foudroie les villes plutôt qu'il ne les assiège, et tout est ouvert à sa puissance. (*O.F.* 214–15)

[31] Migne, *Collection intégrale et universelle des orateurs sacrés*, vol. XXI, 1845, col. 34.
[32] Du Jarry, op. cit., p. 379.

Of course, the *Traité de la concupiscence* does not define Bossuet's position on the things of this world—the tutor to the Dauphin believed in the need for royal magnificence—but even so one wonders whether this sort of eulogy is in place in a meditation on death.

However, I do not wish to dwell on the vexed question of Bossuet's relations to the royal power[33]—it is fairly clear that he was neither the spineless flatterer of Joseph de Maistre nor the fearless John the Baptist figure of Gazier and Rébelliau. My aim at present is rather to characterize Bossuet's eloquence, and in particular his funeral eloquence. In three different sermons, he makes the same radical attack on the folly of men whose vanity is seen even after their death:

Quand je vois ces riches tombeaux sous lesquels les grands de la terre semblent vouloir cacher la honte de leur corruption, je ne puis assez m'étonner de l'extrême folie des hommes, qui érige de si magnifiques trophées à un peu de cendre et à quelques vieux ossements.

(O.O. I. 103–4, 494; V. 470)

I think the question one asks oneself is this: do Bossuet's funeral orations not commit the same sort of folly as the rich tombs he so scorns? Are they not also 'magnifiques trophées' to the dead?

One should not be too sweeping about the style of Bossuet's funeral orations, since it varies so much from speech to speech and even inside each speech. Although I point to one or two passages where Bossuet amply satisfies the theatrical expectations of his audience, this does not mean that one could not find passages which deliberately disappoint these expectations by remaining plain and unemotional. In particular, the four early orations, none of which is devoted to a person of great worldly eminence, remain essentially edifying and undramatic. It is in the six later orations that the Christian preacher comes near to the tragic poet. In all of these Bossuet's language is of the sort demanded by the high rank of the dead man and the aristocratic nature of the congregation. In four of them at least he performs to the full the function of bringing out the emotions of his audience as they contemplate the life and death of Henriette de France, Henriette d'Angleterre, the Princesse Palatine, and the Prince de Condé. In

[33] A lot of ink has been spilt over this question; there is a useful *mise au point* in J. Truchet, *Politique de Bossuet*, Paris, 1966, pp. 7–52.

discussing the Condé oration I indicated some of the concessions which Bossuet makes to human greatness, in particular the way his rich eloquence matches the splendour of Bérain's decorations. On the other hand I neglected the appeal to the emotions. This can best be illustrated from Bossuet's funeral oration for the young Henriette d'Angleterre, who died unexpectedly in 1670.

The whole oration turns on the antithesis of *grandeur* and *misère*. The human greatness of the princess, like all human greatness, is seen to be vanity: 'Je veux dans un seul malheur déplorer toutes les calamités du genre humain, et dans une seule mort faire voir la mort et le néant de toutes les grandeurs humaines.' (*O.F.* 162.) This is the first part. But in the second part Bossuet affirms that in this vain show there is something solid, the hope of salvation which is founded on Christian faith and piety. Naturally it is in the first half that Bossuet appeals most strongly to his audience's emotions, as he oscillates constantly and tragically between the evocation of Henriette's beauty, birth, charm, and intelligence and the reminder of death and destruction. In an article on death and the baroque, André Chastel speaks of this assault on the feelings: 'L'un des grands gestes de l'art baroque reste en somme le mouvement à la fois théâtral et menaçant qui consiste à "ouvrir un tombeau devant la cour".'[34] The quotation is from Bossuet's *Sermon sur la mort*, but the remark applies equally to the funeral orations. Whether baroque is the right word I do not know, but there is certainly something close to the tragic theatre (*Bérénice* and *Iphigénie*, for instance) in moments such as this:

Princesse, le digne objet de l'admiration de deux grands royaumes, n'était-ce pas assez que l'Angleterre pleurât votre absence, sans être encore réduite à pleurer votre mort? et la France, qui vous revit avec tant de joie environnée d'un nouvel éclat, n'avait-elle plus d'autres pompes et d'autres triomphes pour vous, au retour de ce voyage fameux d'où vous aviez remporté tant de gloire et de si belles espérances?

(*O.F.* 161–2)

The emotion is intensified by Bossuet's personal tone (more personal than in any other of his funeral orations), by the use of powerful Biblical metaphors ('Madame cependant a passé du matin au soir, ainsi que l'herbe des champs'), and above all by the vivid narration of the princess's last moments.

[34] A. Chastel, 'Le baroque et la mort', in *Retorica e barocco*, Atti del III congresso Internazionale di Studi Umanistici, Rome, 1955, p. 34.

In all this the oration has a lot in common with tragic and lyric poetry. The difference comes in the second half, where Bossuet moves from lamentation to a hopeful lesson; here he is more concerned to teach, reasoning with his audience rather than stirring their feelings. It is beautifully done, and in theory it ought to work; the audience, softened up by the first half, should grasp eagerly for the strengthening lessons of the second half. Yet inevitably it is the moving first half which stays in the mind. At any rate, this is the version which reached Voltaire:

L'éloge funèbre de Madame, enlevée à la fleur de son âge, et morte entre ses bras, eut le plus grand et le plus rare des succès, celui de faire verser des larmes à la cour. Il fut obligé de s'arrêter après ces paroles: 'O nuit désastreuse! nuit effroyable, où retentit tout à coup, comme un éclat de tonnerre, cette étonnante nouvelle: Madame se meurt, Madame est morte, etc.' L'auditoire éclata en sanglots; et la voix de l'orateur fut interrompue par ses soupirs et par ses pleurs.[35]

It may be that Voltaire is not an ideal witness, but I think his words give us an indication that the gap between funeral oration and tragedy was not so great for some spectators as the preacher might have wished. This strong audience reaction, though better than indifference, must have seemed suspect to the author of the *Sermon sur la parole de Dieu*.

It is not for me to say whether Bossuet was justified in using all the rhetoric of the profane literature of his time. Christianity, like other faiths, has always tried to use the channels of profane communication (from polyphony to popular song) in order to reach an unregenerate audience. But in doing so it runs certain risks. In the first place it is all too easy to accuse Bossuet (like most of his contemporaries) of inconsistency in his hostility to profane rhetoric. Perhaps this is not very important; Bossuet may have been right to change his position according to the circumstances. The attack on profane rhetoric may be read as a sincere attempt to stop the inevitable concessions going too far.

More important, the compromise with human eloquence may obscure or weaken the real message. From Bossuet's point of view, the ideal way of listening to his sermons was to take both the sugar and the pill. But audiences have a way of licking off the sugar. And this, it is fairly clear from Bossuet's sermons, is what many of his listeners did; they were so used to hearing fulminations from the pulpit that they accepted them as a matter of course and concentrated on the value of the performance. 'On s'attend qu'ils reprendront les mauvaises mœurs, on dit qu'ils le font d'office, et l'esprit humain indocile y fait moins de réflexion.' (*O.O.* iv. 48.) And as a result, 'on nous entend quelque temps pendant que nous débitons une morale sensible, ou que nous reprenons les vices communs du siècle. L'homme curieux de spectacles s'en fait un, tant il est vain! de la peinture de ses erreurs et de ses défauts.' (*O.O.* vi. 373.) Condemned to the role of entertainer, the more the preacher attempts to break through and shock, the more he pleases his blasé audience.

This was not true of all spectators, of course. Bossuet's message presumably struck home to some members of his audience. With the rest there was perhaps nothing to be done. Even so, one wonders if he did not go a little too far to meet their tastes—for their tastes were also to some extent his own. If Bossuet complained 'que nous recevons assez de compliments et que nous ne voyons point de pénitence', was his eloquence not partly to blame for this? Ideally one might agree with Jacques Truchet, who condemns those who would see in the *Oraisons funèbres* verbal masterpieces irrespective of their message:

La pire trahison à l'égard de Bossuet consisterait à le présenter comme un magicien du style, dont les phrases garderaient toute leur valeur alors même que l'on n'en reconnaîtrait aucune aux pensées qui les inspirent. Toute étude de son art doit commencer par cette affirmation, que la splendeur de la forme repose ici sur l'élévation de l'idée, la réalité de l'émotion, l'admiration de l'orateur pour les personnages dont il parle et sa ferveur pour la religion qu'il sert, enfin sur le sentiment d'autorité qu'il tire de sa conviction.[36]

While this is true in part, it ignores the vulnerability of the grand style which I have been discussing. Bossuet may have been sincere; this is not the point. But as the cadences swelled and the voice became more impassioned it was surely natural for those listeners who were less fervent than the preacher to step back mentally and admire the orator instead of really absorbing his message. With the passing of time, as the grand style has receded

[36] *Oraisons funèbres*, ed. Truchet, p. xliii. For a classic example of this 'trahison' see Valéry, *Variété*, ii, pp. 41-3.

from us, it is all the more natural for modern readers to see Bossuet in a rather theatrical light.

Bossuet often compared the world to a theatre and life to a play. It was a favourite comparison among his contemporaries and was perhaps justified by the overblown grandeur of much of the art and public life of the time. But Bossuet was of his age, however much he longed for a golden age of directness and simple faith. He was not a man of silence and his eloquence was the eloquence demanded by his contemporaries. Little wonder that he too was caught in the web of theatricality. The preacher is not above the world; he plays his part with the rest of mankind.

5. The King's Poets

A troop of Echoes whose sweet duty
Was but to sing
In voices of surpassing beauty
The wit and wisdom of their King.

(Poe: *The Fall of the House of Usher*)

FROM far back many poets had been dependent on patrons, often royal patrons. The Valois kings, particularly François I, had seen the political value of attaching to their court poets, painters, and artists of all kinds, who better than anyone else could create and maintain a golden public image of the reign.[1] The poets were conscious of their power; Ronsard asserts to his masters as well as to his mistresses that he can dispense immortality. But if this power was flattering, the purse-strings which bound the poet to his patron were irksome. A theme of much sixteenth-century poetry is the opposition between true poetic existence and the corrupting influence of court life. Ronsard gives a subtle picture of the lot of the poet-courtier in his *Discours contre Fortune*, addressed to his patron, the Cardinal de Châtillon. In a poem which thanks Châtillon for favours received and asks for more, Ronsard nevertheless contrasts the state of poetic freedom with the sterility of the pensioned slave:

> Avant qu'aller chez vous, je vivais sans émoi,
> Maintenant par les bois, maintenant à part moi
> J'errais près des ruisseaux, maintenant par les prées
> J'allais, le nourrisson des neuf Muses sacrées.

But patronage, welcome as it is, changed all that. The poet learned to be ambitious; he began to covet benefices. The muses were amazed

> De me voir transformer d'un écolier content
> En nouveau courtisan, demandeur inconstant

---

[1] See M. M. McGowan, 'The French Court and its Poetry', in *French Literature and its Background*, ed. J. Cruickshank, vol. 1: *The Sixteenth Century*, London, 1968.

and

> Apollon, qui soulait m'agréer, me déplut,
> Et depuis mon esprit, comme il soulait, ne put
> Se ranger à l'étude, et ma plume fertile,
> Faute de l'exercer, se moisit inutile.[2]

This is a complaint which we hear made again and again in different ways over the following two centuries. By the eighteenth century it is tending to subside or at least change its character; the patron loses importance as the book-buying public grows. Even so, the relations between many of the *philosophes* and their royal or noble patrons are not very different from those which so irked the poets of the Pléiade. Always the protected man of letters oscillates between grateful flattery and impatient revolt. But the high point of royal protection—or dictatorship— was the reign of Louis XIV, in particular the early part of this reign, when Colbert used a system of pensions and gratifications to elicit from the poets selected by Chapelain a stream of pane- gyric for the King, when the Academy, now under Louis's direct protection, was seen by many of its members as an instrument for furthering the royal glory, and when architects, gardeners, painters, and sculptors were setting up in Versailles the eternal monument of the Sun King.[3]

It is hard now to imagine what such a system must have been like for the intelligent and sophisticated men whose lives were conditioned by it. It gave the docile writer a relatively important part to play and provided for him materially, but was it not full of difficulties for anyone with a spirit of independence? To judge from the writings which have survived, there is no doubt that not everyone found it easy to work in the official propaganda machine. Perhaps Chapelain, Cassagne, Boyer, and many of the *gratifiés* of 1663 were content with their role of official panegyrists (though this is only a conjecture), but some others, including those who have become our classics, were uneasily poised—or torn—between flattery and freedom. La Fontaine, faithful to the disgraced Fouquet and unpensioned in 1663, shows this not only

---

[2] Ronsard, *Œuvres*, ed. G. Cohen, Bibliothèque de la Pléiade, vol. II, pp. 401–2. See H. Weber, *La Création poétique au xviie siècle en France*, Paris, 1956, ch. 2.

[3] See P. France and M. M. McGowan, 'Louis XIV and the Arts', in *French Litera- ture and its Background*, ed. J. Cruickshank, vol. II: *The Seventeenth Century*, London, 1969.

in the contrast between his stance of carefree independence and his reiterated attempts to win official favour with all kinds of fawning verse, but also in his fables, which frequently display a singularly ambiguous attitude to the fox and the lion. And what is one to make of *Le Loup et le Chien*? Molière, much closer to Louis XIV, yet by nature, it seems, a free man, was caught in a similarly awkward position. He was grateful to Louis for his protection in the *Tartuffe* affair; he clearly enjoyed his role as royal entertainer; and yet this role was tiring, the court and the courtiers were in many ways distasteful, and Molière's genius was constrained by his privileged position. *Amphitryon* shows clearly, with the sort of liberty enjoyed by the court jester, how Molière steers his way between base flattery and dangerous disapproval.

The same problems and ambiguities reappear in an acute form in the work of the two friends who in 1677 were ordered to leave everything else and devote themselves to their new task as official historians of the reign of 'Louis le Grand'. These friends, also known as 'Messieurs du Sublime', were Boileau and Racine.

A. BOILEAU: *L'ami du vrai*

In 1704 Boileau's admirer Le Verrier wrote an emblem for a portrait of the old poet:

> Sans peine à la raison asservissant la rime,
> Et même en imitant toujours original,
> J'ai su dans mes écrits, docte, enjoué, sublime,
> Rassembler en moi Perse, Horace et Juvénal.[4]

Boileau was flattered but embarrassed. He liked the idea, thought the quatrain had more force in the first person than in the third (as Brossette had suggested), but did not like it to be supposed that he would address the public so complacently. In reply he composed an epigram:

> Oui, Le Verrier, c'est là mon fidèle portrait,
> Et l'on y voit, en chaque trait

---

[4] Boileau, *Œuvres complètes*, ed. F. Escal, Bibliothèque de la Pléiade, Paris, 1966, p. 272. References in the text are to this edition, which I cite in this section as *O.C.* The edition of C. H. Boudhors, Paris, Les Belles Lettres, 7 vols., 1934–43, is rather a thicket of erudition and is therefore less convenient than the Pléiade volume; it is, however, full of information and original insights and is an indispensable aid to an understanding of Boileau.

L'ennemi des Cotins tracé sur mon visage.
Mais dans les vers altiers, qu'au bas de cet ouvrage,
Trop enclin à me rehausser,
Sur un ton si pompeux tu me fais prononcer,
Qui de l'Ami du Vrai reconnaîtra l'image?

(O.C. 691)

If there is one theme which runs through Boileau's writing from beginning to end, this is it. If he is concerned to create an image of himself, it is that of the honest man, clumsy perhaps, but fearless, speaking out the truth to a world of corrupt courtiers, grasping financiers, crooked lawyers, casuistical Jesuits, and bad poets. Time and again the same expressions recur: 'je suis très sincère', 'je ne saurais flatter', 'un esprit né sans fard', 'la libre vérité fut toute mon étude', 'sa candeur seule a fait tous ses vices', 'un homme sans fard' . . .

In his early satires the 'jeune dogue' barks foolhardily at the corruptions and abuses of Paris. In the ninth epistle, using the myth of a golden age in almost the same way as Rousseau, he attacks the degenerate society of his day, ruled by money, luxury, and duplicity, where 'tout ne fut plus que fard, qu'erreur, que tromperie' (O.C. 136). At the end of his life, far from descending into any sort of senility, he remains on the offensive, but now, with the shadow of his hero Antoine Arnauld behind him, he attacks the arch-enemy of the truth, the casuist (O.C. 149–54). The target varies, but always the basic stance is the same: Boileau is the man who will not be taken in by appearances or bribed into flattery.

The champion of truth was also a lover of poetry, so it is natural that the defence of truth and the exposure of falsehood permeate his literary satire and literary criticism. Of course, falsehood may mean different things in poetry; for instance, there is the hypocritical poem which is written for money or advancement. Boileau, passed over in the distribution of royal largess in 1663, writes virulently about Chapelain and his team of hired panegyrists, widening his attack to include all the contemptible verse which is produced by a degrading system of patronage:

Je ne sais point en lâche essuyer les outrages
D'un faquin orgueilleux qui vous tient à ses gages,
De mes sonnets flatteurs lasser tout l'univers,

Et vendre au plus offrant mon encens et mes vers.
Pour un si bas emploi ma muse est trop altière.

(*O.C.* 14)

But quite apart from the sincerity of the poet, there is another sort
of falsehood in poetry, one which was particularly current in
Boileau's time, the falsehood of verbal inflation. Of this too
Boileau is a consistent enemy, ridiculing the 'fatras' of Brébeuf,
the extravagance of Balzac, or the grandiloquent opening of
Scudéry's epic *Alaric*:

Je chante le vainqueur des vainqueurs de la terre.

(*O.C.* 175)

Most frequently he brings the two together, mocking the hollow
verbosity of the official ode with its 'Alexandre', 'César', 'Mars',
'Alcide', 'Memphis', and 'Byzance' (*O.C.* 103). Boileau rejects
this 'Versailles' style as vehemently as he rejects the insincere
flourishes of what we should now call *précieux* poetry. His criteria
of sincerity and plain speaking are the same as those of Alceste in
the sonnet scene of *Le Misanthrope*, a scene which Boileau claimed
was modelled on his behaviour as a young man (*O.C.* 831).

It is by contrast with this sort of poetry that Boileau—like
Alceste—defines his own style. Not for him the lofty (and therefore false) language of a Scudéry; he is the plain man, calling a
spade a spade—or, as he puts it:

Je ne puis rien nommer, si ce n'est par son nom,
J'appelle un chat un chat, et Rolet un fripon.

(*O.C.* 14)

In practice this means the style conventionally associated with
satire, a style distinguished by a vigorous conversational tone and
a fairly 'low' vocabulary, rich in ridiculous proper names, names
of domestic objects, and other words not acceptable in the elevated
genres. The opening of Satire 6 is a typical example:

Qui frappe l'air, bon Dieu! de ces lugubres cris?
Est-ce donc pour veiller qu'on se couche à Paris?
Et quel fâcheux démon, durant des nuits entières,
Rassemble ici les chats de toutes les gouttières?
J'ai beau sauter du lit, plein de trouble et d'effroi,
Je pense qu'avec eux tout l'enfer est chez moi:
L'un miaule en grondant comme un tigre en furie,

L'autre roule sa voix comme un enfant qui crie.
Ce n'est pas tout encore, les souris et les rats
Semblent pour m'éveiller, s'entendre avec les chats,
Plus importuns pour moi, durant la nuit obscure,
Que jamais en plein jour, ne fut l'abbé de Pure.

(*O.C.* 34)

Not that this is wildly colloquial; seen from the distance of the twentieth century it is clearly a product of the *grand siècle*, but it distinguishes itself from the noble genres and declares itself as 'low' satire with its 'bon Dieu!', 'chats', 'gouttières', 'rats', 'abbé de Pure', and so on. There is exaggeration, but it is comic exaggeration, and not the heroic grandiloquence which is designed to deceive. And in all this Boileau is doing no more than use the traditional language of satire in the line of Régnier and his followers.

Satire and similar 'low' genres were kept distinct from the noble genres in the seventeenth century, but the same people read both. Thus satire gains much of its comic force from its implied insolence to its lofty relations. Parody and burlesque are naturally at their most effective at a time when the noble genres are defined and elevated by a series of linguistic prohibitions, which separate them from ordinary language, purify them, and by so doing render them particularly vulnerable to deflating imitation. The burlesque proper of Scarron, rewriting the classics in the language of the market-place, did not last very long, but it was only one manifestation of a tendency which was much more permanent. The 'faux brave' of the 1630s parodies the splendid eloquence of the heroic drama, Dorante the liar apes Rodrigue the Cid in his *récit*, the *Roman comique* and the *Roman bourgeois* mock the high romance of the ten-volume novels, Racine pokes fun at tragic rhetoric in *Les Plaideurs*. Naturally Boileau the satirist uses parody too.

It is true that in the *Art poétique*, influenced no doubt by the 'sublime' academy of Lamoignon, Boileau has nothing but scorn for Scarron's burlesque:

Imitons de Marot l'élégant badinage,
Et laissons le burlesque aux plaisants du Pont-Neuf.

(*O.C.* 159)[5]

---

[5] Note, however, that in the fourth canto of the *Art poétique* Boileau writes:

J'aime mieux Bergerac et sa burlesque audace
Que ces vers où Motin se morfond et nous glace.

But the reference to Marot suggests that the objection here is to the coarseness of the burlesque rather than to mocking parody as such. And reading his poems and his letters one becomes convinced that 'l'ami du vrai' was also very much a lover of parody. The two go quite well together, of course; parody is a form of linguistic criticism which only amuses, according to Boileau, if it is made quite clear that it is not to be taken seriously. As he puts it rather heavy-handedly in the *Dissertation sur Joconde*, 'le secret donc en contant une chose absurde est de s'énoncer d'une telle manière, que vous fassiez concevoir au lecteur, que vous ne croyez pas vous-même la chose que vous lui contez.' (*O.C.* 312.)

This sort of game with the truth is everywhere in Boileau's writing. Even in the heat of his defence of the Ancients he began a parody of Pindar to attack Perrault (*O.C.* 264). One of his most famous letters is the one addressed to the Duc de Vivonne (*O.C.* 776–80) in which he imagines himself to be successively Balzac and Voiture—Balzac, 'qui ne saurait dire simplement les choses', was a particularly frequent target of parodists in the seventeenth century. Boileau also helped to compose the *Chapelain décoiffé*, a take-off of *Le Cid* which was designed primarily to ridicule Colbert, Chapelain, Cassagne, and the long-suffering La Serre, but which incidentally poked fun at Corneille's noble verse.

These writings and many of Boileau's epigrams are described openly as parodies, but a similar deflation of the language of epic and tragedy is present in many of the Satires and Epistles. One typical pattern here is the abrupt descent from the sublime to the ridiculous, as we see it, for instance, at the beginning of the third satire:

> Quel sujet inconnu vous trouble et vous altère?
> D'où vous vient aujourd'hui cet air sombre et sévère,
> Et ce visage enfin plus pâle qu'un rentier
> A l'aspect d'un arrêt qui retranche un quartier?
>
> (*O.C.* 20)

This is a very obvious juxtaposition of two contrasting registers, and the comic effect is somewhat automatic. More subtly, there is a constant ironic resemblance between the verse patterns of Boileau's alexandrine and those of tragedy. To take one example among hundreds, the fifth epistle gives us a couplet:

> La famille en pâlit, et vit en frémissant
> Dans la poudre du greffe un poète naissant
>
> (*O.C.* 121)

where, in spite of the prosaic subject and vocabulary, the combination of the six-syllable opening and the more periphrastic eighteen syllables which follow it reminds one irresistibly of Racinian tragedy and such lines as

> La Judée en pâlit. Le triste Antiochus
> Se compta le premier au nombre des vaincus.
>
> (*Bérénice*, i. iv)

Indeed the resemblance here is so close that it looks as if actual textual parody was intended.

This game of imitation is seen at its best in *Le Lutrin*—indeed it is the main source of pleasure in *Le Lutrin*. An introductory note defines Boileau's aims: 'C'est un burlesque nouveau, dont je me suis avisé en notre langue: car, au lieu que dans l'autre burlesque, Didon et Énée parlaient comme des harengères et des crocheteurs, dans celui-ci une horlogère et un horloger parlent comme Didon et Énée.' (*O.C.* 1006.) So the language of the poem is predominantly noble, but is constantly undermined by the awareness that the actors and actions are insignificant. Many sequences are directly transposed from the ancient epics, but the implied reference is equally to the epic or the tragedy of Boileau's contemporaries.[6] This is particularly apparent in some of the dialogue; for instance, in the fourth canto there is a speech from protagonist to confidant which is very close in over-all construction and stylistic detail to many tirades of Thomas Corneille or Racine. The *chantre* has found that his rival has had a huge lectern installed in his place:

> La voilà donc, Girot, cette hydre épouvantable
> Que m'a fait voir un songe, hélas! trop véritable.
> Je le vois, ce dragon tout prêt à m'égorger,
> Ce pupitre fatal qui me doit ombrager.
> Prélat, que t'ai-je fait? quelle rage envieuse   5
> Rend pour me tourmenter ton âme ingénieuse?

---

[6] In later editions Boileau omitted some of the most exaggerated parody from his second canto (see *O.C.* 1011–12.)

Quoi! même dans ton lit, cruel, entre deux draps,
Ta profane fureur ne se repose pas!
O ciel! quoi! sur mon banc une honteuse masse
Désormais me va faire un cachot de ma place!   10
Inconnu dans l'église, ignoré dans ce lieu,
Je ne pourrai donc plus être vu que de Dieu!
Ah! plutôt qu'un moment cet affront m'obscurcisse,
Renonçons à l'autel, abandonnons l'office;
Et, sans lasser le ciel par des chants superflus,   15
Ne voyons plus un chœur où l'on ne nous voit plus.
Sortons . . . Mais cependant mon ennemi tranquille
Jouira sur son banc de ma rage inutile,
Et verra dans le chœur le pupitre exhaussé
Tourner sur le pivot où sa main l'a placé!   20
Non, s'il n'est abattu, je ne saurais plus vivre.
A moi, Girot, je veux que mon bras m'en délivre.
Périssons, s'il le faut; mais de ses ais brisés
Entraînons, en mourant, les restes divisés.

                                    (*O.C.* 207–8)

There is no need to look for textual reminiscences in order to feel
the closeness to tragic rhetoric. To take just one or two examples:
the first couplet echoes the awareness of crisis which opens many
tragedies, the confidant's name being placed conventionally at
the caesura; the words 'hydre' and 'dragon' are obviously exaggerated, but the dream was a standby of contemporary tragedy;
the fifth and sixth lines give us the typical apostrophe and again
the impressive division of the couplet after the first hemistich; the
eighth line has a noble metonymy, followed in the next line by
an equally noble periphrasis ('une honteuse masse'); line 11
seems to echo many beautiful 'hanging' appositions of Racinian
tragedy; line 14 is a splendid piece of symmetry, and lines 13–16
as a whole are a standard tragic quatrain hinging on the 'et' of
line 15; the gathering speed of the speech is broken in mid-line
(line 17) as are so many tragic monologues of irresolution; and
the speech comes to a fine dramatic conclusion with the 'non' of
line 21 and the two imperatives of the final couplet. All along there
are the noble words of tragedy ('épouvantable', 'trop véritable',
'fatal', etc.), often combining in the standard rhymes of the noble
genres, but the presence of words such as 'Girot', 'pupitre', 'draps',
'banc', 'office', 'pivot', and 'ais' pulls against them—and from
this tension comes the comic pleasure.

Parody, then; but as we read it, we may well wonder if the description of parody given earlier is adequate. Is this really the parody of a truth-teller who is anxious to expose the frauds of poetic diction? Is it not rather the affectionate pastiche, the homage of the satirist to those who, like Racine, were able to write wholeheartedly and successfully in the vulnerable noble genres? Could there be in the satirist and parodist a heroic writer trying to get out?

Certainly, if we look at it chronologically, we can see Boileau gradually extending his range beyond the limits of satire. Perhaps he was naturally inclined towards a loftier style; he himself admits that as a young man he admired the high romance of *Le Grand Cyrus* (*O.C.* 445). And already in his Satires his style had been criticized by Cotin as too pompous for the genre. Not that Cotin saw in Boileau a sublime poet who was out of place in satire; in his *Critique désintéressée* Boileau appears rather as the envious satirist who for all his efforts will never make a true poet:

O petit Phaéton de la Cour du Palais, ne pensez pas monter sur le char d'Apollon pour avoir fait six satires en toute votre vie: la tête vous pourrait tourner. Ne présumez pas ridiculement de vos forces; n'enviez point à nos poètes épiques, à nos poètes lyriques, à nos poètes tragiques une gloire où vous n'arriverez jamais, tant que vous ne ferez que des satires.[7]

This sort of criticism was to continue throughout Boileau's life, reappearing, for instance, in 1694 in Perrault's remarks on the *Ode sur la prise de Namur*.[8] Small wonder if Boileau sometimes felt inclined to show his powers in fields more exalted than satire.

At the same time the imprudent satirist who had been making trouble for himself by his outspokenness was taken in hand towards 1670 by a number of powerful well-wishers. They admired his talent, but wanted to redirect it. Boileau was encouraged to write more respectably and cautiously—and so in about 1670 he made the transition (not a very great one) from satire to epistle. In particular, he came under the influence of the Président de Lamoignon and was an early member of the private academy which met at Lamoignon's house from 1667 on.[9] Now some

[7] C. Cotin, *La Critique désintéressée sur les satires du temps*, Paris, 1666, pp. 55–6. On Boileau's critics and enemies see E. Magne, *Bibliographie générale de Boileau*, Paris, 1929, vol. II.   [8] See Boileau, *Odes*, ed. Boudhors, pp. 120–2.

[9] On Boileau and the Académie de Lamoignon see A. Adam, *Histoire de la littérature française au XVIIe siècle*, vol. III (Paris, 1952), pp. 113–43, and F. Gaquère, *La Vie et les œuvres de Claude Fleury*, Paris, 1925.

of the thirty-odd members of this group had ideas about poetry
which were noticeably different from many contemporary notions
of elegance and moderation. Among them were Rapin, the Jesuit
father, who later wrote a brief essay on the Sublime, Bossuet,
who talked to the Academy on the high eloquence of the Bible,
and the young Claude Fleury, who defended the noble simplicity
of the Greeks and was later to write on the sublimity of Hebrew
poetry. In spite of some differences of emphasis (Rapin was
considerably less radical in his views than the other two), these
three, and probably other members of the Academy, shared a
common ideal of poetry, an ideal modelled largely on the Bible
and Greek poetry; they praised simplicity and truth to nature and
sought a kind of poetry which would be not just pleasing but
forceful and sublime. This atmosphere can only have encouraged
Boileau in his pursuit of what became widely known as the Sublime. The word owed much of its popularity to the fact that in
1674 Boileau presented to the French public a translation of Longinus' *On the Sublime*,[10] in which he not only translates and introduces the standard work on the subject, but also tries his hand at
heroic or sublime poetry in his translation of excerpts of Greek
poetry which illustrate the treatise. In the same year Boileau also
published his *Art poétique*, which put forward in a diluted form
some of the ideas current in the Lamoignon group. Before long
he and Racine were so much associated with the notion as to be
nicknamed 'Messieurs du Sublime'.

What is the Sublime? In his twelfth *Réflexion* Boileau gives an
example of it, the quatrain from *Athalie* beginning:

> Celui qui met un frein à la fureur des flots

and hazards a definition:

Le Sublime est une certaine force de discours, propre à élever et à
ravir l'âme, et qui provient ou de la grandeur de la pensée et de la
noblesse du sentiment, ou de la magnificence des paroles, ou du tour
harmonieux, vif et animé de l'expression; c'est-à-dire d'une de ces
choses regardées séparément, ou, ce qui fait le parfait Sublime, de ces
trois choses jointes ensemble. (*O.C.* 562-3)

This definition can be expanded by reading Longinus' treaty and
Boileau's various critical writings. The Sublime can eventually

[10] See the excellent work of J. Brody, *Boileau and Longinus*, Geneva, 1958. In what
follows I refer for brevity's sake to Longinus, even though it is now known that
he was not in fact the author of *On the Sublime*.

only be defined by its effect—either you feel it or you don't—
and in this it has affinities with that other dark horse of classical
criticism, the *je ne sais quoi*. But Boileau and Longinus are too conscientious to leave it at that; they suggest ways in which it can
be achieved. Some of these, such as 'une certaine élévation dans
l'esprit', are given by nature, but others, such as 'les figures
tournées d'une certaine manière' (e.g. apostrophe, periphrasis)
and 'la noblesse de l'expression', are much closer to the recipes of
traditional rhetoric. And here we come to the most difficult
point—what is the difference between the Sublime and the 'style
sublime' of the rhetoricians?

It is a point which worried Boileau and he is very careful to
distinguish between the two. The 'style sublime', he says, 'veut
toujours de grands mots'; thus 'Le souverain arbitre de la nature
d'une seule parole forma la lumière' is in the 'style sublime' but
it is not Sublime, merely grandiloquent. The true Sublime in this
case is simple: 'Dieu dit: Que la lumière se fasse; et la lumière se
fit' (*O.C.* 338). The distinction is a vital one for Boileau, since he
must make it clear that the Sublime has nothing to do with the
inflated style which he criticizes or parodies so ruthlessly. And
fortunately Longinus has a chapter devoted to the 'style enflé',
giving such examples as 'le Jupiter des Perses' (Xerxes) or 'des
sépulcres animés' (vultures) (*O.C.* 343).[11] He concludes: 'Il est
certain que l'enflure n'est pas moins vicieuse dans les discours que
dans les corps. Elle n'a que de faux dehors et une apparence
trompeuse; mais au-dedans elle est creuse.' (*O.C.* 344.) The
swollen style is false, but the Sublime is compatible with the truth.

And yet . . . it is not as easy as all that. Longinus told Boileau
what Boileau no doubt knew well enough: 'Le grand, de soi-
même et par sa propre grandeur, est glissant et dangereux' (*O.C.*
386). And we notice, for instance, that the two examples of the
swollen style which I have just quoted are periphrases—yet the
periphrasis is one of the ways to the Sublime. The Sublime is not
always simple—far from it. It may often call for the sort of
language which ennobles; 's'il eût dit la chose simplement', says
Longinus of Demosthenes, 'son discours n'eût point répondu à
la majesté de l'affaire dont il parlait' (*O.C.* 371). In this Longinus
lends support to the amplifying tendency of seventeenth-century

---

[11] Brody points out (op. cit., pp. 92–5) that Boileau adds to his original here, so as
to intensify his attack on the swollen style.

French rhetoric, and Boileau, for all his championing of the plain truth, clearly regards amplification as essential to poetry. To take just one example, he is a great lover of the dignified periphrasis; he explains to Maucroix: 'Plus les choses sont sèches et malaisées à dire en vers, plus elles frappent quand elles sont dites noblement et avec cette élégance qui fait proprement la poésie.' (O.C. 796.) And it is clear that the battle of the Ancients and Moderns led him to exaggerate this position, vaunting his hyperboles, metaphors, and metonymies ('grands mots que Pradon croit des termes de chimie' (O.C. 142). He even comes to say kind things about Balzac, 'car quoique ses beautés soient vicieuses, ce sont néanmoins des beautés, au lieu que la plupart des auteurs de ce temps pèchent moins par avoir des défauts que par n'avoir rien de bon.' (O.C. 644-5.) For a lover of the truth, Boileau was on a slippery path here.

And of course he knew it. He might sing the praises of the Sublime—backed up by Longinus—and he might defend Pindar against Perrault, but very rarely does he unequivocally practise what he preaches. There are, it is true, the fragments of heroic poetry translated in his Longinus (but does translation really commit him to the heroic posture?), and there is the Namur ode (but is this more than a faintly satirical skirmish in his battle with Perrault?).[12] Otherwise Boileau the poet carries within himself a critic. He is too embarrassed to allow himself a whole-hearted sublimity. In letters to Brossette and others he often says that he can go through the motions of worldly ceremony as well as the next man, but you will very rarely catch him taking himself seriously in this vein. If he pulls out the stops of eloquence, it is to thank Brossette for some cheeses—and he calls in Balzac again to help him:

Il vous eût dit que ces fromages avaient été faits du lait de la chèvre céleste ou de celui de la vache Io. Que votre jambon était un membre détaché du sanglier d'Érimanthe. Mais pour moi, qui vais un peu plus terre à terre, vous trouverez bon que je me contente de vous dire que vous vous moquez de m'envoyer tant de choses à la fois. (O.C. 669)

Boileau obviously gains equal pleasure from playing the games of hyperbole and from returning to his solid ground of plain speaking.

[12] Not only does the *Ode* end with the words 'l'auteur du *Saint Paulin*' (Perrault), but it also originally included a stanza openly satirizing Perrault (see O.C. 1023).

The same is true of his poems. I have already examined the
mock-heroic of *Le Lutrin*, which allows Boileau to play with the
forms he will not use seriously, letting them grow and charm his
audience, then destroying them with a 'pupitre' or a 'perruquier'.
The last canto of *Le Lutrin* shows us Boileau's other characteristic
stance. After five mock-heroic cantos he brings his epic round to
a totally serious conclusion, using the allegorical figures of
Justice and Piety to deplore abuses in the Church and the mania
for litigation. This in its turn leads to a full-scale panegyric of
the Président de Lamoignon, who had probably given Boileau
the first idea of *Le Lutrin*. But suddenly Boileau breaks off
(having already praised Lamoignon handsomely), declaring that
he can go no further, that his muse will not rise to describe
the exploits of his protector. And the whole poem finishes
not on a triumphal conclusion, but on an evocation of the
embarrassment of the inexperienced orator, petering out into
silence:

> Il hésite, il bégaie; et le triste orateur
> Demeure enfin muet aux yeux du spectateur.
>
> (*O.C.* 222)

This sort of self-conscious movement is frequent in Boileau's
satires and epistles. We see the poet (or sometimes it is an
imagined listener) watching himself write or listening to himself
talk, smiling ironically and interrupting himself as he launches on
an over-eloquent tirade. And it is this self-consciousness and self-
criticism, this presentation of the actual process of composition,
which gives much of their liveliness and appeal to many of the
epistles—the epistle being traditionally a familiar discourse which
lets us into the poet's secrets. Instead of being asked to admire
the finished piece (for this would be courting disaster), we are
invited by the apparently more modest writer to share in the
difficulties of his profession. Often the real subject of Boileau's
poetry turns out to be poetry. The eleventh epistle, for instance,
presented as if it were spoken to Antoine the gardener, gives us
an ironical yet serious meditation on the problems and rewards of
the poet, self-depreciating in the manner of Montaigne when he
writes about his own essays, but also self-satisfied—like Montaigne
—and ending with the typical self-mocking interruption of a
pastiche sermon:

Je te vais sur cela prouver deux vérités:
L'une, que le travail, aux hommes nécessaire,
Fait leur félicité plutôt que leur misère;
Et l'autre, qu'il n'est point de coupable en repos.
C'est ce qu'il faut ici montrer en peu de mots.
Suis-moi donc. Mais je vois, sur ce début de prône,
Que ta bouche déjà s'ouvre large d'une aune,
Et que, les yeux fermés, tu baisses le menton.
Ma foi, le plus sûr est de finir ce sermon.

(O.C. 147–8)

Thus Boileau weaves his way between eloquence and down-to-earth truthfulness, disarming his potential critic (he hopes) by the constant use of parody and by the introduction into his poems of the ironical poet. He has strong views on many matters, but equally strongly the critic in him prevents him from exposing himself or his beliefs to ridicule by an over-emphatic presentation. Even in the eloquent twelfth epistle, *Sur l'amour de Dieu*, the earnestness of the pleading is shielded, if not by parody, then at least by the self-awareness which leads Boileau to foresee objections concerning his competence to discuss theological matters, and to introduce his concluding section as a 'figure bizarre'. Not for him the 'fougue insensée' of the naïve poet.

Now there was one field above all others in which the over-emphatic was the rule of the game; this was the official poetry of panegyric. We have seen that Boileau, whether out of envy or good sense, ridiculed the mercenary odes which Colbert and Chapelain elicited by the pensions of 1663. But ten years later things had changed. By what he calls 'un coup du sort' Boileau had begun the sharp rise in the world which was to lead him in 1677 to consent to wear the golden chain of historiographer-royal, a post which forced him—against his will, it seems—to abandon the writing of poetry so as to assimilate 'le pénible volume' of Louis XIV's exploits.[13] This poetic silence was only broken—apart from some official trifles—after Boileau's virtual retirement from the court in 1690. Yet, even if this forced silence was as much a burden as an honour, it must be said that Boileau

---

[13] See the eighth epistle. Boileau's dying message to the King was, according to Valincour, 'qu'il était très fâché de ce que lui et M. Racine avaient été chargés d'un travail si contraire à leur génie, qui n'était que pour les vers' (see Boileau, *Satires*, ed. Boudhors, p. xiii and *passim*).

had asked for it. Looking at the poems written before 1677, we find praise of Louis in the fourth book of the *Art poétique*, in two Homeric comparisons in *Le Lutrin*, and in virtually all the epistles and satires. Indeed, Boileau later described his satires as 'étant toutes pleines des louanges du roi, et ces louanges même en faisant le plus bel ornement' (*O.C.* 495). And praise of the King is the central subject of the *Discours au Roi* and of the first, fourth, and eighth epistles. How did 'l'ami du vrai' manage to live and write as a courtier?

It would help if we knew what Boileau's real feelings were towards Louis and his regime, but these are often so well disguised that it is impossible to be certain. But we do know, at a rather anecdotal level, that he was vigorously opposed to Colbert between 1663 and 1668; the original *Chapelain décoiffé* was probably directed almost as much against Colbert as against Chapelain.[14] We know too that he remained throughout his life hostile to wars of conquest; he regularly referred to Alexander the Great as a madman,[15] whereas Racine used him as a flattering image of Louis—it is therefore all the more interesting to find Boileau describing himself in the eleventh epistle as the 'chroniqueur des gestes d'Alexandre' (*O.C.* 145). This attitude is naturally more marked in Boileau's last years, when he could write to Brossette: 'j'ai bien peur que les trois quarts du royaume ne s'en aillent à l'hôpital couronnés de lauriers.' (*O.C.* 688.) Moreover, he gave unfailing support to Arnauld and thus implicitly to the Jansenist cause. This may well have been read as a gesture of opposition, particularly towards the end of his life, when his polemic with the Jesuits led the King to withdraw the privilege for the twelfth satire. And Boileau said nothing about the Revocation of the Edict of Nantes, when others were applauding.

These, then, are some signs of hostility towards the regime, but we cannot conclude from them that Boileau was opposed to Louis XIV personally, particularly in the period of his worldly success. It is reasonable to suppose that Boileau was pleased—as he often declared himself to be—at being appreciated by a king who had, after all, enormous prestige. Apparently he admired the élite which he places alongside the people and the provinces as the audience

[14] On Boileau's early years and his reputation as a 'mal pensant' see A. Adam, *Histoire de la littérature française au XVIIe siècle*, vol. III, pp. 49–113.
[15] See in particular Satire VIII (*O.C.* 43).

that he and Racine aim to please: the King, Condé, Enghien, Colbert, Vivonne, La Rochefoucauld, Marsillac, Pomponne—or perhaps he was simply glad to be able to quote these big names among his protectors, particularly in the crisis of 1677 (*O.C.* 129). It is impossible to say for certain.

We can, however, say for certain what Boileau did not like, and that is the formality of court life, with its demands of vigilance, tact, hypocrisy, and flattery—the life La Bruyère describes for us. Pradon thought it was clever to taunt Boileau with this:

> Dans ces palais dorés que tu figures mal!
> Crois-moi, tu n'es pas là dans ton pays natal[16]

but Boileau was doubtless happy to agree and vastly relieved, it seems, to retire to his so-called solitude of Auteuil (Racine called it his 'hôtellerie', for Boileau was no misanthrope). Not that he was incapable of going through the motions of court life; by 1677 he had repressed a good deal of the abrupt frankness of his early years and could coin some of the typical courtier's *mots* which he—or rather Longinus—ridicules in the *Traité du sublime*. Thus, in a linguistic argument with the King, he remarked: 'Cela est assez beau que de toute l'Europe je sois le seul qui résiste à votre Majesté'—'cela fit assez agréablement ma cour,' he later remarked to Brossette (*O.C.* 705). But he was never really at home at court and was glad to rely on Racine's superior skill, asking his colleague to look over letters to the King and Madame de Maintenon. And in his letters to Racine, particularly the series written from Bourbon in 1687, it is impossible to miss the irony in his voice as he apes the courtier: 'Pour moi je suis persuadé qu'il fait bon suivre ses ordonnances en fait même de médecine . . . Un prince qui a exécuté tant de choses miraculeuses est vraisemblablement inspiré du Ciel et toutes les choses qu'il dit sont des oracles'—and then the return to reality: 'Cependant je vous dirai que je suis aussi muet que jamais.' (*O.C.* 744.) No doubt he was flattered at Louis's interest in his health, but this was not enough to extinguish his critical sense.

The ambiguity of this letter is close to the ambiguity of Boileau's court poetry. The self-consciousness and parody of which I spoke earlier permeate his praise of Louis. Moreover, this is done deliberately, for Boileau, coming to court with his reputation

[16] Boileau, *Satires*, ed. Boudhors, p. xxxi.

of plain, blunt satirist and truth-teller, puts this reputation to advantage and develops his own form of flattery, the flattery which either rejects or mocks the more obviously insincere forms in the name of the unadorned yet splendid truth and which centres on an evocation of the pitfalls of the panegyric. This is developed theoretically in so far as official historiography is concerned in the *Remerciement à l'Académie française*. Here Boileau seeks to outflank the critics who had said that poets, being used to adornment and amplification, were not suitable as historians. He admits the principle, but argues that on the contrary he has been chosen precisely because of his reputation for honesty:

Il n'a pas trouvé mauvais qu'au milieu de tant d'écrivains célèbres qui s'apprêtent à l'envi à peindre ses actions dans tout leur éclat, et avec tous les ornements de l'éloquence la plus sublime, un homme sans fard, et accusé plutôt de trop de sincérité que de flatterie, contribuât de son travail et de ses conseils à bien mettre en jour, et dans toute la naïveté du style le plus simple, la vérité de ces actions, qui étant si peu vraisemblables d'elles-mêmes, ont bien plus besoin d'être fidèlement écrites que fortement exprimées.   (*O.C.* 608)

It will be seen that the 'homme sans fard' nevertheless manages to say the right thing; the second part of the speech goes on to give a glowing picture of Louis's reign.

But the theory had been worked out well before this, notably in the first epistle, which ends with ten lines saying exactly the same thing as the *Remerciement*, and in the ninth epistle (1675), where Boileau distinguishes between 'la louange adroite et délicate' and 'le plus grossier éloge'. The ninth epistle is ostensibly written in praise of truthfulness, but once again the notion is not entirely free of ambiguity; could it be that Boileau is simply trying to use his reputation to best advantage? It is here that we meet the famous line:

> Rien n'est beau que le vrai; le vrai seul est aimable
> (*O.C.* 134)

but in a context which casts a rather peculiar light on it, since the epistle manages to suggest that Colbert, Condé, and Seignelay are too intelligent to be taken in by flattery, while at the same time praising them (and the King) quite fulsomely. The dubious sincerity of the truth-teller is particularly evident in the praise of

Boileau's former enemy Colbert and his 'amour pour les beaux-arts'.

In this poem, then, the appeal is largely to the intelligence of the patron; he is invited to show his superiority by not taking himself too seriously, by sharing in the poet's amusement at the excessive solemnity of conventional forms of address. A recurring feature of Boileau's letters to his social superiors (e.g. Vivonne, Luxembourg, Guilleragues, Pontchartrain, Revel) is the challenge not to stand on their dignity: 'Je savais assez bien de quel air il fallait écrire à Mgr de Vivonne général des galères de France; mais oserait-on se familiariser de même avec le libérateur de Messine, le vainqueur de Ruyter, le destructeur de la flotte espagnole? Seriez-vous le premier héros qu'une extrême prospérité ne pût enorgueillir?' In this way Boileau combines familiarity and flattery—and incidentally preserves some of his own dignity. With Louis too he seems to be trying to set up a relationship which is half that between friends and half that between king and courtier—or even king and court jester. Exactly as in *L'Impromptu de Versailles* Louis is offered the superior pleasure of seeing the artist at work, sharing his difficulties, and laughing with him at his rivals. The pattern recurs in several poems; it is perhaps seen at its clearest in the fourth epistle, addressed to the King and celebrating what was called by Charpentier 'le merveilleux passage du Rhin' and by Boileau simply 'le passage du Rhin'.

The poem (*O.C.* 113–17) was originally preceded by a note 'au lecteur' which sets the tone.[17] Boileau cannot guarantee the detailed accuracy of his description, 'parce que franchement je n'y étais pas'; all he can be certain of, he says ironically, is the 'histoire du fleuve en colère que j'ai apprise d'une de ses naïades'. Even before we start reading we are on our guard. The poem itself begins with a page of oratorical precautions on Boileau's constant theme, the difficulty, for him personally, of writing heroic panegyric. This is perhaps in part a genuine apology, but it is also an opportunity for amusing Louis with a picture of the poet wrestling with the difficulty of fitting the Dutch conquests into alexandrines—a quite false difficulty, since Boileau obviously enjoys writing couplets like:

> Comment en vers heureux assiéger Doesbourg,
> Zutphen, Wageninghen, Harderwic, Knotzembourg?

[17] Boileau, *Épîtres*, ed. Boudhors, pp. 76–7.

This comic concentration on the unfortunate poet does not, however, distract Boileau from the business of flattery; indeed it is no
more than a development of the typical courtier's *bon mot*:

> Ce pays, où cent murs n'ont pu te résister,
> Grand roi, n'est pas en vers si facile à dompter.

This is, incidentally, exactly the sort of flattery which Longinus
ridicules in Isocrates.

Then comes the appeal to truth, but this time inverted, so as to
prepare the reader for what is essentially a parody:

> Muses, pour le tracer, cherchez tous vos crayons:
> Car, puisqu'en cet exploit tout paraît incroyable,
> Que la vérité pure y ressemble à la fable,
> De tous vos ornements vous pouvez l'égayer.

(It is instructive to compare this with the passage quoted from the
Remerciement à l'Académie.) And finally, before launching on the
heroic narration, Boileau takes a backhand swing at all the poet-
flatterers whom he has ridiculed in his *Discours au Roi* and his
first epistle:

> Vous savez des grands vers les disgrâces tragiques,
> Et souvent on ennuie en termes magnifiques.

All this warns us sufficiently what we are to expect.

As in an epic, the narration begins not with the actual protagonists, but with the mythological machinery, introduced in
a blandly flowing period like those of La Fontaine's *Adonis*. The
effect is immediately one of falsehood and pastiche—as some of
Boileau's critics pointed out. Thus Desmarets de Saint-Sorlin:

> Et quand du Dieu du Rhin l'on feint la fière image
> S'opposant en fureur à ton fameux passage,
> On ternit par le faux la pure vérité.[18]

[18] Dedication of the second edition of *Clovis*, quoted by Magne, *Bibliographie
générale*, vol. II, pp. 161–2. Magne also analyses Lignières's attack on the fourth
epistle.
  There is a passage in the *Mercure Galant* (vol. III, pp. 29–37) which appears to be
a mockery of Boileau's epistle, and not, as Adam suggests, a source of inspiration,
since the epistle first appeared in August 1672 and the number of the *Mercure* is dated
1673. Boileau may have been perfunctory, but not to the extent of borrowing
Donneau de Visé's jokes. Adam is inclined to think that Boileau's perfunctoriness
indicates 'une faiblesse d'inspiration qui ne réussit pas à s'élever sans effort et à se
maintenir à une certaine hauteur de ton' (*Histoire*, vol. III, pp. 121–2). Perhaps, but

It was for this sort of reason that people had doubts about
Boileau's appointment as royal historian. The impression of
pastiche grows as the poem progresses and sometimes reaches
almost burlesque proportions:

> Le Rhin tremble et frémit à ces tristes nouvelles,
> Le feu sort à travers ses humides prunelles . . .
> A ces mots essuyant sa barbe limoneuse,
> Il prend d'un vieux guerrier la figure poudreuse.

Before long 'le fameux fort de Skink' makes its appearance; fore-
warned by Boileau's preamble, we are not likely to pronounce
this name with proper solemnity. And so it goes on; Louis is
compared to Jupiter, as Xerxes had been in Longinus' 'style enflé',
and 'Mars et Bellone' accompany Gramont, as they might have
done in the poems mocked in the first epistle. Nor is this all; there
are many actual echoes of the noble style of Chapelain, Corneille,
and Brébeuf, borrowings which were immediately denounced by
Boileau's critics.

In all this Boileau is either perfunctory and unintelligent, or
else he is inviting the intelligent reader to enjoy his own amusement at the expense of the poetry of official occasions. And surely
it must be the latter, for suddenly, apparently vastly relieved,
Boileau breaks the flow, just as he does at the end of *Le Lutrin*:

> Du fleuve ainsi dompté la déroute éclatante
> A Wurts jusqu'en son camp va porter l'épouvante.
> Wurts, l'espoir du pays, et l'appui de ses murs;
> Wurts... Ah! quel nom, grand roi, quel Hector que ce Wurts!
> Sans ce terrible nom, mal né pour les oreilles,
> Que j'allais à tes yeux étaler de merveilles!

The repetition of the proper name shows Boileau amusing himself
with the idiocy of his position and inviting the King to join him.

And so he is ready for his peroration, which takes us back to the
themes of the preamble. If only Louis would conquer Asia there
would be some good linguistic material for the official poet, says
Boileau. And indeed he is sure he will conquer Asia:

> Puisqu'ainsi dans deux mois tu prends quarante villes,
> Assuré des beaux vers dont ton bras me répond,
> Je t'attends dans deux ans aux bords de l'Hellespont.

might this not be to Boileau's credit? See the comment of Boudhors on this and
similar poems in his edition of Boileau's works.

Now this could be taken for the most vulgar flattery of the sort which Boileau had often ridiculed, for instance, at the beginning of the first epistle. This is presumably how Bussy-Rabutin took it, if it is true, as a letter of the Comte de Limoges suggests, that he rhymed 'Tarare-pon-pon' with 'Hellespont'.[19] But in the context of the poem, and bearing in mind Boileau's unchanging feelings about wars of conquest, it seems rather to be a hyperbolic pirouette, which no intelligent reader could take seriously. Here, as throughout the poem, Boileau appears to combine flattering allusions and the even more flattering insinuation that the King is above flattery.

But of course it could be taken for insolence. Boileau's critics immediately seized on the 'turlupinades' of the epistle, as they seized on much else in his writing, to portray him as the eternal satirist, incapable of genuine praise and now discrediting not just Chapelain but the King himself. It is by no means certain that Louis could take this sort of joke. Although he is reported as reproaching Racine with excessive flattery in his Academic Discourse of 1685, the King could be quite prickly, if praise was not fulsome enough. At any rate, Boileau remarks to Racine in a letter of 1693: 'vous n'ignorez pas combien notre maître est chatouilleux sur les gens qu'on associe à ses louanges.' (O.C. 765.) Certainly the history of the first epistle makes one doubt the success of Boileau's technique. He had concluded the original version of this poem with the fable of the oyster, thinking that this would 'délasser agréablement l'esprit des lecteurs qu'un sublime trop sérieux peut enfin fatiguer',[20] but Boileau was advised by his protectors to cut out the fable and put in its place a fawning passage on Louis's patronage of the arts (and we know what Boileau thought of the patronage system before 1670).

So perhaps Louis was not amused. However this may be, it is certainly possible to see in the ambiguities of Boileau's official poetry not so much a subtle flattery as a disguise under which the unrepentant 'ami du vrai' could preserve a sort of independence. More than this, it may have allowed him to imply a certain amount of unwelcome criticism; the jokes and the panegyric of the first epistle are the sugar on the pill of an anti-war argument. That parody was a shield is certainly apparent in such official writing

[19] Bussy-Rabutin, *Correspondance*, ed. Lalanne, Paris, 1858–9, vol. II, p. 246.
[20] *Épîtres*, ed. Boudhors, p. 75.

as the operatic fragment which Boileau was obliged to write and
probably in the pompous little inscription which he composed
for a bust of the King:

> C'est ce roi si fameux dans la paix, dans la guerre,
> Qui seul fait à son gré le destin de la terre.
> Tout reconnaît ses lois, ou brigue son appui.
> De ses nombreux combats le Rhin frémit encore;
> Et l'Europe en cent lieux a vu fuir devant lui
> Tous ces héros si fiers, que l'on voit aujourd'hui
> Faire fuir l'Ottoman au-delà du Bosphore.
>
> (*O.C.* 259)

And what are we to make of this Homeric comparison, where the
warlike Louis makes his unexpected appearance in the middle of
the burlesque heroics of *Le Lutrin*?

> Ainsi, lorsque tout prêt à briser cent murailles,
> Louis, la foudre en main, abandonnant Versailles,
> Au retour du soleil et des zéphirs nouveaux,
> Fait dans les champs de Mars déployer ses drapeaux;
> Au seul bruit répandu de sa marche étonnante,
> Le Danube s'émeut, le Tage s'épouvante,
> Bruxelle attend le coup qui la doit foudroyer,
> Et le Batave encore est prêt à se noyer.
> Mais en vain dans leurs lits un juste effroi les presse . . .
>
> (*O.O.* 209)

It is hard to weigh up the likely impact of such passages on a
contemporary audience, who read Boileau with less reverence and
a greater attention to hidden meanings than the subsequent
generations which swallowed the bait of 'Rien n'est beau que le
vrai'. I think that one can at least see here, as in all Boileau's sublime or official poetry, a heavy dose of mocking ambiguity.

Eventually, having kept up his defences more or less effectively,
Boileau became a free man again. Unlike Racine, who for all his
radical pessimism about courts and kings remained a prisoner in
that world to the end, Boileau came into it half against his will,
played the game, succeeded, and then drifted away again, protected by his deafness. In such poems as the twelfth epistle we see
again the candour of the early Boileau—and this time without any
parody. And it is interesting to reflect that his very last poem, the
twelfth satire, is devoted to an attack on 'l'équivoque'. The centre

of this poem is an exposure of the casuistical doctrine of the Jesuits, but the ripples spread to cover all sorts of 'discours imposteurs', which Boileau castigates as of old. In 1694 he had written to Arnauld that he could not bring himself to praise Perrault, but that his Jesuit friends might show him 'des moyens pour dire de bouche sans blesser la vérité que j'estime ce que je n'estime pas' (*O.C.* 793). And yet had not Boileau been guilty of just this sort of Jesuitical equivocation in his court poetry? Although he proclaims to equivocation:

> Tu sais bien que jamais chez toi, dans mes discours,
> Je n'ai d'un faux brillant emprunté le secours
>
> (*O.C.* 91)

we know that this is not strictly true, even if Boileau guarded himself with mocking parody.

Finally one wonders how much the satire on equivocation expressed Boileau's own regret at being forced into a sort of falsehood which his moral sense must have rebelled against. One remembers the strong words he had translated in Longinus' treatise: 'Mais nous, qui avons appris dès nos premières années à souffrir le joug d'une domination légitime . . . ce qui arrive ordinairement de nous, c'est que nous nous rendons de grands et magnifiques flatteurs.' (*O.C.* 400.) Perhaps Boileau would have been happier in a free republic. But it is far from certain that he would have been a better poet. For I think it is clear that, at any rate in such poems as the fourth epistle and *Le Lutrin*, the reader's pleasure comes from the juxtaposition of two registers, the noble inflation of heroic and royal poetry and the deflating awareness of the truth. Of course, there is more to Boileau than this; he was quite genuinely in his life and in many of his poems 'l'ami du vrai', and one admires the vigorous eloquence of such poems as the first satire and the twelfth epistle. But if Boileau is good to read, it is also because of his inevitable compromises and his awareness of the pitfalls of eloquence, the power of parody, and the fragility of the Sublime.

B. RACINE: *le savant de la cour*

If Boileau stumbled somewhat incompetently through court life, making of his incompetence the basis of a second-degree flattery and the starting-point for some subtle and ambiguous poetry, his friend Racine, by contrast, was an accomplished performer in an absolutely conventional way—or, as Stendhal puts it, a 'plat hypocrite', a flatterer. I should like now to explore the rhetoric of Racine's success, his skill as a court writer, and then, briefly, to ask how his tragedies fit into this rhetorical strategy.[21]

Raymond Picard's *La Carrière de Jean Racine*[22] demonstrates vividly the efficiency with which Racine made his way in the world. Starting from an unpromising position, a commoner and an orphan with Jansenist connections, Racine became successively a member of the French Academy (at the age of thirty-four), Trésorier de France at Moulins, official historian to Louis XIV, member of the Petite Académie, and finally, the peak of his career, Gentilhomme Ordinaire de la Chambre du Roi. During the last twenty-five years of his life—with the possible exception of his very last year—he was close to Louis XIV and protected successively by the two women who dominated Louis's reign.

How did Racine achieve this? Initially, of course, thanks to the theatre. But whatever the fundamental reasons for Racine's semi-farewell to the theatre in 1677, it does at least show that theatrical success was not essential to Racine's career. On the contrary, one might say that Racine's success in the theatre in his own lifetime was only one product of the quality on which he depended, his eloquence. 'Racine a bien de l'esprit', said Louis XIV to Madame de Sévigné,[23] and his words were echoed some years later in Dangeau's brief epitaph: 'Je n'ai jamais connu d'homme qui eût tant d'esprit que celui-là' (*Corpus*, 335).

There are many other testimonies to this 'esprit', this ability to choose words well and use them effectively. Some of them have nothing to do with courtly flattery: thus Valincour's account of Racine reading a passage from Sophocles in impromptu translation

---

[21] An earlier version of this study appeared in *Esprit créateur*, Summer 1968. A much fuller treatment of the role of rhetoric *inside* Racine's tragedies will be found in my book *Racine's Rhetoric*, Oxford, 1965.

[22] R. Picard, *La Carrière de Jean Racine*, 2nd ed., Paris, 1961. Professor Picard's companion volume, *Corpus Racinianum*, Lyons, 1956, together with its supplements published separately in 1961 and then in the journal *Jeunesse de Racine* (1963 and 1966), is an invaluable collection of contemporary documents relating to Racine. I have drawn heavily on it for this chapter, and refer to it in the text as *Corpus*.

[23] Madame de Sévigné, *Lettres*, ed. Gérard-Gailly, Bibliothèque de la Pléiade, vol. III, p. 351.

and rooting his audience to the spot: 'rien n'a jamais approché du trouble où me jeta ce récit; et au moment où j'écris, je m'imagine voir encore Racine le livre à la main, et nous tous consternés autour de lui.'[24] Racine, we remember, was a great success as unofficial reader to the King, a function which is recalled by the scene in *Esther* where the insomniac Assuérus is comforted by listening to the annals of his reign (Racine was annalist as well as reader).

It was not only as a reader that Racine was able to adapt himself effectively to his audience. In conversation, though he seems to have been fundamentally 'vif naturellement tout ce qu'il se peut' (*Corpus*, 334), he learnt to suffer fools gladly, when it suited him to do so. Rather than talk to the great about his own works, he made them feel that they were the intelligent ones: 'mon talent avec eux n'est pas de leur faire sentir que j'ai de l'esprit, mais de leur apprendre qu'ils en ont' (*O.C.* 1. 25). This is the courtier's great gift. On the other hand, if the occasion called for a more positive eloquence, he could play the part required. In a highly suggestive juxtaposition Spanheim asserts: 'S'il était prédicateur ou comédien, il surpasserait tout en l'un et l'autre genre.' (*Corpus*, 213.) And we know how Racine taught his profane and sacred actresses the art of effective declamation.

These are so many tantalizing glimpses of 'le savant de la cour' in action. It would be good to have recordings of some of these conversations, but failing oral records we do have written monuments to Racine's eloquence. As we can see from his prefaces and the *Lettres sur les imaginaires* (let alone the plays), Racine knew how to choose arguments and place words so as to wound and crush his opponents. His written works also provide ample evidence of his ability to please and flatter.

In the first place we may note briefly the persuasive skill which Racine gives to the men and women in his plays.[25] In fact, much of this persuasion falls on deaf ears, since flattery is not effective in the face of passion and obsession, but the technique is good. One notices, for instance, the almost automatic way in which

[24] Louis Racine, *Mémoires sur la vie et les ouvrages de Jean Racine*, in Racine, *Œuvres complètes*, ed. R. Picard, Bibliothèque de la Pléiade, 2 vols., Paris, 1950–2. This edition is cited hereafter as *O.C.* (Note that in later impressions of the *Pléiade* edition, page numbers in vol. 1 are 18 below those in the first edition: thus page 24 becomes page 6.)
[25] See P. France, *Racine's Rhetoric*, ch. 6, for more details.

Osmin, favourite of the Vizir Acomat, drops remarks which will successfully ingratiate him with his protector:

> Ils regrettent le temps, à leur grand cœur si doux,
> Lorsque assurés de vaincre ils combattaient sous vous.
> *(Bajazet,* I. i)

When it is a question of preparing their interlocutors for a course of action they may not like, Racine's orators go in for a full-scale *captatio benevolentiae*, whether they are courtiers, like Paulin:

> Je n'attendais pas moins de cet amour de gloire
> Qui partout après vous attacha la victoire.
> *(Bérénice,* II. ii)

or kings, like Agamemnon:

> La Thessalie entière, ou vaincue, ou calmée,
> Lesbos même conquise en attendant l'armée,
> De toute autre valeur éternels monuments,
> Ne sont d'Achille oisif que les amusements.
> *(Iphigénie,* I. ii)

In *Esther*, presumably in part for reasons of local colour, the flattery becomes even more fulsome.[26]

Racine's own first attempt at public flattery was *La Nymphe de la Seine* (1660), a highly conventional epithalamion which goes through the motions efficiently and with a certain grace. It is the work of a twenty-year-old beginner, who was willing to take the advice of the accredited expert, Chapelain (*O.C.* II. 382–6). Soon after, Chapelain put the young Racine's name on the list of writers who were to be paid for services rendered in the cause of royal propaganda. Racine responded quickly with two more poems; the first congratulates France on Louis's recovery from measles, while in the second, *La Renommée aux Muses*, Louis is compared, not for the first time, to Augustus and Alexander. And in 1665 comes the full-length play, *Alexandre le Grand*.

One could hardly claim that *Alexandre* is designed solely to sound forth the praises of Louis. Racine is clearly anxious to win an audience with a play which flatters contemporary tastes for the heroic and the *galant*. But although he certainly wants to please the general public, as he says again and again, his prefaces and dedicatory epistles show him anxious at all times to appeal

[26] See in particular Act II, sc. v.

to a social élite. In some respects he could have echoed Boileau's sentiments:

> Et qu'importe à nos vers que Perrin les admire? . . .
> Pourvu qu'ils sachent plaire au plus puissant des Rois,
> Qu'à Chantilly Condé les souffre quelquefois . . .[27]

In *Alexandre* Racine's principal target was the centre of this élite, the young king who could see himself flatteringly reflected in the brilliant and amorous conqueror. The whole play, with its decorative eloquence, contributes to the golden legend and reaches its high point (at least in terms of flattery) in the dazzling image of Alexandre-Louis which immediately precedes his first entrance:

> Mais de ce même front l'héroïque fierté,
> Le feu de ses regards, sa haute majesté,
> Font connaître Alexandre. Et certes son visage
> Porte de sa grandeur l'infaillible présage . . .
> *(Alexandre*, III. iii)

This was value for Chapelain's money. (It is interesting to note that not long after this, similar portraits were composed by Pierre Corneille—in *Attila*, II. v—and by Molière—in *Mélicerte*, I. iii.) To clinch it, Racine dedicates his play to the King; in his dedicatory epistle he brings out the parallel between Louis and Alexander (in spite of Louis's lack of military exploits) and foresees the day when he will move on from depicting the heroes of antiquity to recording the deeds of their modern successor.

The dedicatory epistle was, of course, one of the tests of a writer's 'esprit'. Racine dedicated his first five tragedies respectively to the Duc de Saint-Aignan, the King, Henriette d'Angleterre, the Duc de Chevreuse, and Colbert, a pretty illustrious group. All of these epistles naturally express modesty about the work dedicated, gratitude for favours received, and praise of the patron's good taste and other qualities. For Louis the terms of the dedication are superlative (excess is hardly possible), but in all the other dedications Racine executes subtle variations on the traditional dedication so that the flattery shall not seem too indiscriminate, nor the flatterer too crawling.[28] Addressing Henriette d'Angle-

---

[27] Boileau, *Œuvres complètes*, ed. F. Escal, Bibliothèque de la Pléiade, Paris, 1966, p. 129.

[28] Such pieces as Corneille's notorious dedication of *Cinna* to the financier Montoron had made the dedicatory epistle particularly vulnerable. See W. Leiner, *Der Widmungsbrief in der französischen Literatur*, Heidelberg, 1965.

terre, he sets up a kind of complicity between the princess and her poet, insisting on her instinctive taste and judgement in matters of literature. In the other three dedications Racine uses the old rhetorical device of saying something while pretending not to say it (preterition); the modesty of his patrons, he says, prevents him from praising them, yet he cannot help doing so. Thus, after detailing the Duc de Chevreuse's qualities, and in particular his modesty, he stops short: 'Mais je me laisse emporter insensiblement à la tentation de parler de vous' (O.C. 1. 402). It is the same with Colbert, whom Racine had already seized the opportunity of praising in the dedication to *Britannicus*. Colbert was above all the busy man, with no time for frills and flattery, so Racine adopted the appropriate tactics: 'J'aurais ici une belle occasion de m'étendre sur vos louanges, si vous me permettiez de vous louer. Et que ne dirais-je point de tant de rares qualités . . .' (O.C. 1. 481), and so on. Here already, in a rather obvious form, we see provisional solutions to the problems which teased Racine as official historian.

After *Bérénice* Racine no longer needed to write dedications, but as he became increasingly the poet of Louis XIV and eventually 'le savant de la cour', he had plenty of opportunity to use his tact and eloquence. He was expected to turn his hand to a variety of petty literary tasks—producing libretti for Lully, or checking the style of the constitution of Saint-Cyr. In 1679, when Madame de Maintenon wanted an epistle dedicating the 'works' of the seven-year-old Duc du Maine to his mother, Madame de Montespan, it was (by all accounts) Racine who took on the job, filling the epistle with delicately flattering allusions to the young duke's illegitimate birth and his royal father, the modern Alexander or Caesar. Bayle was impressed: 'Il semble qu'on n'y touche pas ou qu'on ne veuille qu'effleurer. Cependant on loue jusqu'au vif, et on va loin en peu de paroles . . .' (*Corpus*, 143.)

These were merely occasional tasks: more officially Racine's eloquence was required by his duties as member of the French Academy and the Petite Académie and as official historian of the reign of Louis XIV. The academic discourse, like the dedication, was a genre which allowed or even required heavy flattery; as Bayle said, 'on sait assez, avant que de lire cette sorte d'ouvrages, qu'un Roi y est toujours le plus grand monarque de l'Univers, sans en excepter ni Alexandre, ni César.' (*Corpus*, 122.) So Racine the academician hardly attempts to temper the conventional eulogy, carrying it to ridiculous lengths at the conclusion of his *Discours pour la réception de l'abbé Colbert*: 'Tous les mots de la langue, toutes les syllabes nous paraissent précieuses, parce que nous les regardons comme autant d'instruments qui doivent servir à la gloire de notre auguste protecteur.' (*O.C.* II. 343–4.) The second, more famous harangue contains no such absurdities, but it concludes with a long, eloquent, even fulsome eulogy of the King, which was too much for Antoine Arnauld (letter to Racine, 7 April 1685) and even, it seems, for Louis himself: 'Je vous louerais davantage, si vous ne me louiez pas tant,' he is reported to have said to Racine (*O.C.* II. 281).

This 'bon mot du roi', as Racine calls it, suggests some of the difficulties facing him as historian. The royal historians were pulled in two directions. Their history was above all an instrument for spreading and immortalizing the glory of the King— they had therefore to avoid the gaffe of Mézeray, who had lost his pension by criticizing Louis's economic policy in his history of France. But the historian was also supposed to tell the truth. He should do this partly because that was what history was about, as Racine repeatedly notes in his extracts from Lucian ('l'éloge et l'histoire sont éloignés infiniment' (*O.C.* II. 197)), but also because Louis's exploits were already—they said—so incredible that any poetic exaggeration or adornment would smack of flattery and make the whole history suspect. This is why many enemies of Racine and Boileau doubted—or claimed to doubt— the ability of mere poets, who were already in the habit of embellishing antiquity, to preserve the dignified truthfulness which suited their task. The exiled Bussy-Rabutin, who would not have minded being official historian himself, writes acidly to Madame de Sévigné of the low breeding of his successful rivals; when she tells him of a clever reply made by Racine to the King ('les places que vous attaquiez furent plus tôt prises que nos habits ne furent faits'), he comments, with some justification: 'La réponse de Racine au Roi est bonne pour un courtisan, mais elle ne vaut rien pour un historien, et je craindrais bien pour la gloire de notre maître, qu'il ne nous donnât souvent dans son histoire de ces sortes d'exagérations qui ne plaisent qu'aux intéressés, et qu'il ne fût toujours poète en prose.' (*Corpus*, 94.)

Racine and Boileau were aware of the pitfalls threatening the official historian. Their answer, in general terms, was to adopt a sober rhetoric which would, by comparison with other rhetorics, give the impression of being the unadorned truth and would thus be more pleasing to a master who liked praise, but not when it was called flattery. When Versailles was built, the academician Charpentier had devised a series of 'inscriptions pleines d'emphase' for Le Brun's paintings of the great exploits of Louis's reign. In 1685 these were replaced by simple inscriptions of Racine's and Boileau's invention. Boileau explained the principle involved to the King: 'Il suffit d'énoncer simplement les choses pour les faire admirer. *Le passage du Rhin* dit beaucoup plus que *le merveilleux passage du Rhin*.'[29] It was a question of choosing not so much the most truthful as the most effective form—since in any case the picture did the flattering. The same problem and the same solution reappear in the work of the Académie des Inscriptions, which had to think of mottoes for a medallic history of the golden reign and which was well served by Racine's unfailing tact and inventiveness.

Finally, in the written history proper, eloquence serves glory rather than truth. Dangeau wrote in his journal for 31 December 1684:

Madame de Montespan fit présent au Roi, le soir après souper, d'un livre relié d'or et plein de tableaux de miniature, qui sont toutes les villes de Hollande que le Roi prit en 1672. Ce livre lui coûte quatre mille pistoles, à ce qu'elle nous dit. Racine et Despréaux en ont fait tous les discours et y ont joint un éloge historique de Sa Majesté.

(*Corpus*, 135)

This expensive volume, the *Précis historique des campagnes de Louis XIV*, together with Racine's brief *Relation du siège de Namur* (always sieges and captured cities!), is all that has survived of the combined historical labours of Racine and Boileau. The text lives up to the golden binding. The language is constantly formal, pompous, far from the familiarity which Racine had noted as recommended by Lucian. It is true that Racine stops short of comparing Louis yet again to Alexander or Caesar, but otherwise he uses all the traditional resources of epideictic rhetoric (magnification of difficulties encountered, diminution of the effort needed to overcome them, enumeration, gradation, vivid historic presents, superlative vocabulary, insistent rhythm, and ennobling

[29] Boileau, *Œuvres*, p. 611.

metaphor) to emphasize the magnitude of Louis's achievements. And of course there can be no doubt about the extreme partiality of Racine's golden image of the reign. Nothing brings out more clearly the difference between courtier's history and a relatively pure (though still tendentious) history of the past than a comparison between the first lines of the *Précis historique*:

Avant que le Roi déclarât la guerre aux états des Provinces Unies, sa réputation avait déjà donné de la jalousie à tous les princes de l'Europe. Le repos des peuples affermi, l'ordre rétabli dans ses finances, ses ambassadeurs vengés, Dunkerque retiré des mains des Anglais, et l'Empire si glorieusement secouru, étaient des preuves illustres de sa sagesse et de sa conduite; et par la rapidité de ses conquêtes en Flandres et en Franche-Comté, il avait fait voir qu'il n'était pas moins excellent capitaine que grand politique   (*O.C.* II. 207)

and the beginning of his *Abrégé de l'histoire de Port-Royal*:

L'Abbaye de Port-Royal, près de Chevreuse, est une des plus anciennes abbayes de l'ordre de Cîteaux. Elle fut fondée, en l'année 1204, par un saint évêque de Paris, nommé Eudes de Sully, de la maison des comtes de Champagne, proche parent de Philippe-Auguste. C'est lui dont on voit la tombe en cuivre, élevée de deux pieds, à l'entrée du chœur de Notre-Dame de Paris.   (*O.C.* II. 37)

In this way Racine the courtier tried to find the narrow way between fulsome flattery and unpopular honesty. His success in this was differently gauged by different contemporaries. The Port-Royalists, after their reconciliation with Racine, used him as their man at court; while appreciating his skill in dealing with people, they also praised his courage and honesty. Nicole, congratulating Racine on becoming Gentilhomme Ordinaire, writes: 'Je me réjouis . . . qu'en allant son chemin sans crainte, on ne soit tombé en aucun inconvénient' (*Corpus*, 210). Many would have agreed with this, among them Racine's son Louis, who rather amusingly insists on his father's honest independence while giving us all the material we need to construct a picture of the supple time-server. With endearing innocence he quotes a witticism about Racine's desire, expressed in his will, to be buried at Port-Royal: ' "C'est ce qu'il n'eût point fait de son vivant," dit un seigneur connu par des réflexions de cette nature.' (*O.C.* I. 113.)

These words echo the way many of Racine's contemporaries felt about him. They may have been inspired by envy or malice, but the refrain is constant: Racine is in all things an opportunist, a flatterer, and a hypocrite, whose devotion is only put on to please the reformed King and Madame de Maintenon. Even his apparent independence in supporting Port-Royal is a more subtle form of hypocrisy, according to Spanheim: 'Le jansénisme en France n'est plus à la mode; mais pour paraître plus honnête homme et pour passer pour spirituel, il n'est pas fâché qu'on le croie janséniste.' (*Corpus*, 212.) And though Racine's friends proclaimed that he had found the right formula for writing royal history, his enemies were not to be disarmed and continued to brand him as a flatterer.

Well, clearly, even allowing for Racine's Jansenist connections, we are not going to find in him an opponent of Louis XIV. It is in vain that we search his correspondence for any clear sign of a critical approach to the regime. (It is interesting, however, that in 1697 Racine received a letter from Vauban which was so critical of recent foreign policy that Vauban asked Racine to burn it (*Corpus*, 311).) There is little reason to doubt that Racine, like many other artists of his time, did feel genuine enthusiasm for many aspects of Louis XIV's reign. But I should like to ask now what bearing Racine's plays have on all this, since, after all, the plays are what cause us to ask questions about Racine the courtier in the first place. Are they the plays of a courtier?

Of course we have to remember that most of the plays were written before Racine became 'le savant de la cour'. Nevertheless, Racine was known as a eulogist before he made his name as a play-wright; as early as 1665 he clearly uses *Alexandre* as an instrument of flattery. And thereafter, whatever the deeper implications of his plays, Racine as dramatist is making his contribution to the courtly ceremony of worldliness. *Mithridate*, so Dangeau tells us, was Louis XIV's favourite play. *Iphigénie* was performed at Versailles in a setting of ornate splendour. And *Esther*, with its impeccable blend of piety and entertainment, provided the centre for one of the most striking ceremonies of Louis's reign. On a superficial level all Racine's plays, like most of the art of the period, satisfy an aristocratic taste for an elegant, ordered art which will reassure in its ritual perfection.

In *Alexandre* this surface splendour serves a glossy world-view which is flattering to King and aristocracy. In subsequent plays this is not so. The 'demolition of the hero' has often been com-mented on; here I want to see what happens specifically to the

King. In the first place he is often besieged by flatterers. The villainous counsellor, an exponent of Machiavellian politics, was a traditional feature of serious drama in the seventeenth century,[30] Corneille's later plays are full of these supple, amoral schemers, from the Photin of *Pompée* to the Sillace of *Suréna*. Racine too gives us a small gallery of them—Créon in *La Thébaïde*, Narcisse in *Britannicus*, Acomat (perhaps) in *Bajazet*, Œnone in *Phèdre*, Aman in *Esther*, Mathan in *Athalie*. Let Mathan speak for them as he advises Athalie:

> Dans le vulgaire obscur si le sort l'a placé,
> Qu'importe qu'au hasard un sang vil soit versé?
> Est-ce aux rois à garder cette lente justice?
> *(Athalie,* II. v)

It is interesting to note that this sort of character takes more of our attention in Racine's last plays, written when he had reason to be personally preoccupied with the question of flattery. It is in these plays that we find his most vigorous denunciations of flattery, particularly in *Phèdre*:

> Détestables flatteurs, présent le plus funeste
> Que puisse faire aux rois la colère céleste!
> *(Phèdre,* IV. vi)

and in Joad's warning to Joas:

> De l'absolu pouvoir vous ignorez l'ivresse,
> Et des lâches flatteurs la voix enchanteresse.
> Bientôt ils vous diront que les plus saintes lois,
> Maîtresses du vil peuple, obéissent aux rois;
> Qu'un roi n'a d'autre frein que sa volonté même;
> Qu'il doit immoler tout à sa grandeur suprême . . .
> *(Athalie,* IV. iii)

Now these fulminations could be read as lessons to the King, rather in the manner of a court preacher. Indeed, this is how some contemporaries saw them.[31] But should we not rather see them as the sort of roundabout flattery which condemns flattery? The implication is that the King may occasionally be led astray, but

[30] See M. Baudin, 'The King's Minister in Seventeenth-Century French Drama', *Modern Language Notes,* 1939.
[31] Act IV, sc. iii of *Athalie* was apparently vigorously applauded just before the Revolution for its attack on flattery (see G. Mongrédien, *Athalie de Racine*, Paris 1929, pp. 95–8).

is not fundamentally to blame; thus Assuérus, as soon as he sees the light, is converted. So if, as is far from certain, Racine is criticizing Louis's religious policy in *Esther* and *Athalie*, it is the ministers rather than the King himself who take the blame. It is the same story with Phèdre and Œnone; Racine writes in his preface to *Phèdre*: 'J'ai cru que la calomnie avait quelque chose de trop bas et de trop noir pour la mettre dans la bouche d'une princesse qui a d'ailleurs des sentiments si nobles et si vertueux. Cette bassesse m'a paru plus convenable à une nourrice . . .' (*O.C.* I. 763.) The flatterer is a scapegoat.

If we look at Racine's earlier plays, however, we find that kings are not usually led astray by wicked counsellors—Narcisse is an exception. Phœnix, Burrhus, Paulin, Arbate, Arcas, and Théramène are all honest servants, anxious for the greater moral good of their masters and urging them on in the path of duty. They cannot be blamed for what goes wrong. And clearly something does go wrong with the Alexandre image of royalty. From Pyrrhus on (not to speak of the disasters of *La Thébaïde*), Racine's kings are unhappy or weak or evil. In Pyrrhus we see a rapid change from the impressive orator of Act I, scene ii to the still attractive but unstable and childish lover of Act I, scene iv. If his fickle weakness did not produce such tragic results it would be comic. And if his behaviour as a lover is a terrible come-down after Alexandre's easy victories, so too is his military prowess. At first we see him as the conqueror of Troy, worthy son of Achilles, but as the play progresses, the memories of Andromaque and Hermione give us instead the cruel and bloody murderer of helpless girls and old men. See the way in which the accumulation of participial clauses, one of the standard devices of eulogy (see the passage quoted above from Racine's history), is made to serve Hermione's deadly irony:

> Du vieux père d'Hector la valeur abattue
> Aux pieds de sa famille expirante à sa vue,
> Tandis que dans son sein votre bras enfoncé
> Cherche un reste de sang que l'âge avait glacé;
> Dans des ruisseaux de sang Troie ardente plongée;
> De votre propre main Polyxène égorgée
> Aux yeux de tous les Grecs indignés contre vous:
> Que peut-on refuser à ces généreux coups?
>
> (*Andromaque*, IV. v)

Néron is a step lower on the scale. He too is weak and easily swayed, but in him we see also a more positive evil, pleasure in the suffering of others. This is the 'monstre naissant'. The whole play could be seen as a reply to *Cinna*, which shows the conversion of man of blood to magnanimous ruler; *Britannicus* shows the opposite change. Agrippine says of her son:

> Il commence, il est vrai, par où finit Auguste;
> Mais crains que l'avenir détruisant le passé,
> Il ne finisse ainsi qu'Auguste a commencé
> (*Britannicus*, I. i)

words which bring to mind a passage in the dedication to *Alexandre*: '. . . devant Elle, on n'a point vu de roi qui à l'âge d'Alexandre ait fait paraître la conduite d'Auguste . . . et qui ait commencé sa carrière par où les plus grands princes ont tâché d'achever la leur.' (*O.C.* I. 194.) Titus, on the other hand, does follow the advice of his good counsellor; *Bérénice* shows us the victory of a noble monarch, who conquers his passions in a way which Louis XIV was occasionally able to imitate—with the encouragement of his ministers and preachers. Yet although the play does contain an idealized portrait and a model for kings, it can hardly be said to offer a pleasing picture of the royal condition. Titus is able to place his duty and reputation before anything else, as the good king should, but, as in some later plays of Pierre Corneille, the dominant impression is of the bleak personal consequences of this political decision:

> Mais il ne s'agit plus de vivre, il faut régner.
> (*Bérénice*, IV. v)

And so it goes in all Racine's tragedies. The kings and queens are not all as evil or as weak as Roxane and the absent Acomat. Indeed many of them have a certain nobility; Mithridate and Assuérus are more or less converted and end in glory. But all the time the implication seems to be that men are not up to the part of king; they are all inwardly flawed or mocked by fate. For all his final apotheosis, Mithridate is old, defeated, cruel, dishonest, and pathetically a victim of his own emotion. Agamemnon, 'roi des rois', is made to feel his own weakness in the face of his family and his powerlessness in the face of the political (or religious) situation. Thésée the giant-killer is also Thésée the inglorious seducer; the darling of Neptune is mocked and destroyed by Neptune. Even the young king Joas, whose restoration causes such rejoicing, is doomed to degenerate:

> Comment en un plomb vil l'or pur s'est-il changé?
> Quel est dans le lieu saint ce pontife égorgé?
>
> (*Athalie*, III. vii)

The Palace, scene of so many of Racine's plays, is either a place of sterile splendour (*Bérénice*) or, more often, a place of double-dealing, lust, and cruelty, where the innocent Junie, the honest Bajazet, or the pious young Éliacin cannot survive. In some plays there is no alternative to this world of the Palace, except for occasional glimpses of ships and the sea. Certainly the pessimistic vision of royal power does not lead to the elaboration of an alternative political system. But in some plays, notably *Britannicus* and *Athalie*, there is another and better place, the monastery or the temple. And one thinks of the world-denying retreat to the 'désert' which is such a notable theme of life and literature in seventeenth-century France. (Did Racine really want to become a Carthusian in 1677?) Remembering this and Racine's own connections with Port-Royal, we may well ask how far his plays imply a radical Christian view of political power, the sort of view expressed in Pascal's cynical words on force and justice and the sort of view which Bossuet had to reconcile with his more optimistic view of the divinely sanctioned monarch serving God on his throne. This 'Jansenist' picture of Racine's theatre is strongly expounded in Lucien Goldmann's *Le Dieu caché*; it seems to me more satisfactory than the image of an amoral, apolitical Racine which is presented in caricatural form by Jean Giraudoux.[32]

'Racine a bien de l'esprit', enough wit and eloquence to establish himself in a society whose foundations his major writings must be seen as undermining. Whatever the world-view expressed in them, their presentation made them acceptable among the rituals of court life. Indeed, even an anti-worldly vision, beautifully expressed, may well have been as acceptable in tragedy as it was in the pulpit—though it is by no means the norm in tragedy of the time. This does not mean that it was taken to heart. We

---

[32] J. Giraudoux, *Littérature*, Paris, 1941, pp. 27–55. For a balanced view of this question see Odette de Mourgues, *Racine, or the Triumph of Relevance*, Cambridge, 1967, ch. 6.

cannot possibly know how fully Racine's first spectators, including the King, were able to respond to his tragic drama, how far they felt it to be critical of the values they lived by. Apart from an anecdote to the effect that Louis stopped dancing in court ballets after hearing the condemnation of the play-acting Néron in *Britannicus* (Act IV, scene iv),[33] there is nothing to suggest that he felt himself at all undermined by Racine's destructive picture of the world of the Palace. We can hardly suppose that he saw himself, or that Racine wanted him to see himself, as Néron, or even as Mithridate or Agamemnon. We are left, therefore, with the tantalizing ambiguity of the sure-footed courtier and tragic dramatist, using his rhetorical skill to make his way in the world, but also to suggest the degradation of this world and its rulers.

[33] See Louis Racine, *Mémoires,* in *O.C.* I. 47–8, and Boileau, *Œuvres,* p. 834.

IV

THE VOICE OF NATURE

Quand on voit le style naturel, on est tout étonné et ravi,
car on s'attendait de voir un auteur, et on trouve un
homme.

(Pascal: *Pensées*)

La rhétorique, à l'entendre, ne s'est jamais proposé que
d'arracher l'écrivain aux conventions et aux phrases: de
le rendre au naturel, à la vérité. Mais il nous semble plutôt
qu'elle n'a jamais formé que des faiseurs de phrases, et des
arrangeurs de mots. D'où suivent ici l'originalité, la révolte
et la Terreur . . .

Mais quand le rhéteur dit, et répète, qu'il faut éviter de
laisser le compas dans le cercle, ou le mètre dans le mur, et
que la véritable rhétorique commence au dégoût de la
rhétorique (comme la philosophie à la haine de la philosophie), que fait-il, que prévoir à son tour, et déjà comprendre la Terreur? Si Montaigne connaît Cicéron, Cicéron
s'attend à Montaigne.

(Jean Paulhan: *La Rhétorique renaît de ses cendres*)

R HETORICAL language is often opposed to spontaneous or natural speech. One of the things about school rhetoric (or at least bad school rhetoric) was the way it inculcated a routine, pressing individual perceptions and experience into a mould of conformity. Its techniques were available to all and used by all; its lessons were a codification of past wisdom rather than an incitement to novelty. Not surprisingly then, it was seen principally as an obstacle by many powerfully individual writers, who felt obliged to define their manner by opposition to the old formulas which governed orthodox writing and speaking. Such writers often appear to be jettisoning rhetoric and spurning the sheep-like flock of book-producers; what they are doing, in fact, is to re-define and renew rhetoric, keeping it alive by questioning its norms and forms, but still, as communicators, working well within the frame of reference I outlined in Chapter I. For of course there is no getting away from rhetoric.

The prime example and greatest influence is Montaigne, the bookish critic of mere books, who inherits an old noble tradition of scorn for the mere pen-pusher—which remains vigorous throughout our period—yet who finds in writing a satisfaction which no amount of mock (or real) modesty can conceal.[1] Montaigne sets a high value on the sort of writing which preserves the life, vigour, and spontaneity of individual speech, his own sort of writing in fact. In so far as rhetoric had lost touch with this, it had become a sterile and self-defeating discipline. Reading Montaigne, one feels again the force of Pascal's paradox: 'La véritable éloquence se moque de l'éloquence'—the ability to communicate and persuade, which is the *raison d'être* of rhetoric, is in fact hindered by the sort of rhetoric which is often taught. To say this is to be very ungrateful to the old art, which knew all about the debate

---

[1] I am indebted to my colleague Margaret McGowan for allowing me to read the manuscript of her forthcoming book on Montaigne's persuasive stance and techniques. On Montaigne and Diderot see J. Schwartz, *Diderot and Montaigne*, Geneva, 1966.

between art and nature and to which even the most idiosyncratic writer owes more than he cares to say, but still it remains true (a truism even) that the great writer is both a destroyer and a creator of rhetoric.

6. Diderot: the Order of Dialogue

Méfiez-vous de celui qui veut mettre de l'ordre
(Diderot: *Supplément au Voyage de Bougainville*)

ONE day in 1760, at the Baron d'Holbach's country house, Melchior Grimm had an argument with Charles-Georges Leroy about method and genius. Unable to agree, they appealed to the Neapolitan Abbé Galiani, who told them a story. The cuckoo and the nightingale were arguing which of them had the better song. The cuckoo said: 'Je dis peu de choses, mais elles ont du poids, de l'ordre, et on les retient', and the nightingale replied: 'J'aime à parler; mais je suis toujours nouveau et je ne fatigue jamais. J'enchante les forêts; le coucou les attriste. Il est tellement attaché à la leçon de sa mère, qu'il n'oserait hasarder un ton qu'il n'a point appris d'elle. Moi, je ne reconnais point de maître. Je me joue des règles. C'est surtout lorsque je les enfreins qu'on m'admire. Quelle comparaison de sa fastidieuse méthode avec mes heureux écarts!' Seeing the splendid ears of a passing donkey, they appealed to his judgement; he listened to their songs, first the cuckoo, then the irrepressible nightingale, but he cut the nightingale short and declared: 'Je me doute que tout ce que vous avez chanté là est fort beau, mais je n'y entends rien. Cela me paraît bizarre, brouillé, décousu. Vous êtes peut-être plus savant que votre rival, mais il est plus méthodique que vous, et j'en suis, moi, pour la méthode.' And Galiani said to Leroy, pointing to Grimm: 'Voilà le rossignol. Vous êtes le coucou, et moi je suis l'âne qui vous donne gain de cause. Bonsoir.' And Denis Diderot, for whom this was no new question, wrote it all down in one of his nightingale letters to Sophie Volland (*Corr.* III. 166–9).[1]

It was indeed one of the questions which constantly recurred in Diderot's thinking. In his art criticism, for instance, the nightingale of disorderly genius and the cuckoo of patient method reappear again and again. The emphasis changes. He will sometimes

---

[1] Diderot's *Œuvres complètes*, ed. J. Assézat and M. Tourneux, 20 vols., Paris, 1875–7, are referred to in this chapter as *A.T.* His *Correspondance*, ed. G. Roth and J. Varloot, 16 vols. Paris, 1955–70, is referred to as *Corr.*

take a painter to task for his confusion, thus Boucher: 'une confusion d'objets entassés les uns sur les autres, si déplacés, si dis-
parates, que c'est moins le tableau d'un homme sensé que le rêve
d'un fou' (*A.T.* x. 256). But 'le rêve d'un fou' is not always a term
of blame for Diderot and at other times the tables seem to be
turned, thus for architecture in the *Essais sur la peinture*: 'ce
système de mesures d'ordres vitruviennes et rigoureuses semble
n'avoir été inventé que pour conduire à la monotonie et étouffer
le génie.' (*A.T.* x. 512.) The same work gives us a balanced view
which represents his mature position: 'l'ordonnance, en poésie
ainsi qu'en peinture, suppose un certain tempérament de jugement
et de verve, de chaleur et de sagesse, d'ivresse et de sang-froid,
dont les exemples ne sont pas communs en nature.' (*A.T.* x. 504.)
The *Salon* of 1767 speaks of the rhetoric of disorder, the sweet
disorder of classical poetics: 'Les instruments y sont disposés avec
goût. Il y a, dans ce désordre qui les entasse, une sorte de verve.'
(*A.T.* xi. 97.) This refers to a Chardin still life; it might well be
applied to the *Salons* themselves. Here, as in many of his other
writings, Diderot is self-consciously the nightingale, enjoying his
freedom and scornful of the cuckoo's order.

Rhetoric was always concerned with order. The teachers of
rhetoric, in Diderot's case the Jesuits, taught the classical *dispositio* of exordium, narration, proof, and peroration. They did not
suppose, of course, that this order could be rigidly applied to all
subjects and all occasions; more generally, they tried to inculcate
the habit of giving to all messages the sort of shape which is
clearly grasped by the listener or reader and thus makes communication more effective. Whatever frills might later be added,
the orator and the writer were to begin by sorting out their
material, arranging it clearly and logically. This was true of play-
writing; Diderot, an innovator in this field, nevertheless remained
quite classically convinced of the importance of planning: 'Surtout s'imposer la loi de ne pas jeter sur le papier une seule idée de
détail que le plan ne soit arrêté' (*A.T.* vii. 321). It was true too
of philosophical writing. In the case of philosophy, however, the
advocacy of order was not just a rhetorical one, concerned simply
with the best way of putting a message across; it sprang also from
the heart of the subject, as Diderot's contemporaries understood it.

The great ambition of the philosopher-scientists of the eighteenth century was to introduce order into the apparent chaos of

phenomena, or rather, as they would have said, to lay bare the order which had been there all the time. Newton had done this triumphantly for the movement of bodies and the dance of the stars. The much more difficult task remained of discovering the laws underlying the complexities of animal life and human society. Although the *philosophes* mainly declared themselves disciples of Newton in the avoidance of 'hypotheses' and the distrust of *a priori* 'systems', they nevertheless worked on the assumption that the universe in all its aspects is indeed governed by such laws. The aim was to come as near as possible to a position from which things would be seen to fall into place in their essential unity; thus d'Alembert in his Preliminary Discourse to the *Encyclopédie*: 'L'Univers, pour qui saurait l'embrasser d'un seul point de vue, ne serait, s'il est permis de le dire, qu'un fait unique et une grande vérité.'[2] Here, quite clearly, the search for order is not a rhetorical one; the aim is discovery, not communication. But it was natural that this should lead to an emphasis on the need for a similar order in the communication of philosophical beliefs or scientific findings. There is no necessary connection between the two; it may be that the best form for conveying the regular laws of the universe is in fact an irregular one. The confusion is a natural one, however, and is perhaps attributable in part to the influence of rhetoric, which early in life gave boys the habit of setting out their case in as orderly a manner as possible.

Diderot, author of *De l'interprétation de la nature* and editor of the *Encyclopédie*, shared many of the ideas of his contemporaries concerning the value of order. It was this quality which attracted him in 1767 to the physiocratic doctrine expounded by La Rivière in a work bearing the promising title *L'Ordre essentiel*. Justifying his admiration to his sceptical friend Damilaville, Diderot explained:

Premièrement, c'est que dans *L'Ami des hommes*, *Le Traité de l'impôt* et autres ouvrages sur la même matière, les vérités sont éparses, isolées, sans liaison, sans force; et qu'ici elles découlent les unes des autres, enchaînées par une logique dont je ne connais aucun exemple.

(*Corr.* VII. 76)

And again, insisting now on his personal need to have things sorted out:

Tous les écrits, toutes les conversations, toutes les lectures m'avaient tellement embrouillé la tête sur les questions d'économie et de politique,

2 D'Alembert, *Œuvres*, ed. Bossange and Belin, Paris, 1821-2, vol. 1, p. 33.

que j'ai dit cent fois que la plus mince de ces questions était plus difficile qu'un problème de calcul différentiel ou intégral. Voilà le premier qui m'ait éclairé, qui m'ait instruit, qui m'ait convaincu et qui ait dissipé les fantômes que les autres m'avaient faits. (*Corr.* VII. 77)

Diderot's physiocratic faith did not last, but in his first enthusiasm he appreciated in La Rivière's work both the philosophical success in discovering the essential order behind the puzzling phenomena of political economy, and the rhetorical or pedagogical qualities of the exposition. Indeed, the two seem to go naturally together, almost as in Boileau's notion that 'ce que l'on conçoit bien s'énonce clairement'. The discovery of order calls for orderly communication and both together are greeted with relief by the perplexed layman. The same reassuring virtues of order and method are again saluted in 1771 in Bemetzrieder's *Leçons de clavecin.* It is true that Diderot had some part in the writing of these dialogues,[3] but he claims that he did not do much more than tidy up the French style of his German author. He is not therefore simply praising himself when he writes: 'Je crois que ce traité est le seul qui jusqu'à présent conduise au but par principes et avec méthode; il me semble avoir réduit l'art à des règles aussi sûres et invariables que les autres sciences.' (*Corr.* XI. 97.) The praise goes in the first place to the philosophical achievement, but does not neglect the skilful order adopted by the communicator.

One could quote many more instances of Diderot's concern for order, but the most important is surely the *Encyclopédie,* which was after all the great undertaking of his life.[4] He begins his programmatic article 'Encyclopédie' by using a false etymology to define the word as 'enchaînement des sciences' and goes on: 'En effet, le but d'une *encyclopédie* est de rassembler les connaissances éparses sur la surface de la terre, d'en exposer le système général aux hommes avec qui nous vivons . . .' (*A.T.* XIV. 415.) It would seem that the words 'le système général' imply that there is indeed one order, a natural 'enchaînement des sciences', which the *Encyclopédie* has to lay bare to its reader. This would be in accordance

---

[3] See R. Niklaus, 'Diderot and the *Leçons de clavecin et principes d'harmonie* par Bemetzrieder (1771)', in *Modern Miscellany presented to Eugene Vinaver,* Manchester, 1969. The *Leçons,* which I have not considered at length because of their doubtful authorship, are an excellent example of the didactic dialogue discussed later.

[4] On this question see H. Dieckmann, *Cinq Leçons sur Diderot,* Geneva, 1959, ch. 2. This book is one of the best introductions to Diderot, particularly to the aspect which concerns me here.

with the implications of the Preliminary Discourse and the almost Ramist diagram accompanying the prospectus, where all the fields of knowledge are logically derived from the three essential functions of the mind.

In fact, however, Diderot's conception of encyclopedic order as expressed in this article is as much rhetorical as philosophical. While he is willing to admit that the material in the encyclopedia could well have been arranged according to a different scheme, he justifies the scheme adopted on the grounds that it is the one most likely to appeal to the average reader:

Qu'on suive telle autre voie qu'on aimera mieux, pourvu qu'on ne substitue pas à l'homme un être muet, insensible et froid. L'homme est le terme unique d'où il faut partir, et auquel il faut tout ramener, si l'on veut plaire, intéresser, toucher jusque dans les considérations les plus arides et les détails les plus secs. (*A.T.* XIV. 453)

The sum of available knowledge is now compared, for instance, to a vast countryside; the task of the encyclopedist is to find a viewpoint which will give the reader as clear and comprehensive a view as possible. There is no single perfect viewpoint; the God's-eye view imagined by d'Alembert in his Preliminary Discourse does not exist for man. Instead

Plus le point de vue d'où nous considérerons les objets sera élevé, plus il nous découvrira d'étendue, et plus l'ordre que nous suivrons sera instructif et grand. Il faut par conséquent qu'il soit simple, parce qu'il y a rarement de la grandeur sans simplicité; qu'il soit clair et facile; que ce ne soit point un labyrinthe tortueux où l'on s'égare, et où l'on n'aperçoive rien au-delà du point où l'on est, mais une grande et vaste avenue qui s'étende au loin, et sur la longueur de laquelle on en rencontre d'autres également bien distribuées, qui conduisent aux objets solitaires et écartés par le chemin le plus facile et le plus court.

(*A.T.* XIV. 452-3)

These roads over the landscape are like the branches of the tree of knowledge, which help the reader to introduce an admittedly arbitrary, but still indispensable, pattern into the mass of phenomena. And the tree appears again to provide a metaphor for the *dispositio* of each particular science. Always the reader must be led from the trunk to the large branches and thence to the small branches and the twigs.

As editor, Diderot's first task was to put things in the right

order: 'un bon esprit (et il faut supposer au moins cette qualité
dans un éditeur) saura mettre chaque chose à sa place.' (*A.T.* xiv.
459.) In their turn his contributors were expected to proceed
methodically: 'J'exige seulement de la méthode, quelle qu'elle
soit.' (*A.T.* xiv. 460.) The 'quelle qu'elle soit' makes it clear that
this method is not to be a strait jacket, like the dichotomies of
Ramus. Diderot mentions, for instance, the usefulness of the
'méthode d'invention', which leads the reader along the road of
discovery—what Descartes had called the 'analytic' method. But,
whatever the method, there must be the sort of order which
enables a reader to master the subject: 'c'est l'ordre qui soulage
la mémoire. Mais il est difficile qu'un auteur prenne cette attention
pour le lecteur qu'elle ne tourne à son avantage.' (*A.T.* xiv. 460.)
Here again, communication and discovery are linked, but the
primacy goes to rhetoric.

The *Encyclopédie* provides the most striking illustrations of
Diderot's advocacy of orderly communication. One might also
mention his participation in the contemporary movement to bring
some order into the French language and make it a vehicle fit for
philosophical discourse.[5] Or, on a more general level, one could
point to his often-repeated praise of the control exercised by the
great artist. This appears most strongly about 1770, notably in
Le Paradoxe sur le comédien, at a time when Diderot felt vulnerable
to the criticisms of those who shared the opinion later expressed
by Marmontel:

Dans ses écrits, il ne sut jamais former un tout ensemble: cette première
opération, qui ordonne et met tout à sa place, était pour lui trop lente et
trop pénible. Il écrivait de verve avant d'avoir rien médité: aussi a-t-il
écrit de belles pages, comme il disait lui-même, mais il n'a jamais fait
un livre.[6]

This has often been said about Diderot; we do not need to accept
it as a final judgement, but it is clear that Diderot himself was
aware of his apparent failings in respect of order. We can perhaps
detect in his descriptions of the artist of genius a note of personal
regret: 'Ce n'est pas l'homme violent qui est hors de lui-même qui
dispose de nous; c'est un avantage réservé à l'homme qui se

    [5] See J. Proust, 'Diderot et les problèmes du langage', *Romanische Forschungen*,
1967, pp. 1–27. See also Herbert Josephs, *Diderot's Dialogue of Gesture and Language*,
Ohio, 1969.
    [6] Marmontel, *Mémoires*, ed. M. Tourneux, Paris, 1891, vol. ii, p. 244.

possède.' (*A.T.* VIII. 367.)[7] The emphasis here is not narrowly on order, but on the rhetorical control over one's material, one aspect of which is *dispositio*. It is significant that the *Paradoxe* ends with the image of the orator feigning emotion so as to move others.

I have begun this chapter on Diderot by stressing the importance he placed on order, since this is a neglected aspect of his writing. Obviously, Diderot is not primarily a man of order, as we normally understand the word. Generations of readers have been perplexed and often irritated by the chaos of such works as the *Lettre sur les sourds et muets*. Often they have reacted like Marmontel, patronizingly allowing Diderot to have had brilliant ideas which he was never able to express. Some have actually presented his disorder as a potentially dangerous influence, which undermines the traditional virtues of symmetry, clarity, and stability. More recently, the tendency has been to reverse the argument, scorning the narrow-mindedness of those who ask for the traditional formal qualities and praising Diderot's broken and open forms as peculiarly modern.[8] But whether we choose to praise or blame, there is no denying that his writings flout certain traditional canons of orderly disposition.

If we look, for instance, at the *Encyclopédie*, which I have chosen to illustrate Diderot's concern for *dispositio*, we find a great chaos of disparate information and opinion, a jumble of different styles and manners, all arranged in the arbitrary sequence of the alphabet.[9] It is true that the cross-references do allow, as the editors hoped, a reasonably complete treatment of the subject, but the reader is hardly put in the position of clear-sighted mastery which Diderot evokes in his article 'Encyclopédie'. And even this article, in which he dwells at such length on order, is not shaped in accordance with the traditional precepts. It is more regularly arranged than the *Lettre sur les sourds et muets*, and different subjects

---

[7] In the *Paradoxe sur le comédien* Diderot confesses his own tendency, when in love, to lose rhetorical control and blurt out his thoughts all too spontaneously: 'Je m'en souviens, je n'approchais de l'objet aimé qu'en tremblant; le cœur me battait, mes idées se brouillaient; ma voix s'embarrassait, j'estropiais tout ce que je disais . . .' (*A.T.* VIII. 386.)

[8] See in particular the valuable article of Georges May, 'Diderot, artiste et philosophe du décousu', in *Europäische Aufklärung, Herbert Dieckmann zum 60. Geburtstag*, ed. H. Friedrich and F. Schalk, Munich, 1967.

[9] In the article 'Encyclopédie', Diderot notes: 'L'ordre alphabétique donnerait à tout moment des contrastes burlesques; un article de théologie se trouverait relégué tout au travers des arts mécaniques.' (*A.T.* XIV. 458.)

are discussed one at a time; but always one is conscious of the element of improvisation, or 'verve', as Marmontel calls it. Thus, in the middle of a discussion of the irregularity of the *Encyclopédie*, Diderot suddenly and ironically remarks: 'On se pique, on veut avoir des morceaux d'appareil. C'est même peut-être en ce moment ma vanité.' (*A.T.* xiv. 456.) In this way he gives an impression of the zigzags of conversation and combines ambitious philosophy with casual talk.

Should we then think that Diderot knew the value of order as a condition of successful communication, but was incapable of giving the right sort of shape to his writings? It is clearly not so simple as that. Against the remarks quoted above one can set a much greater number in which Diderot attacks the traditional notions of order and method. The attack is conducted on at least three different fronts.[10] In the first place, the textbook order, rigidly followed, was often unsuitable for a particular subject. This was the objection made to the three-part division of sermons; Diderot applied it to the symmetrical arrangement of Chambers's *Cyclopaedia*, claiming that where a subject did not fit it was either trimmed or, more frequently, amplified to fill the available space: 'Les articles de Chambers sont assez régulièrement distribués, mais ils sont vides: les nôtres sont pleins, mais irréguliers.' (*A.T.* xiv. 456.) Diderot favoured the more flexible sort of order which leaves room for constant discovery. In a number of frequently quoted passages from his correspondence and from the *De l'interprétation de la nature*,[11] he speaks of the fruitful disorder of dreams, madness, and casual conversation, where the writer or speaker is led on by analogies to unexpected new ideas. Similarly, when it was a question of communication rather than discovery, too

[10] A further possibility, which I do not explore in this chapter, is that Diderot cultivated disorder and ambiguity as protective devices in an age of repressive censorship. I think it would be easy to exaggerate the importance of this; one has only to think of the sort of books which were published, with or without permission, to see that political pressure was not an absolutely compelling factor. Diderot does say, however, that inconsistency was forced on philosophers by intolerance; as for himself: 'Moi, je me suis sauvé par le ton ironique le plus délié que j'ai pu trouver, les généralités, le laconisme, et l'obscurité.' (*Corr.* xiii. 27.) This may apply to the *Encyclopédie* and to such early writings as the *Pensées philosophiques*, but not to those works (his most important ones) which were not printed in his lifetime.

[11] See in particular the passage quoted below, p. 204, and paragraph xxxi of *De l'interprétation de la nature* (*A.T.* ii. 24–5). Also, among others, the *Salon* of 1767 (*A.T.* xi. 134), *Corr.* ix. 94, 204, and the article 'Pyrrhonienne' in the *Encyclopédie*.

orderly a form seemed unsuitable to express a complex reality. Whether he looked at the physical world or the behaviour of men, Diderot was struck by movement, change, and uncertainty; thus in the cosmos:

Qu'est-ce que ce monde, monsieur Holmes? Un composé sujet à des révolutions, qui toutes indiquent une tendance continuelle à la destruction; une succession rapide d'êtres qui s'entresuivent, se poussent et disparaissent; une symétrie passagère; un ordre momentané.
(*A.T.* I. 311)

and similarly in the instrument with which we seek to apprehend this reality, our language:

Nous n'avons dans la mémoire que des mots que nous croyons entendre, par l'usage fréquent et l'application même juste que nous en faisons; dans l'esprit que des notions vagues . . . (*AT.* v. 458)

These are the sort of considerations which Helvétius fails to take into account in his *De l'homme*; instead, he chops his way methodically and blindly through the forest of reality. Although Diderot does not make the explicit connection between the bewildering variety of the world and the inadequacy of rhetorical order, all these notions of complexity and uncertainty combine to make a strong case against the confident divisions and symmetries of *dispositio* and to cause Diderot to search for a more tentative order better adapted to his vision of the flux of things.

The second reason for distrusting the traditional *dispositio* is that it is felt as a strait jacket on the writer's freedom. The epigraph to the present chapter, 'Méfiez-vous de celui qui veut mettre de l'ordre' (*A.T.* II. 247), is taken from the *Supplément au Voyage de Bougainville*. There it has a political meaning; like several passages in Diderot's later writing it expresses his distrust of enlightened despots. But it seems to me legitimate to apply it to the activities of writing and speaking. In the previous paragraph, we were obliged to deduce some of Diderot's reasons for rejecting too formal a *dispositio*, but on this question of personal liberty he is quite explicit. The second sentence of *De l'interprétation de la nature* makes the point clearly: 'Je laisserai les pensées se succéder sous ma plume, dans l'ordre même selon lequel les objets se sont offerts à ma réflexion; parce qu'elles n'en représenteront que mieux les mouvements et la marche de mon esprit.' (*A.T.* II. 9.) The same

notion recurs frequently;[12] often it has defensive overtones, as
when Diderot justifies his digressions in the *Lettre sur les aveugles*
and the *Lettre sur les sourds et muets*. He knew that in indulging his
taste for freedom at the expense of order he was flouting the
traditional canons of composition, but he was unwilling to change
his ways. Even when writing about philosophy or science, he
was loath to give up that irresponsibility which is so winningly
described in the opening paragraph of *Le Neveu de Rameau*.

By committing himself to a persuasive form, the writer is cutting himself off from all sorts of fascinating possibilities. The real
enemy, in fact, is not so much the old *dispositio* as the book itself.
'Un livre est pour un auteur un grand obstacle à la vérité. J'ai sur
vous l'avantage de n'avoir point écrit', says Diderot to Hemsterhuis;[13] the annotator is in a stronger position than his subject. In
a less extreme form, the remark is echoed time and again in
Diderot's writings, perhaps most memorably at the beginning of
the *Essai sur les règnes de Claude et de Néron*: 'Je ne compose point,
je ne suis point auteur; je lis ou je converse, j'interroge ou je
réponds.' (*A.T.* III. 10.) It is hard to tell how much such asser-
tions are uneasy self-justification and how much they really express Diderot's feelings, but there is no doubt that the editor of
the *Encyclopédie* can be placed in the great line of French authors
who have proclaimed their distaste for the status of professional
writer. In many cases this appears to be an aristocratic pose, for
instance with Montaigne, but with Montaigne as with Diderot
it corresponds to the awareness that the composition of books
is a degrading and imprisoning activity for a free spirit. How
much more so the submission to the strict order of class-room
rhetoric!

So far the reasons for attacking order have been equally reasons
for attacking rhetoric, the enemy of truth and self-expression. But
the third front of attack is situated inside rhetoric; this time the
objection to the traditional orderly *dispositio* is made in the name

---

[12] Diderot's art criticism often shows his awareness of the difficulty of fixing the
changeable; his well-known comments on his own portrait by Van Loo (*A.T.* XI.
20–3) are echoed in his *Essais sur la peinture* (*A.T.* X. 473): 'Quel supplice n'est donc
pas pour eux [the painters] le visage de l'homme, cette toile qui s'agite, se meut,
s'étend, se détend, se colore, se ternit selon la multitude infinie des alternatives de
ce souffle léger et mobile qu'on appelle l'âme!'

[13] F. Hemsterhuis, *Lettre sur l'homme et ses rapports*, with Diderot's unpublished
comments, ed. G. May, New Haven, Conn., 1964, p. 179.

of effective communication. Diderot was aware, as indeed the more intelligent teachers of rhetoric were, that an over-methodical approach can be boring and self-defeating. 'En bien des circonstances, rien ne fatigue tant en pure perte que la méthode. Elle gêne l'esprit, elle captive la mémoire, elle applique.' (*A.T.* VI. 375–6.) In the writings of his contemporary Helvétius, Diderot was able to see some of the disadvantages of method. Just as he criticized *De l'homme* for steam-rollering the complexity of reality, so he saw in *De l'esprit* the inability of a mediocre and methodical mind to find the sort of order needed for persuasion.[14] The passage devoted to Helvétius's method is worth quoting at length:

Il est très méthodique; et c'est un de ses défauts principaux: premièrement, parce que la méthode, quand elle est d'appareil, refroidit, appesantit et ralentit; secondement, parce qu'elle ôte à tout l'air de liberté et de génie; troisièmement, parce qu'elle a l'aspect d'argumentation; quatrièmement, et cette raison est particulière à l'ouvrage, c'est qu'il n'y a rien qui veuille être prouvé avec moins d'affectation, plus dérobé, moins annoncé qu'un paradoxe. Un auteur paradoxal ne doit jamais dire son mot, mais toujours ses preuves: il doit entrer furtivement dans l'âme de son lecteur, et non de vive force. C'est le grand art de Montaigne, qui ne veut jamais prouver, et qui va toujours prouvant, et me ballottant du blanc au noir et du noir au blanc. D'ailleurs, l'appareil de la méthode ressemble à l'échafaud qu'on laisserait toujours subsister après que le bâtiment est élevé. C'est une chose nécessaire pour travailler, mais qu'on ne doit plus apercevoir quand l'ouvrage est fini. Elle marque un esprit trop tranquille, trop maître de lui-même. L'esprit d'invention s'agite, se meut, se remue d'une manière déréglée; il cherche. L'esprit de méthode arrange, ordonne et suppose que tout est trouvé ... Voilà le défaut principal de cet ouvrage. Si tout ce que l'auteur a écrit eût été entassé comme pêle-mêle, qu'il n'y eût eu que dans l'esprit de l'auteur un ordre sourd, son livre eût été infiniment plus agréable, et, sans le paraître, infiniment plus dangereux.

(*A.T.* II. 272–3)[15]

---

[14] Similarly, Diderot remarks sadly on the dead hand of his friend d'Holbach, whose translation of Hobbes's *Human Nature* 'peut-être ne fera pas la moindre sensation, grace à la manière longue, plate, diffuse, dont notre ami le baron l'a rendu' (*Corr.* XII. 46). Here it is a question of *elocutio* rather than *dispositio*, but the common enemy is boredom.

[15] It is interesting to compare Dr. Johnson's remark, recorded by Boswell in the *Journal of a Tour to the Hebrides* (ed. Chapman, London, 1930, p. 184): 'I fancy mankind may come, in time, to write all aphoristically, except in narrative; grow weary of preparation, and connection, and illustration, and all those arts by which a big book is made.' So far, he seems to have been wrong.

202 THE VOICE OF NATURE

Notice Diderot's extreme rhetorical consciousness of the audience. Again and again, he comes back to this advocacy of a disarming appearance of naturalness; knowing the public and sharing its taste, he wanted to preserve in his published correspondence with Falconet 'un air de négligence qui plaît toujours' (*Corr.* VII. 62). The aim is to please and amuse the reader. To do this, the writer must avoid appearing openly as a persuader; the philosopher who knows the world will say to his Maréchale: 'Je ne me suis pas proposé de vous persuader.' As Diderot notes, this is Montaigne's stance. And, like Montaigne and many writers after him, Diderot's ideal writer will be the opposite of the pedant; he will never give the impression of writing a book, but always of talking as light-heartedly as the subject allows.

Such at least is Diderot's normal position; it is worth noting, however, that in his article 'Encyclopédie', when discussing the manner most suited to an encyclopedia, he declares himself against fashionable frivolity: 'Il faut absolument bannir d'un grand livre ces à-propos légers, ces allusions fines, ces embellissements délicats qui feraient la fortune d'une historiette.' (*A.T.* XIV. 486.) There is, it is true, a distinction to be made between a 'natural' and a witty way of writing, but even so it is interesting to see Diderot defending the 'grand livre'. His attitude to the book, like his attitude to order, was distinctly ambiguous. Perhaps this apparent contradiction can be partly accounted for by the fact that in the *Encyclopédie* and similar works Diderot was aiming to enlighten a large and indeterminate audience, whereas in other writings, many of which remained unpublished, he was addressing a smaller, more intimate audience, whether it be the august readers of the *Correspondance littéraire* or his Parisian circle, or above all his friends Grimm and Sophie Volland. In the first case he would naturally figure as the book-writer, the pedagogue even, but in the second he was the friend and the man of good company. I do not think, however, that one should draw too sharp a line between these two forms of writing. Professor Dieckmann has shown in his masterly treatment of Diderot's attitude to his readers how Grimm and Sophie combine the functions of private audience and envoys of posterity.[16] In the private letters to Sophie we often hear the eloquence of Diderot the public figure; conversely, in the very public article 'Encyclopédie', one is struck by the very personal tone of much

[16] H. Dieckmann, *Cinq Leçons sur Diderot*, ch. 1.

that he says. He may swing between two extremes, but typically his stance is half-public, half-private, his voice that of a man talking in a room where there are both friends and strangers; sometimes he will talk eloquently to the whole company, but from time to time he will drop his voice and say something private, ironical, and self-deprecating to his friends.

In any case, Diderot is a talker and one who often rates speech higher than writing. We know from many witnesses that he was himself an exceptional conversationalist.[17] When launched, he seems to have talked inexhaustibly, moving unpredictably from one subject to another, arriving at the most unexpected conclusions. He was a good listener too, if the speaker was worth listening to. In his correspondence he often praises the talk of others, and in many of his letters to Sophie Volland he gives a brilliant rendering of conversations. Similarly he is very much alive to the appearance of real speech in literary works; he exclaims of Sedaine's *Le Philosophe sans le savoir*: 'Et foutre non, cela n'est pas écrit, mais cela est parlé.' (*Corr.* v. 212.) Normally, though, there is a regrettable gap between the spoken word and its written rendering; at the beginning of his *Entretiens sur le Fils naturel*, which are presented as the record of actual conversation, Diderot apologizes: 'Voici nos entretiens. Mais quelle différence entre ce que Dorval me disait, et ce que j'écris! . . . je ne vois plus Dorval; je ne l'entends plus. Je suis seul, parmi la poussière des livres et dans l'ombre d'un cabinet . . . et j'écris des lignes faibles, tristes et froides.' (*A.T.* VII. 86.)

Why this high value set on the spoken word in an age when the written word and the mathematical symbol were increasingly dominating the intellectual world? In the first place, as every rhetorician knew, the spoken word persuades more effectively than the written, because it carries more easily the full force of personality and conviction. In this context the speaker is not so much the charming entertainer as the overpowering orator. For Diderot, however, there was a more important rhetorical reason for preferring speech to writing. This was the awareness of an anti-pedantic tradition in educated French society of the *ancien régime*, where a high value was placed on the social art of conversation as against the solitary production and consumption of written

[17] See May, art. cit., and B. Waisbord, 'La Conversation de Diderot', *Europe*, Jan.–Feb. 1963.

works. Diderot, believing man to be essentially sociable, was always inclined to see the act of talking as more important than the subject treated—and here again he reminds one of Montaigne, the 'incomparable auteur de l'art de conférer'. There is a nice fragment of a letter in which some richly suggestive notes on an apparently chaotic conversation with d'Holbach are placed in the prestigious tradition of Montaigne's *Des coches* and rounded off with the revealing remark: 'Toutes ces idées, vraies ou fausses, trompent les heures d'une manière délicieuse. Elles amusent l'ami avec lequel on cause.' (*Corr.* IX. 96.) One is reminded of the endless conversations of *Jacques le fataliste*, whose function is less to discover the truth than to fill the time until the end of the road. In the same way the philosopher presents himself to Catherine the Great as a sort of verbal entertainer, not the writer of treatises, but an inconsequential talker: 'J'écris à votre Majesté comme elle me permet de causer avec elle. Je me livre à tous les écarts de ma tête.' (*Corr.* XIII. 92.) Here again, Diderot's natural taste adapts itself easily to a persuasive purpose.

These, then, may be called the rhetorical reasons for preferring speech to writing, in that they are concerned with the effect of communication on an audience. Such a preference could, however, be motivated in other ways, and notably in ways akin to what I have described as Diderot's first two reasons for opposing the traditional order of rhetoric. Thus, whereas the methodical treatment of written books bends subjects to a fixed order which does not necessarily suit them, the freedom of conversation allows the speaker to adapt to a complex and changing subject. And whereas the writer imprisons himself by committing himself to writing, in conversation he remains free to shift his position, expressing to the full his own variety and inconsistency. In both cases the stress is on the apparent lack of logical sequence in normal conversation. Diderot gave several memorable descriptions of this disorder, which he presents as a hidden and more subtle order. One which is often quoted comes in a letter to Sophie Volland:

C'est une chose singulière que la conversation, surtout lorsque la compagnie est un peu nombreuse. Voyez les circuits que nous avons faits. Les rêves d'un malade en délire ne sont pas plus hétéroclites. Cependant, comme il n'y a rien de décousu ni dans la tête d'un homme qui rêve, ni dans celle d'un fou, tout tient aussi dans la conversation...

(*Corr.* III. 172–3)

It will be seen that the order of conversation comes near to the order which Diderot saw as most likely to lead to the discovery of new truths.

Whether for rhetorical or philosophical reasons, then, we see Diderot setting up the casual, apparently disjointed logic of conversation against the more formal order which usually presided over the written book, and particularly the philosophical treatise. Yet we saw earlier how in some contexts he values orderly *dispositio*. All his attacks on method do not amount to a total rejection of order; his criticism of Helvétius's method implies the desirability of reaching an audience and the need to find a hidden order which is more effective than the obvious *dispositio* of *De l'esprit*. He was in fact a writer who was fully aware of the problems of communication, someone in love with books and the writing of books, yet suspecting that the order usually adopted by philosophers was both inadequate to their message and unsuitable for persuasion. Conversation provided one model, but how was it possible to preserve the virtues of the order of conversation in a written book, to write books without becoming a book-writer, to commit thoughts to paper and yet remain uncommitted, to persuade and still remain free?

Diderot tried various ways. The *Pensées philosophiques* are disconnected aphorisms in the tradition of La Rochefoucauld or Pascal. In the *Lettre sur les aveugles* and the *Lettre sur les sourds et muets* he takes advantage of the convention of the letter form to allow himself the freedom to digress; he also gives a certain reality to the convention in that his letters are addressed to real people whose promptings and likely reactions influence the development of his thought. In such works as the *Observations sur le Nakaz*, the *Réfutation d'Helvétius*, and the *Essai sur les règnes de Claude et de Néron*, he weaves his own words around a given text. It is the original text which provides such order as there is, while Diderot is left free to develop his ideas as the mood takes him. But obviously, the form which appears to give the nearest approach in writing to the living order of conversation is the dialogue.[18]

[18] On Diderot and dialogue see Dieckmann, op. cit., ch. 3; R. Mortier, 'Diderot et le problème de l'expressivité: de la pensée au dialogue heuristique', *Cahiers de l'Association internationale des études françaises*, 1963; C. Guyot, 'L'homme du dialogue', *Europe*, Jan.–Feb. 1963; E. Zants, 'Dialogue, Diderot and the New Novel in France', *Eighteenth Century Studies*, 1969.

It has often been observed that Diderot had a natural tendency towards dialogue. His thinking depended to a great extent on outside stimuli, suggestions, contradictions, or chance reading to set it in motion. He seems to have required the counter-thrust of argument to preserve his momentum. We may compare him to 'le premier' of the *Paradoxe sur le comédien*, who complains at one point: 'Eh bien, n'avez-vous rien à m'objecter?' (*A.T.* viii. 371.) The letter and the refutation or annotation both involve a sort of interlocutor, someone who listens and has to be contradicted. On other occasions Diderot invents one. In the *Discours sur la poésie dramatique*, which is a cross between a treatise and a personal letter to his great friend Melchior Grimm, he breaks from time to time into dialogue. In the *Réfutation d'Helvétius* he already has Helvétius's written words to lean on, but he goes further and actually puts words into the dead author's mouth. And in the *Contes* and *Jacques le fataliste* he cannot do without an interlocutor. The act of writing for no one in particular seems absurd; so he invents his reader:

Lorsqu'on fait un conte, c'est à quelqu'un qui l'écoute; et pour peu que le conte dure, il est rare que le conteur ne soit pas interrompu quelquefois par son auditeur. Voilà pourquoi j'ai introduit dans le récit qu'on va lire . . . un personnage qui fasse à peu près le rôle du lecteur. (*A.T.* v. 311)

Always the model for writing is speech.

In many cases, however, the form chosen by Diderot is a full-scale dialogue, in which all or most of the work consists of the directly quoted words of two or more speakers. This quasi-dramatic form had a long and magnificent history at the time when Diderot was writing; it enjoyed in the three hundred years before the Revolution a popularity in Europe which is hard for us to imagine today.[19] The form could be used for almost any subject; thus Diderot's friend, the Abbé Galiani, attacked the economic doctrines of the physiocrats in his *Dialogues sur le commerce des blés* (1770). It was assumed that the ordinary reader would be seduced by the appearance of conversation, where he might be repelled by the aridity of a methodical book. The dialogue form was very

[19] I do not know of any good general treatment of this very important form; it is a vast subject, which deserves to find its historian. Suggestive remarks on the tradition will be found in W. J. Ong, *Ramus, Method and the Decay of Dialogue*, Cambridge, Mass., 1958, and *The Barbarian Within*, New York, 1962. See also B. Beugnot, *L'Entretien au xvii* siècle*, Montréal, 1971.

useful from a pedagogical point of view in that it allowed a writer to put forward possible objections against his own position in an interesting way, thus involving the reader in the argument and leading him to the correct answer. This is what happens in the dialogues of Malebranche and Berkeley, both of whom make agreeable conversations from the material of previously published treatises.[20] They are quite open about their motives for choosing this form, thus Berkeley: 'In this treatise . . . it has been my aim to introduce the notions I advance into the mind in the most easy and familiar manner.'[21] This didactic use of dialogue may be very effective; Berkeley makes excellent use of the dramatic possibilities of the form, keeping the reader in suspense while all the time proceeding methodically to his foreordained conclusion. Typically then, the good philosophical dialogue combines an attractive and even gripping presentation with the sort of orderly *dispositio* which might equally well be found in a treatise. Shaftesbury, another prominent exponent of the form, says as much in a comment on his own dialogues: ''Tis not only at the bottom as systematical, didactic and preceptive as that other piece of formal structure, but it assumes withal another garb and more fashionable turn of wit. It conceals what is scholastical under the appearance of a polite work.'[22] Commonly, in Malebranche for instance, the dialogue is given chapter headings, just as if it was in fact a treatise.

It was, however, possible for the dialogue to be something more than a book dressed up as speech for greater effect. Among the dialogues of Plato, the fountain-head of the tradition, there are those in which something of the real life of debate is maintained. The *Symposium*, for instance, is both a well-ordered presentation of views on love and a living scene between real people. It culminates in a eulogy of one of the protagonists, Socrates, which is very important because, in a work such as this, unlike the dialogues of Berkeley or Malebranche, the speakers' characters are as significant as the opinions they express. In the words of Paul Friedländer, these dialogues 'are philosophical life, appealing to the reader to share its experience, to enter into the conversation of the dialogue, to offer resistance, or to become a follower. They

[20] N. Malebranche, *Entretiens sur la métaphysique et sur la religion*, ed. A. Cuvillier, 2 vols., Paris, 1961; G. Berkeley, *Three Dialogues between Hylas and Philonous* in *Works*, ed. A. A. Luce and T. E. Jessop, vol. II.
[21] Berkeley, op. cit., vol. II, p. 168.
[22] Shaftesbury, *Characteristics*, ed. J. M. Robertson, 2 vols., 1963, vol. II, p. 333.

do not philosophize about existence; they are existence, not always, but most of the time.'[23]

It hardly needs saying that not many subsequent philosophical dialogues equal the dramatic presentation of the *Symposium*. Nor are there many where the issues are presented in a truly open manner, where the dialogue conveys the urgency of unresolved debate rather than the agreeable serving-up of pre-established conclusions. There are some, however. Hume's *Dialogues concerning Natural Religion* continue to stir up readers and puzzle interpreters, who cannot agree which character speaks for the author. I do not wish to discuss this work, but I should like at this stage to quote at some length from the prefatory letter, since this gives a brilliant account of the problems and possibilities of the 'Platonic' dialogue:

Accurate and regular argument, indeed, such as is now expected of philosophical enquirers, naturally throws a man into the methodical and didactic manner, where he can immediately, without preparation, explain the point, at which he aims, and thence proceed, without interruption, to deduce the proofs, on which it is established. To deliver a SYSTEM in conversation scarcely appears natural; and while the dialogue-writer desires, by departing from the direct style of composition, to give a freer air to his performance, and avoid the appearance of *author* and *reader*, he is apt to run into a worse inconvenience, and convey the image of *pedagogue* and *pupil*. Or if he carries on the dispute in the natural spirit of good company, by throwing in a variety of topics, and preserving a proper balance between the speakers, he often loses so much time in preparations and transitions, that the reader will scarcely think himself compensated, by all the graces of dialogue, for the order, brevity, and precision, which are sacrificed to them.

There are some subjects, however, to which dialogue-writing is peculiarly adapted, and where it is still preferable to the direct and simple method of composition.

Any point of doctrine, which is so *obvious*, that it scarcely admits of dispute, but at the same time so *important*, that it cannot be too often inculcated, seems to require some such method of handling it, where the novelty of the manner may compensate the triteness of the subject, where the vivacity of conversation may enforce the precept, and where the variety of lights, presented by various personages and characters, may appear neither tedious nor redundant.

[23] P. Friedländer, *Plato*, tr. H. Meyerhoff, New York, 1963, vol. I, p. 235.

Any question of philosophy, on the other hand, which is so *obscure* and *uncertain*, that human reason can reach no fixed determination with regard to it, if it should be treated at all, seems to lead us naturally into the style of dialogue and conversation. Reasonable men may be allowed to differ, where no one can reasonably be positive, opposite sentiments, even without any decision, afford an agreeable amusement, and if the subject be curious and interesting, the book carries us, in a manner, into company, and unites the two greatest and purest pleasures of human life, study and society.[24]

These contemporary remarks are an excellent introduction to thinking about Diderot's dialogues. They stress the rhetorical attractions of the dialogue, its 'graces', its 'freer air', and the 'agreeable amusement' it affords, but they suggest that these worldly graces may conflict with a serious and orderly treatment of a subject. At the same time they show how the dialogue may correspond to something more acceptable than the desire to dress up the truth, that it may in fact be *the* appropriate form for certain subjects—and for certain authors, Diderot might have added. Bearing Hume's words in mind, I should like now to examine the nature of Diderot's various dialogues. In doing so I shall concentrate on the question of order from which I started, but this will lead to more general considerations about the use of the dialogue form.

One should perhaps begin, briefly, with the *Promenade du sceptique* (1747), even though only a part of this is in true dialogue form.[25] The most striking formal characteristic of this early work is the rather obviously literary presentation. The speaker at first is a conventional narrator, a philosopher-soldier, who is soon recounting a dialogue between himself and his wise friend Cléobule. This is a disguised preface—an interesting one, because Diderot here uses the dialogue to express his own uncertainty about the value of writing for a wide audience. Thereafter the bulk of the work purports to be the words of Cléobule, speaking without interruption from the original narrator, who appears merely as the 'tu' to whom the speech is addressed. In the course of his

24 Hume, *Dialogues concerning Natural Religion*, ed. N. Kemp-Smith, Oxford, 1935, pp. 157–8.
25 On the relationship of thought and form in this work see the article of H. Dieckmann, 'Diderot's *Promenade du sceptique*', in *Studies on Voltaire and the Eighteenth Century*, no. 55, 1967, pp. 417–38.

laboured allegory about the Church, Philosophy, and the World, Cléobule occasionally resorts to dialogue. In the first two instances these dialogues are Voltairean pieces which present the conversation of a bigot and a reasonable man in such a way that the reader has no alternative but to laugh at the bigot. The function of these passages is clearly to introduce some variety into Cléobule's monotonous allegory. But the third and most important piece of dialogue comes nearer to the Platonic tradition. It is a short discussion between an atheist, a deist, a sceptic, and a Spinozist, in which the deist appears to be winning until he is unexpectedly routed by the Spinozist. We are not told the deist's answer; Cléobule merely says: 'on y pèse actuellement nos raisons; et si l'on y prononce jamais un jugement définitif, je t'en instruirai.' (*A.T.* I. 235.)

It will be seen that at this point the dialogue has something of the openness and unpredictability of real conversation. Further, the presentation of the argument as a discussion between fictional characters allows Diderot to distance himself from it, avoiding the stance of pedagogue. Indeed, the relatively complex structure of the work gives the author a convenient hiding-place. By the time we reach the Spinozist's onslaught, which in any case may not correspond to Diderot's real convictions, we are listening to a conversation being retold by a witness, whose words in turn are given to us by a fictitious narrator—and this narrator has apologized in typical Diderot fashion for the inadequacy of his rendering: 'Je ne doute point qu'en passant par ma plume, les choses n'aient beaucoup perdu de l'énergie et de la vivacité qu'elles avaient dans sa bouche.' (*A.T.* I. 180.) This complexity and use of receding planes, which we find in so much of Diderot's writing, seems to correspond not only to the need for self-protection, but also to a more positive taste for the appearance of disorder; like Cléobule, Diderot prefers 'un désordre toujours nouveau à la symétrie qu'on sait en un moment' (*A.T.* I. 178). Nevertheless, for all these disguises, the *Promenade* remains a pretty conventional literary piece. The characters in the allegory and the dialogue wear the traditional Greek names, Ariste, Cléobule, Athéos, Philoxène, which are a recurring feature of even the best philosophical dialogues of the period. These names fit perfectly into the unreal allegory-setting, though they jar slightly with the reference to the battle of Fontenoy on the first page of the book. And for all the complexity of presentation, the over-all order remains clear: a classic division into three, the 'Allée des Épines', the 'Allée des Marronniers', and the 'Allée des Fleurs'. Apart from the surprise of the Spinozist, it is 'la symétrie qu'on sait en un moment' rather than the 'désordre toujours nouveau'.

There is also a threefold division in Diderot's next dialogue, the *Entretiens sur le Fils naturel* (1757), but here the division resembles less the division of a subject into three for easier assimilation than the division of a play into acts. There is indeed a strong dramatic element in these dialogues. As if to illustrate the subject under discussion, we are told a good deal about the appearance and movements of the main speaker, Dorval. Both he and his interlocutor, 'Moi', who is a pale Diderot, are clearly characterized and speak with distinctive voices, the narrator calmly and critically, Dorval with eloquence and enthusiasm. This is particularly striking at the beginning of the second *entretien*, where we are shown Dorval meditating on a wild scene and exclaiming:

O Nature, tout ce qui est bien est renfermé dans ton sein! Tu es la source féconde de toutes vérités! . . . Il n'y a dans ce monde que la vertu et la vérité qui soient dignes de m'occuper . . . L'enthousiasme naît d'un objet de la nature. Si l'esprit l'a vu sous des aspects frappants et divers, il en est occupé, agité, tourmenté. L'imagination s'échauffe; la passion s'émeut. (*A.T.* VII. 103)

The passage has a close connection with the dramatic theories of the dialogues, which are placed under the twin signs of nature and passion, but these theories are given greater force through being spoken by a man who so clearly lives his ideas and whose manner of speaking bears a marked resemblance to the dramatic style advocated by Diderot. Dorval is indeed a real character to us (or should be) before we even read the dialogues, since he is also one of the protagonists of the play which is under discussion, *Le Fils naturel*. He is also supposedly the author of the play, which is presented as a rendering of what actually happened to Dorval and his friends. This play with fact and fiction is typical of Diderot; it enables him to give greater immediacy to his writing, for rather than listening to a Spinozist talking to a deist, we are hearing Diderot, whom we know to be a real person, talking to a character who is on the borders of the real, even if we know him to be a fiction. At the same time, the dramatic form again allows the writer to withdraw from total commitment. While 'Moi' is clearly Diderot the encyclopedist philosopher, Dorval is equally clearly Diderot in some respects, even though he may share some characteristics with Jean-Jacques Rousseau. The doubling-up is particularly neat on the final page, where Dorval says to 'Moi': 'Oui . . . retournez à Paris . . . Publiez le septième volume de l'*Encyclopédie* . . . Venez vous reposer ici . . . et comptez que *le Père de famille* ne se fera point, ou qu'il sera fait avant la fin de vos vacances . . .' (*A.T.* VII. 167.) In this way Diderot is able to put forward his views with the eloquence of Dorval, but also to preserve the cooler tone of 'Moi', showing himself aware of all the objections that could be brought against his ideas.

The order of these dialogues is not then the typically logical order of didactic exposition. The first two dialogues are propelled forward by 'Moi' 's apparently random comments on *Le Fils naturel*. In this respect the dialogues belong to the same family as the commentaries on Hemsterhuis, Helvétius, or the Nakaz, in which the writer is freed from the slavery of composition and weaves his parasitic work round an existing text (in this case both text and commentary are by Diderot). The commentary form lends itself to all sorts of excursions and apparent digressions—Diderot is very conscious of this and makes Dorval remark at the end of one such parenthesis: 'Mais où en sommes-nous de notre examen? Puisque c'est vous qui m'égarez, vous vous chargez sans doute de me remettre dans la voie.' (*A.T.* VII. 124.) It may be noted in passing that this sort of composition by interruption and parenthesis is characteristic of Diderot. Rather than deal completely with one thing before moving to another, he prefers to advance simultaneously on several fronts. He gives us a thread to hold on to as we advance with him; in *Jacques le fataliste* it is the story of Jacques's love, here it is the scene-by-scene comments of 'Moi'.

These comments are, of course, no more than a pretext for the exposition of Dorval-Diderot's ideas. In the first *entretien* this is mainly fragmentary, whetting our appetite for a more complete treatment. In the second *entretien*, after the apostrophe to Nature which sets the tone for what follows, Dorval expounds his theories of gesture and declamation at some length and with few interruptions from 'Moi', only to return to the commentary, as if this were the main subject of the work: 'Mais nous voilà bien loin de ma pièce.' (*A.T.* VII. 109.) Thereafter the dialogue alternates between long speeches by Dorval and more rapid exchanges, usually involving questions of detail. This alternation recalls the combination of tirade and stichomythia of classical tragedy and serves the same purpose, the avoidance of tedium. Eventually, however, towards the end of the second *entretien*, the commentary comes to an end; the conversation now has enough impetus to do without this prop. The third *entretien*, like the second, begins with a long speech from Dorval, which again provides a starting-point for a discussion which is full of digression and changes of direction.

The *Entretiens* are not without order. After the brief introductory dialogue, which suggests some of the themes that will be discussed, there is a broad over-all division, with the second *entretien* concentrating more on questions of gesture, style, and staging and the third developing Diderot's ideas on the theatrical genres. These subjects are announced at the end of the preceding dialogues, so that we know roughly what to expect, and at the end of the third *entretien* there is a recapitulation of the main points of reform suggested by Dorval:

La tragédie domestique et bourgeoise à créer.
Le genre sérieux à perfectionner.
Les conditions de l'homme à substituer aux caractères, peut-être dans tous les genres.
La pantomime à lier étroitement avec l'action dramatique.
La scène à changer, et les tableaux à substituer aux coups de théâtre . . .
La tragédie réelle à introduire sur le théâtre lyrique.
Enfin la danse à réduire sous la forme d'un véritable poème, à écrire et à séparer de tout autre art d'imitation.

(*A.T.* VII. 161)

This is a very schematic account and is hardly more faithful to the spirit of the *Entretiens* than the similar table of contents at the end of the chaotic *Lettre sur les sourds et muets*, but it does suggest that Diderot is making an effort to help his reader. In the same way, in the course of the dialogue, he has 'Moi' provide a brief summary of Dorval's wandering ideas: 'Je vous entends: Le burlesque . . . Le genre comique . . . Le genre sérieux . . . Le genre tragique . . . Le merveilleux.' (*A.T.* VII. 135.)

To this extent the dialogue is a treatise in disguise. But it is a far cry from the didactic dialogues of a Malebranche. There is some ordering of the material, but Diderot's method is close to that of

UNIVERSITY LIBRARIES
CARNEGIE-MELLON UNIVERSITY
PITTSBURGH, PENNSYLVANIA 15213

a serious conversation, where the same subject is touched on from various angles, often with repetitions and paraphrases, and always with recourse to examples and anecdotes, which may appear to digress from the immediate point, but help to illuminate the subject as a whole. And finally, it avoids the earnestness which the persuasive order of monologue easily falls into. Dorval's enthusiastic propaganda for the *drame* is put in an almost casual setting; indeed, he himself insists that he may talk about these things, but is not really interested in publishing them: 'J'ai commencé, il y a longtemps, à chercher mon bonheur dans un objet qui fût plus solide, et qui dépendît plus de moi que la gloire littéraire.' (*A.T.* VII. 166.) When a writer speaks directly to his public, he cannot normally suggest that they are not listening to him, but the dialogue form allows this awareness to be expressed; at one point Dorval is obliged to break off his remarks and say: 'Mais vous êtes distrait . . . vous rêvez . . . vous ne m'écoutez pas.' (*A.T.* VII. 146.) Similarly, where a dissertation is expected to reach a conclusion, a dialogue will naturally peter out into desultory talk and, traditionally, a supper.

Diderot's second theatrical dialogue, *Le Paradoxe sur le comédien*, also ends with a supper, or at least the prospect of one. Particularly towards the end, it shows an even greater awareness than the *Entretiens* of the gaps in communication. This ironical use of dialogue is very clear in the following passage, which follows a tirade from 'le premier':

> LE PREMIER. Ne le pensez-vous pas?
> LE SECOND. Je ne pense rien. Je ne vous ai pas entendu.
> LE PREMIER. Quoi! nous n'avons pas continué à disputer?
> LE SECOND. Non.
> LE PREMIER. Et que diable faisiez-vous donc?
> LE SECOND. Je rêvais.
>
> (*A.T.* VIII. 421)

Typically, Diderot's dialogues exhibit this consciousness of the traps of monologue and enable him to distance himself safely from the exaggerated exposition of his own ideas. In the case of the *Paradoxe*, the text tells us that 'le premier' is Diderot, the author of *Le Père de famille* and *Est-il bon? Est-il méchant?* But 'le second', who is given an excessively naive notion of the role of emotion in acting, has views not unlike those of the Diderot of 1757, the author of the *Entretiens sur le Fils naturel*. Once again dramatic *dédoublement* affords the real author a hiding-place.

With its frequent digressions and interruptions, the *Paradoxe* has some of the apparent disorder of conversation. Its brusque opening ('N'en parlons plus') is like the opening of a play—one thinks, for instance, of the first lines of *Le Misanthrope*. But, compared with the *Entretiens*, the *Paradoxe* remains very much an essay. There is little attempt to localize the action or give any physical details to back up the voices of interlocutors who are simply 'le premier' and 'le second'. Nor is the balance kept at all even between the two speakers. It is true that in the last twenty pages or so, when 'le premier' has had his say, 'le second' is given more time, but he is not allowed to lead, as 'Moi' does with his comments on *Le Fils naturel*. His part is like that of the confidant in classical tragedy; at the beginning his questioning launches the reluctant 'premier' on an exposition of his ideas, and thereafter his questions and exclamations keep the dialogue moving along. At times he is even reduced to confirming what 'le premier' has said; there are moments when the dialogue reads like a set of liturgical responses:

> LE PREMIER. Celui qui dans la société se propose, et a le malheureux talent de plaire à tous, n'est rien, n'a rien qui lui appartienne, qui le distingue, qui engoue les uns et qui fatigue les autres. Il parle toujours, et toujours bien; c'est un adulateur de profession, c'est un grand courtisan, c'est un grand comédien.
>
> LE SECOND. Un grand courtisan, accoutumé, depuis qu'il respire, au rôle d'un pantin merveilleux, prend toutes sortes de formes, au gré de la ficelle qui est entre les mains de son maître.
>
> LE PREMIER. Un grand comédien est un autre pantin merveilleux dont le poète tient la ficelle, et auquel il indique à chaque ligne la véritable forme qu'il doit prendre.
>
> (A.T. VIII. 397)

Here it is easy to see that Diderot is simply dressing up a monologue in dialogue form, presumably to make it more lively. Conversely, there are occasions where he has not made the effort, where 'le premier' asks rhetorical questions, which should perhaps have been objections in the mouth of 'le second' if the dialogue form had been adopted whole-heartedly. This becomes very obvious in an interesting passage towards the end, where the conversation stops and a hitherto unheard narrator starts to speak, describing 'le premier' muttering his thoughts; the narrator introduces these thoughts in the following way:

Les idées de l'homme au paradoxe sont les seules dont je puisse rendre compte, et les voici aussi décousues qu'elles doivent le paraître lorsqu'on supprime d'un soliloque les intermédiaires qui servent de liaison.
(*A.T.* VIII. 416)

The dialogue form appears here as a rhetorical preparation which makes an author's jottings easier to follow; Diderot has not bothered to dress up the next page or two in this way, although he returns to dialogue at the end of the work. In general, the use of dialogue in the *Paradoxe* is about as perfunctory as the use of allegory in the *Promenade du sceptique*. It is a hastily assumed disguise rather than something integral to Diderot's thought—this appears most clearly of all when 'le premier' finishes his disquisition with what is a barely concealed bibliographical note by the author:

Au reste, la question que j'approfondis a été autrefois entamée entre un médiocre littérateur, Rémond de Saint-Albine, et un grand comédien, Riccoboni . . . C'est une anecdote que j'ignorais et que je viens d'apprendre. (*A.T.* VIII. 410)

This 'que je viens d'apprendre' breaks the dialogue convention wide open and makes it clear that this is really an essay written by Diderot.

We have seen that in the *Entretiens* there is a certain over-all ordering of material. This is not the case with the *Paradoxe*. Even though the work takes the form of a monologue which is not effectively interrupted or deflected, it remains more or less untouched by classical *dispositio*. This is partly because the subject of discussion is less complex than that of the *Entretiens*; the *Paradoxe* is basically the development of a single idea, that great actors are cold observers rather than sensitive beings. This is the sort of idea which could have been treated in the manner of the rhetorical *chria*, but Diderot prefers to proceed in a much less orderly manner. It is impossible to reduce the work to a neat table of contents; the most that can be said is that after a brief lead-in (hardly an *exordium*), consisting typically of comments on another book, the main theme is stated and developed at some length. Once this has been done, the rest of the dialogue consists of a variety of approaches to the subject, digressions to related areas, and the accumulation of anecdotes which bolster up the argument. As usual with Diderot, the complexity of structure increased with successive drafts, as new developments and anecdotes were added, but even the first version, which appeared in the *Correspondance littéraire* of 1770, already shows the same disdain for classical order. If anything, the composition reminds one of certain musical forms, perhaps the theme and variations. It does not build up to a climax, however. At one point it seems that everything has been said; 'le second' remarks: 'Je pense qu'il vous reste peu de chose à dire', but 'le premier' replies: 'Vous vous trompez' (*A.T.* VIII. 403), and the dialogue proceeds, always inconclusively, for a further twenty pages. Diderot is conscious of this disorder, if that is the word for it; at the beginning 'le premier' says, apologetically: 'Je n'ai pas encore bien enchaîné mes raisons, et vous me permettrez de vous les exposer comme elles me viendront, dans le désordre de l'ouvrage même de votre ami.' (*A.T.* VIII. 365.) This suggests that what follows will be the familiar commentary, but in fact Diderot's disorder is entirely self-generated. And in the end I think it would be agreed that this wilful disorder, when associated with the affirmation of a paradox in what is after all quite a short work, is in reality an effective order of persuasion. As we have seen, however, it is not really the order of dialogue.

Diderot's two dialogues on the theatre are unusual, for him, in presenting only two speakers, one of whom gives a fairly complete exposition of the author's ideas. The short *Entretien d'un philosophe avec la Maréchale de* *** (1774) is not dissimilar in that the character called 'Diderot' (or 'Crudeli' in another version) is patently a mouthpiece for the philosopher Diderot. Nevertheless, the Maréchale is not overshadowed; it is she who starts the argument and, as it progresses, she refuses to let herself be won over. At one point she says to her interlocutor: 'Je ne sais trop que vous répondre, et cependant vous ne me persuadez pas.' The philosopher's answer is characteristic: 'Je ne me suis pas proposé de vous persuader.' (*A.T.* II. 518.) Far more than in the two theatrical dialogues, Diderot is anxious to avoid the pedagogue–pupil relation which Hume warned against. This is the aspect of the work which was picked out for praise in the first published version, when the dialogue was presented as a translation from the Italian of Crudeli. The preface declared:

Ce dialogue n'est pas sans profondeur, mais elle y est partout dérobée par la naïveté et la simplicité du discours. Il serait à souhaiter que les matières importantes se traitassent toujours avec la même impartialité, et dans le même esprit de tolérance. Le philosophe ne prétend point amener la dame à ses opinions, et celle-ci, de son côté, écoute ses raisons sans humeur, et ils se séparent l'un de l'autre en s'aimant et en s'estimant. En traduisant ce dialogue, il nous paraissait assister véritablement à leur conversation; nous espérons qu'on éprouvera le même effet à la lecture. (*A.T.* II. 506)

Formally, then, the main feature of this *Entretien* is the relaxed, urbane tone of polite conversation. It is important that the talk should not seem ponderous; one of the ways in which this is managed is the frequent reference to the fact that the philosopher has really come to see the Maréchal, not his wife. Several times he begins to break off the conversation with a 'Mais, Monsieur le Maréchal . . .', only to be kept to the subject by his tenacious interlocutor. He is just whiling away time talking to the lady of the house, allowing her to push him into playing the part of the philosopher. Thus, although at one point (*A.T.* II. 511–12) there is something of the formal order of a properly conducted argument, where the philosopher establishes a definition of good and evil which is acceptable to the Maréchale, this is presented as almost a parody, with the lady's 'Et j'ai fait de la philosophie!' echoing Monsieur Jourdain's joy in discovering prose. The implication is that the order usually associated with philosophy is pedantic and unnecessary. Not that the conversation of Diderot and the Maréchale is positively disorderly. As a piece of polite talk it proceeds with a certain formality; the partners listen to one another and do not interrupt. There is, too, a fairly logical progression from one subject to another. Thus, towards the end, the talk moves from a discussion of the consoling function of Christianity to a consideration of the immortality of the soul, thence to the question of the creation and the nature of matter and spirit, men and animals. But it must be said that none of these topics is more than touched on; this is not the steady progress of the serious thinker, but the rapid flight of the intelligent talker. Once or twice Diderot elaborates, but for the most part it is up to the reader, having been stimulated by the talk, to fill in all the developments for himself. This is something like the order which Diderot admired in Montaigne, 'qui ne veut jamais prouver, et qui va toujours prouvant'. The dialogue is persuasive in intention, but it hopes to be more effective by virtue of this elegant lightness of touch.

Describing the *Entretien*, Diderot wrote to Catherine the Great: 'Ce sont quelques pages, moitié sérieuses, et moitié gaies.' (*Corr.* XIV. 85.) The same sort of juxtaposition of terms can be seen in the various descriptions of *Le Rêve de d'Alembert* (1769) found in letters to Sophie Volland. Diderot remarks, for instance: 'J'ai fait un dialogue entre d'Alembert et moi; nous y causons assez gaiement, et même assez clairement, malgré la sécheresse et l'obscurité du sujet.' So much for the first dialogue; for the second one, the dream proper, the terms change somewhat: 'cela est de la plus haute extravagance et tout à la fois de la philosophie la plus profonde.' Gaiety has become extravagance, but the aim seems to be the same, to 'donner à la sagesse l'air de la folie, afin de lui procurer ses entrées' (*Corr.* IX. 126-7). If we are to take this at face value, the apparently non-serious side to these dialogues—and this will include their lack of traditional order—is to be seen as rhetorical in intention, an aid to effective communication rather than a necessary consequence of the subject under discussion.

Before considering this point, it may be helpful to recall the over-all construction of the three dialogues which make up the *Rêve*. The first of them, the *Entretien entre d'Alembert et Diderot*, is a typical philosophical dialogue, comparable to the *Entretiens sur le Fils naturel*, in which a persuasive character called Diderot tries to convince his sceptical friend d'Alembert of the truth of his materialistic theory of universal sensibility. The second, *Le Rêve de d'Alembert*, opens with d'Alembert asleep at home. His friend, Mademoiselle de Lespinasse, tells the doctor, Bordeu, of the apparently delirious things which he has said in his sleep; when Bordeu elaborates on d'Alembert's dream-words, she mocks him. Their conversation is interrupted by a continuation of the dream, in which we hear d'Alembert talking directly. Thereafter the conversation between Bordeu and Mademoiselle de Lespinasse continues; by now she is playing the part of willing learner. D'Alembert wakes up and joins them, asking questions and remaining fairly sceptical; eventually the doctor has to hurry off to see a patient. The third and shortest dialogue, the *Suite de l'entretien*, is simply a continuation of the conversation between Bordeu and Mademoiselle de Lespinasse, in which she asks him some

tricky questions about sexual morality. It will be seen that it is
by no means a homogeneous work. The first section is a conversation between equals, where questions are put and answers only
very tentatively proposed. The second and third are more one-
sided; the opposition to what we take to be Diderot's ideas is not
so forceful, consisting mainly of the common-sense scepticism of
Mademoiselle de Lespinasse—and even this gives way fairly
quickly to the stance of eager listener. A further distinction should
be made, that between the dream sequences, which are chaotic
and eloquent, and the much more level-headed discussion which
follows them.

The dialogue takes different forms, then, but this does not
prevent Diderot from giving his work a certain unity of tone. The
distinctions which I have made do not strike the reader very
strongly, because the whole work is cast in the form of a series
of realistic conversation pieces. Diderot had begun with the idea
of writing a more traditional 'dialogue of the dead' between
Democritus, Hippocrates, and Leucippe, but decided that although this might give dignity to the work, it would involve too
many sacrifices. The primary sacrifice concerned the contemporary
scientific subject-matter, but one may also imagine that it suited
his rhetorical purposes better to bring his dialogue as near as
possible to the reality of conversation as his readers knew it. For
this reason the dialogues bristle with contemporary references, the
individual speakers are clearly characterized and speak for most of
the time with distinctive voices, they are given actions and gestures as well as words, and the setting in time and space is vividly
evoked. The talk is lively, often witty, and close to the dialogue of
drama. In fact Diderot, in his *Lettre d'envoi*, describes the work as
a 'comédie'; it has, he says, 'de l'originalité, de la force, de la
verve, de la gaieté, du naturel et même de la suite' (*A.T.* IX.
251–2).[26]

'De la suite'—what sort of order is meant by this? Is it again
the subtle order of conversation which Diderot admired in Montaigne's *Des coches*? Certainly there is an appearance of attractive

---

[26] For a different point of view see the interesting article of G. Daniel, 'Autour
du *Rêve de d'Alembert*; réflexions sur l'esthétique de Diderot', *Diderot Studies*, XII,
1969, pp. 13–73. Daniel suggests either that this rather traditional praise of the
classic dramatic qualities of the dialogue is not meant seriously, or else that it shows
Diderot to be afraid of his own genius. For him, 'dramatic' qualities are subordinated
to a dream-like unity, at any rate in the second of the dialogues.

disorder, which seems calculated to charm an audience bored by treatises. There is the constant recourse to the anecdote; this may be necessary, as Bordeu says, to make abstractions come alive, but it tends to break the expository flow. The line of argument is interrupted by the actions of the protagonists, Mademoiselle de Lespinasse's piece of by-play with the valet, for instance, and d'Alembert's erotic dream—a dream which appears to be merely gratuitous titillation, until one realizes that it connects with a great deal of the surrounding dialogue and in particular with the subsequent discussion of the physiology of dreams. Exactly like the *Entretien avec la Maréchale*, the second dialogue is punctuated by the attempts of Bordeu to escape and rush off to his patient— here again this lends rapidity and a certain inconsequentiality to the talk. More generally, the dialogue is full of digressions and parentheses, the most striking being the one where Mademoiselle de Lespinasse is about to put forward her image of the spider, when she is interrupted by the dream talk of d'Alembert—and this in its turn encloses a brief discussion on the relation between needs and organs. As in the *Lettre sur les aveugles*, Diderot admits these 'écarts', half-apologetically, half-defiantly. At one point Bordeu objects: 'du train dont nous y allons on effleure tout, et l'on n'approfondit rien', but Mademoiselle de Lespinasse replies: 'Qu'importe? nous ne composons pas, nous causons.' (*A.T.* ii. 166.)

All of these factors combine to suggest to the reader that this is not really a book, not a pedantic attempt to put a theory over to us, but the record of a real conversation between living people. But underneath this theatrical appearance, it is not difficult to detect the bare bones of a potential treatise. The first dialogue poses in general terms the problems of the traditional dualism of matter and spirit and suggests that the theory of universal sensibility and spontaneous generation may enable us to explain the phenomena of life and thought. The second dialogue 'sert d'éclaircissement au premier', as Diderot wrote to Sophie Volland (*Corr.* ix. 126); it takes up the same themes, using some of the same examples (above all, that of the egg). The dream is used to break some of the normal eighteenth-century assumptions concerning fixity of species and to set the question in the wider context of the evolution of the universe, where everything is possible. Man having been given his proper place in the natural order, Diderot can proceed to a more detailed exposition of his materialistic psycho-physiology, describing the operation of the nervous system, and discussing the nature of memory and the relation of the 'sensorium commune' to the rest of the system. This leads him to deal more rapidly with related questions, the value of sensibility, the phenomena of sleep and dreaming, the question of free will and its ethical consequences. Finally, after a deliberate recapitulation, which takes us back to the question that opened the first dialogue, the *Rêve* ends with a few notes on imagination and abstraction. The third dialogue is merely a corollary, drawing out some of the sexual implications of the preceding physiological exposition.

Particularly in the second half of the *Rêve*, the dialogue form sometimes seems a very thin disguise for didactic monologue.[27] Mademoiselle de Lespinasse is made a very rapid learner, often answering Bordeu as we saw 'le second' answering 'le premier' in the *Paradoxe sur le comédien*. When Bordeu says:

Si cette infinie diversité de toucher n'existait pas, on saurait qu'on éprouve du plaisir ou de la douleur, mais on ne saurait où les rapporter. Il faudrait le secours de la vue. Ce ne serait plus une affaire de sensation, ce serait une affaire d'expérience et d'observation,

she replies:

Quand je dirais que j'ai mal au doigt, si l'on me demandait pourquoi j'assure que c'est au doigt que j'ai mal, il faudrait que je répondisse non pas que je le sens, mais que je sens du mal et que je vois que mon doigt est malade. (*A.T.* ii. 146)

Diderot, sensing the artificiality of the procedure, finds it necessary to bring in a little humorous dialogue here to make the talk more real ('Docteur, vous embrassez mademoiselle; c'est fort bien fait à vous'). Similarly he seems slightly embarrassed at having put the spider image in her mouth and makes her exclaim, very much like the Maréchale: 'j'ai fait de la prose sans m'en douter.'

It is possible, then, to imagine the work stripped of its attractive dialogue presentation (and stripped also of its striking metaphors and similes), as the rhetoricians taught their pupils to strip down the speeches of Cicero. It might resemble the *Éléments de physio-*

---

[27] Daniel (art. cit., p. 46) puts this in more positive terms: 'Tout se passe comme si Diderot, en composant le dialogue, s'était amusé à répartir les différents éléments d'une pensée, et ceux de la phrase ou de la période qui l'expriment, entre plusieurs voix, engagées, non dans une conversation, mais dans une sorte de duo d'opéra, avec tout ce que cela comporte d'artifice et de stylisation.'

logie, which were composed in the same period. This is to situate the *Rêve* in the tradition of scientific popularization, of which Fontenelle's *Entretiens sur la pluralité des mondes* is the classic representative—significantly, the *Rêve* contains a somewhat ambiguous exchange on the elegant style of Fontenelle's dialogues (*A.T.* II. 134). One would have to stress the different aesthetic norms governing the different performances—Diderot's dialogues striving more than Fontenelle's towards an appearance of natural disorder, reflecting his own taste and that of his contemporaries—but one might assert that the relation between content and form is comparable in the two works.

Putting it like that suggests that the rhetorical explanation of the form of the *Rêve* is inadequate. Few readers of Diderot would be willing to place these dialogues alongside the *Entretiens* of Fontenelle. Although the irregular conversational form is designed, as Diderot put it, to 'procurer ses entrées à la sagesse', it fulfils other equally important functions.[28] In the first place, one must remember that although the dialogues were designed to be read by someone eventually, they do not appear to have been aimed in the first instance at a wide public—typically, Diderot speaks of reading them aloud to Sophie. He also mentions the pleasure 'de se rendre compte à soi-même de ses opinions' (*A.T.* IX. 251). This suggests that the form of the work may correspond as much to Diderot's personal attitude to his subject as to any designs on an audience. He knew that the hypotheses which so excited him were for the time being no more than hypotheses; it was essential that they should be put forward not dogmatically, but tentatively. It is for this reason that he uses the dream form; the dream evokes the inspiration of creative genius, but it also enables Diderot to distance himself from some of his more absurd flights of fancy. In addition it allows him the irony of putting into d'Alembert's mouth ideas which the waking geometer would never have admitted. But the irony is directed against himself as well; this is seen notably in the use of the doubter, Mademoiselle de Lespinasse, to mock all these spendid hypotheses as either delirious or time-wasting. She asks Bordeu: 'Qu'appelez-vous un sujet grave?'; he replies with what is virtually a table of contents

[28] See H. Dieckmann, *Die künstlerische Form des Rêve de d'Alembert*, Cologne, 1966, and the discussion contained in it, particularly the exchange between Professor Dieckmann and Professor Iser.

of the *Rêve*, and she retorts: 'Moi, j'appelle cela des folies auxquelles je permets de rêver quand on dort, mais dont un homme
de bon sens qui veille ne s'occupera jamais.' (*A.T.* II. 135.) It is
true that she is soon converted, but here, as at the end of the *De
l'interprétation de la nature*, there is a lurking scepticism about the
value of investigating the huge and difficult subjects which interest
Diderot:

Si les hommes étaient sages, ils se livreraient enfin à des recherches
relatives à leur bien-être, et ne répondraient à mes questions futiles
que dans mille ans au plus tôt; ou peut-être même, considérant sans
cesse le peu d'étendue qu'ils occupent dans l'espace et dans la durée,
ils ne daigneraient jamais y répondre.[29]   (*A.T.* II. 60)

Diderot combats this scepticism at the end of the dialogue between
d'Alembert and himself, but it is a constant part of his philosophical attitude and one which finds expression in the fluidity and
contradictions of dialogue. In the end, perhaps, it is impossible
to separate this function of dialogue from the more consciously
rhetorical purpose; the disguise of dialogue suits Diderot's philosophical attitude just as it serves his persuasive intention, since
this sceptical, tentative attitude was just the thing to appeal to an
intelligent and essentially literary public.

   Disorder in the *Rêve de d'Alembert* has yet another function apart
from rhetorical appeal and the expression of a personal attitude.
I mentioned earlier the long digression which separates Mademoiselle de Lespinasse's announcement of the spider theme from
her actual statement of it. She is just about to embark on this
metaphorical description of the role of the brain in the nervous
system, when the sleeping d'Alembert starts to talk again; in a
'belle excursion' which lasts some four pages (*A.T.* II. 137–40),
he speaks of the 'flux perpétuel' of the universe, the great chain
of being, the philosophical impossibility of distinguishing individuals in the 'grand tout'. Only when he has finished can
Mademoiselle de Lespinasse expound her spider theory. This sort
of suspense is one of Diderot's favourite tricks—it is the main-
spring of *Jacques le fataliste*—but here it serves a philosophical
purpose in that it forces us to examine the possible connections
between the main line of argument and the 'digression'. The links

---

[29] On Diderot's literary scepticism in relation to scientific questions see J. Roger,
Les Sciences de la vie dans la pensée française du xviiie siècle, Paris, 1963, pp. 676–8.

are numerous; one which is subsequently brought out is the
suggestion, previously made in *De l'interprétation de la nature*, that
the spider image applies to the cosmos just as it applies to man.
The 'grand tout' may have the same sort of unity which we can
see in the microcosm.

In this case, then, the broken order is not merely a persuasive
device, but corresponds to the reality of the subject, leading us to
wonder whether the universe may not be full of unexpected connections and analogies. The sense of these would be lost in the
linear progress of a methodical treatise, but it is preserved in the
looping, circular, parenthetic form which Diderot so loves. The
actual use of dialogue is not essential —Diderot can make the letter
work in the same sort of way—but in a dialogue it is easier to
introduce this feeling of complexity and movement without being
accused of obscurity or incompetence. In a different way, we are
still in the field of rhetoric, which always favoured adapting the
dispositio to the subject-matter. But it must be said that this is a far
cry from the norms of philosophical rhetoric.

The *Rêve de d'Alembert* is one of Diderot's most important
philosophical dialogues. It will be possible to deal more rapidly
with the *Supplément au Voyage de Bougainville* (1772) and the *Entretien d'un père avec ses enfants* (1773), although they are among his
most attractive works. The *Supplément* really needs to be read in
conjunction with the two stories, *Ceci n'est pas un conte* and *Madame
de la Carlière*, since they are continuous with one another and all
deal with the relation between the sexes. They too are couched in
dialogue form, and, in *Madame de la Carlière* in particular, the conversation of story-teller and listener constantly breaks the smooth
line of the anecdote which gives its name to the story. The alternative title, *De l'inconséquence du jugement public sur nos actions particulières*, suggests that we are on the border line of story and
philosophical dialogue and points forward to the sub-title of the
Supplément, 'Sur l'inconvénient d'attacher des idées morales à certaines actions physiques qui n'en comportent pas'. The *Supplément*
itself is one of the clearest indications of Diderot's taste for complicated structures. We find in it the same use of parenthesis and
receding planes as in *Jacques le fataliste*. Here the basic element, the
equivalent of the author/reader dialogue in *Jacques*, is the conversation of *A* and *B*, two men of the world. This serves as a frame
for pieces of monologue and dialogue which purport to come

from an unpublished supplement to Bougainville's recent account of his journey round the world. In its turn this 'supplement' is interrupted from time to time by the comments of *A* and *B* and once by the telling of a story from another book, Raynal's *Histoire des deux Indes*. In general, one can say that this complex, broken form serves to amuse us by its variety, but also, as we shall shortly see, to distance Diderot from his Tahitians. What now of the detailed conduct of the different parts of the book?

The talk between *A* and *B* is the normal Diderot dialogue, apparently fairly desultory, digressing from time to time and yet allowing points to be well made. One notices, for instance, how the preamble, which takes the form (yet again) of comments on another book, gradually brings us from a consideration of 'savage' customs and of the 'civilized' Jesuit rule in Paraguay to the real theme of the book, which is the comparison between life in Tahiti and life in Paris. Throughout, *B* is the *meneur du jeu*; *A* comments ironically on this dominance, which is a recurrent feature of Platonic dialogue: 'Il semble que mon lot soit d'avoir tort avec vous jusque dans les moindres choses; il faut que je sois bien bon pour vous pardonner une supériorité aussi continue!' (*A.T.* II. 213.) *B*, on the other hand, is reluctant to preach; 'mais vous m'engagez là dans un cours de morale galante' (*A.T.* II. 243), he protests, and his ideas on sexual morality and natural law are only gradually drawn out of him by *A*'s perseverance as a questioner. But in the end, in spite of a deliberately low-key conclusion, one finds that the questions have been thoroughly debated; all the material from the dialogues and the supposed supplement is drawn together in a series of conclusions, the sort of *aide-mémoire* that Diderot puts at the end of many of his more rambling works.

The intercalated Tahitian passages are differently put together. The long dialogue between Orou and the ship's chaplain resembles Voltaire's philosophical dialogues, both in its style ('Le vieil ouvrier, qui a tout fait sans tête, sans mains et sans outils') and in its construction. There is some attempt to make it sound like a real conversation, but it remains very obviously a device of satire and didactic exposition. The Tahitian Orou is unwilling to be deflected from his complete and eloquent account of the sexual customs of his country. The 'adieux du vieillard' are even more obviously a set piece. One can easily imagine it as a rhetorical exercise: compose the speech of a Tahitian elder deploring the evils brought to his island by European explorers. The traditional rhetoric of the passage is apparent in the choice of words, in the copious use of figures of speech, and not least in the *dispositio*. An exordium addressed to the Tahitians is followed by a long speech to Bougainville, which divides into three sections, the first devoted to property, the second to natural and artificial needs, the third to sexual customs and venereal disease; the speech ends with a long and passionate peroration, taking up again the ideas which have been treated earlier. It is all very eloquent, rather too eloquent for Diderot to commit himself to it wholeheartedly. It is here that the use of receding planes serves him well, allowing him to dissociate himself from his own eloquence and comment on the excessively literary character of the speech. *A* remarks: 'Ce discours me paraît véhément; mais à travers je ne sais quoi d'abrupt et de sauvage, il me semble retrouver des idées et des tournures européennes', and *B* explains that 'C'est une traduction du tahitien en espagnol et de l'espagnol en français.' (*A.T.* II. 218.)

The ironical interruption of the flow of eloquence by the dry comments of men of the world can work in two ways. Either it can help the reader to accept a rhetoric which by itself might make him smile, or else it can show him that he should not take the eloquent passage too seriously. If the first of these is uppermost in the *Supplément*, it is perhaps the second which is more in evidence in a comparable passage in the *Entretien d'un père avec ses enfants*.[30] Here, 'Moi', the philosopher Denis Diderot, talking to his family by the fireside at Langres, delivers a stirring harangue on the duty of doctors to let criminals die; this ends with him imagining himself a doctor denouncing a sick criminal:

Je ne m'occuperai point de rendre à la vie celui dont il m'est enjoint par l'équité naturelle, le bien de la société, le salut de mes semblables, d'être le dénonciateur. Meurs, et qu'il ne soit pas dit que par mon art et mes soins il existe un monstre de plus. (*A.T.* v. 286)

But the doctor to whom this is addressed is not even listening. His next words are addressed to Diderot's father: 'Bonjour, papa. Ah ça, moins de café après dîner, entendez-vous?'

This is a good example of the way dialogue can be used to avoid the dogmatic tone and to suggest complexity and uncertainty.

[30] On the *Entretien* see M. Rœlens, 'L'Art de la digression dans l'*Entretien d'un père avec ses enfants*', *Europe*, Jan.–Feb. 1963, and P. France, 'Public Theatre and Private Theatre in the Writings of Diderot', *Modern Language Review*, 1969.

Partly because it consists, like many of Diderot's works, of a first draft interspersed with later additions of various dates, the *Entretien* is an unusually convoluted piece. It has a lot of speakers, a lot of anecdotes, and constant interruptions and new directions. This complexity of composition undoubtedly helps to create the illusion of dramatic life, making the work more attractive to the average reader and avoiding the solemnity with which such a subject (the citizen and the law) would normally be treated. Some of the digressions appear as no more than whimsical ornament, so that the reader is encouraged to react as to the *Entretien avec la Maréchale*: 'Ce dialogue n'est pas sans profondeur, mais elle y est partout dérobée par la naïveté et la simplicité du discours.' (*A.T.* II. 506.) We are disarmed by the appearance of reality and by touches of irony such as the one quoted above. But it would be incorrect to see the broken order of this *Entretien* simply as a rhetorical device for putting across a message. In spite of the sub-title: 'Du danger de se mettre au-dessus des lois', there is no such single message to be extracted from this work; the whole point of it lies in the impossibility of resolving the differences of opinion which sometimes separate honest men. This sort of unresolved contradiction seems, as Hume said, to call for dialogue, but even better than an orderly dialogue of the traditional sort, where characters assumed clearly defined roles of questioner and answerer inside a quite formal structure, is the loose and broken order of Diderot's dialogue, where the unpredictable twists and turns, starts and stops of an ordinary conversation mime the flickering uncertainty which lies in wait for the intelligent person thinking about questions such as these. With most of the dialogues considered so far, it is possible (at a pinch) to imagine the work taking some other, more openly didactic, form. With the *Entretien* this is impossible.

It is even more impossible with *Le Neveu de Rameau*. This is the last dialogue I shall consider. It is true that *Jacques le fataliste* is largely in the form of conversations, but it is not a philosophical dialogue in the same sense as the works which I have been talking about. Although there are recurrent themes for discussion—most obviously the old favourite, freedom and determinism—it cannot be said that *Jacques* is seriously devoted to the exploration of philosophical questions.[31] At most, it may be said to put such questions

[31] The narrator intervenes in a discussion of freedom and determinism to remark: 'Vous concevez, lecteur, jusqu'où je pourrais pousser cette conversation sur un sujet

good-humouredly in their place. This is not the case with the
Neveu. Although it is a satire, in which much of the interest lies
in the portrayal of an extraordinary man in action, there is nevertheless a constant teasing at interrelated questions (centred round
art and morality and the definition of the natural), which places
this dialogue at least in part in the Platonic line.

I do not wish to make a detailed study of the *Neveu*; it is the
best known of Diderot's dialogues and the one which has called
forth the most comment and analysis.[32] It will perhaps be enough
to say a few things about the way the dialogue form is used here,
as compared with the works already discussed. I shall concentrate
once again on order. Almost everyone who reads this dialogue is
impressed by its extraordinary liveliness, the feeling of real speech
which one associates more with plays and novels than with philosophical dialogues. In passages such as the following we hear
people, not an author:

> LUI. La paix chez soi? morbleu, on ne l'a que quand on est le ser-
> viteur ou le maître; et c'est le maître qu'il faut être ... J'ai eu une
> femme. Dieu veuille avoir son âme; mais quand il lui arrivait
> quelquefois de se rebéquer, je m'élevais sur mes ergots; je déployais
> mon tonnerre, je disais, comme Dieu, 'Que la lumière se fasse',
> et la lumière était faite. Aussi en quatre années de temps nous
> n'avons pas eu dix fois un mot plus haut que l'autre. Quel âge a
> votre enfant?
> MOI. Cela ne fait rien à l'affaire.
> LUI. Quel âge a votre enfant?
> MOI. Et que diable! laissons là mon enfant et son âge, et revenons
> aux maîtres qu'elle aura.
> LUI. Pardieu! je ne sache rien de si têtu qu'un philosophe. En vous
> suppliant très humblement, ne pourrait-on savoir de monseigneur
> le philosophe quel âge à peu près peut avoir mademoiselle sa fille?
> MOI. Supposez-lui huit ans.
>
> (*A.T.* v. 413)

dont on a tant parlé, tant écrit depuis deux mille ans, sans en être d'un pas plus
avancé.' (*A.T.* VI. 15.) Of course, *Jacques* has often been harvested for ideas and has
yielded good crops, but such an exercise seems to me to miss the point of the book.

[32] A good analysis is to be found in H. Josephs, *Diderot's Dialogue of Gesture and
Language*, Ohio, 1969. An indication of the main lines of debate can be gained from
the *Entretiens sur le Neveu de Rameau*, ed. M. Duchet and M. Launay, Paris, 1967. *Le
Neveu*, like Montaigne's essays, tempts us to undertake a coherent interpretation;
this is as it should be, but it would be naïve to suppose that 'research' will provide
a definite answer. Diderot's story of the man and his two sons (*De l'interprétation de la
nature*, paras. 28–9, *A.T.* II. 23) applies here as elsewhere.

Among other features, one notices the zigzagging order, the lightning digression to Genesis, and the way the dialogue suddenly turns back on itself with 'Quel âge a votre enfant?' These surprises are an essential feature of the *Neveu*. The dialogue moves sinuously and spasmodically, sometimes opening out into an extended discussion of a single subject, such as the merits of the new Italian music, but then interrupting this with apparently irrelevant remarks or with the description of one of Rameau's 'pantomimes'. The point has often been made and need not be laboured. What then is the function of this disorder? I do not think it will do to say that, because the *Neveu* is the most private of all Diderot's works, the broken order is purely expressive and has no designs on an audience; we cannot say for whom the work was written, but it was written with great care, frequently revised, and almost certainly intended for some happy few. In part, like the *Rêve de d'Alembert*, it meets the taste for the naturalness of the spoken word as against the pedantry of the written order. More than this, there is the attraction of a deliberate complex structure, where the reader is kept holding many threads at once. Where the 'Moi' of the *Entretiens* had been commenting on *Le Fils naturel*, the 'Lui' of the *Neveu* is trying to tell the story of his expulsion from favour, but in both cases this basic movement is constantly interrupted by great parentheses which matter more than the guiding thread. As in the *Rêve*, central themes (the question of education, for instance) keep recurring, giving us the exercise and the pleasure of grouping them together in the mind. The complexity of structure obliges the reader to re-create the work himself, and this, as Diderot said when criticizing Helvétius, is one of the secrets of successful communication.

In most of the dialogues this attractive complexity serves a well-defined persuasive end—and this holds good even for works like the *Rêve de d'Alembert*, which was not designed for immediate publication. The dialogue may enable Diderot to adopt a distant, half-sceptical attitude towards his own beliefs, but this, like the appearance of real talk, is calculated to make us look sympathetically at the author's thesis. In the *Entretien d'un père avec ses enfants* this is not the case, but there at least we do have one single dilemma to consider. In the *Neveu* there is not even this unifying element. To apply a philosophical sub-title to the work would be to impose a false unity on it. Neither can one easily imagine a table of contents for it. It is true that it might be subdivided roughly along these lines:

A. Introduction.
B. The question of genius.
C. The problems of a parasite.
D. Education.
E. Vice, virtue, and society.
F. Flattery and parasitism in Paris.
G. Sublimity in evil.
H. Comparison of Italian and French music.
I. General discussion of morals, music, and society.
J. Conclusion.

Such a scheme is at best a very approximate *aide-mémoire*. It fails, for instance—and must fail—to mention the way in which particular themes, ideas, and images reappear in different and unexpected contexts. Above all, by not saying anything about the protagonists, it fails to show the really important thing, which is the changing relationship between 'Moi' and 'Lui'. But it does bring out the obvious fact that this dialogue is not arranged in accordance with the philosophical order which characterizes the dialogues of Berkeley or even, with reservations, the *Rêve de d'Alembert*.

The truth of the matter is that if the dialogue is disorderly it is primarily because disorder is its subject. (In saying this, am I falling into the trap of imposing false unity?) The epigraph is a quotation from the Horatian caricature of the ever-changing Priscius, set under the sign of a minor god of change, Vertumnus. Rameau's nephew is inconstancy personified: 'Rien ne dissemble plus de lui que lui-même.' The philosophical narrator, like Diderot the writer of dialogues, is willing to allow his thoughts a charming disorder:

J'abandonne mon esprit à tout son libertinage; je le laisse maître de suivre la première idée sage ou folle qui se présente, comme on voit, dans l'allée de Foi, nos jeunes dissolus marcher sur les pas d'une courtisane à l'air éventé, au visage riant, à l'œil vif, au nez retroussé, quitter celle-ci pour une autre, les attaquant toutes et ne s'attachant à aucune. Mes pensées, ce sont mes catins. (*A.T.* v. 387)

He does not want to lay down the law to Rameau and refuses to be drawn into discussion with him, preferring to let him pour out his own peculiar disorder. As a philosopher, 'Moi' hopes to profit

by this; it is to be a sort of Saturnalia, 'une fois l'an', when disorder is loosed on the world and allows the orderly philospher
a more complete vision of things: 'Il secoue, il agite; il fait
approuver ou blâmer; il fait sortir la vérité.' But 'Lui' refuses to
be a mere Saturnalia figure; in a traditional way, he turns the
tables on the philosopher:

Moi, je suis le fou de Bertin et de beaucoup d'autres, le vôtre peut-
être dans ce moment, ou peut-être vous le mien: celui qui serait
sage n'aurait point de fou; celui donc qui a un fou n'est pas sage; s'il
n'est pas sage il est fou; et peut-être, fût-il roi, le fou de son fou.
(*A.T.* v. 443)

As they talk, it seems that not 'Lui' but 'Moi' is the exception to
the general order of things. Very much like the strait jacket of
rhetorical *dispositio*, the order of the philosopher is rejected as
having nothing to do with the real world. Thus 'Lui' challenges
the methods of natural science:

Montre-t-on bien sans la méthode? et la méthode, d'où naît-elle?
Tenez, mon cher philosophe, j'ai dans la tête que la physique sera toujours une pauvre science, une goutte d'eau prise avec la pointe d'une
aiguille dans le vaste océan, un grain détaché de la chaîne des Alpes!
Et les raisons des phénomènes? En vérité, il vaudrait autant ignorer que
de savoir si peu et si mal (*A.T.* v. 415)

just as he throws doubt on the certainties of ethics and linguistics:

Mais, monsieur le philosophe, il y a une conscience générale, comme il
y a une grammaire générale, et puis des exceptions dans chaque langue
. . . chaque état a ses exceptions à la conscience générale auxquelles je
donnerais volontiers le nom d'idiotismes de métier. (*A.T.* v. 419)

In both cases 'Moi' remains unconvinced by 'Lui''s arguments,
which he describes in the first instance as 'spécieux' and in the
second as 'tout cet entortillage'. Later, however, when Rameau
rejects the traditional order of music in the name of nature, 'Moi'
can only listen in silence—and of course these are Diderot's own
ideas:

C'est au cri animal de la passion à dicter la ligne qui nous convient;
il faut que ces expressions soient pressées les unes sur les autres; il faut
que la phrase soit courte, que le sens en soit coupé, suspendu . . . Il
nous faut des exclamations, des interjections, des suspensions, des
interruptions, des affirmations, des négations; nous appelons, nous

invoquons, nous crions, nous gémissons, nous pleurons, nous rions franchement. (*A.T.* v. 466)

Here at any rate there is no doubt but that the true order is disorder.

It is an open question how the discussion ends. The narrator sticks to his 'Saturnalia' view of 'Lui':

Les folies de cet homme, les contes de l'abbé Galiani, les extravagances de Rabelais, m'ont quelquefois fait rêver profondément. Ce sont trois magasins où je me suis pourvu de masques ridicules que je place sur le visage des plus graves personnages. (*A.T.* v. 483)

But although 'Moi' may continue to affirm the dignity of philosophy, the dialogue itself ends in total uncertainty. The individual reader may prefer to gamble with 'Moi' on the possibility of philosophical integrity; he may be won over by Rameau's corrosive cynicism; more probably, he will do neither, but will remain suspended in a doubt which he may find entertaining or worrying. But whatever his private conclusion, a great part of the experience of reading this dialogue will have been the incursion of disorder into the tidy world of theory; this disorder is expounded by 'Lui', but, more impressively, it is forced on us by the very shape of the work.

Le Neveu de Rameau is probably Diderot's furthest advance into the realm of disorder. It would be risky to claim that it embodies his essential vision. As we saw at the beginning of this chapter, he was sufficiently a man of his times to share the desire to understand the world rationally, to perceive or create order in the apparent chaos of phenomena. Yet he saw more clearly than most that, outside the domain of Newtonian physics and mathematics, the time had not yet come (and perhaps never would) for a full understanding of the laws governing such complex fields as the life of animals or the social and moral behaviour of humans. The order of Helvétius was to him a grotesque over-simplification, a real obstacle to knowledge. It was essential to preserve an awareness that any conclusions were only provisional and tentative, that the world was far more varied than the words and forms which were commonly used to describe it.

It cannot be said, however, that the 'disorder' of Diderot's writings is always designed to embody this awareness. Thus it appears, from my all too 'Helvetian' analysis, that dialogue can

work in different ways. Often it follows the old tradition of
le beau désordre, a device to seduce a non-specialist audience,
whether wide or intimate, with the charming appearance of real
talk. This may be rather different from what was taught in the
Jesuit colleges, but it is still rhetoric in the sense of the art of persuading an audience of the probable truth of a pre-existing view.
But there is another rhetoric of dialogue, where the dialogue
corresponds to a real complexity and uncertainty of thought and
feeling. This is an expressive rather than a persuasive rhetoric. In
Le Neveu de Rameau, for instance, one cannot regard the irregular
order of the dialogue as simply a new and improved way of
insinuating the truth into the mind of a recalcitrant reader; the
disorder is the heart of the matter. If rhetoric were no more than
the mother of lies, the knack of public speaking, and run-of-the-
mill popularization, then we should not want to use the word for
works such as this; it is only by shifting to a less dismissive use
of the word, where rhetoric means more or less the same thing
as literary art, that we can speak of the rhetoric of *Le Neveu de
Rameau*.

7. Jean-Jacques Rousseau

Vitam impendere vero: to devote one's life to truth. The motto which Rousseau adopted as his own is a hard one to live by. For him, however, truth-telling usually meant no more than speaking your own mind honestly; if what you think does not correspond with objective reality, you cannot be blamed, for you have been deceived in good faith. To forestall criticism, the Vicaire Savoyard declares at the beginning of his *profession de foi*:

> Je ne suis pas un grand philosophe, et je me soucie peu de l'être. Mais j'ai quelquefois du bon sens, et j'aime toujours la vérité. Je ne veux pas argumenter avec vous, ni même tenter de vous convaincre; il me suffit de vous exposer ce que je pense dans la simplicité de mon cœur. Consultez le vôtre durant mon discours; c'est tout ce que je vous demande. Si je me trompe, c'est de bonne foi; cela suffit pour que mon erreur ne me soit point imputée à crime: quand vous vous tromperiez de même, il y aurait peu de mal à cela. (*O.C.* IV. 565–6)[1]

In its distinction between the sincere layman and the philosopher or the persuader, this is characteristic of Rousseau's persuasive stance.

But even if truthfulness is equated with sincerity, it is no easy virtue. Again and again Rousseau proclaims himself a man of truth; he says of the *Confessions*, for instance: 'Oui, je le dis et le sens avec une fière élévation d'âme, j'ai porté dans cet écrit la bonne foi, la véracité, la franchise, aussi loin, plus loin même, au moins je le crois, que ne fit jamais aucun autre homme.' (*O.C.* I. 1035.) Nevertheless, it is obvious from his autobiographical writings

---

[1] *O.C.* refers to Rousseau's *Œuvres complètes*, ed. B. Gagnebin and M. Raymond, Bibliothèque de la Pléiade, 4 vols. to date, Paris, 1959–69. Vol. I contains the autobiographical writings; vol. II *La Nouvelle Héloïse*, the plays, and literary essays; vol. III the political writings; and vol. IV the *Émile* and writings on education, ethics, and botany. The *Essai sur l'origine des langues*, which does not figure in these volumes, is referred to as *E.O.L.* and only chapter references are given. Similarly the *Lettre à d'Alembert sur les spectacles* is referred to as *L. d'A.*; page numbers are those of the Garnier edition of *Du contrat social* and other texts. The correspondence up to 1762 is referred to in the edition of J. Leigh, 10 vols. to date, Geneva, 1965– (*Corr. Leigh*) and after 1762 in the edition of T. Dufour, 20 vols., Paris, 1924–34 (*Corr. Dufour*).

that the problem plagued him. He was worried by the actual lies he had told, both the unimportant ones which he manages to excuse in the fourth *Promenade* of the *Rêveries* and the tormenting ones which were, he says, a partial cause of his writing the *Confessions*. He was worried too by the apparent contradictions between his words and his life, his abandoned children, his attachment to music and the arts, his relations with the rich and powerful—the aim of the dialogues *Rousseau juge de Jean-Jacques* is to dissolve such contradictions and show the perfect identity between the writer and the man. Here, however, I want to explore how he approached what is in a way the most fundamental aspect of the problem: when, if ever, can human language communicate the truth? Or, in less absolute terms, what sort of language or rhetoric is most appropriate for truth-telling?

This is an old question; it has been close to the centre of almost all the preceding chapters. For Rousseau it was not quite the same as for Descartes or d'Alembert. For him the question was not whether worldly eloquence helps or hinders philosophical communication; it was rather a question of the adequacy of a shared language and a common rhetoric to express his own personal truth. One of Rousseau's central preoccupations was what Jean Starobinski calls 'la transparence',[2] the desire for direct, uninterrupted communication (or communion) with others, through which he would appear in their consciousness as he knew himself to be. In his own words, 'je voudrais pouvoir en quelque façon rendre mon âme transparente aux yeux du lecteur.' (*O.C.* i. 175.) In what R. J. Ellrich has called 'the fantasy of perfect communication'[3] it is not so much the ideas which have to be presented undeformed as the original man himself with his hopes, his loves, his fears, his aspirations. The contact with others must not be simply intellectual but emotional as well.

One of Rousseau's recurrent ideals is that of wordless communion, the silence of the 'matinée à l'anglaise' in *La Nouvelle Héloïse*:

---

[2] J. Starobinski, *Jean-Jacques Rousseau. La transparence et l'obstacle*, Paris, 1957. This valuable study contains many pages which are directly relevant to the subject of this chapter.

[3] R. J. Ellrich, *Rousseau and his Reader: the Rhetorical Situation of the Major Works*, Chapel Hill, N.C., 1969. I am considerably indebted to this monograph, which gives a persuasive account of the evolution of Rousseau's relations with his imagined or real reader.

Après six jours perdus aux entretiens frivoles des gens indifférents, nous avons passé aujourd'hui une matinée à l'anglaise, réunis et dans le silence, goûtant à la fois le plaisir d'être ensemble et la douceur du recueillement. Que les délices de cet état sont connues de peu de gens! Je n'ai vu personne en France en avoir la moindre idée. 'La conversation des amis ne tarit jamais', disent-ils. Il est vrai, la langue fournit un babil facile aux attachements médiocres. Mais l'amitié, Milord, l'amitié! sentiment vif et céleste, quels discours sont dignes de toi? Quelle langue ose être ton interprète? Jamais ce qu'on dit à son ami peut-il valoir ce qu'on sent à ses côtés? (*O.C.* II. 558)

and again, two pages later:

Que de choses se sont dites sans ouvrir la bouche! Que d'ardents sentiments se sont communiqués sans la froide entremise de la parole!
(*O.C.* II. 560)

This is the ideal, only possible among true friends and as fragile as the idyll of Clarens. In the corrupt world, the world of book-writing, the use of conventional signs, above all language, is unavoidable. The problem is to give to this mediated communication the force and immediacy of silent communion.

It seems that Rousseau found something like this in music, particularly Italian music. The appeal of French music lay principally in its complex harmonies; for him this was an artificially cultivated taste: 'N'ayant que des beautés de convention, elle ne flatte à nul égard les oreilles qui n'y sont pas exercées.' (*E.O.L.* XIV.)[4] Italian music, on the contrary, depended on melody, which was a 'natural' medium for conveying emotion—and we know what overtones went with this word 'natural'. The Italian music teacher in *La Nouvelle Héloïse* explains to Julie: 'C'est de la seule mélodie que sort cette puissance invincible des accents passionnés' (*O.C.* II. 132), and Rousseau echoes this in the *Essai sur l'origine des langues*: 'Elle [la mélodie] n'imite pas seulement, elle parle; et son langage inarticulé, mais vif, ardent, passionné, a cent fois plus d'énergie que la parole même.' (*E.O.L.* XIV.)

It can be objected, of course, that producing strong emotions is different from telling the truth or baring one's soul. Rousseau, who made a compilation of Plato's various denunciations of the

---

4 Harmony is discussed more fully in the *Lettre sur la musique française* and in the ensuing polemic with Rameau, particularly the *Examen de deux principes avancés par M. Rameau*. While Rousseau allows that basic harmonies are natural, this is far from true of the complicated harmonies of Rameau and his followers.

mimetic arts[5] before writing his own attack on the theatre in the
Lettre à d'Alembert, could not in all conscience place a very high
value on music. In his more severe moments he has to admit that
like the other arts it is at best a harmless amusement, a way of
keeping a corrupt people off the streets. In an autobiographical
fragment dating from the height of his prophetic period he confesses: 'J'avoue à ma honte que je me suis toute ma vie occupé de
musique beaucoup plus qu'il ne convient à un homme sage et cet
art de rendre les sentiments par des sons m'a toujours inspiré une
passion qui méritait bien d'être punie et modérée par un peu
d'inquiétude.' (*O.C.* I. 1116.) For all that, music was one of the
great loves of Rousseau's life, and the Italian musicians of *La
Nouvelle Héloïse* are portrayed as sincere and passionate men, far
removed from the cold detachment of Diderot's 'comédien'.[6] One
of Saint-Preux's letters describes the perfect and easy communion
between performers and audience:

A chaque phrase, quelque image entrait dans mon cerveau ou quelque
sentiment dans mon cœur; le plaisir ne s'arrêtait point à l'oreille, il
pénétrait jusqu'à l'âme; l'exécution coulait sans effort avec une facilité
charmante; tous les concertants semblaient animés du même esprit;
le chanteur maître de sa voix en tirait sans gêne tout ce que le chant et
les paroles demandaient de lui . . .   (*O.C.* II. 133)

In spite of the 'semblaient' this gives an idyllic picture of un-
hampered emotional contact which might provide a model for the
activities which concern us here, speech and writing.

We saw earlier that music was wordless language with 'cent
fois plus d'énergie que la parole même'. Rousseau was not alone
among his contemporaries in proclaiming the emotive superiority
of music and gesture over language.[7] Nor was he alone in tracing
a history of the decline in expressiveness of the word, a decline
associated with the invention of writing.[8] The three friends of the

---

[5] *De l'imitation théâtrale* (not yet published in the Pléiade edition).

[6] Compare the article 'Expression' in Rousseau's *Dictionnaire de la musique*: 'Vainement le compositeur saura-t-il animer son ouvrage, si la chaleur qui doit y régner ne
passe à ceux qui l'exécutent.'

[7] There is some ambiguity in Rousseau's attitude to gesture. While he recognizes
the power of visual signs, he knows too that for the communication of emotion
a longer message (such as music or speech) is more effective: 'L'impression successive du discours, qui frappe à coups redoublés, vous donne bien une autre émotion
que la présence de l'objet même, où d'un coup d'œil vous avez tout vu.' (*E.O.L.* I.)

[8] On this subject see J. Starobinski, 'Rousseau et l'origine des langues', in
Europäische Aufklärung, Herbert Dieckmann zum 60. Geburtstag, ed. H. Friedrich and

Panier Fleuri, Rousseau, Condillac, and Diderot, all agreed that 'l'écriture, qui semble devoir fixer la langue, est précisément ce qui l'altère; elle n'en change pas les mots, mais le génie; elle substitue l'exactitude à l'expression. L'on rend ses sentiments quand on parle, et ses idées quand on écrit.' (*E.O.L.* v.) The original language, long before writing, was the language of poetry: 'les premières langues furent chantantes et passionnées avant d'être simples et méthodiques.' (*E.O.L.* II.) They had, in fact, some of the advantages of music.

For the true *philosophe*, Fontenelle or Condillac, the gain in precision outweighed the loss of power.[9] For Rousseau it was more complicated. 'L'ami de la vérité', as he often called himself, naturally wanted a language which would not distort truth. But his truth was not the analytical truth of the philosopher-scientist. For the scientist the truth could only be obscured by the sort of words which communicated the speaker's or writer's emotions; Rousseau's truth was inseparable from his emotions. He tends therefore to value the forceful, eloquent language which adds to the referential quality of civilized prose 'l'accent oratoire et pathétique, c'est-à-dire l'art de parler à l'oreille et au cœur dans une langue sans articuler des mots' (*O.C.* II. 133). In his *Essai sur l'origine des langues*, although he is saying much the same thing as Condillac, his approval clearly goes to 'original' speech at the expense of civilized, rational language:

par un progrès naturel, toutes les langues lettrées doivent changer de caractère et perdre de la force en gagnant de la clarté... plus on s'attache à perfectionner la grammaire et la logique, plus on accélère ce progrès, et ... pour rendre bientôt une langue froide et monotone, il ne faut qu'établir des académies chez le peuple qui la parle. (*E.O.L.* VII)

In the *Émile* there is a similar tension. The man-made child of nature shows that he belongs to an age when things are valued above words: 'en général il doit avoir un langage simple et peu figuré. Il parle ordinairement au propre et seulement pour être entendu.' (*O.C.* IV. 546.) Émile's language at the age of fifteen is not that of early man, which was essentially figurative and musical; it is more akin to the eloquence which is appropriate to ideal civilized man and which Starobinski describes as 'une langue

F. Schalk, Munich, 1967. See also Rousseau's notes on pronunciation in *O.C.* II. 1248-52.

9 See above, p. 71.

évoluée qui rappelle l'origine perdue'.[10] If the boy speaks plainly, this is mainly because he has few passions as yet; it does not mean that he is 'tout à fait flegmatique et froid'. When he is roused his language has force and vehemence:

> Le noble sentiment qui l'inspire lui donne de la force et de l'élévation; pénétré du tendre amour de l'humanité, il transmet en parlant les mouvements de son âme; sa généreuse franchise a je ne sais quoi de plus enchanteur que l'artificieuse éloquence des autres, ou plutôt lui seul est véritablement éloquent, puisqu'il n'a qu'à montrer ce qu'il sent pour le communiquer à ceux qui l'écoutent. (O.C. IV. 547)

Nature has endowed him with the sort of communicative warmth which Rousseau so admired in the orators of antiquity, particularly Demosthenes: 'Entraîné par la mâle éloquence de Démosthène il [Émile] dira: c'est un orateur; mais en lisant Cicéron, il dira: c'est un avocat.' (O.C. IV. 676.) Cicero was still one of the mainstays of rhetoric teaching in eighteenth-century France.

In the supposed language of primitive man, in the speech of Émile, and in the eloquence of ancient Greece, Rousseau sees then a persuasive vigour which he rarely finds in contemporary speech and writing. All around him he hears 'le bavardage des académies' (O.C. IV. 676), 'le bourdonnement des divans' (E.O.L. xx), the 'maussade jargon' of woman-dominated societies (L. d'A. 207), the 'vanité du babil' of professional men of letters (O.C. I. 803). In his eyes the *philosophes* are sophists, happy to debate for or against any proposition. They are merely the adult versions of the children whom a traditional education (with its stress on verbal performance) had taught to juggle with words without any care for meaning. The result is that their works are cold and unconvincing. Rousseau, by contrast, is the man of passionate sincerity, whose ardent conviction communicates itself to his readers—for of course we can see Rousseau's own face lurking behind the masks of the primitive man, the Greek orator, and the young Émile. His is the 'généreuse franchise'; the 'artificieuse éloquence' is that of his contemporaries.

As one might expect, Rousseau's adversaries (as he called them) did not interpret his eloquence in the way he would have wished. The more determined among them claimed that Rousseau did not believe a word of what he wrote and was simply perform-

---

[10] Starobinski, art. cit., p. 297.

ing in order to make a name in the world. Or if they did not
actually accuse him of insincerity, they managed to praise his
eloquence in a back-handed way, implying that his only quality
was a rhetorical gift which enabled him to seduce the simple
reader. Thus his compatriot Charles Bonnet wrote to Albrecht
von Haller in 1761:

Ce peintre n'a que le coloris et point du tout le dessein. Pour parler
sans figure, je ne connais pas d'auteur qui ait moins de logique. Il a
prouvé à la honte d'un siècle qui pense, qu'on peut se faire une réputation brillante à force de paradoxes. Le Français sera toujours prenable
par les oreilles; toujours l'harmonie du style le séduira, et quiconque
sait *phraser* est sûr d'être lu et admiré par cette nation amie des frivolités.

(*Corr. Leigh*, VIII. 47)

Bonnet speaks of harmony, but it is above all the notion of warmth
which reappears in appraisals of Rousseau's style; d'Alembert,
who was no lover of 'chaleur', says of this quality in a critique of
the *Émile*: 'c'est là, selon l'opinion publique, le caractère distinctif
de ses ouvrages, c'est là ce qui en fait le succès, c'est là ce qui le fait
préférer par bien des lecteurs à tous nos écrivains, sans en excepter
aucun'—he goes on to suggest that this is mere physical stimula-
tion and has little to do with truth.[11] Of course, most of those who
wrote to congratulate Rousseau on his ardent style were not praising the manner so as to belittle the matter, as d'Alembert and
Bonnet do, but still it is possible to infer from their praise that his
eloquence, far from being intimately bound up with his convictions, was a weapon which could be used in any cause—and indeed
a good number of people did attempt to borrow his pen to defend
causes quite remote from him, as he himself complains in *Rousseau
iuge de Jean-Jacques*.[12]

In the *Lettre à d'Alembert*, Rousseau describes the actor as someone skilled in 'l'art de se contrefaire, de revêtir un autre caractère
que le sien, de paraître différent de ce qu'on est, de se passionner de
sang-froid, de dire autre chose que ce qu'on pense, aussi naturellement que si l'on le pensait réellement' (*L. d'A.* 186). There is, he
claims, a basic difference between the actor and the orator or the

---

[11] J. d'Alembert, *Œuvres*, ed. Bossange and Belin, Paris, 1821–2, vol. IV, p. 465.
On 'chaleur' see the passage from d'Alembert's *Éléments de philosophie* quoted above,
p. 103.
[12] 'Il lui faudrait dix mains et dix secrétaires pour écrire les requêtes, placets,
lettres, mémoires, compliments, vers, bouquets, dont on vient à l'envi le charger,
vu la grande éloquence de sa plume et la grande bonté de son cœur.' (*O.C.* I. 907–8.)

preacher (the two other prime examples of rhetoric in action):
whereas the actor plays an assumed role, the orator or preacher 'ne
représente que lui-même, il ne fait que son propre rôle, ne parle
qu'en son propre nom, ne dit ou ne doit dire que ce qu'il pense:
l'homme et le personnage étant le même être, il est à sa place'
(L. d'A. 187). While Rousseau was constantly anxious to suppress
the distinction between 'l'homme' and 'le personnage' in his own
life and writing, all the insistence on the eloquence of his pen
tended to place him in the camp of the actor. For this reason, when
his enemy Tronchin praised his style in the *Lettres de la campagne*,
Jean-Jacques was driven in his reply, the *Lettres de la montagne*
(placed once again under the motto *Vitam impendere vero*), to warn
his readers against his own eloquence: 'Je prie les lecteurs de
vouloir bien mettre à part mon beau style, et d'examiner seulement si je raisonne bien ou mal.' (*O.C.* III. 686.)

Defensive moves such as this should not lead us to think that
Rousseau really believed that 'chaleur' was a bad thing; to those
who argued that 'il est essentiel à la vérité d'être dite froidement',
he replied: 'lorsqu'une vive persuasion nous anime, le moyen
d'employer un langage glacé?' (*O.C.* III. 685–6.) Indeed, not only
this 'chaleur' but also the more formal aspects of fine writing
counted more for him than one might imagine from some of his
more radical anti-literary statements. In a well-known passage
from the *Confessions*, he speaks of the difficulties of composition,
noting that 'il y a telle de mes périodes que j'ai tournée et retournée
cinq ou six nuits dans ma tête avant qu'elle fût en état d'être mise
sur le papier' (*O.C.* I. 114). This is meant to demonstrate that he
is not a glib rhetorician, but it shows too the classical importance
he attaches to *l'art de bien dire*. Above all he is attentive to the
sound of his sentences. When Rey's proof-reader presumes to
change his French, he writes indignantly: 'Je trouve ma phrase
élégante et harmonieuse, la vôtre dure et plate.' (*Corr. Leigh*, V.
119.) On another occasion he decides, for reasons of euphony, not
to correct an error of fact: 'Je crois pourtant qu'il sera mieux de ne
rien changer à la phrase, parce qu'un entretien entre gens de condition ne demande pas toute l'exactitude historique, qu'il faut que
ces noms barbares passent comme un trait, et que la phrase est
tellement cadencée que l'addition d'une seule syllabe en gâterait
toute l'harmonie.' (*Corr. Leigh*, VII. 131–2.) It is true that the context here is only a fictional letter in *La Nouvelle Héloïse*, but the

letters to Rey are full of passages such as this; Rousseau is a jealous father to his writings and wants them to appear as beautiful as possible, even as regards the type-face and the quality of the paper.

Nor is he averse to accepting the role of literary expert. In a youthful manuscript entitled 'Idée de la méthode dans la composition d'un livre' he shows himself a conscientious exponent of orthodox literary techniques who knows that once you have decided on your subject, 'il n'est question que de l'amplifier et de lui donner l'arrangement le plus propre à convaincre et à plaire' (*O.C.* II. 1242).[13] Much later, in his correspondence with such Swiss friends as Du Peyrou, Moultou, and De Luc, he often gives advice on style. Sometimes this is the advice of a plain man who is not concerned with Parisian delicacy—he tells Du Peyrou not to worry about grammatical mistakes, since these often make writing more 'lumineux' and 'c'est en cela, et non dans toutes les pédanteries du purisme, que consiste le véritable art d'écrire' (*Corr. Dufour*, XIII. 221). But at other times, particularly to De Luc, his advice is more that of the rhetorician or even the grammarian; he criticizes such faults as prolixity, lack of harmony, and even provincialisms.[14] He knows full well that for the wider reading public (and even for himself?) sincerity and solidity are not enough— thus on a book sent him by Rey: 'j'y ai trouvé une érudition prodigieuse et plusieurs points de critique bien et savamment discutés; mais l'ouvrage est écrit d'un très mauvais ton et d'une diffusion à faire perdre patience à l'Allemand le plus flegmatique . . .' (*Corr. Dufour*, X. 276.)

If in Paris Rousseau presents himself as the Swiss, in Switzerland he is the man with experience of Paris. It is from a Parisian viewpoint that he criticizes his compatriots' verbal clumsiness: 'Ils parlent très bien, très aisément; mais ils écrivent platement et mal, surtout quand ils veulent écrire légèrement, et ils le veulent toujours. Comme ils ne savent pas même en quoi consiste la grâce et le sel du style léger, lorsqu'ils ont enfilé des phrases lourdement sémillantes, ils se croient autant de Voltaires et de Crébillons.' (*Corr. Dufour*, IX. 14.) When he speaks at the beginning of the first Discourse of the charms of eighteenth-century politeness

---

[13] This piece is well worth studying; it displays unequivocally Rousseau's awareness of the persuader's need for art and subterfuge. Of course it dates from before the 'reform', but even so . . .

[14] See for instance *Corr. Dufour*, X. 218; XI. 116–17, 192, 359; XII. 82, 238.

('un ton philosophe sans pédanterie, des manières naturelles et pourtant prévenantes'), this is not just an oratorical precaution; he never ceased to recognize the merits of Parisian style and tone. *La Nouvelle Héloïse* shows him with a foot in each camp. In most respects Switzerland wins hands down, but not in the use of words; Saint-Preux learns, as Rousseau had learnt, that the corruptions of Paris have their literary compensations. Conversely, the 'editor's notes' repeatedly draw our attention to the un-Parisian eloquence of the characters, half apologizing for it, half blaming the supposed reader for being amused by it.

In the unpublished dialogue preface to *La Nouvelle Héloïse*, there is a curious passage where Rousseau explains that if his Swiss characters write in a prolix and rather bombastic way, this is precisely because they are sincere and have no experience of fashionable society:

Ce n'est que dans le monde qu'on apprend à parler avec énergie. Premièrement, parce qu'il faut toujours dire autrement et mieux que les autres, et puis que, forcé d'affirmer à chaque instant ce qu'on ne croit pas, d'exprimer des sentiments qu'on n'a point, on cherche à donner à ce qu'on dit un tour persuasif qui supplée à la persuasion intérieure. Croyez-vous que les gens vraiment passionnés aient ces manières de parler vives, fortes, coloriées, que vous admirez dans vos drames et dans vos romans? Non; la passion, pleine d'elle-même, s'exprime avec plus d'abondance que de force; elle ne songe même pas à persuader; elle ne soupçonne pas qu'on puisse douter d'elle.

(*O.C.* II. 14–15)

What Rousseau (or one of his interlocutors) says here is troubling if we apply it to his own case, since he knew quite well that his own writing did not lack energy or force. If it means, as the other speaker in the dialogue wrily observes, that 'la faiblesse du langage prouve la force du sentiment', then Jean-Jacques himself comes to look more like the worldly performer than the incompetent man of feeling. How then could he distinguish himself from the insincere rhetorician?

Logically, it is impossible to make such a distinction. Rousseau says, in contradiction to the passage just quoted, that 'rien n'est plus semblable à l'éloquence que le ton d'un homme fortement persuadé' (*O.C.* I. 1113), but of course the sentence can be turned round: 'rien n'est plus semblable au ton d'un homme fortement persuadé que l'éloquence.' In speech you may be able to detect insincerity intuitively when you are confronted with another person and can hear his voice and watch his face and his movements— it is perhaps for this reason that Rousseau pinned such hopes on reading the *Confessions* aloud to select gatherings. But even here the language of the heart can be imitated, as the actor and the orator have always known. In the written book there are absolutely no guarantees. Nevertheless, in various ways, Rousseau keeps up the fight to prove that his eloquence is the real thing and not a wily counterfeit.

In the first place, in spite of what I have just said, he appeals to the reader's feelings. Although others may make huge efforts to persuade, Rousseau claims that his are the only writings which carry conviction and penetrate to the reader's inmost being. *Rousseau juge de Jean-Jacques* begins with an interesting distinction between 'faste' and 'force' (*O.C.* 1. 667–8). The Frenchman says that the monster Jean-Jacques is 'ce même homme dont les pompeuses productions vous ont si charmé, si ravi par les beaux préceptes de vertu qu'il y étale avec tant de faste'. But 'Rousseau' rejects the word 'faste': 'Dites, de force. Soyons justes, même avec les méchants. Le faste n'excite tout au plus qu'une admiration froide et stérile, et sûrement ne me charmera jamais. Des écrits qui élèvent l'âme et enflamment le cœur méritent un autre nom.' Even so, as the Frenchman points out, this proves nothing about the sincerity of the writer: 'Faste ou force, qu'importe le mot, si l'idée est toujours le même? Si ce sublime jargon tiré par l'hypocrisie d'une tête exaltée n'en est pas moins dicté par une âme de boue?' But for 'Rousseau' the difference is considerable; not only does 'la force' produce virtuous resolution and action in the reader, it also appears virtually inconceivable that such writings should be the work of a hypocrite. The same sort of point is made elsewhere; as R. J. Ellrich has shown, Rousseau tends to demand an ideal reader, who will immediately understand his words as they were meant to be understood and will sense in them the emotion which produced them.[15] All other readers (and this includes a large part of the public) are rejected as unworthy; thus in the *Confessions*, speaking of *La Nouvelle Héloïse*, Rousseau says: 'Quiconque, en lisant ces deux lettres, ne sent pas amollir et fondre son cœur dans l'attendrissement qui me les dicta, doit fermer le livre.' (*O.C.* 1. 438.)

---

[15] Ellrich, *Rousseau and his Reader, passim.*

Still, it remains a fact that some readers are not affected, and that even those who are may choose to explain this by reference to the author's rhetorical skill. Rousseau's answer to these—and here we come to the central point of this chapter—is to deny that he has any rhetorical skill, to insist that he is impulsive, incompetent, and untaught, or, to come back to the contrast of *La Nouvelle Héloïse*, to place himself in the Swiss camp. One of his best descriptions of himself as the artless speaker is to be found in an autobiographical fragment of 1755 or 1756, where he is taking stock after the success of his early writings:

La vive persuasion qui dictait mes écrits leur donnait une chaleur capable de suppléer quelquefois à la force du raisonnement; élevé pour ainsi dire au-dessus de moi-même par la sublimité de mon sujet, j'étais comme ces avocats plus célèbres qu'éloquents qu'on prend pour de grands orateurs, parce qu'ils plaident de grandes causes, ou plutôt comme ces prédicateurs évangéliques qui prêchent sans art mais touchent parce qu'ils sont touchés . . . c'est un grand avantage pour bien parler que de dire toujours ce qu'on pense, la bonne foi sert de rhétorique, l'honnêteté de talent et rien n'est plus semblable à l'éloquence que le ton d'un homme fortement persuadé. (*O.C.* I. 1113)

Whatever else we call Rousseau, we are not to call him a professional writer. The *Émile* is full of scorn for books; the 'métier de faiseur de livres' is seen as no more than a futile luxury trade: 'Je ne veux point qu'il soit brodeur, ni doreur, ni vernisseur, comme le gentilhomme de Locke; je ne veux qu'il soit ni musicien, ni comédien, ni faiseur de livres.' (*O.C.* IV. 473.) The note to this sentence expresses some embarrassment at the obvious fact that he himself had written books, but even so he can declare firmly in *Rousseau juge de Jean-Jacques*: 'J'ai fait des livres, il est vrai, mais jamais je ne fus un livrier.' (*O.C.* I. 840.) He says this partly to show that he stands to gain nothing by writing (his real trade being that of copying music), partly also to show that he is not naturally endowed with the glibness of the professional. In the long passage just quoted he says he was lifted above himself by the sublimity of his subject. It is only when he feels the flame of inspiration that he can inspire others. Otherwise he is awkward in conversation and finds writing a burdensome occupation.

This is above all the case with letter-writing, 'genre dont je n'ai jamais pu prendre le ton, et dont l'occupation me met au supplice'. He cannot lightly adopt the right style for a given correspondent

or a particular occasion, so that even the most trivial letters cost
him hours of fatigue.[16] He is driven therefore to proclaim, half-
defiantly, that he can only write or speak in one way, his own, and
that his correspondents will just have to make the best of it. Most
of all, he writes in this way to those who might feel themselves
entitled to a more polite sort of language, notably to his friends
and protectors, the Luxembourgs. Here is one of his rather con-
torted protestations:

N'ayant jamais voulu vivre qu'avec mes amis, je n'ai qu'un langage,
celui de l'amitié, de la familiarité. Je n'ignore pas combien de mon
état au vôtre il faut modifier ce langage; je sais que mon respect pour
votre personne ne me dispense pas de celui que je dois à votre rang:
mais je sais mieux encore que la pauvreté qui s'avilit devient bientôt
méprisable; je sais qu'elle a aussi sa dignité, que l'amour même de la
vertu l'oblige de conserver. Je suis ainsi toujours dans le doute de
manquer à vous ou à moi, d'être familier ou rampant.

(Corr. Leigh, VI. 83)

Here and not infrequently elsewhere in his letters, Rousseau reminds one of his hero Alceste and the 'je ne dis pas cela'. He does
not want to be taken for 'un arrogant et un malappris' (O.C. I.
518), but he also wants it be clear that he is a truth-teller. And this
stance, while it corresponds to a real need in his nature, is one that
can be turned to advantage, as we saw when discussing Boileau;
it is flattering to be treated roughly by the 'ami de la vérité'. Anyone who objects will disqualify himself as a friend or even as an
honest man. In fact, most people do not object; as Rousseau knew
well enough, audiences like being shocked,[17] and his own books
sold well precisely because they were not the work of a flattering
professional writer: 'Mon métier pouvait me nourrir si mes livres
ne se vendaient pas, et voilà précisément ce qui les faisait vendre.'
(O.C. I. 403.)

There is nothing naïve, then, about Rousseau's failure to observe the customary forms; he knew quite well what he was doing
and was indeed highly sensitive to the tone of his own writings
and those of others. With his correspondents he discusses the

---

[16] Even so, the voluminous correspondence shows letter-writing to have been one
of the main occupations of his later life.

[17] In the Lettre à d'Alembert, Rousseau notes of fashionable audiences: 'C'est
précisément leur aversion pour les choses communes qui les ramène quelquefois
aux choses simples.' (L.d'Al. 136.)

appropriate mode of address ('Mon cher citoyen', etc.) and again
reminds one of Boileau in the horror he expresses for the normal
epistolary flourishes. Reading the letters of his friends, he reacts
very strongly to any slight verbal touches which might indicate
contempt, condescension, or similar unwelcome feelings towards
him, while he himself hopes to get away with all sorts of rudeness.
And on the occasions when he feels he has dealt well with a difficult rhetorical situation, he is more proud of his achievement than
some of his Diogenes-like pronouncements would lead one to
expect. Thus, naturally enough, with kings; as everyone knows,
Rousseau's embarrassment led him to avoid meeting Louis XV,
and not the least part of this embarrassment was the same question
raised by his correspondence with the Maréchal de Luxembourg:
'Je voulais, sans quitter l'air et le ton sévère que j'avais pris, me
montrer sensible à l'honneur que me faisait un si grand monarque.
Il fallait envelopper quelque grande et utile vérité dans une
louange belle et méritée.' (O.C. 1. 380.) He could not hope to do
this viva voce, but felt he had achieved something like it in his
written reply to King Stanislas; in a Machiavellian way, he congratulates himself on cutting up Stanislas's Jesuit adviser 'sans
ménagement', while adopting a different, but still dignified, tone
towards the King: 'J'y saisis l'occasion qui m'était offerte d'apprendre au public comment un particulier pouvait défendre la
cause de la vérité contre un souverain même. Il est difficile de
prendre en même temps un ton plus fier et plus respectueux que
celui que je pris pour lui répondre.' (O.C. 1. 366.)

Letters, even open letters, obviously present special rhetorical
problems; the letter-writer is addressing a definite reader whose
affection or respect may be valued and who can be expected to
answer back, to wound if he is wounded and flatter if he is flattered. This is not true to the same extent of the reading public.
The book-writer can in some measure invent his own audience,
choose some elements of his actual public and disdain others, or
disregard the expectations of the real audience without fear of any
immediate reprisal. But in eighteenth-century France more than
today, the literary expectations of the audience were homogeneous
and were embodied in the taste and judgement of the writer.
Rousseau, as we have seen, knew all about the norms of polite
literature, sometimes accepting them, sometimes despising them.
In his published writings he at the same time plays the Parisian

game, using the consecrated rhetoric with the skill of an expert, and refuses the game, appearing as the barbarian who does not know the rhetoric, but only the truth, *his* truth.

Barbarus his ego sum, quia non intelligor illis was the epigraph attached by Jean-Jacques to his prize-winning *Discours sur les sciences et les arts* in 1750. He used it again at the beginning of his self-justifying dialogues, twenty-five years later. It is a curious motto, carrying some of the tension between culture and nature which I have spoken of in the first part of this chapter. The original 'barbarian' was Ovid among the Scythians. But Rousseau takes it literally; he is the man of nature addressing the over-civilized world. Indeed, in the course of the *Discours*, the primitive Scythians are praised as examples of manly virtue. But is there anything of the barbarian about the *Discours* itself? In what ways, if any, does its rhetoric depart from the norms of the eighteenth-century prize speech?

I think the answer must be that even if there is something shocking (though not original) about the stand taken by Rousseau against the sciences and the arts, there is little that is unorthodox about his language. We saw in an earlier chapter how Malebranche had the reputation of making imaginative attacks on imagina-tion.[18] In the same way, Rousseau could be (and was) accused of using eloquence to attack (among other things) eloquence. The *Discours* is in the mainstream of highflown, persuasive writing, powerful but easily placed in a tradition (and thus perhaps neutral-ized). In the preface and the short introduction one does catch, it is true, signs of a strongly individual manner, notably in the heavy use of the first person, the brutal affirmations, and the defiant short sentences. Rousseau's voice is briefly heard in the superlatives of the opening blast: 'Voici une des grandes et des plus belles ques-tions qui aient jamais été agitées', in the careless rapidity of 'Un mot encore, et je finis', and in the uninhibited personal force of the final sentence of the introductory page: 'A ce motif qui m'encou-rage, il s'en joint un autre qui me détermine: c'est qu'après avoir soutenu, selon ma lumière naturelle, le parti de la vérité; quel que soit mon succès, il est un prix qui ne peut me manquer: je le trouverai dans le fond de mon cœur.' (*O.C.* III. 3–5.)

[18] See above, pp. 79–80.

But soon 'nous' takes the place of 'je'. Once we have finished the preliminaries we hear immediately the grandiloquence of the orator (and, of course, the *Discours* was originally meant to be heard) in the accumulation of infinitive clauses of the first paragraph. This does not continue unabated throughout the discourse—after all, variety is one of the most important recommendations of rhetoric; the enumeration of the first paragraph is followed by the short concluding sentence: 'Toutes ces merveilles se sont renouvelées depuis peu de générations.' At different points in the discourse the rhetorical colouring is stronger or weaker, but almost always one is conscious of a bare outline of argument dressed up in the grand clothes which the occasion demanded—it would be relatively easy to strip down most of the work as the rhetoricians taught their pupils to strip down the oratory of antiquity. Not only in the notorious prosopopoeia of Fabricius and in such obvious places as the peroration and the transition from the first to the second part of the discourse, but throughout the work, we hear the formal voice of the man haranguing an academy:

Oublierais-je que ce fut dans le sein même de la Grèce qu'on vit s'élever cette Cité aussi célèbre par son heureuse ignorance que par la sagesse de ses Lois, cette République de demi-Dieux plutôt que d'hommes? tant leurs vertus semblaient supérieures à l'humanité. O Sparte! opprobre éternel d'une vaine doctrine! Tandis que les vices conduits par les beaux Arts s'introduisaient ensemble dans Athènes, tandis qu'un Tyran y rassemblait avec tant de soin les ouvrages du Prince des Poètes, tu chassais de tes murs les Arts et les Artistes, les Sciences et les Savants. (*O.C.* III. 12)

The vocabulary here is all of the elevated sort (on the heroic section of Virgil's wheel). It is not so metaphorical as in some parts of the *Discours*; one barely notices the image in 's'élever' and 'dans le sein de' or the personification in 'les vices conduits par les beaux Arts' and 'les Arts et les Artistes, les Sciences et les Savants'. The tropes, like the capital letters, serve principally to preserve the noble tone. Far more noticeable are the figures of pattern and passion. Rousseau tells us how he meditated his periods for days and nights before committing them to paper (*O.C.* I. 352)—here we see the result. The first sentence consists of two balanced and internally symmetrical definitions of Sparta, buttressed by two clauses of virtually the same length. In the traditional way the place is thus evoked in periphrases before being named in a brief apostrophe which stands at the centre of the paragraph and is itself built on the chiasmus pattern (noun–adjective : adjective–noun) so familiar in French classical tragedy : 'opprobre éternel d'une vaine doctrine'—indeed this only just escapes being a perfect alexandrine. The long period which follows balances the opening sentence almost symmetrically, although its internal patterning is different—now we have two 'tandis' clauses of almost the same length leading up to the doubly symmetrical conclusion: 'tu chassais de tes murs les Arts et les Artistes, les Sciences et les Savants.' In an entirely conventional way, it is splendid stuff to read aloud. Not that Rousseau wants simply to lull his readers into belief; he aims also to communicate the movement of his own emotions, first the suggestion of sudden recollection (though this is no more than a formal transition, a reminiscence of the oratory of antiquity), then the apostrophe and exclamation of enthusiasm. We have every reason to suppose that the enthusiasm was genuine enough, but unfortunately the rhetoric which communicates it is virtually indistinguishable from that which boys learnt and practised in the Jesuit schools.

Faced with such a show it is hardly surprising that, while many contemporaries were moved and convinced, others treated the *Discours* as the work of a sophist. The clever rhetorician is precisely one of Rousseau's targets in his attack on the arts and sciences; in the polemic which followed the publication of the work, he was made aware that he himself, however deeply he might feel, was hard to distinguish from the unmoved orator. In self-defence, then, he was led to dissociate himself from the periphrastic grandiloquence of the academic style. Where his critics had said that 'Il est aussi bien des lecteurs qui les goûteront mieux [les vérités] dans un style tout uni, que sous cet habit de cérémonie qu'exigent les discours académiques', he replied: 'Je suis fort du goût de ces lecteurs-là.' (*O.C.* iii. 33.) In his reply to Stanislas he remarks of the early Christians that 'ce fut d'une manière très savante que la plupart d'entre eux déclamèrent contre le progrès des sciences' (*O.C.* iii. 48); as if to deflect such attacks from his own work, he protests that he is an ordinary man, 'grossier, maussade, impoli', and that style does not interest him: 'je sais, il est vrai, que la première règle de tous nos écrivains est d'écrire correctement, et, comme ils disent, de parler français; c'est qu'ils

ont des prétentions, et qu'ils veulent passer pour avoir de la correction et de l'élégance. Ma première règle, à moi qui ne me soucie
nullement de ce qu'on pensera de mon style, est de me faire
entendre.' (*O.C.* III. 101.) When Gautier, the professional teacher
of rhetoric, accuses him of substituting eloquence for argument,
he counterattacks rather crudely: 'c'est en prodiguant la pompe
oratoire dans une réfutation, qu'il me reproche à moi de l'avoir
employée dans un discours académique.' (*O.C.* III. 65.) He goes on
to criticize 'les vaines déclamations des collèges' (Gautier's home
ground) and insists that his work is not of this sort. It was obvious, nevertheless, that his own subject was very much like the sort
of school *exercices* which I described in Chapter 1, the *chria* such
as 'nothing is better [or worse] than the tongue'—and indeed
Rousseau's discourse provided a subject for oratorical contests in
the secondary schools.

We see, then, that the arguments following the first Discourse
led Rousseau to think about his style. If in later years he tends
not to rate his first work very highly, it is not only because
it set him on the road to ruin, not only because 'de tous ceux
qui sont sortis de ma plume, c'est le plus faible en raisonnement et le plus pauvre de nombre et d'harmonie', but also, one
suspects, because, more than any of his other serious writings, it
is cast in the mould of orthodox contemporary eloquence. It is
interesting to note that in his reply to Stanislas he quotes the
familiar example of the uncouth Apostles, whose untutored eloquence conquered the world. Like the Apostles, Rousseau was
untaught (or self-taught), and he tended always to see his mission
in a religious light. He was too much of a man of letters to believe
that style did not matter—he does not really side with the Pope
who held that 'c'était une chose honteuse d'asservir la parole de
Dieu aux règles de la grammaire' (*O.C.* III. 48)—but even so, the
example of the Apostles provided a pole of attraction. His later
works are no longer the productions of a conformist (if sincere)
competitor for a prize; in part at least, their language reflects their
author's personal reform, his change of clothes, of home, of life.
There are many differences from work to work: the *Discours sur
l'inégalité* still contains much of the pomp of the first Discourse,
being ostensibly written for the same audience; *Du contrat social*[19]

---

[19] On the style of the *Contrat social* see the valuable study of M. Launay, 'L'art de
l'écrivain dans le *Contrat social*', in his *Jean-Jacques Rousseau et son temps*, Paris, 1969.

is a delibertately austere piece, Rousseau's nearest approach to the language of the treatise; the *Lettre à d'Alembert*, as its title suggests, is more personal than either of these. I do not intend to examine any of these works here, but rather to concentrate on the rhetoric of the *Émile*, the keystone of the philosophical edifice.

The book opens, as one might perhaps expect, with protestations of modesty and incompetence—'ce recueil de réflexions et d'observations, sans ordre et presque sans suite' (*O.C.* IV. 241). Rousseau adopts his usual position of the plain lover of truth who says what he thinks without dressing it up in the garb of oratory: 'celui qui vous parle n'est ni un savant ni un philosophe, mais un homme simple, ami de la vérité, sans parti, sans système.' (*O.C.* IV. 348.) But this plain man has some professional things to say about speech, writing, and persuasion. We have already seen something of the sort of speech which is expected of Émile; it is interesting also to see how the tutor talks to the boy. In general, Rousseau believes that you should not talk too much to children—actions speak louder than words. But when Émile is older, persuasive words are needed. The important thing here is not to rely on cold reasoning: 'Toujours raisonner est la manie des petits esprits. Les âmes fortes ont bien un autre langage; c'est par ce langage qu'on persuade et qu'on fait agir.' (*O.C.* IV. 645.) This means using gesture, sign, and action as well as words: 'Je mettrai dans mes yeux, dans mon accent, dans mon geste, l'enthousiasme et l'ardeur que je lui veux inspirer. Alors je lui parlerai et il m'écoutera, je m'attendrirai et il sera ému.' (*O.C.* IV. 648.) All this, as Rousseau observes, is very much in the line of ancient eloquence. Then we are given an example of the kind of language which is appropriate to important occasions:

Vous n'avez point une âme abjecte, je le sais bien; vous ne violerez jamais votre foi; mais combien de fois peut-être vous vous repentirez de l'avoir donnée! Combien de fois vous maudirez celui qui vous aime, quand, pour vous dérober aux maux qui vous menacent, il se verra forcé de vous déchirer le cœur! Tel qu'Ulysse, ému du chant des Sirènes, criait à ses conducteurs de le déchaîner, séduit par l'attrait des plaisirs, vous voudrez briser les liens qui vous gênent; vous m'importunerez de vos plaintes; vous me reprocherez ma tyrannie quand je serai le plus tendrement occupé de vous; en ne songeant qu'à vous rendre heureux, je m'attirerai votre haine. O mon Émile . . .

(*O.C.* IV. 652)

Now it is possible that in the sort of circumstances described by Rousseau such language can really carry and communicate a passionate 'chaleur'. From a distance of two centuries it is all too clearly the standard eloquence of its time, less general in its application than that of the first Discourse, but very much the same sort of thing. 'Faste' and force' are still hard to tell apart.

This is the tutor talking to Émile; in the bulk of the book, where we hear Rousseau addressing his reader, such elevated and conventional eloquence is only one of the elements of persuasive rhetoric—and in many ways the least impressive one. The language of exclamation and apostrophe, of enumeration and symmetry, appears at fairly regular intervals, punctuating calmer, more expository passages and providing a fitting garment for such high points in the narrative as the wedding-night of Sophie and Émile. But whereas in the first Discourse this style dominated the whole and gave it a pompous uniformity, the *Émile* strikes one above all by its variety, by the unexpected combination of different sorts of writing. The basic fabric of the work is straightforward and didactic, far more so than in the first or even the second Discourse. For much of the time Rousseau is the unpretentious *philosophe*, expounding problems and facts, suggesting solutions. But constantly a personal note breaks into this exposition: we hear the author talking to us (or his image of us), exhorting us, mocking us, answering our objections, or speaking of himself, his experiences as a boy, his problems as a writer, his beliefs as a man. In particular this individual voice speaks with a brutal vigour which is very different from the noble eloquence of the passage quoted above; Rousseau is Diogenes, discarding any oratorical precautions as he insults his contemporaries with savage irony or states his own convictions in short, challenging sentences. This is the style of the 'homme à paradoxes', whom Jean-Jacques prefers to the boring 'homme à préjugés'; he is aware that he will be criticized for not watering down his affirmations with such qualifications as 'it seems to me', but is unrepentant: 'Que si je prends quelquefois le ton affirmatif, ce n'est point pour en imposer au lecteur; c'est pour lui parler comme je pense. Pourquoi proposerais-je par forme de doute ce dont, quant à moi, je ne doute point? Je dis exactement ce qui se passe dans mon esprit.' (*O.C.* IV. 242.) As in Diderot, this defiance of the norms of polite rhetoric asserts the writer's individuality, stimulates the reader, and avoids the drone of the tedious treatise. This brutal force is not unprecedented (one thinks immediately of some of the great masters, Montaigne and Pascal, for instance), but it undoubtedly accounts for much of Rousseau's power to galvanize the reader. It can most easily be seen in the first few pages of the book, where a whole vision of human nature is stated or suggested in striking formulas; it can be seen also, in combination with the other modes I have mentioned, at almost any point in the work. Let us look at the first few pages of Book III (*O.C.* IV. 426–32).

The first three paragraphs are calmly philosophical, describing the twelve-year-old boy and introducing a discussion of the 'troisième âge'. There is no personal intervention of Rousseau, except as the author introducing his material. One notices, however, the forceful shaping of the sentences, as in the aphoristic conclusion to the first paragraph—'Comme homme il serait très faible, comme enfant il est très fort'—and in the long and evocative enumeration which makes up most of paragraph 3. At this point the exposition is interrupted by an imagined objection, and immediately Rousseau is the vehement debater, personally challenged and asserting his own position against that of the upper-class reader: 'je parle de mon élève, non de ces poupées ambulantes qui voyagent d'une chambre à l'autre, qui labourent dans une caisse et portent des fardeaux de carton.' The opinions of his contradictors are summarily dismissed—'Voilà la philosophie du cabinet; mais moi j'en appelle à l'expérience'—and a whole series of examples is brought in to prove this.

Having made his point, Rousseau continues with his introductory exposition (paragraphs 5 and 6), posing the problem and suggesting the general answer which Book III will develop. Then he goes on to discuss the sort of studies which are suitable for a boy of Émile's age. At first this discussion takes a philosophical tone; the argument is studded with such words as 'puisque', 'donc', and 'par conséquent'. In the middle of this reasonable talk, however, comes the brutal assertion that 'Des connaissances qui sont à notre portée, les unes sont fausses, les autres sont inutiles, les autres servent à nourrir l'orgueil de celui qui les a'. A similar point is made in the sharp conclusion to paragraph 7: 'Il ne s'agit point de savoir ce qui est, mais seulement ce qui est utile.'

So far, the language has been relatively down-to-earth, but now, suddenly (in paragraph 9), comes a flight of eloquence which sounds very much like the rhetoric of the pulpit. It has all the usual exclamations and apostrophes, first to the 'ténèbres de l'entendement humain' and then to the prospective reader, 'toi qui vas le conduire dans ces périlleux sentiers'. Tropes and pattern rhetoric both contribute to create a sudden impression of high oratory: 'Crains l'attrait spécieux du mensonge et les vapeurs enivrantes de l'orgueil. Souviens-toi, souviens-toi sans cesse que l'ignorance n'a jamais fait de mal, que l'erreur seule est funeste, et qu'on s'égare point par ce qu'on ne sait pas, mais par ce qu'on croit savoir.' And then, just as suddenly (paragraph 10), we are back in the humbler world of the treatise. Rousseau is still addressing his reader directly, but he calls him 'vous', not 'tu', as he gives him advice on the use of geometry. The 'vapeurs enivrantes de l'orgueil' are replaced by technical terms such as 'moyenne proportionnelle'. This soon leads back, however, to a less technical development (paragraph 11) on the source of children's curiosity. The more general discussion is marked by a certain heightening of style, notably the accumulation of antithetical constructions which enables Rousseau to press home his essential distinctions. One of his favourite images, that of the philosopher on a desert island, performs a similar didactic function at the end of this paragraph and allows him to begin paragraph 12 with the formidable aphorism: 'L'île du genre humain, c'est la terre'—this is one of those unexpected sparks which continue to light up the mind when we have put down the book.

With paragraph 13 the objector appears again, and the next page is devoted to a to-and-fro discussion with the reader. Using the pronouns 'nous' and 'vous', Rousseau reasons with us, exhorts us, makes fun of us, and throws at us such striking and unqualified formulations as 'point d'autre livre que le monde, point d'autre instruction que les faits'. This sort of absolutism forces the attention, which is held as the lesson is insistently drummed in with antitheses and staccato rhythms: 'L'enfant qui lit ne pense pas, il ne fait que lire; il ne s'instruit pas, il apprend des mots.' The discussion with the reader reaches its climax in paragraph 16, where the direct address, the mocking exclamations, and the questions propel our interest forward into the next, very different paragraph. For now (paragraph 17) we hear another Rousseau, neither the philosopher, nor the preacher, but the poet. We are no longer directly addressed, instead we can read an evocation of

Rousseau's recollected feelings at the hour of sunrise. The vocabulary of this often-quoted purple passage is perhaps rather conventionally 'poetic' ('le père de la vie', 'part comme un éclair', etc.), but the total effect is moving in an unexpected way, since we had been led to expect an account of a practical geography lesson. And indeed this is what we are to have, or rather a lesson on the rhetoric of secondary education, since the poetic evocation is followed by the ironical comment: 'Plein de l'enthousiasme qu'il éprouve, le maître veut le communiquer à l'enfant; il croit l'émouvoir en le rendant attentif aux sensations dont il est ému lui-même. Pure bêtise! . . .' and this, after rhetorical questions and some more forceful axioms, leads into the actual lesson on the position of the sun.

In the constant change of the *Émile* we hear a living voice, the voice of a free man who may use the hackneyed old rhetoric but is not its slave. The personal presence, the unexpectedness of the transitions, and the vigorous brevity of Rousseau's affirmations and paradoxes all serve his didactic purpose admirably; it is hard to read the *Émile* in the detached manner which seems appropriate to the first Discourse. One does not feel called upon to make a literary judgement, but rather to respond personally to what is felt as a personal commitment. None of this means, however, that the *Émile* is perceived as a spontaneous piece of writing; even a brief analysis shows the presence of the skilful verbal artist—and this is as true of what I call the 'brutal' style as of the passages of high eloquence.

Some years later Rousseau was to compose his *Confessions*. In all his writings he wanted to be heard as the truth-teller, but now more than ever he had to appear totally sincere, not a performing writer but a man baring his soul. He was conscious of the great difficulty of the undertaking; this lay not only in choosing what to write and what to omit, but equally in finding a way of writing about it. Even more than in the *Émile* it was essential to avoid seeming a 'livrier'. The trouble was that when he wanted to speak directly to his readers (or his listeners in the case of the readings of the *Confessions*), their natural inclination was to treat his writings as performances, mere books which could be savoured, criticized, and corrected in the same way as other literary productions. Rousseau was shocked by the reaction of Condillac, to whom he had entrusted *Rousseau juge de Jean-Jacques*:

Il me parla de cet écrit comme il m'aurait parlé d'un ouvrage de littérature que je l'aurais prié d'examiner pour m'en dire son sentiment. Il me parla de transpositions à faire pour donner un meilleur ordre à mes matières: mais il ne me dit rien de l'effet qu'avait fait sur lui mon écrit, ni de ce qu'il pensait de l'auteur. (*O.C.* I. 982)

It is a familiar plight—we saw something very like it in Bossuet. To avoid it, one must write in a new way, purify one's language of its associations with the common rhetoric of literature. Rousseau describes his theoretical solution to the problem in the unpublished introduction which was to have preceded the 1764 Neuchâtel edition:

Si je veux faire un ouvrage écrit avec soin comme les autres, je ne me peindrai pas, je me farderai. C'est ici de mon portrait qu'il s'agit et non pas d'un livre. Je vais travailler pour ainsi dire dans la chambre obscure; il n'y a point d'autre art que de suivre exactement les traits que je vois marqués. Je prends donc mon parti sur le style comme sur les choses. Je ne m'attacherai point à le rendre uniforme; j'aurai toujours celui qui me viendra, j'en changerai selon mon humeur sans scrupule, je dirai chaque chose comme je la sens, comme je la vois, sans recherche, sans gêne, sans m'embarrasser de la bigarrure. En me livrant à la fois au souvenir de l'impression reçue et au sentiment présent je peindrai doublement l'état de mon âme, savoir au moment où l'événement m'est arrivé et au moment où je l'ai décrit; mon style inégal et naturel, tantôt rapide et tantôt diffus, tantôt sage et tantôt fou, tantôt grave et tantôt gai, fera lui-même partie de mon histoire. (*O.C.* I. 1154)

The main aim is to reduce the obstacle of reflection and artifice which normally stands between feeling and expression. 'J'aurai toujours celui qui me viendra'—writing is to be as natural as breathing and the guarantee of spontaneity is to be the 'bigarrure', the disdain for the unity (or uniformity) of the professional writer.[20]

There is not space here to attempt a complete study of the language of the *Confessions*,[21] but one can at least say that, while Rousseau's ideal may be unattainable, he does often give an

---

[20] Similarly with music, in the *Confessions* Rousseau gives this description of his early compositions: 'mon travail inégal et sans règle était tantôt sublime et tantôt très plat, comme doit être celui de quiconque ne s'élève que par quelques élans de génie et que la science ne soutient point.' (*O.C.* I. 334.)

[21] Interesting remarks on the language of the *Confessions* will be found in Sainte-Beuve's 'Les Confessions de Jean-Jacques Rousseau', *Causeries du Lundi*, vol. III, 1850. See also W. von Wartburg, *Évolution et structure de la langue française*, Berne, 1934, pp. 206-10.

impression of direct and spontaneous writing. This is not true of the famous first page ('Je forme une entreprise qui n'eut jamais d'exemple . . .'), where rhythm and symmetry indicate clearly the presence of a rhetorical design: 'Je sens mon cœur et je connais les hommes. Je ne suis fait comme aucun de ceux que j'ai vus; j'ose croire n'être fait comme aucun de ceux qui existent. Si je vaux pas mieux, au moins je suis autre.' (*O.C.* I. 5.) This opening trumpet-blast is akin to the brutal effrontery which we noted in the *Émile*; it works because it flouts the oratorical conventions of modesty and self-effacement, but also because it uses some of the old devices, notably prosopopoeia ('Je dirai hautement . . .').

The contrast between these paragraphs and the beginning of the narrative is striking. After the resounding declarations comes the calm statement: 'Je suis né à Genève en 1712.' Not that this narrative is without literary pretensions; if Jean-Jacques let his pen follow his thoughts, his thoughts naturally cast themselves in a mould which owes a lot to the rhetoric of the time. In this same first paragraph of narrative, for instance, the sentences are constructed and cut up in a manner worthy of Montesquieu, with discreet symmetry and telling brevity:

Le sort qui semblait contrarier leur passion ne fit que l'animer. Le jeune amant, ne pouvant obtenir sa maîtresse, se consumait de douleur; elle lui conseilla de voyager pour l'oublier. Il voyagea sans fruit, et revint plus amoureux que jamais. Il retrouva celle qu'il aimait tendre et fidèle. Après cette épreuve il ne restait qu'à s'aimer toute la vie; ils le jurèrent, et le ciel bénit leur serment. (*O.C.* I. 6)

This elegant and unpretentious narrative is to be the staple of the work, particularly in the early books where Rousseau is concerned less to plead a cause than to set down his memories. It does not exclude, however, the sort of 'bigarrure' which is spoken of in the unpublished introduction; very much as in the *Émile*, the calm narrative is broken by Rousseau's constant tendency to hyperbolic assertion, by the unexpected use of familiar or picturesque expressions, by passages of lyrical evocation, and by flights of more traditional-seeming eloquence. And all the time there is the presence of 'je', both the Jean-Jacques of the past and the Rousseau who is recalling the past, since the second of these is as much the subject of the work as the first. To this end, he lets us know how he feels as he writes and what his difficulties are—all this is part of the 'bigarrure' of spontaneity. In particular, one is conscious of the ironic eye of the narrator, playing with the follies of his earlier self, amusing himself by presenting the young Jean-Jacques in mock-heroic terms—'O vous, lecteurs curieux de la grande histoire du noyer de la terrasse, écoutez-en l'horrible tragédie, et vous abstenez de frémir, si vous pouvez!' (*O.C.* 1. 22.) As we saw in Boileau's poems, this sort of parody is an effective way of distancing oneself from conventional rhetoric and thus, paradoxically, appearing genuinely truthful.

It is difficult to give a brief illustration of the variety and power of the *Confessions*, but if we take as an example the beginning of Book VI, the description of life at Les Charmettes (*O.C.* 1. 225–7), it will show some of the characteristics of Rousseau's new rhetoric of self-revelation:

> *Hoc erat in votis: modus agri non ita magnus,*
> *Hortus ubi et tecto vicinus jugis aquae fons,*
> *Et paulum sylvae super his foret . . .*

Je ne puis pas ajouter: '*Auctius atque di melius fecere*'; mais n'importe, il ne m'en fallait pas davantage; il ne m'en fallait pas même la propriété, c'était assez pour moi de la jouissance: et il y a longtemps que j'ai dit et senti que le propriétaire et le possesseur sont souvent deux personnes très différentes, même en laissant à part les maris et les amants.

Ici commence le court bonheur de ma vie; ici viennent les paisibles, mais rapides moments qui m'ont donné le droit de dire que j'ai vécu. Moments précieux et si regrettés! ah! recommencez pour moi votre aimable cours, coulez plus lentement dans mon souvenir, s'il est possible, que vous ne fîtes réellement dans votre fugitive succession. Comment ferai-je pour prolonger à mon gré ce récit si touchant et si simple, pour redire toujours les mêmes choses, et n'ennuyer pas plus mes lecteurs en les répétant que je ne m'ennuyais moi-même en les recommençant sans cesse? Encore si tout cela consistait en faits, en actions, en paroles, je pourrais le décrire et le rendre en quelque façon; mais comment dire ce qui n'était ni dit, ni fait, ni pensé même, mais goûté, mais senti, sans que je puisse énoncer d'autre objet de mon bonheur que ce sentiment même? Je me levais avec le soleil, et j'étais heureux; je me promenais, et j'étais heureux; je voyais Maman, et j'étais heureux; je la quittais, et j'étais heureux; je parcourais les bois, les coteaux, j'errais dans les vallons, je lisais, j'étais oisif; je travaillais au jardin, je cueillais les fruits, j'aidais au ménage, et le bonheur me suivait partout: il n'était dans aucune chose assignable, il était tout en moi-même, il ne pouvait me quitter un seul instant.

Rien de tout ce qui m'est arrivé durant cette époque chérie, rien de ce que j'ai fait, dit et pensé tout le temps qu'elle a duré, n'est échappé de ma mémoire. Les temps qui précèdent et qui suivent me reviennent par intervalles; je me les rappelle inégalement et confusément: mais je me rappelle celui-là tout entier comme s'il durait encore. Mon imagination, qui dans ma jeunesse allait toujours en avant, et maintenant rétrograde, compense par ces doux souvenirs l'espoir que j'ai pour jamais perdu. Je ne vois plus rien dans l'avenir qui me tente; les seuls retours du passé peuvent me flatter, et ces retours si vifs et si vrais dans l'époque dont je parle me font souvent vivre heureux malgré mes malheurs.

Je donnerai de ces souvenirs un seul exemple qui pourra faire juger de leur force et de leur vérité. Le premier jour que nous allâmes coucher aux Charmettes, Maman était en chaise à porteurs, et je la suivais à pied. Le chemin monte: elle était assez pesante, et craignant de trop fatiguer ses porteurs, elle voulut descendre à peu près à moitié chemin pour faire le reste à pied. En marchant elle vit quelque chose de bleu dans la haie, et me dit: 'Voilà de la pervenche encore en fleur.' Je n'avais jamais vu de la pervenche, je ne me baissai pas pour l'examiner, et j'ai la vue trop courte pour distinguer à terre les plantes de ma hauteur. Je jetai seulement en passant un coup d'œil sur celle-là, et près de trente ans se sont passés sans que j'aie revu de la pervenche ou que j'y aie fait attention. En 1764, étant à Cressier avec mon ami M. du Peyrou, nous montions une petite montagne au sommet de laquelle il a un joli salon qu'il appelle avec raison Belle-Vue. Je commençais alors d'herboriser un peu. En montant et regardant parmi les buissons, je pousse un cri de joie: '*Ah! voilà de la pervenche!*' et c'en était en effet. Du Peyrou s'aperçut du transport, mais il en ignorait la cause; il l'apprendra, je l'espère, lorsqu'un jour il lira ceci. Le lecteur peut juger par l'impression d'un si petit objet, de celle que m'ont faite tous ceux qui se rapportent à la même époque.

Cependant l'air de la campagne ne me rendit point ma première santé. J'étais languissant; je le devins davantage. Je ne pus supporter le lait; il fallut le quitter. C'était alors la mode de l'eau pour tout remède; je me mis à l'eau, et si peu discrètement, qu'elle faillit me guérir, non de mes maux, mais de la vie. Tous les matins, en me levant, j'allais à la fontaine avec un grand gobelet, et j'en buvais successivement, en me promenant, la valeur de deux bouteilles. Je quittai tout à fait le vin à mes repas. L'eau que je buvais était un peu crue et difficile à passer, comme sont la plupart des eaux des montagnes. Bref, je fis si bien, qu'en moins de deux mois je me détruisis totalement l'estomac, que j'avais eu très bon jusqu'alors. Ne digérant plus, je compris qu'il ne fallait plus espérer de guérir. Dans ce même temps il m'arriva un accident aussi singulier par lui-même que par ses suites, qui ne finiront qu'avec moi.

The book opens, in what might seem a rather pompous way, with a Latin tag, Horace on the joys of country life; the effect of this is immediately mitigated, however, by some unemphatic comments, where the author talks familiarly to the reader ('il y a longtemps que j'ai dit et senti'); the humorous final clause, 'même en laisssant à part les maris et les amants', is really an aside, and gives the desired impression of a man writing down what comes into his head.

The second paragraph is totally different. It opens with one of the fateful statements which ring out regularly in the *Confessions*, punctuating the passage of time and giving dramatic form to the flux of events: 'Ici commence le court bonheur de ma vie; ici viennent les paisibles, mais rapides moments qui m'ont donné le droit de dire que j'ai vécu.' The tone rises as Rousseau apostrophizes the 'moments précieux et si regrettés', and with the apostrophe comes all the pattern rhetoric of high emotional eloquence, above all the rapturous enumeration and repetition of the sentence beginning: 'Je me levais . . .' This passage is not without elements of discursive prose ('How can I describe my past happiness?'), but they are subordinated to the musical communication of emotion; Rousseau's prose is moving in the same way as some of the high moments of Racinian tragedy.

There is something of the same song-like quality, though muted now, in the following paragraph. The patterns are simpler and less obtrusive, but from the anaphora ('rien de . . . rien de . . .') of the beginning to the 'heureux malgré mes malheurs' of the end, it is clear that this is the language of literature, characterized above all by the discreet balancing of word against word and clause against clause, as in the sentence: 'Mon imagination, qui dans ma jeunesse allait toujours en avant, et maintenant rétrograde, compense par ces doux souvenirs l'espoir que j'ai pour jamais perdu.' The paragraph allows a gradual transition from the high emotion of the second paragraph to the more factual narrative of the fourth, where Rousseau is very much the plain man, taking the reader into his confidence and explaining what he is doing: 'Je donnerai de ces souvenirs un seul exemple qui pourra faire juger de leur force et de leur vérité.' The total effect is harmonious, but in the sentence construction there are no obvious departures from the patterns of normal conversational French. The same tone continues in the next paragraph, though now with a touch of irony at the expense of the unfortunate young Jean-Jacques: 'je me mis à l'eau, et si peu discrètement, qu'elle faillit me guérir, non de mes maux, mais de la vie.' And then, at the end of the paragraph, comes another of those punctuating sentences which announce a turning-point and prepare us for the next stage in the narration: 'Dans ce même temps il m'arriva un accident aussi singulier par lui-même que par ses suites, qui ne finiront qu'avec moi.'

These few pages are reasonably representative of the constant variety of the *Confessions*. While only the most credulous reader would believe that the 'bigarrure' and impressive simplicity meant that the author was careless of literary qualities, it would be equally wrong to assume that the sort of rhetoric which now appears dated ('Moments précieux et si regrettés! ah! recommencez pour moi votre aimable cours') indicates any lack of sincerity. It is impossible totally to discard the stylistic conventions of contemporary literature, impossible not to use much of the rhetoric which can equally well be used by clever performers. It is no good appealing to the reader's intuition as a proof of authenticity. When Rousseau speaks of 'une douceur d'âme qu'on sentit n'être point jouée' in the *Lettre à d'Alembert* (*O.C.* I. 502) or of the fiery passion of his Discourses, he is very vulnerable. *He* may have known that his eloquence sprang from conviction, no one else could. Indeed, he himself often presents his behaviour and language in his 'prophetic' period as aberrant and even affected[22]— thus he says of his tone in conversation: 'Je me fis cynique et caustique par honte; j'affectai de mépriser la politesse que je ne savais pas pratiquer. Il est vrai que cette âpreté, conforme à mes nouveaux principes, s'ennoblissait dans mon âme, y prenait l'intrépidité de la vertu, et c'est, je l'ose dire, sur cette auguste base qu'elle s'est soutenue mieux et plus longtemps qu'on aurait dû attendre d'un effort si contraire à mon naturel.' (*O.C.* I. 368.) This betrays the awareness of the rhetorician that to tell the truth we have to lie.

In the same way, in the *Confessions*, Rousseau's achievement is not to dispense with rhetoric, but to invent a rhetoric of 'bigarrure' and simplicity which enables him, as a conscious orator, to impress and convince his readers. As a writer, he could not completely avoid the traps of what he usually refers to contemptuously as 'literature', but he could break sufficiently with the cultural norms of his time to be perceived as more than a well-bred writer. D'Alembert, who was no friend of his, explained his success in these terms:

[22] On this question see Starobinski, *Jean-Jacques Rousseau*, pp. 58–77.

Il s'est mis à son aise avec le public de tous les rangs et de toutes les espèces; et cette liberté, qui se trouve heureusement jointe en lui avec beaucoup de talent, lui donne un prodigieux avantage. C'est pour s'être mis à son aise comme lui, que Diogène a dit beaucoup plus de choses dignes d'être retenues qu'aucun philosophe de l'antiquité, quoiqu'il ne fût peut-être pas le plus grand des philosophes.[23]

Clearly, the *barbarus his ego sum* was effective. It was in vain that such enemies as the *Mémoires de Trévoux* or Voltaire accused him of writing eloquently against eloquence. This may be fair criticism of the first Discourse, but in works such as the *Émile* and particularly the *Confessions*, the eloquence of the protester is not the same as the eloquence against which he is protesting. In part at least, it breaks out of the chains of contemporary literature and points to the possibility of a new way of speaking and living together.

In time, of course, Rousseau's revolutionary rhetoric was to become a norm—all new rhetorics grow old and create the same problems as those they originally solved. Once Rousseau has written, his manner enters the common cultural inheritance as a potential obstacle to new writers. Or perhaps this is to present it in too dramatic a light; for many writers there is only gain in the enrichment of the common rhetorical stock, and nothing shameful or even irksome in using as well as possible the various forms of rhetoric which they inherit. But for others there is a problem. Of all the writers I have discussed, Rousseau is the one who most clearly prefigures some modern attitudes to rhetoric, the disgust with verbal performance combined with a love of words, the determination to break out of the old pattern and create a new style in the writer's own image, the aspiration to direct, unmediated communication. As time passes, we recognize more distinctly in writers such as Rousseau the many threads linking them to their predecessors and contemporaries. He has lost some of his revolutionary power, but still we recognize in him a writer who is great not just because he uses the old rhetoric well, but because he transforms it. His absolutist dreams of perfect verbal communication may be absurd, but it was because of them, because of his dissatisfaction with the accepted modes of speech and writing, that he was able to use words so powerfully. 'La véritable éloquence se moque de l'éloquence.'

[23] D'Alembert, *Œuvres*, vol. IV, p. 464.

BIBLIOGRAPHICAL ESSAY

A. *General questions*

AFTER an eclipse dating back at least as far as the Encyclopedists, but made total by the success of Romantic views of literary creation, rhetoric has been showing signs of new life. In America, where the tradition of formal rhetorical training was strong, the revival of the subject has been proportionately vigorous, but Europe too has been touched by the movement. The word rhetoric is now an accepted part of the critical arsenal, even if it has to do service in a number of rather different causes. I want in this bibliographical essay to give a brief and necessarily incomplete account of some of the work which has been done in the field of French rhetoric and to mention some of the more important sources for those who wish to study the rhetoric of the *ancien régime*.

In a properly rhetorical way, one could say that the revival of the subject has taken three main directions. The first can be seen in the attempts to rejuvenate rhetoric in its original function, as the art of effective verbal communication. Obviously this still continues to be taught, more or less methodically, in schools and elsewhere, but in Europe, at least, it is not usually thought of as having anything to do with the old rhetoric. There are, however, a certain number of works which proclaim themselves as modern rhetorics, notably C. Perelman and L. Olbrechts-Tyteca, *La Nouvelle Rhétorique, traité de l'argumentation* (2 vols., Paris, 1958). This work sets out to study the techniques of verbal persuasion as they affect philosophers; there are other more practical books, mainly American, which set their advice on speech and writing in the ancient tradition, thus C. Brooks and R. P. Warren, *Modern Rhetoric* (2nd ed., New York, 1958), and E. P. J. Corbett, *Classical Rhetoric for the Modern Student* (New York, 1965).

The second element in the revival of rhetoric is more interesting to the student of literature, though it too is tangential to the main point of the present study, which is historical. This is the attempt to build on the model of classical rhetoric a modern science, whose principal aim is to describe the language of literature. In this, rhetoric is part of the cluster of subjects known as stylistics (from another point of view, stylistics is a part of rhetoric). The early pioneers of stylistics, many of whom were not particularly concerned with literary language, had no time for traditional rhetoric. But in the first half of the twentieth century various writers, even outside America, helped to keep the name of rhetoric from total disrepute; in France the main names to spring to mind are those of Jean Paulhan and Paul Valéry. Paulhan defends and defines rhetoric in his *Les Fleurs de Tarbes* (Paris, 1941) and in the 'Traité des figures ou la rhétorique décryptée' (*Cahiers du Sud*, 1949, later reprinted with similar essays in his *Œuvres complètes*, vol. II, Paris, 1966). Valéry writes in *Tel Quel*: 'L'ancienne rhétorique regardait comme des ornements et des artifices ces figures et ces relations que les raffinements successifs de la poésie ont fait enfin connaître comme l'essentiel de son objet'; in a variety of works, but particularly in two lectures, 'L'enseignement de la poétique au Collège de France' and 'Première leçon du cours de poétique', which were published together under the title *Introduction à la poétique* (Paris, 1938), Valéry suggests a programme of literary study which he himself links more than once with the name of rhetoric.

Together with the Russian Formalists, the American New Critics, and certain structural linguists, Valéry has been a major influence on the Paris theorists (many of them connected with the review *Tel Quel* and subsequently with two more specialized periodicals, *Communications* and *Poétique*), who in the last few years have given something of a vogue to the term 'rhetoric' and launched it on a wider career than that of literary analysis. Roland Barthes, one of the main figures in this movement, suggests a programme of study in 'L'Analyse rhétorique' (in *Littérature et société*, Éditions de l'Institut de sociologie de l'Université libre de Bruxelles, 1967). In various chapters of his two fascinating volumes entitled *Figures* (Paris, 1966 and 1969), G. Genette has related the concerns of modern literary analysis—and indeed of modern literary creation—to those of the old rhetoricians. T. Todorov has sketched a system of tropes and figures in his *Littérature et signification* (Paris, 1967), while more recently still a group calling itself μ (for metaphor) and led by J. Dubois has published a *Rhétorique générale* (Paris, 1970) which sets out to rewrite the *elocutio* section of the old books in the language of modern linguistics. On a wider scale, the French 'formalists' have applied the methods of linguistics to what might be called the rhetorical analysis of complete works, above all of stories and tales, breaking them down into their constituent parts—see in particular Number 8 of *Communications*, entitled 'L'analyse structurale du récit'.

In other countries too there have been attempts to elaborate a new critical rhetoric. In America the tendency has been to dwell less on the figures of rhetoric or even the formal analysis of complete works than on the relation between author (or book) and reader. The 'Aristotelian' school of Chicago, in opposition to the interpretative New Criticism, has attempted to show how given works are solutions of rhetorical problems—perhaps the most widely known of such studies is Wayne C. Booth, *The Rhetoric of Fiction* (Chicago, 1961). The classic works of A. Warren and R. Wellek (*Theory of Literature*, New York, 1949) and Northrop Frye (*Anatomy of Criticism*, Princeton, 1957), while they go well beyond the limits of rhetorical analysis, provide a valuable introductory framework for anyone studying the subject.

These are only a few of the attempts to revive rhetoric as a tool for present-day use, whether in communicating or analysing communication. They have undoubtedly given support to the increasing interest in rhetoric as a part of the cultural history of Europe. If the subject still appears to be alive, we have a greater incentive to study its earlier manifestations.

Of the general works that include some treatment of European rhetoric, one must mention E. R. Curtius, *European Literature and the Latin Middle Ages* (tr. W. R. Trask, London, 1953), R. R. Bolgar, *The Classical Heritage and its Beneficiaries* (Cambridge, 1954), and the older works of J. E. Spingarn, *A History of Literary Criticism in the Renaissance* (New York, 1899), and G. E. B. Saintsbury, *A History of Criticism and Literary Taste in Europe* (3 vols., London, 1900–4). More recently H. Morier has written a *Dictionnaire de poétique et de rhétorique* (Paris, 1961). These are mostly, however, rapid treatments compared to the full and systematic description of the field of traditional rhetoric in Heinrich Lausberg's formidable *Handbuch der literarischen Rhetorik* (2 vols., Munich, 1960). Lausberg tends to describe the corpus of rhetorical theory in somewhat static terms, his aim being to provide an aid to the reading of ancient and medieval literary texts rather than a historical treatment of the evolving function and nature of rhetoric.

I do not in fact know of any satisfactory historical account of the development of European rhetoric. The historical part of A. E. Chaignet's *La Rhétorique et son histoire* (Paris, 1888) is entirely devoted to classical rhetoric (this book is an interesting last-ditch defence of the subject and one of the last traditional rhetorics to be written in France—in a curious way its old-fashioned preface prefigures some aspects of the rhetorical criticism of the twentieth century). Many of the main stages have, however, been studied in monographs. Of the various books on classical rhetoric, G. A. Kennedy, *The Art of Persuasion in Greece* (London and Chicago, 1963), and M. L. Clarke, *Rhetoric at Rome* (London, 1953), are reasonably accessible to the non-specialist. Medieval rhetoric has been very differently interpreted; C. S. Baldwin, *Medieval Rhetoric and Poetics* (New York, 1928), stressing the degeneration of the subject, is vigorously contradicted in an important article by R. McKeon, 'Rhetoric in the Middle Ages' (*Speculum*, 1942). The impressive and difficult work of W. J. Ong, *Ramus, Method and the Decay of Dialogue* (Cambridge, Mass., 1958), contains a lot of excellent material on the move from medieval to Renaissance rhetoric. W. S. Howell, *Logic and Rhetoric in England, 1500–1700* (New York, 1956), is a serious study which casts a good deal of light on developments in France. Finally, on the relation between rhetoric and the baroque at the same period, see the mixed collection of articles in *Retorica e barocco* (Atti del III. Congresso internazionale di studi umanistici, Rome, 1955).

This selection of books should provide a context for the study of rhetoric in the French *ancien régime*. The rest of this essay will be concerned, first with the rhetoric books themselves, secondly with modern studies of rhetorical theory in France, and finally with books and articles on French rhetoric in action in the period preceding the Revolution.

B. *The rhetoric books*

The essential texts are of course not French at all, they are the classics, Plato's *Phaedrus*, Aristotle's *Rhetoric*, Cicero's *De Oratore*, *Orator*, and *De Inventione*, the *Rhetorica ad Herennium*, Quintilian's *Institutio Oratoria*, and various other writings, including the pseudo-Longinus *On the Sublime*, the fourth book of St. Augustine's *De Doctrina Christiana*, and the ever-popular rhetorical exercises or *progymnasmata* of Hermogenes and Aphthonius. Besides forming the basis of much of the writing in the vernacular, these works were translated, more or less faithfully, from Greek into Latin, Greek into French, and Latin into French throughout our period. B. Munteano, in a chapter of his *Constantes dialectiques en littérature et en histoire* (Paris, 1967) entitled 'La survie littéraire des rhéteurs anciens', traces the presence of classical rhetoric in seventeenth-century France. Among the most important translations are the versions of Aristotle by J. Cassandre (1654), of Cicero by P. Jacob (1652), of Quintilian by the Abbé de Pure (1663), and of course Boileau's *Traité du sublime* (1674). In his study, *Boileau and Longinus* (Geneva, 1958), J. Brody shows in what ways Boileau modifies the position of the pseudo-Longinus.

There were a great many modern Latin textbooks. In the sixteenth century Erasmus' *De Duplici Copia Verborum ac Rerum* was unfailingly popular (see Bolgar, *Classical Heritage*, pp. 273–5 and *passim*). The *Rhetorica* of Omer Talon, a companion piece to his master Ramus' *Dialectica*, was influential, though less so in France than in England. The handbook of Father Soarez, *De Arte Rhetorica* (1562), continued to be used throughout the seventeenth century, by Jansenists as well as Jesuits. A good idea of the aims of Latin rhetoric teaching in the Jesuit colleges can be obtained from the *Ratio Studiorum*; something of the probable practice can be seen in the textbook of Father F. Pomey, *Novus Candidatus Rhetoricae* (1659), and its successor, the *Candidatus Rhetoricae* (1711) of Father J. Jouvancy (sometimes spelt Jouvency). A French abridgement of this last work was published by H. Ferté in 1892.

French rhetorics are rare in the sixteenth century. In 1521 P. Fabri published *Le Grand et Vrai Art de pleine rhétorique* (republished by A. Héron, Rouen, 1889), which continues the medieval tradition by combining advice on prose eloquence and versification. The *Rhétorique française* (1555) of A. Fouquelin (also spelt Foclin, Focquelin, etc.) is virtually a translation of Talon's Latin rhetoric. Two years later appeared the *Rhétorique* of P. de Courcelles which is in fact only an *inventio*, but richly illustrated with French verse. In general, though, there was little demand for French rhetorics at this period. In the seventeenth century, by contrast, and particularly after 1650, such works appeared in large

numbers. There is a fairly exhaustive list of them compiled by
P. Kuentz in *Dix-septième Siècle*, 1968, pp. 133–40. Of the full-
length rhetorics, probably the most serious are the following:
F. la Mothe le Vayer, *La Rhétorique du Prince* (1651); R. Bary, *La
Rhétorique française* (1653); B. Lamy, *De l'art de parler* (1675);
Abbé D. E. de Bretteville, *L'Éloquence de la chaire et du barreau*
(1689). Lamy's is the most interesting of these, in that it attempts
to break with the classical pattern. The later editions are fuller
than that of 1675 (the 4th ed. of 1699 was reprinted in 1969 in the
series Sussex Reprints).

Alongside these conventional treatises there were other more
eccentric productions, such as N. de Hauteville, *L'Art de bien
discourir* (1666), and J. de la Sourdière, sieur de Richesource, *La
Méthode des orateurs* (1668, one of many similar works by the same
author). There were also collections of model speeches; two fairly
typical ones are R. Bary, *Actions poétiques sur la rhétorique* (1658)
and P. d'Ortigues de Vaumorières, *Harangues sur toutes sortes de
sujets avec l'art de composer* (1687)—later editions of this work contain an interesting addition, the *Dissertation sur les oraisons funèbres*
of the Abbé du Jarry.

Although the essential rhetoric was that taught in the schools
(usually in Latin before 1700), much interesting writing on the
subject is to be found in a variety of dialogues, letters, reflections,
and similar works. The ideas of the pioneer J. L. Guez de Balzac
will be found in his *Œuvres*, ed. L. Moreau (2 vols., Paris, 1854).
The rhetoric of Port-Royal can be studied in the books of P. Nicole
(*Traité de la beauté des ouvrages de l'esprit*, 1689, translated from a
Latin text of 1659) and A. Arnauld (*Réflexions sur l'éloquence*, 1700,
a debate concerning the need for orthodox rhetoric), and in the
manuscript 'Règles de la traduction; des locutions figurées' by
Racine's teacher Antoine Lemaistre (Bibliothèque nationale, Fonds
français, Nouvelles acquisitions 1359). The Jesuit Dominique
Bouhours was a critic of the Jansenists and an arbiter of taste; his
most important works from the point of view of rhetoric are *Les
Entretiens d'Ariste et d'Eugène* (1671) and *La Manière de bien penser
dans les ouvrages de l'esprit* (1687); his views are echoed in the rather
précieux work of the Abbé J. B. Morvan de Bellegarde, *Réflexions
sur l'élégance et la politesse du style* (1697). A more austere position
than that of Bouhours was adopted in the camp of the Ancients,
the partisans of the 'Sublime'; see R. Rapin, *Réflexions sur la*

poétique d'Aristote (1674, modern edition by E. T. Dubois, Geneva, 1970) and *Les Comparaisons des grands hommes de l'antiquité* (2 vols., 1684); Claude Fleury, *Dialogues sur l'éloquence judiciaire* (written in 1664, published by F. Gaquère, Paris, 1925); Fénelon, *Dialogues sur l'éloquence* (written in the late seventeenth century but first published in 1718) and *Lettre à l'Académie* (ed. E. Caldarini, Geneva, 1970); and finally, of course, Boileau's many writings, of which the most relevant are probably the translation of the *Traité du sublime* and the *Réflexions sur Longin*. To conclude a very selective list, there are a certain number of philosophical works which are extremely relevant to rhetoric, in particular Pascal's *Pensées*, Malebranche's *De la recherche de la vérité*, and the *Logique* of Port-Royal, written by Arnauld and Nicole.

All the books mentioned in the last paragraph, and many more besides, have a close bearing on the questions discussed in the rhetoric books. Similarly for the eighteenth century the student of rhetoric will do well to look at books which are not specifically rhetorical treatises, such as J. B. Dubos, *Réflexions critiques sur la poésie et la peinture* (2 vols., 1719); C. Batteux, *Cours de belles-lettres* (4 vols., 1747) and *De la construction oratoire* (1763); Buffon, *Discours sur le style* (1753); Voltaire, *Conseils à un journaliste* (1737, in *Œuvres complètes*, ed. L. Moland, vol. xxii), to mention only one or two representative or influential works. The contributions of some of the *philosophes* to rhetorical theory are indicated in Chapters 3, 6, and 7 above. Periodicals such as the *Mémoires de Trévoux* and Grimm's *Correspondance littéraire* contain much interesting material, as does the *Encyclopédie*—see, for instance, its articles entitled 'Collège', 'Élocution', 'Éloquence', 'Figure', 'Goût', 'Langue', 'Orateur', 'Rhétorique', 'Trope'.

Nevertheless, the backbone of the subject is the practice of the schools; in the eighteenth century, among many other works on rhetoric (see A. Cioranescu, *Bibliographie de la littérature française du 18e siècle*, vol. i, pp. 210–12), we have a succession of full-scale French rhetorics written by well-known teachers. One of the most complete and most sensible is that of B. Gibert, *La Rhétorique* (1730), an augmented version of his Latin rhetoric. Gibert, a professor in Paris for some fifty years, also engaged in a polemic about the nature of true rhetoric with François Lamy, the essential documents being the fifth volume of Lamy's *De la connaissance de soi-même* (1700), the volume entitled *Réflexions sur l'éloquence* (mentioned above under the name of Arnauld), Gibert's broadside, *De la véritable éloquence* (1703), Lamy's reply, *La Rhétorique de collège trahie par son apologiste* (1704), and Gibert's last word, *Réflexions sur la rhétorique* (3 vols., 1705–7). But his most important work is his critical history of rhetoric from its origins to his own day, *Les Jugements des savants sur les auteurs qui ont traité de la rhétorique* (3 vols., 1713–19), which is a valuable guide to the subject as seen by a professional in its heyday. Subsequently Gibert had unkind things to say about the work of his more famous contemporary C. Rollin, *De la manière d'enseigner et d'étudier les belles lettres* (4 vols., 1726–8); this treatise, an account of Rollin's practice as a teacher, often known as the *Traité des études*, contains a good deal on rhetoric— the second volume consists entirely of a French rhetoric. Rollin's pupil J. B. L. Crévier subsequently wrote a two-volume *Rhétorique française* (1765), which continued in use for several generations. It is an orthodox work, written at the end of a long teaching career, as is the *Rhétorique française* (1804) of L. Domairon, who had started his career as a Jesuit teacher, but after the Revolution transferred his services to the schools of the Republic.

All of these are good, solid works, showing rhetoric as a thriving, well-established discipline. A less orthodox treatment is that of Condillac, whose *Art d'écrire* (in *Œuvres philosophiques*, ed. G. Le Roy, vol. I, 1947) is virtually a rhetoric, except that it is not concerned with speech. It is an interesting blend of ancient and modern. The treatise *Des tropes* (1730) by the grammarian C. C. Dumarsais became a classic treatment of one aspect of rhetoric; together with the commentary of P. Fontanier (1818), it was reissued in 1967 by Slatkine Reprints of Geneva with an introduction by G. Genette. Fontanier subsequently gave the theory of the figures its final form in *Les Figures du discours* (1830), which has also been reissued with an introduction by G. Genette (Paris, 1969). Dumarsais and Fontanier are the chosen ancestors of the *Tel Quel* rhetoricians.

And of course, rhetoric books continued to be published throughout the nineteenth century. They would provide an interesting area of study, but they are outside the scope of the present essay. Some useful indications will be found in J. Bruneau, *Les Débuts littéraires de Gustave Flaubert* (Paris, 1962), particularly pp. 52–68.

c. *Studies of rhetorical theory*

The preceding section was intended to point to some of the peaks (often rather cloudy ones) in the French rhetorical tradition. There is, to my knowledge, no over-all survey of the evolution of this tradition over the two centuries preceding the Revolution, but there are several books which in their different ways can be read as introductions to the subject.

On rhetoric in education one can always consult the old work of G. Compayré, *Histoire critique des doctrines d'éducation en France* (2 vols., 3rd ed., Paris, 1881), though this has been superseded in some respects. G. Snyders, *La Pédagogie en France aux XVIIᵉ et XVIIIᵉ siècles* (Paris, 1965), has quite a lot to say about rhetoric, though he rather exaggerates the divorce between rhetoric and real life. But the best studies of rhetoric teaching are those of Father F. de Dainville, in particular *La Naissance de l'humanisme moderne* (Paris, 1940) and a recent article, 'L'évolution de l'enseignement de la rhétorique au XVIIᵉ siècle' (*Dix-septième Siècle*, 1968). Like Snyders, Dainville confines himself to the Jesuit colleges, but the Jesuits were easily the most important teaching order. I do not know of any specific study of rhetoric teaching in other schools and colleges, but some indications will be found in such general studies as: H. C. Barnard, *The Port-Royalists on Education* (Cambridge, 1918); P. D. Bourchenin, *Étude sur les académies protestantes en France aux XVIᵉ et XVIIᵉ siècles* (Paris, 1882); H. E. Lantoine, *Histoire de l'enseignement secondaire en France au XVIIᵉ siècle* (Paris, 1874); P. Lallemand, *Essai sur l'histoire de l'éducation dans l'ancien Oratoire de France* (Paris, 1887). And of course, studies of individual writers often say something about the sort of rhetorical training they probably received—thus, to take the examples of Bossuet (Jesuits) and Racine (Jansenists), we have: J. Truchet, *La Prédication de Bossuet* (2 vols., Paris, 1960); T. Goyet, *L'Humanisme de Bossuet* (2 vols., Paris, 1965); R. C. Knight, *Racine et la Grèce* (Paris, 1950); P. France, *Racine's Rhetoric* (Oxford, 1965); W. McC. Stewart, 'L'éducation de Racine' (*Cahiers de l'Association internationale des études françaises*, 1953).

Most studies of rhetorical theory limit themselves to a part of the period which concerns us, but there are one or two more general works, notably the collection of essays by B. Munteano, *Constantes dialectiques en littérature et en histoire* (Paris, 1967), which is essential reading for anyone interested in the subject. Munteano stresses the passionate and persuasive side of rhetoric; it is worth comparing his approach with that adopted by G. Genette, whose essay 'Figures' (in *Figures*, 1, Paris, 1966) presents rhetoric as self-proclaiming artifice. Three other French works should be mentioned here: D. Mornet, *Histoire de la clarté française* (Paris, 1929), which devotes a lot of space to *dispositio*, Y. Le Hir, *Rhétorique et stylistique de la Pléiade au Parnasse* (Paris, 1960), and A. Kibedi Varga, *Rhétorique et littérature. Études de structures classiques* (Paris, 1970). Finally there is a German study on wider aspects of the subject: B. W. Wloka, *Die moralpädagogischen und psychologischen Grundlagen der französischen Rhétorique-Bücher des XVII. und XVIII. Jahrhunderts* (Breslau, 1935).

If we look now at more detailed treatments of moments in the history of French rhetoric, for the sixteenth century one must again mention W. J. Ong's *Ramus, Method and the Decay of Dialogue*, which is full of illumination and takes one well outside the field of rhetoric. Ong has also devoted a short article to Fouquelin's *Rhétorique*, 'Fouquelin's French Rhetoric and the Ramist Vernacular Tradition' (*Studies in Philology*, 1954). Otherwise, apart from the excellent work of Dainville, there is little to report on sixteenth-century French rhetoric. L. A. Sonnino, *A Handbook of Sixteenth-Century Rhetoric* (London, 1968), is a useful glossary of rhetorical terminology, though it is more concerned with England than France.

For the seventeenth century, a good starting-point is the recent double number of *Dix-septième Siècle* (nos. 80–1, 1968) entitled 'Points de vue sur la rhétorique', which contains not only seven articles on the theory and practice of rhetoric, but also a bibliography and a rather sketchy glossary of technical terms. Of the general items mentioned in this bibliography, two are of particular interest: I. Söter, *La Doctrine stylistique des rhétoriques du XVIIe siècle* (Budapest, 1937), an early attempt to exploit a neglected field, and H. M. Davidson, *Audience, Words and Art* (Ohio, 1965), devoted chiefly to the writings of Rapin and the rhetorical position of Pascal and the Jansenists. Then there are quite a few more detailed studies. The theory of preaching has often been discussed, usually in connection with Bossuet; a good introduction will be found in the article of J. Truchet, 'La substance de l'éloquence sacrée d'après le XVIIe siècle français' (*Dix-septième Siècle*, 1955). In

the field of legal rhetoric, the young Claude Fleury is worth studying and insufficiently known in spite of the valuable work of
F. Gaquère, *La Vie et les œuvres de Claude Fleury* (Paris, 1925) and
the introduction to his edition of Fleury's *Dialogues sur l'éloquence
judiciaire* (Paris, 1925).

The borderline dividing rhetoric and poetics is imprecise; this
is not the place to list the many studies of classical poetics, but
anyone interested in the rhetoric of the period will need to know
such basic works as J. Scherer, *La Dramaturgie classique en France*
(Paris, 1950), R. Bray, *La Formation de la doctrine classique en France*
(Paris, 1927), and D. Mornet, *Histoire de la littérature française
classique* (Paris, 1940). In Italian there is a series of useful studies
by A. Pizzorusso, *La poetica di Fénelon* (Milan, 1959), 'La poetica di
La Bruyère' (*Studi francesi*, 1957), and 'Morvan de Bellegarde e una
retorica delle *bienséances*' (*Rivista di letterature moderne e comparate*,
1959).

Similarly rhetoric shades off into grammar and the theory of
correct usage; here the classic work of F. Brunot, *Histoire de la
langue française*, has a lot to tell the student of rhetoric—the relevant
volumes for the period concerning us are III, IV, and VI. Father
Dominique Bouhours constantly worked at the frontiers of
rhetoric and grammar; his theories have been studied by T.
Rosset, *Entretiens, doutes, critique et remarques du Père Bouhours sur la
langue française* (Grenoble, 1908). Another important figure who
is both linguist and rhetorician (among other things) is Bernard
Lamy; he has recently aroused some interest and his *De l'art de
parler* is the subject of a long article by G. Rodis-Lewis, 'Un
théoricien du langage au XVIIᵉ siècle: Bernard Lamy' (*Le Français
moderne*, 1968).

Apart from the recent editions of Dumarsais and Fontanier, the
rhetoric books of the eighteenth century seem to have aroused
little interest, although they are examined in the general works of
Munteano, Genette, Mornet, Brunot, and others. A good deal
more attention has been given (quite understandably) to theories
of language and aesthetics; one thinks, for instance, of such works
as M. Foucault, *Les Mots et les Choses* (Paris, 1966); N. Chomsky,
Cartesian Linguistics (New York, 1966); and W. Folkierski, *Entre
le classicisme et le romantisme* (Paris, 1925). All this has a bearing on
rhetoric, of course (what has not, one is sometimes tempted to
ask), but no one seems to have felt the need to write specifically

about the rhetoric of Gibert, Rollin, or Crévier. At this period rhetoric was a thriving discipline and still had an immense influence on people's linguistic behaviour, but it was no longer a conquering discipline.

D. *Studies of rhetoric in action*

If it is hard to delimit the field of rhetorical theory, it is even harder to do the same for studies of rhetoric in the work of poets, preachers, or philosophers. Almost any stylistic study is bound to touch on rhetoric, but I cannot hope now to include all such studies and must refer the reader to H. Hatzfeld, *A Critical Bibliography of the New Stylistics applied to the Romance Literatures, 1900–1952* (Chapel Hill, N.C., 1952), H. Hatzfeld and Y. Le Hir, *Essai de bibliographie critique de stylistique française et romane 1955–1960* (Paris, 1961), and to subsequent general bibliographies in such periodicals as *Studi francesi* and *Revue d'histoire littéraire de la France*. The following list is therefore arbitrary and incomplete; not all the works contained in it are primarily rhetorical in emphasis, but all of them use the notion and some of the terminology of rhetoric in their discussion of the style and general approach of French writers:

F. M. Higman, *The Style of John Calvin* (Oxford, 1967)

R. Griffiths, *The Dramatic Technique of Antoine de Montchrestien: Rhetoric and Style in French Renaissance Tragedy* (Oxford, 1970)

W. Leiner, *Der Widmungsbrief in der französischen Literatur, 1580–1715* (Heidelberg, 1965)

M. W. Croll, *Style, Rhetoric and Rhythm* (Princeton, 1966)

J. Hennequin, 'La rhétorique dans les oraisons funèbres prononcées à la mort du roi Henri IV' (*Dix-septième Siècle*, 1968)

J. Descrains, 'La Rhétorique dans les homélies de Jean-Pierre Camus aux États généraux de 1614' (*Dix-septième Siècle*, 1968)

H. Gouhier, *La Pensée métaphysique de Descartes* (Paris, 1962)

J. Morel, 'Rhétorique et tragédie' (*Dix-septième Siècle*, 1968)

M. Fumaroli, 'Rhétorique et dramaturgie dans *L'Illusion comique* de Corneille' (*Dix-septième Siècle*, 1968)

J. Truchet, *La Prédication de Bossuet* (2 vols., Paris, 1960)

H. M. Davidson, *Audience, Words and Art* (Ohio, 1965)

P. Topliss, *The Rhetoric of Pascal* (Leicester, 1966)

J. Cousin, 'Rhétorique latine et classicisme français' (*Revue des cours et conférences*, 1932–3)

G. Couton, *La Poétique de La Fontaine* (Paris, 1957)

P. France, *Racine's Rhetoric* (Oxford, 1965)

L. Spitzer, 'Die klassische Dämpfung in Racines Stil' (*Archivum Romanicum*, 1928)

R. Ginsberg, 'The Argument of Voltaire's *L'Homme aux quarante écus*: a Study in Philosophic Rhetoric' (*Studies on Voltaire and the Eighteenth Century*, LVI, 1967)

R. J. Ellrich, 'The Rhetoric of *La Religieuse* and Eighteenth Century Forensic Rhetoric' (*Diderot Studies*, II, 1961)

R. J. Ellrich, *Rousseau and his Reader: the Rhetorical Situation of the Major Works* (Chapel Hill, N.C., 1969)

T. Todorov, *Littérature et signification* (Paris, 1967)

Although, as I have said, this list is limited to books and articles devoted specifically to questions of rhetoric, and although it is undoubtedly far from complete even within those limits, it still seems a short one, at least when one compares it with some of the other rubrics of literary study (biography, influences, metaphorical themes, etc.). Rhetoric may be enjoying a new vogue, but it has not yet had time to establish itself as a normal tool for French literary study. Perhaps it never will, but at least it is clear now that, as J. Truchet puts it in the closing sentence of his introduction to the number of *Dix-septième Siècle* entitled 'Points de vue sur la rhétorique', 'étudier le XVIIe siècle c'est étudier, si l'on y tient absolument, l'homme éternel, mais . . . c'est d'abord étudier un type—j'allais dire une race—d'hommes spécifique: l'homme du XVIIe siècle. La rhétorique se situe de plein droit au cœur de cette étude.' The same holds for the eighteenth century.

Note. Since I wrote this (in 1970), the new Parisian rhetoric described on p. 266 has continued to flourish, notably in the periodicals *Communications*, *Poétique* and *Littérature*. See in particular *Communications* 16 (1970), 'Recherches rhétoriques'; and *Poétique* 5 (1971), 'Rhétorique et philosophie'.

Index